Success Is Never
Final

Success Is Never Final

Empire, War, and Faith in Early Modern Europe

GEOFFREY PARKER

BASIC
BOOKS

A Member of the
Perseus Books Group

For Paul Kennedy

Contents

List of illustrations   ix
List of tables   xi
Acknowledgements   xii
Note on conventions   xiii

Introduction   1

PART I
PHILIP II: THE WORLD IS
NOT ENOUGH

1. David or Goliath? Philip II and His World in the
   1580s   16
2. Of Providence and Protestant Winds: The Spanish
   Armada of 1588 and the Dutch Armada of 1688   39
3. Treason and Plot in Elizabethan Diplomacy: The
   'Fame of Sir Edward Stafford' Reconsidered   67
4. Philip II, Maps and Power   96

PART II
THE CENTURY OF
THE SOLDIER

5. The Treaty of Lyon (1601) and the Spanish Road   126
6. The Etiquette of Atrocity: The Laws of War in Early
   Modern Europe   143
7. The 'Military Revolution' in Seventeenth-century
   Ireland   169

8. The Artillery Fortress as an Engine of European
   Overseas Expansion, 1480–1750   192

PART III
SIN, SALVATION AND
SUCCESS DENIED

9. Success and Failure during the First Century of the
   Reformation   222
10. The 'Kirk by Law Established' and the
    'Taming of Scotland': St Andrews, 1559–1600   253

   Appendix: The Disciplinary Work of the
   St Andrews Kirk-session, 1573–1600   283

   Notes   288
   Text acknowledgements   399
   Index   400

Illustrations

1. 'The World is not Enough' medal, 1583 [Museu Numismático Português, Lisbon, Inv. 2918] 26

2. Sailing orders for the Spanish Armada, 1588 [Archivio di Stato, Florence, *Mediceo del Principato* 4919/340] 48

3. Sailing orders for the Dutch armada, 1688 [University of Nottingham, Department of Manuscripts and Special Collections, *Portland Papers*, Pw A 2197] 49

4. The Escorial Atlas: map of Spain and Portugal, c. 1585 [Biblioteca del Monasterio de San Lorenzo de El Escorial, *Manuscript* K.I.1/1] 105

5. The coastline of Atlantic Europe, 1586 [Biblioteca Nacional, Madrid, *Manuscrito Reservado* 237/16] 111

6. Bernardino de Escalante's campaign plan against England, 1586 [Biblioteca Nacional, Madrid, *Manuscript* 5785/186] 112

7. The itinerary for troops marching through Franche-Comté, 1573 [Archives départementales du Doubs, C *États* 264 unfol., endorsed 'Pour le passage de la gendarmerie et pour les estappes'] 115

8. The duke of Alba reconnoitres the Maas, 1568 [Archivo de la Casa de Alba 166/2, unfol., endorsed 'Relación de Juan Despuche y Don Alonso de Vargas sobre el país y el río'] 116

9. A map of the Low Countries by Christopher 'Sgrooten, 1572–3 [Bibliothèque Royale, Brussels, *Manuscrit* 21, 596/11–12, 'Superioris Holandiae pars'] 118

10. A 'news map' from the 'Atlas' of Gaspar de Robles, 1572–3 [Harry Ransom Humanities Research Center, University of Texas at Austin, *Kraus Catalog* 124/36, no. 18] 119

11. The Spanish Road as seen by France, 1606 [By permission of the

British Library. British Library, *Additional Manuscript* 21, 117/ 34v] 135

12. The 'New Route' between Antwerp and Milan, 1621 [Katholieke Universiteit, Leuven, Central Library: Tabularium, *Een-bladsdrukken*] 139

13. The siege of Limerick by the forces of Henry Ireton, 1651 [Reproduced by permission of the Master and Fellows of Worcester College, Oxford] 175

14. The fortifications of Dublin according to the Down Survey, 1650s 183

15. The siege of Ballyshannon (County Kildare), 1648 [By permission of the British Library. British Library, *Additional Manuscript* 21, 427/34v–5] 184

16. The siege of Duncannon fort (County Waterford) by General Thomas Preston, 1645 188

17. The development of the artillery fortress to 1648 [M. Dögen, *Architectura militaris moderna* (Amsterdam, 1647), 12–13 (courtesy of the Beinecke Library, Yale University)] 197

18. The reduction of the forts around Makassar, 1667 [Wouter Schouten, *Reys-togten naar en door Oost Indien* (2nd edn., Amsterdam, 1708), plate facing p. 92 (courtesy of the Universiteitsbibliotheek, Leiden)] 215

19. A Swedish father teaches his children religion, 1840s 248–9

Tables

1. Ordinations at Merseburg (Saxony), 1515–34 233
2. Survival of Scottish church records, 1560–1700 265
3. Kirk-session cases in St Ninians parish, 1653–1719 268
4. Offenders disciplined by the St Andrews kirk-session, 1573–1600 270
5. Activity of the St Andrews kirk-session, 1573–1600 279

Acknowledgements

Most of the essays in this volume have already appeared in print, although I have revised them for this occasion, and I am most grateful to the editors of the journals and volumes concerned for permission to reprint them here. In addition, I thank the co-authors of chapters 2, 3 and 7 for their gracious consent to include our joint work: respectively, Jonathan Israel, Mitchell Leimon and Rolf Loeber. Finally, I am grateful to Richard Duguid, Stuart Proffitt and Sue Phillpott at Penguin; to Don Fehr at Basic Books; to Carol Heaton and her team; and to Kay Freeman, Matthew Keith and Alexander Lassner of the Ohio State University, for their help in getting this volume ready for the press.

Although other obligations are acknowledged individually in the notes to each chapter, I would like to record one further debt here. Ever since we first met in 1985, Paul Kennedy has supported me as mentor, colleague and friend. As a token of esteem, gratitude and affection, I have dedicated this volume to him.

Columbus, February 2001

Note on conventions

As far as possible, all foreign currencies have been given with a rough conversion into £s sterling at the following exchange rates prevailing at the time:

> 4.8 thalers
> 4.5 crowns (*écus, escudos, scudi*)
> 10 Dutch florins
> 10 *livres tournois*
> } £1 sterling

This can be a misleading exercise because, then as now, exchange rates varied according to time and place. Thus although the *livre tournois* maintained a parity of roughly 10:1 with the £ sterling for the first third of the seventeenth century it fell thereafter, reaching 14:1 by 1654. Data to make detailed conversions are available in J. J. McCusker, *Money and Exchange in Europe and America, 1600– 1775. A Handbook* (Chapel Hill, 1978).

DATES AND PLACE-NAMES

1. Unless otherwise indicated, dates after 1582 appear according to the Gregorian Calendar (New Style (N.S.)), even for countries like Britain that did not abandon the Julian Calendar (Old Style (O.S.)) until later.
2. Where a recognized English version of a foreign place-name exists, I have used it (thus Vienna, Rome, Brussels); otherwise I have preferred

the style used today in the place itself (thus Bratislava and not Pressburg or Pozsony). Likewise, with personal names, where an established English usage exists I have adopted it (Philip II, Henry IV, Gustavus Adolphus).

TRANSLATIONS

Unless otherwise stated, all translations from foreign sources are my own. Readers who wish to locate the original Spanish citations may do so in G. Parker, *El éxito nunca es definitivo. Imperio, guerra y fe en la Europa moderna* (Madrid: Taurus, 2000).

Introduction

The ten studies in this volume all concern failure, a topic that fascinated many historians in the late twentieth century. Hugh Trevor-Roper, one of the most influential British scholars of his generation, studied a succession of men who, in a misguided quest for total success, brought about their own destruction. His first book, *Archbishop Laud*, offered a classic biography of Charles I's unsuccessful primate; his second provided a detailed study of *The Last Days of Hitler*. Then came biographies of the crooked sinologist Edmund Backhouse (*The Hermit of Peking*), and of the cultivated but unattractive spy, Kim Philby.[1] J. H. Elliott, perhaps the most influential British historian of the next generation, studied for over thirty years the heroic failure of Spain's seventeenth-century statesman, the count-duke of Olivares. Losers also attracted the attention of many 'micro-historians' in the later twentieth century. Natalie Zemon Davis wrote a book and contributed to a film about a French veteran executed for pretending to be his comrade-in-arms Martin Guerre (and sleeping with his wife), while Carlo Ginzburg chronicled the progress of the freethinking miller Menocchio to his death at the hands of the Venetian Inquisition. Judith Brown told the story of Benedetta Carlini, deposited in a nunnery near Florence at age nine, who later faked stigmata and claimed that Jesus spoke to her in dreams; she also had a lesbian relationship with another nun and, after her various heterodox activities became known, spent the last thirty-five years of her life in solitary confinement. Other historians have produced anthologies of heroic failures: recent biographical collections bear engaging titles such as *The Nobility of Failure. Tragic Heroes in the History of Japan* or *Worsted in the Game: Losers in Irish History*.[2]

One might object that success has also attracted historians, and produce a long list of counter-examples, but failure has proved more common than success – especially in war and government. As the British politician Enoch Powell put it: 'All political lives end in failure.' Moreover, in most cases, amazing success preceded the fall: Laud, Hitler and Olivares all came within an ace of achieving their political goals. The false Martin Guerre defeated every effort of his wife's family to destroy him, and perished only when his real namesake turned up. Menocchio survived one trial and the Inquisitors released him; but he proved incapable of keeping his mouth shut, as his sentence required, and this brought him before the court a second time as a 'relapsed heretic', an offence for which the sentence was death. Benedetta Carlini gained a widespread reputation of sanctity before her unmasking, which seems to have made her careless and domineering, both with her lover and with the other nuns. Most of Japan's 'tragic heroes' triumphantly defied the dictates of convention and common sense until defeated by more flexible adversaries. Richard Talbot earl of Tyrconnel, one of those 'worsted in the game', first rose to be viceroy of Ireland. Success, as Winston Churchill once observed, is never final.

Few people ever plan properly for failure and yet, as the eminent mathematician John von Neumann pointed out, 'Failure must not be thought of as an aberration, but as an essential, independent part of the logic of complex systems. The more complex the system, the more likely it is that one of its parts will malfunction.' Human affairs have a tendency to become disorderly, and their random deviations from the predicted pattern require constant correction. In warfare, the greatest single obstacle to success has always been what Carl von Clausewitz in the nineteenth century termed 'friction':

Everything in war is very simple, but the simplest thing is difficult. The difficulties accumulate and end by producing a kind of friction that is inconceivable unless one has experienced war . . . Countless minor incidents – the kind you can never really foresee – combine to lower the general level of performance, so that one always falls short of the intended goal.[3]

The essays collected in this volume focus on the balance between success and failure during the early modern period in three related areas: imperialism, war and faith. Those in Part I concern Philip

II, who inherited extensive possessions in Europe and America and expanded them until he ruled the first global empire in history – an empire, as even his enemies admitted, on which 'the sun never set'. The king left a broad paper trail, thanks to his habit of transacting as much business as possible in writing and to his private secretary's practice of dating and filing each scrap of paper received from the royal desk. This enables historians to follow in remarkable detail Philip's efforts to overcome individual problems, and to evaluate whether his eventual failure stemmed more from personal errors than from structural defects.

The balance of evidence suggests that the monarchy inherited by Philip II was never viable: that he could only defend it with great difficulty and at prohibitive cost. The unification of the Iberian peninsula in the 1580s, something its kings had striven to achieve for centuries, at first seemed a source of unparalleled strength; but before long it exacerbated existing problems and made them insurmountable (chapter 1). In a letter written shortly after the king's death, one of Spain's leading diplomats offered a shrewd analysis of this strategic dilemma. 'I believe we are gradually becoming the target at which the whole world wants to shoot its arrows; and you know that no empire, however great, has been able to sustain many wars in different areas for long.' 'I doubt,' he concluded, 'whether we can sustain an empire as scattered as ours' (see page 37 below). Philip II had persisted for forty-three years, confident that he would finally succeed and achieve his goals; yet even possession of the greatest material resources, the best espionage network and the finest cartographic services in Europe did not suffice. Above all, the king failed to achieve his greatest goal: the invasion and conquest of England. In the summer of 1588, the English fleet outmanoeuvred and outgunned the Spanish Armada, which had taken almost three years to assemble and drained the resources of Philip's entire empire (chapters 2, 3 and 4).

Part II seeks to show that although military innovations have often produced short-term success, few conferred permanent advantage. The 'Spanish Road', devised by Philip II and his ministers in the 1560s to convey their troops and treasure from Lombardy to the Low Countries, and thus to maintain Spanish influence in Northwest Europe, functioned poorly in the seventeenth century (chapter 5). The terror tactics adopted by the duke of Alba in the Netherlands in 1572 regained most of the rebellious provinces, but stiffened the resistance of the rest; Count Tilly's decision to storm and sack Magdeburg in 1631, although it pleased his soldiers and his master the emperor, scared many neutral rulers into joining the emperor's enemies. Even Oliver Cromwell's selective use of terror in Ireland in 1649, although it laid the foundations for the 'Protestant Ascendancy', ultimately made Ireland ungovernable (chapter 6). Likewise, the construction of expensive artillery fortresses with bastions and outworks, each requiring months and occasionally years to capture, transformed the art of war wherever they appeared. Eventually, however, they led either to equally costly imitations that precluded further military advance, or to overconfident demilitarization that created vulnerability in the face of those who persisted with new experiments (chapters 7 and 8). In any case fortifications alone, however comprehensive, could never produce final success without winning the hearts and minds of those who lived in the shadow of the walls.

Religious faith (the subject of Part III) provided perhaps the most effective means of securing and keeping allegiance in early modern Europe, even in the teeth of military repression and atrocities. Paradoxically, however, most religious leaders seemed capable of seeing only failure: they constantly feared that those who had changed their confessional allegiance once would do so again, and that most conversions lacked conviction. For a century after the rise of Protestantism, Christians of all denominations complained frequently about the ignorance or indifference of their congregations. They devised complicated – perhaps unrealistic – tests to 'measure' devotion and expressed bitter disappointment when the results confirmed their fears (chapter 9). Even when they found a rare oasis of piety and morality, such as the small university town of St Andrews in Scotland in the 1590s, elation did not last: within a few years, its religious rulers began to complain anew (chapter 10).

These ten essays share more than just a fascination with the ability of humans to focus on failure amid success and to snatch defeat from the jaws of victory. First, almost all of them materialized in response to an outside stimulus: in no case did I awake one morning and think 'I want to write an article on this subject.' Rather, each originated either with the command of a colleague possessing irresistible authority ('Thou shalt write something for me on . . .') or with an unsolicited but tempting request ('We are putting together a conference with a theme that I know will appeal to you . . .'). The exact circumstances appear in the introduction to each chapter. Although the general subject always bore some relationship to my research interests, the summons or request led me to examine new aspects or to see new linkages that would otherwise have escaped me.[4]

Second, the essays share a common methodology. First, they reflect my belief that the proliferation of serial records in sixteenth-century Europe enables historians to measure, or at least to indicate scales of magnitude, to an extent seldom possible in earlier periods. This is particularly true in three areas: military affairs, where governments regularly 'counted' in order to ascertain what happened to their money and supplies; the economic sphere, where merchants and entrepreneurs needed to keep track of their goods and their profits; and religious matters, where ecclesiastical authorities wanted to find out how many followers each of them had and how much of the Christian message they knew. Serial history is not statistical history: we would search in vain for complete and reliable figures in any of these areas (or in other apparently comprehensive serial data, such as records generated by the criminal courts of early modern Europe).[5] Nevertheless, if we try to measure the same things as those who compiled the data – if, for example, we seek to 'grade' early modern religious leaders where they themselves 'would have chosen to be tested' – we gain insights that establish a scale, and therefore a better framework, for comprehension, interpretation and generalization.

We should never do this in isolation, however, and the desire to find appropriate comparisons forms a third shared characteristic of the chapters in this volume. It is unfair to 'grade' Philip II's imperialism without bearing in mind the limitations under which all early modern rulers operated – such as the problems created by distance when mounting a combined operation. A comparison between the invasions of England launched in 1588 and in 1688 therefore helps to isolate the importance of some essential variables (chapter 2). For example, many people both at the time and subsequently have blamed Philip II for trying to send the Spanish Armada into the English Channel too late in the year, even though the king assured his dispirited commanders that 'since it is all for His cause, God will send good weather'. A century later, however, William of Orange set sail on 13 November and, although his English opponents considered this entirely mad, thanks to the 'Protestant wind' the Dutch armada landed intact at Torbay just two days later! Units of William's invasion army went on to occupy Whitehall, the Tower and all other key locations in and around London before Christmas.[6] Just as Philip II had claimed, God could indeed send 'good weather' when He chose.

A fourth common denominator in these studies concerns the nature of historical explanations. I find very attractive the controversial 'punctuated equilibrium' model of human evolution advanced by Niles E. Eldredge and Stephen J. Gould: an underlying tendency towards balance, with occasional 'events' causing a dramatic change that destroys the prevailing equilibrium and produces other compensatory changes until a new balance emerges.[7] This model also works well in at least some areas of historical evolution. For example, the invention of powerful bronze artillery in Europe – and only in Europe – in the fifteenth century transformed the nature of warfare by making offence far superior to defence. Francesco Guicciardini – Florentine soldier, diplomat and historian – believed that the mould of land warfare in his native Italy had been shattered for ever by the arrival in 1494 of a French army with modern siege guns. Previously, he wrote,

When war broke out, the sides were so evenly balanced, the military methods so slow and the artillery so primitive, that the capture of a castle took up almost a whole campaign. Wars lasted a very long time, and battles ended with very few or no deaths. But the French came upon all this like a sudden tempest that turns everything upside down ... Wars became sudden and violent, conquering and capturing a state in less time than it used to take to occupy a village; cities were reduced with great speed, in a matter of days and hours rather than months; battles became savage and bloody in the extreme.[8]

Before long, however, compensatory changes took place: above all, military engineers devised a system of artillery fortresses, known as the 'modern system' within Italy (the land of its birth) and as the

'Italian style' everywhere else, which proved resistant to heavy artillery bombardment. A new equilibrium gradually emerged, with defence again superior to offence (chapter 8).

Religious history, too, conforms to a 'punctuated equilibrium' model. The criticisms of the church of Rome launched by Martin Luther and others after 1517 eventually created a series of competing creeds that emphasized doctrine and understanding over practice and mystery. For about a generation, the vision of Luther and other Protestants made rapid headway, especially in the towns of northern Europe. By 1560 only 60 per cent of Europe remained obedient to Rome, and most parishes – and many lay families – possessed a vernacular Bible. Then the Catholic church fought back. The third session of the council of Trent (1562–3) enacted measures, duly enforced by the popes and by many Catholic rulers, to improve doctrinal knowledge among both clergy and laity. Although some responses – such as the use of a simple question-and-answer catechism – imitated proven Protestant successes, others systematized traditional practices: veneration of relics, the intercession of saints, the central role of the priesthood. In 1593, the Index of Prohibited Books forbade the publication of all vernacular works that conveyed the words of Scripture in any form. Thanks to these firm countermeasures, the Catholic church regained much ground: by 1650, 80 per cent of Europe owed obedience to Rome and the rest remained fragmented between various creeds – an equilibrium that endured until the twentieth century.

Concentration on such 'punctuations' has turned me into something of a historical mechanic, just as interested in 'how' as in 'why' things happen. Historians who begin by wondering 'why' seem to me anachronistic. Sixteenth-century military engineers, for example, did not sit down and ask why they should devise the artillery fortress: instead, they studied how they could best counter the impact of the newly powerful artillery and, after almost half a century of trial and error, a group of architects led by the San Gallo family devised a sort of 'star wars' based on interlocking configurations of angled bastions. The advantages of the new system immediately became apparent, and other architects (most of them Italians) gradually spread the new style first to the rest of the continent and then to Europe's enclaves around the world. Likewise, Martin Luther did not set out to create a new, separate church, but rather sought to persuade the papacy to remedy some specific abuses that seemed to him intolerable. Only when Rome refused to listen – preferring to silence him, first with the offer of a cardinal's hat and then through excommunication and banishment – did Luther decide that the pope must be Antichrist, with whom no compromise could be reached. Even so, the breach with Rome took place in stages: Luther did not stop wearing his monk's habit until 1525, eight years after publicly voicing his first criticisms.[9] Although the reformers may have wanted to proceed more rapidly, their secular masters feared that changes in religious traditions might produce disorder – a fear amply justified by the Peasants' War in South Germany in 1524–5, in which Protestant ideas and some Protestant personnel played a leading role. Admittedly, a few places experienced a rapid and peaceful transition from one creed to another (like St Andrews in Scotland, whose inhabitants on 11 June 1559 awoke in the capital of Catholic Scotland and went to bed that night with the Protestants in firm control: page 265 below). Most, however, passed through numerous stages, each centred on a concrete issue, over a period of years. Thus England's Reformation in the 1530s comprised a series of partial measures – to end appeals to Rome, to recognize the Royal Supremacy, to dissolve first the smaller and then the larger monasteries, and so on.[10] 'How' the Reformation happened therefore explains 'why'. Eventually, it is of course appropriate to ask 'why' – including why some areas failed to embrace the Reformation at all – but in my view that question should be posed, as it normally was at the time, only after asking 'how'.[11]

Fifth and finally, these essays seek to address – both collectively and individually – issues of current concern. I have always admired Hugh Trevor-Roper's insistence that historians should strive to provide a perspective from the past on present problems. In his valedictory lecture to Oxford University in 1980, he remarked:

Historians of every generation, I believe, unless they are pure antiquaries, see history against the background – the controlling background – of current events. They call upon it to explain the problems of their own time, to give to those problems a philosophical context, a *continuum* in which they may be reduced to proportion and perhaps made intelligible.[12]

In this volume, the essays in Part I should remind those who seek to manage apparently irresistible global empires of how 'a kind of friction that is inconceivable unless one has experienced [it]' can undermine any venture. Part II stresses that even the greatest military triumph has only limited consequences: sooner or later, a new challenge will confront the victor. Part III anticipates the bitter experience of Eastern Europe's Communist leaders in 1989, who found that although new ideologies may seem deeply rooted and even enthusiastically shared for a time, they can disappear with remarkable speed. Taken together, these ten studies offer a reminder, for those who still need one, that success is indeed never final.

PART I

PHILIP II: THE WORLD IS NOT ENOUGH

I still remember the place and the hour when I decided to study the life of King Philip II. As I walked through the streets of Madrid one clear spring day in 1969, I kept thinking about a letter written by the king four centuries before that I had just read in the Instituto de Valencia de Don Juan (a magnificent private archive filled with sixteenth-century documents):

These things can only make me sorrowful and exhaust me; and thus you must believe me when I say that I have become so tired by them, and by what is happening in this world, that if it were not for [things] . . . that cannot be set aside I do not know what I would do with myself . . . Certainly, I cannot cope with this modern world, and I realize that I should be in some other station in life less exalted than the one that God has bestowed upon me, which torments me so.

These troubled words were written by Philip II in the margin of a memorandum from his chief minister, Cardinal Diego de Espinosa. His lament ended: 'Burn this paper once you have read it, because it is of no real use.' In spite of this plea, however, the document survived. Instead, on its dorse, a secretary wrote the admonition: 'Beware! Only His Majesty may see this.'[1] 'Well,' I thought to myself as I walked along, 'if I am lucky enough to find more documents like this, I could write a new biography of the "Prudent King".'

I knew that many biographies of Philip II already existed, but none of them revealed the monarch who wrote that moving lament. In the early seventeenth century, while those who had known Philip still lived, some wrote memoirs that recorded interesting personal details: Antonio de Herrera y Tordesillas, who first suggested the epithet

'Prudent' for the king; José de Sigüenza, the monk who looked after his relics at the Escorial; Lorenzo van der Hammen, a courtier; finally, in 1628, Balthasar Porreño, a parish priest related to one of the king's architects. After that, however, few studies of value appeared for three centuries. Then, in the 1940s, historians – some Spanish, notably Manuel Fernández Álvarez; others foreign, above all Fernand Braudel – began to publish perceptive studies of Philip and his world based on the abundant state papers in Simancas castle (Spain's National Archives).

They made little or no use, however, of the king's private correspondence contained in the Instituto de Valencia de Don Juan, or in the British Library in London, the Bibliothèque Publique et Universitaire in Geneva, and the Archivo y Biblioteca de Zabálburu in Madrid. These four repositories contain three types of 'private' material from the king's desk. First, between 1573 and 1591 Philip's personal secretary Mateo Vázquez filed every piece of paper he received from the king, noting the exact time at which he received it. Vázquez also collected a second set of documents: the confidential letters written by ministers abroad 'to be delivered into the king's hands'. Philip II encouraged his viceroys and generals to bring sensitive and secret matters directly to his attention, without passing through the central bureaucracy, and he often responded directly via his personal secretary (who sometimes kept a copy). Finally, Vázquez collected the papers of ministers when they died: some he passed on to the state archives in Simancas, but others he retained for his own collection. The 'arch-secretary' thus assembled a vast collection of documents that enables historians to measure the pulse of the entire Spanish monarchy for over two decades. The only integral publication of Philip's private correspondence with Vázquez devoted almost four hundred pages to printing the contents of a single manuscript volume! Well over one hundred similar manuscript volumes exist today.[2]

The collection passed through many hands after the secretary's death in 1591 until in 1711 they reached the archive of the counts of Altamira. There, disaster struck: in the nineteenth century, many documents disappeared and the rest eventually became scattered at random between London, Geneva and Madrid. Today, the various confidential documents handled by Philip and his secretary on the same day may be in London and Geneva, with the king's comments on them in one Madrid archive and Vázquez's draft replies in the other. The lack of a modern 'concordance' of Vázquez's papers represents the most serious obstacle facing those who seek to study Philip II today. Without it, any study of the king's policy, and of his reaction to the various crises that assailed his monarchy, remains a hit-and-miss affair.[3]

Since 1969, I have seen and read perhaps half of the surviving Altamira documents concerning Philip II (as well as many more royal papers in other collections), using them to write a biography, two monographs and several articles. The 'other' half of the collection surely contains sensational insights, however, and several historians have started to quarry it – especially those who produced the host of works (containing well over twenty-five thousand pages) that commemorated the quatercentenary of the king's death in 1998. By now, more has probably been written about Philip II than about any other European ruler except Napoleon and Hitler.[4]

I

Richard Kagan and I have met frequently since we began our graduate studies under John Elliott's direction at Cambridge in 1965. We often coincided in foreign archives and libraries, comparing notes and exchanging references afterwards, and June 1992 found us both researching in Madrid; but nothing prepared me for Richard's suggestion one day over lunch (weakened by six hours of struggle with Philip II's calligraphy, we ate it Spanish style, about 3 p.m.). 'John will be sixty-five three years from now,' he announced, 'and his students have decided that you and I should edit a Festschrift to be presented to him on his birthday.' Richard remained uncharacteristically reticent on exactly who had issued this mandate, but the ensuing discussion swiftly resolved two critical issues: the theme of the volume and the criteria for selecting the contributors. The second proved easier than the first. Elliott had 'formed or deformed' (as Richard put it) about a dozen doctoral students at Cambridge and London; and, although he had not directed dissertations during his years at Princeton's Institute of Advanced Study, he invited many post-doctoral students to work with him there. We therefore decided that the Festschrift would include only John's own advisees. The interests of these potential authors ranged all over the globe, from the work of Robert Evans on the Austrian Habsburgs to the studies of Peter Bakewell on the silver mines of Mexico and Peru, so Richard and I gave much thought to finding a theme that could include as many of them as possible.

The idea of a dialogue – sometimes harmonious, sometimes divisive – between the centre and the periphery of the early modern state lies at the heart of much of John Elliott's historical writing. It served as the fulcrum of his first two books on Spain (Imperial Spain and The Revolt of the Catalans) as well as of his later writings on the relation-

*ship between the Old World and the New. His Inaugural Lecture as
Professor of History at King's College, London, in 1968, perceived
the various revolts of mid-seventeenth-century Europe as essentially
conflicts between the loyalties owed to one's patria (normally representing a province or a principality) and those owed to one's monarch. It therefore seemed an obvious theme for the Festscrift.[1] We
secured contributions from fourteen former pupils and on 24 June
1995, his sixty-fifth birthday, we presented the volume to our mentor
on the lawn of Oriel College, Oxford.[2]*

*Most contributors took their inspiration from one of Elliott's works.
Mine came from an essay he published in 1991 on the relations between
Spain and Portugal.[3] I knew from my studies of Philip II that the king
and his contemporaries attached special significance to the acquisition
of Portugal, which reunited the entire Iberian peninsula for the first
time in a millennium. The death of the childless King Sebastian in
battle in 1578, leaving Philip next in line to the succession (except for
one aged clerical relative, who died a few months later), seemed like a
miracle to many of Philip's subjects. The ease with which Spain's army
and navy annexed the country in 1580 provided another clear sign
of divine favour. Finally, the conquest by massive amphibious
expeditions of the Azores, which alone resisted Philip's succession, in
1582 and 1583 led to unparalleled euphoria in Spain and encouraged
some of the king's advisers to call upon him to '[make] arrangements
for the invasion of England'. Even two decades later, these events
seemed to stand out as the king's finest achievement. Of the twenty-
four canvases exhibited in the church of San Lorenzo in Florence for
his exequies in 1598, at least four depicted aspects of the annexation
of Portugal. Nevertheless, enforcing the king's claim to the throne
provoked great hostility. In Spain, many feared the consequences of
a war that 'pitted Christians against Christians, Catholics against
Catholics' (page 24 below); in Portugal, many of Philip's new subjects
plotted against him or sought refuge in 'Sebastianismo' (a messianic
belief that the last king of the Avis line, Sebastian, still lived and would
return to claim his rightful inheritance). Above all, the other great
powers of Europe perceived the unification of the Spanish and Portuguese empires as a threat, which increased the risk of an international
coalition against Philip II.[4]*

These ramifications all undermined the advantages that the annexation of Portugal brought to Spain; a detailed discussion appears below. Since writing the chapter, however, I have become aware of another more deadly consequence. The spectacular Portuguese inheritance only came to Spain thanks to repeated intermarriage between the two ruling dynasties of the peninsula over several generations. Don Carlos, Philip's mentally unstable eldest son by his first wife Maria Manuela of Portugal, had four generations of inbreeding behind him. Instead of eight great-grandparents, Don Carlos could count only four; instead of sixteen great-great-grandparents he had only six.[5] Philip later married two other close relatives. Mary Tudor was his cousin; Anna of Austria was both his cousin and his niece. In Anna's case, the consanguinity appalled the pope. Although he regularly issued marriage dispensations to royal families in such cases, in December 1568 Pius V refused his consent, 'having always seen the bad results that follow from such marriages of the first degree'. It took eight months for the king to wear him down.[6]

Philip's global empire was thus structurally flawed. Even had the king achieved more of his ambitious foreign policy goals – say, the conquest of England and suppression of the Dutch Revolt – it would not have improved the Habsburg gene pool. Rather, it would have accumulated an even greater legacy for Philip II's inbred successors to squander. Better management of the monarchy might have delayed the fragmentation of the empire acquired by Charles V and Philip II, but nothing short of abandoning the dynasty's policy of matrimonial imperialism – the very strategy that underlay its success – could have prevented it. The systematic use of endogamy to create and consolidate a global empire, although it triumphed in the case of Portugal, ultimately proved counterproductive because the system literally contained within itself the seeds of its own destruction. After two more generations of inbreeding, which produced the impotent and retarded Carlos II, the dynasty came to an end.

David or Goliath?
Philip II and His World in the 1580s

The coronation of Philip II as king of Portugal at Tomar on 16 April 1581 created the first empire upon which the sun never set. Nevertheless, the king did not look forward to the ceremony: 'As you know,' he confided in a letter to his daughters, 'they want to dress me in silk brocade, very much against my will'; but, on that historic day, he rose to the occasion. Putting aside the mourning that he had worn since the death of his fourth wife, six months before, according to an eyewitness the king emerged 'clothed in brocade, with the sceptre in his hand, so he looked very fine. Don Diego de Córdoba [a courtier] said he looked like King David.'[7]

Philip had already announced his accession to the outposts of the Portuguese empire: in November 1580 he ordered the city of Goa to obey his orders thenceforth, and the viceroy proclaimed him king there in September 1581, sending on news to Malacca, the Moluccas and other parts of Portuguese Asia.[8] The only resistance to the Spanish succession arose in the Azores, but amphibious expeditions conquered first São Miguel in 1582 and then, with a force of 98 ships and 15,000 men, Terceira in 1583. Philip's possessions now ran from Madrid through Mexico, Manila, Macao and Malacca to India, Mozambique and Angola, and so back to Madrid.

Even before the union of crowns, a Spanish astrologer had commented on the fact that the 'banners and standards' of his sovereign 'have crossed more than one third of the world, from Sicily to Cuzco and to the province of Quito, a distance which includes nine hours of difference, for when it is nine o'clock at night here it is midday there. And if we measure its breadth from one side to the other it covers one quarter of the earth, over 90 degrees.'[9] A practical demonstration of the increased confidence generated by the union occurred during the lunar eclipse of 17 November 1584: the newly founded Academy of Mathematics in Madrid sent out in advance a dossier of instructions, including details on how and when to record observations on paper, not only to Antwerp, Toledo and Seville, but also to Mexico City, Manila and perhaps even Macao. In addition, to ensure the most accurate results, the council of the Indies dispatched a noted astronomer to America along with special instruments to observe the eclipse, and thus (the council hoped) to establish the exact longitude of Mexico City (see page 108 below).

Intoxication with Habsburg power was not new. The election in 1519 of Charles V as Holy Roman Emperor gave rise to a spate of polemics calling upon the new ruler to imitate the achievements of his namesake Charlemagne and unite all Christendom; and Charles's coronation by the pope in 1530 unleashed a fresh torrent of prophetic pamphlets in which the emperor appeared as a second Augustus. Juan Ginés de Sepúlveda, later appointed tutor to Philip II, wrote one of the more extreme of these imperialist tracts and no doubt tried to pass his ideas on to his young charge.[10] Somewhat later, Prince Philip's journey from Spain to the Netherlands in 1548 occasioned a further literary effusion urging the Habsburgs to acquire the 'Universal Monarchy'.[11] Before long, some of Philip II's subjects saw this in global terms. No sooner had a small party of Spaniards commanded by Miguel López de Legazpi landed at Cebu in the Philippines than Friar Martín de Rada dreamed of using the archipelago as a base from which to conquer China – a suggestion enthusiastically endorsed by others: by Andrés de la Mirandola, the royal factor in Manila, in 1569; by the Augustinian Diego de Herrera, a member of Legazpi's expedition, in 1570; and by Legazpi's successor as governor, Don Francisco de Sande, in 1576. Only two or three thousand European troops would be required, Sande claimed, and only one mainland province needed to be attacked, because 'in conquering one province, the conquest of all is made'.[12] Shortly afterwards, Giovanni Battista Gesio, an expert on geography residing at the Spanish court, argued that the Philippines should become a military base 'like Italy and Flanders, with a garrison of numerous experienced troops' because the islands could serve as a launching-pad for the conquest and conversion of Japan, divided and weakened by civil war, and perhaps also of China. The king sharply rejected these wild ideas: 'It seems to us here,' a royal order of April 1577 declared, 'that it is inappropriate to discuss the conquest of China at this time.'[13]

Other imperialist dreams could still seduce the Spanish government, however. The coincidence of the spectacular victory of Lepanto over the Turks with the birth of a son and heir to Philip II in 1571 provoked a veritable torrent of euphoric letters from the king's chief minister, Cardinal Diego de Espinosa, drawing attention to these indubitable signs of God's special providence towards Spain 'which leaves us with little more to desire but much to expect from His divine mercy'. Espinosa even compared Lepanto with the drowning of Pharaoh's army in the Red Sea, while the king commissioned a vast commemorative canvas of the two events from Titian, the foremost painter of the age. Meanwhile in Italy, many speculated that Philip would continue in God's grace to reconquer the Holy Land and revive the title 'emperor of the east'.[14] A few years later, yet another spate of 'universalist' polemics followed the death in 1578 of the childless King Sebastian of Portugal at the battle of Alcazarquivir – a circumstance in which some detected God's hand, 'because Divine Providence would not have permitted such a remarkable event without a great cause'. In the rhetorical phrase of the Dominican preacher, Fray Hernando del Castillo: 'Uniting the kingdoms of Portugal and Castile will make Your Majesty the greatest king in the world . . . because if the Romans were able to rule the world simply by ruling the Mediterranean, what of the man who rules the Atlantic and Pacific oceans, since they surround the world?'

The unification of the peninsula soon came to be seen as a vital step on Spain's road to global mastery. According to Giovanni Battista Gesio, acquiring Portugal 'would be the principal, most effective, and decisive instrument and remedy for the reduction of the Dutch [rebels] to obedience', as well as a useful means of controlling England. In the terse phrase of Hernando del Castillo, 'The gain or loss [of Portugal] will mean the gain or loss of the world.'[15]

Naturally, not all contemporaries welcomed this expansive vision. William Cecil, Lord Burghley, chief minister of Elizabeth I, observed in 1584 that, with the Portuguese empire under Philip II's belt, 'I know not what limits any man of judgment can set unto his greatness.' England would surely now become a prey to Philip's 'insatiable malice, which is most terrible to be thought of, but most miserable to suffer'; while the following year, Henry of Navarre likewise expressed his fear of 'the ambition of the Spaniards who, having acquired domination of so many lands and seas, believe no part of the world to be inaccessible to them'.[16] Even within Spain, some felt misgivings about the union with Portugal. In February 1580 the Jesuit Pedro de Ribadeneira warned one of the king's ministers about the evils of wars that 'pitted Christians against Christians, Catholics against Catholics', and lamented the high taxes which already meant that 'although the king is so powerful and so feared and respected, he is not as well liked as he used to be'. A war for Portugal might expose new and unwelcome tensions in Spain, and allow the king's enemies abroad to find and exploit a 'fifth column' of discontented subjects within the peninsula.[17]

Nevertheless, Ribadeneira conceded, the only thing worse than fighting to secure Portugal would be to let someone else acquire it! Even though uniting the peninsular kingdoms would threaten the European balance of power (just as Charles V's election as Holy Roman Emperor had done in 1519), allowing the Lusitanian inheritance to pass to someone else would point a dagger at the heart of Spain itself. The central question facing Philip II and his ministers after 1580 was therefore how to ensure that the assets conferred by the new inheritance outweighed the liabilities.

Initially, the government tried to foster a new spirit of integration. Just twelve days after the 'governors' of Portugal had recognized his claim to the throne, but before securing the kingdom itself, Philip II issued an edict that abolished the *puertos secos*, the sixty or so customs posts in Castile which collected taxes on all goods crossing the frontier; and at the Cortes of Tomar in 1581 he abolished them on both sides of the frontier.[18] Much subsequent legislation, particularly economic measures, henceforth applied to all the Iberian kingdoms: thus the various orders to embargo North European shipping, from 1585 onwards, went to Lisbon and Oporto as well as to Bilbao, Valencia and Seville.[19] The king even went to live in Portugal for almost three years, from 1580 to 1583, and took steps to 'Castilianize' the royal palaces: Juan de Herrera and Filippo Terzo came from the Escorial with orders to do 'everything necessary to complete the work on Your Majesty's palaces' in the kingdom, while experts from Castile were summoned to put the royal gardens 'in the same order and perfection as those at the Casa del Campo and Aranjuez'. At the same time, labourers and engineers toiled to make the Tagus navigable from Lisbon to the heart of Castile, and cartographers from both Spain and Portugal collaborated to produce an atlas of twenty-one manuscript maps of the entire Iberian peninsula all on the same large scale of 1:430,000.[20]

Philip II had no intention of effecting a total integration of his peninsular dominions, however. To take a tiny but representative example of his respect for autonomy and tradition, in August 1581 one of his secretaries drew up a warrant in favour of a Venetian delegation intending to return home overland, calling upon the authorities of each community along the way 'from this city of Lisbon to Madrid and from there to Barcelona' to provide the travellers with lodging and transport 'at just and reasonable prices, without charging them any more than these things cost locally'. After signing this routine order, probably one of scores to cross his desk that day, the king spotted a major flaw. He scratched out his signature and added: 'This order, saying "From here to Madrid and from there to Barcelona" will not do. It must read "from the frontier between the kingdoms of Portugal and Castile to Madrid, and from there to the frontier between the kingdoms of Castile and Aragon". Let it be done that way.'[21] The king realized that protocol and local privileges required separate orders for both Portugal and the crown of Aragon.

This solicitude for the particularist sensibilities of his new subjects began to wane after 1583, however, when Philip returned to Castile. Now the king's administrative contact with Portugal centred on the weekly package of letters, concerning all sorts of matters that required royal decisions, sent by his viceroy in Lisbon to Madrid. Those for the year 1586, for example, which survive intact in a register of 728 folios, dealt *inter alia* with a request from the archbishop of Goa for 'some relics, and especially wood from the True Cross'; the possibility of lifting the ban on card games; a junta to be established 'to codify the laws of this kingdom into a single corpus'; 'the importance of expelling the Jews from Lisbon'; the machinations of 'Duarte Lopes, ambassador of the king of Congo'; and the need to appoint a bishop for, and found Christian churches in, Japan.[22] Dwarfing these spiritual and material issues, almost half of the letters in the volume concerned defence: sending a naval squadron to the Azores in order to protect the returning

East Indiamen against possible attack by English pirates, and building fortresses in Brazil, Africa and the Atlantic islands, likewise against the English.[23] It was the shape of things to come. Though English (and, to a lesser degree, French) merchants and mariners had occasionally challenged Portugal's monopoly on seaborne trade with Asia and Brazil, and though England and Portugal suspended commercial relations in 1568, the two nations soon composed their differences.[24] During his circumnavigation between 1577 and 1580, Francis Drake took care not to harm Portuguese property. His conduct during the West India raid of 1585–6 was quite different, however: first Drake harried Spanish Galicia and then he attacked the Portuguese Cape Verde islands before moving on to ravage the Spanish Caribbean.[25]

Although none of the letters from Lisbon during the year 1586 bears an apostil or any other evidence of the king's personal attention, Philip II took Drake's depredations as a *casus belli* and plunged his entire monarchy into a bitter war with England which lasted until 1604. The chronicler Pero Rois Soares of Lisbon significantly entitled his account of the year 1585: 'Chapter 82, which gives the reason why war broke out with England, the cause of so many evils for this kingdom, as you shall hear'.[26]

At first, however, the government's aggressive stance proved popular, and drew upon the new imperialist spirit bred in various parts of the peninsula by the union of crowns. The iconography of the king's ceremonial entry into Lisbon in 1581, for example, reflected a newly confident spirit of expansion. Thus one of the triumphal arches showed Janus surrendering the keys of his temple 'as if to the lord of the world, who holds it securely under his rule'; while another bore the legend 'The world, which was divided between your great-grandfather King Ferdinand the Catholic and your grandfather King Manuel of Portugal, is now linked into one, since you are lord of everything in the East and West.'[27] Meanwhile, in Castile, the verses of the soldier-poets Fernando de Herrera, Alonso de Ercilla and Francisco de Aldana, which circulated widely in the 1580s, all displayed a self-intoxicating rhetoric that called for Spain to conquer the world.[28] A medal struck in 1583 made the same point more concisely – it showed the king with the inscription PHILIPP II HISP ET NOVI ORBIS REX ('Philip II, king of Spain and of the New World') on the obverse, and on the reverse, around a terrestrial globe, the uncompromising legend NON SUFFICIT ORBIS ('The World is not Enough': see Figure 1). Another medal design of 1585, in a conscious attempt to go beyond the famous PLUS ULTRA motto of Charles V, displayed the zodiac with the phrase ULTRA ANNI SOLISQUE VIAS ('Beyond the solar circuit of the year': a slight emendation of Virgil's formula for the Roman emperor Augustus in the *Aeneid*) 'because God has given him [Philip II] a greater inheritance; and with his great power he could be lord of Cambodia and China and of other vast provinces if he wished'.[29]

Equally ambitious suggestions again flowed in from the periphery of the empire. In 1583, at the suggestion of the bishop of Manila, governor of the Philippines again urged his master to sanction an expedition to conquer China. The following year the devout but pragmatic Matteo Ricci in China wrote scathingly of the pusillanimity of his hosts:

Because when two or three Japanese warships come and land on the coast of China, they burn their boats and capture villages and even large cities, putting everything to the torch and sack, without anyone offering resistance . . . It is true that the Chinese have many fortresses, and the towns all have their walls with which to resist the fury of the pirates; but the walls are not of geometric design [i.e., they lacked bastions] nor do they have traverses or moats.

Others quickly drew the obvious conclusions. The recipient of Ricci's letter, a royal official in Portuguese Macao, added a covering note alleging that: 'With less than 5000 Spaniards Your Majesty could conquer these lands [China] and become lord of them, or at least of the maritime areas, which are the most important in all parts of the world. And with half-a-dozen galleons and as many galleys you would be master of all the coast of China and the adjacent provinces.'[30]

That same year, 1584, the Portuguese bishop of Malacca advocated pooling all Iberian resources in the Far East in order, first, to secure the simultaneous conquest of Southeast Asia, and then to annex southern China. The bishop envisaged an expeditionary force of 4000 Portuguese troops leaving Goa to attack and destroy the hostile sultanate of Acheh in Sumatra, while simultaneously 2000 Spanish soldiers would sail to, and occupy, first Patani and then Siam before moving on

1 'The World is not Enough' medal, 1583

After the 'union of crowns' in 1580, a new conceit boldly commemorated the creation of Philip II's global empire. A medal of gilded bronze, probably cast in 1583, shows the king on one side and, on the other, a globe surmounted by a horse together with the uncompromising legend NON SUFFICIT ORBIS – 'The world is not enough.' Early in 1586 Francis Drake and his expeditionary force saw the same device in the Governor's Mansion in Santo Domingo: it had by then apparently become the 'logo' of the monarchy and Drake's men considered it a 'very notable marke and token of the vnsatiable ambition of the Spanishe King and his nation'.

effortlessly (and, he seems to have assumed, without casualties) to conquer the city of Canton, 'so rich and sumptuous, and all those other regions of the south [of China], which are many, and very great and very wealthy. And thus His Majesty will be the greatest lord that ever was in the world.'[31] The following year, one of Philip II's judges at Manila went even further and called for the king 'to evict and expel the Muslims from all the Philippine islands, or at least to subject them and make them pay tribute, vanquishing those in Java, Sumatra, Acheh, Borneo, Mindanao, Solo, the Moluccas, Malacca, Siam, Patani, Pegu and other kingdoms which venerate Mohammed'. And in 1586, a 'general assembly' of the Spanish inhabitants of the Philippines, led by the bishop and the governor, drew up a lengthy memorandum urging the king to undertake the conquest of China and sent Father Alonso Sánchez, SJ, to Spain with orders to present their arguments to the king.[32]

Meanwhile, in Europe, jubilation at the marquis of Santa Cruz's conquest of the Azores in 1582 reached such heights that, according to some *madrileños*, 'even Christ was no longer safe in Paradise, for the marquis might go there to bring him back and crucify him all over again'.[33] Nor did the celebrations stop at verbal hyperbole: a bowl commemorating the Terceira campaign of 1583 (found among the wreckage of one of the Spanish Armada vessels that foundered off Ireland) shows Spain's warrior patron saint with new attributes. He still rides a charger, with his sword-arm raised to strike down his foes; but these foes are no longer cowering infidels. Instead they are the swirling waves of the ocean, waves now subdued by Spain along with the human enemies who sought refuge amongst them.[34] The euphoria even affected Santa Cruz who in August 1583, flushed by his success in the Azores, pointed out to the king that: 'Victories as complete as the one God has been pleased to grant Your Majesty in these islands normally spur princes on to other enterprises; and since Our Lord has made Your Majesty such a great king, it is just that you should follow up this victory by making arrangements for the invasion of England next year.' The marquis recommended using the newly expanded Iberian resources of his master to concentrate an expeditionary force of overwhelming strength in preparation for a rapid descent on the English coast as close to London as possible.[35]

Gradually, the conquest of England – just like the conquest of Portugal a few years before – came to be seen as the only means of assuring imperial security. An important strategic assessment prepared in 1585, just after Francis Drake raided Galicia, argued that 'to fight a purely defensive war [against England] is to court a huge and permanent expense, because we have to defend the Indies, Spain and the convoys travelling between them'.[36] Even the prudent duke of Medina Sidonia, when asked his opinion in 1586 on mobilizing a fleet against England, urged 'that this should be set in hand at once, and in earnest, and let it be understood that it will not suffice simply to oppose what the English send: the fleet will need to go into the Channel'.[37] The central government agreed. Early in 1587, a senior minister argued, 'with the English established in Holland and Zeeland, together with their infestation of the Americas and the high seas, it seems that defensive measures cannot deal with everything. Rather, it obliges us to put their house to the torch.' And if that 'house' could not be England, 'then let us take from them Ireland, which could be used as a pawn to exchange for the places they hold in the Netherlands, that voracious monster which gobbles up the troops and treasure of Spain'. By the spring of 1588, with 19,000 soldiers embarked on 130 ships at Lisbon, and a further 80 ships (plus 194 barges) and 27,000 soldiers standing by in Flanders, Philip II and his ministers believed that 'all our wars and affairs afoot today are reduced to this one enterprise': the invasion and conquest of England.[38]

Such an expensive policy – the Armada alone cost 30,000 crowns (£6666) a day – gravely affected the other parts of Philip II's vast empire. Thus in February 1588, the king rejected the request of his viceroy of India for the dispatch of 'more troops, ships and munitions than normally leave [for India] each year' in order to attack Acheh because 'The large number of ships of all sorts, troops, munitions and military equipment' assembled for the descent on England 'consume so much that it was not in any way possible (even though we have tried very hard) to send more than five ships' to Goa. The king's only concession was to hope that Acheh might still be assaulted if the Armada succeeded: 'For what cannot be done now may still happen, if Our Lord wishes to provide the occasion by doing something over here that would be so much for his service, and of such general and such great importance for Christianity, and for the general and particular good of all my kingdoms.'[39]

Now a similar element of 'providentialism' coloured the strategic thinking of almost all states in the century following the Reformation, as religious and political issues became tightly intertwined and the Bible came to serve as a guide to secular as well as spiritual salvation. Most nations in this period regarded themselves as the new 'chosen people', granted a special mandate for empire by God. Thus Philip II's English, Dutch and French enemies also regarded their victories as the result of direct divine intervention. In the words of Oliver Cromwell's schoolteacher, Thomas Beard: 'Nothing in this world comes to pass by chance or adventure, but only and alwaies by the prescription of [God's] will.' After the destruction of the Spanish Armada in 1588, a Dutch commemorative medal boasted, 'God blew and they were scattered'; while a French sympathizer wrote: 'God is wonderful in His works, which smash the designs of this world just when people are ready to shout "victory".'[40]

Spain's rulers espoused similar messianic views with unusual passion. The medieval kings of Castile had laid claim to divine protection, to the power to command miracles, and to a divinely appointed mission; those of medieval Aragon boasted prophecies that their line would produce a 'second David'. The two traditions combined in the persons of Ferdinand of Aragon and Isabella of Castile, Philip's great-grandparents. Chroniclers claimed that their deeds fulfilled ancient prophecies, while God guided their every step, provided miracles for them, and protected them from harm. They hailed Ferdinand, in particular, as a *rey pastor* (king and shepherd – with the double sense of priest) and a 'New David' who would emulate the deeds of the Old Testament kings. In recognition of their work for the Christian faith, the pope accorded Ferdinand and Isabella the title *Reyes Católicos*, 'the Catholic Monarchs'.[41]

Philip II, who inherited the title 'Catholic King', went further – much further. The opening speeches in his name to the Cortes of Castile normally began by stating that his government worked 'first and foremost for the things that concern the service of God, Our Lord, and the defence and conservation of His Holy faith and of the Catholic religion'. They then reviewed recent expensive enterprises undertaken for 'the holy purpose that His Majesty has always in view, to further the holy Christian faith'; and concluded with an appeal for taxes to be voted 'for the service of God Our Lord, and for the general good of these kingdoms and of Christendom – since all these things are linked'. At the start of the reign, as he struggled to find sufficient funds to carry on his government, Philip believed that: 'Everything depends on the will of God, so we can only wait to see how best He can be served. I trust that, because He has removed other worse obstacles, He will remove this one too and give me the means to sustain my kingdoms, so that they will not be lost.' Most expressive of all, he once reassured a dispirited minister with the extraordinary boast: 'May God give you life and health, because you are engaged in His service and in mine, which is the same thing.'[42]

These remarkable statements contained at least three related 'layers' of messianic vision. First, Philip believed that God had chosen him to rule expressly to achieve His purpose for the world. Second, he was equally convinced that God held him under special protection, to enable him to achieve these goals (although the process might prove neither obvious nor easy). Third, he felt certain that, if necessary, God would intervene directly in order to help him to succeed.

In accordance with this vision, Philip II pursued policies that he believed God would favour and, to this end, he spent a great deal of his life in prayer, presumably laying out his options before God as well as begging for divine support. His devotions often dictated the pace of government business. 'I could not send you anything more tonight because today we had a sermon,' he once informed a minister; or again, 'I could not see the rest [of these papers] yesterday, nor until now today, because of the mass.'[43] Every Lent, and at times of particular crisis, he went on retreat and, as a matter of principle, transacted no business of state while in seclusion. The king's constant and comprehensive cycle of religious devotions no doubt allowed him to step back temporarily from political concerns and to clear his mind, renewing his strength to cope with problems of state. (In addition, they occasionally allowed him to catch up on his sleep. He once confessed to his daughters that he had just 'heard two of the longest sermons of my life, although I slept through part of them'.)[44]

The king also devoted prodigious state resources to pious purposes that, he hoped, would please God. The most notable, and the most expensive, was the monastery of St Lawrence at El Escorial, built under Philip's close personal supervision between 1563 and 1584. Politically, it stood as a monument to the Habsburgs' defeat of their arch-enemy, since it commemorated Philip's victory over the French at St Quentin on St Lawrence's Day, 1557. Polemically, it served as a visible bastion against the rising tide of heresy, since its liturgy and its religious iconography ceaselessly affirmed the validity of Catholic doctrine. Dynastically, it provided a magnificent complex in which the royal family could live, rule, pray and die as exemplars of Counter-Reformation piety, and also a mausoleum where the king could bury his relatives and sanctify their memory. In all, it cost at least seven million crowns (£1.5 million) – almost as much as the Spanish Armada and rather more than the Treasury's annual income.

Philip also sought assistance from others in identifying God's purpose. From time to time, he asked his advisers – many of whom were clerics – 'to tell me in all things what you think is best for the service of God, which is my principal aim, and therefore for my service'.[45] Occasionally, he also referred particularly thorny issues to special Committees of Theologians (*Juntas de Teólogos*): how to plan for the council of Trent; which policy to pursue towards heresy in the Netherlands; whether or not to enforce his claim to the Portuguese throne. Several times a week, he seems to have consulted his confessor over whether a specific measure was 'legitimate' (*lícito en consciencia*).[46]

Once he had identified God's purpose, Philip acted to mobilize supernatural assistance to attain his goals. On the one hand, he sought the support of the saints and, to this end, assembled at the Escorial no less than 7422 relics, including 12 entire bodies, 144 complete heads and 306 whole limbs of various saints. Now, for a Catholic, one relic reveals devotion, and a few may reflect exemplary piety; but 7422 relics suggest unbridled obsession. When his agents brought the body of St Leocadia back from the Netherlands to her native city of Toledo in 1587, the king helped to carry the casket into the cathedral, and watched as Cardinal Quiroga, archbishop of Toledo, took out each bone in turn and placed it on the altar. Then Philip said, 'Cardinal, I would like a relic', to which Quiroga (also an accomplished courtier) suavely responded: 'They all belong to Your Majesty. Take whichever you want.' Philip chose one of the saint's thighbones for the Escorial. During his final illness, the only sure way to rouse the dying Philip from his coma was to say loudly: ' "Don't touch the relics!" (pretending that someone was about to take one), and the king immediately opened his eyes.'[47]

The king also mobilized the devotions of his subjects in support of his messianic goals. In the 1560s, he signed hundreds of orders asking secular and religious leaders to organize prayer cycles in favour of the union of the church, the success of the council of Trent, the defeat of the Turks, the suppression of the Dutch Revolt, the health of the queen, the end of a plague epidemic. In the 1570s, he established a comprehensive prayer-chain throughout Castile to seek divine guidance and protection for his cause, and he instructed his prelates to seek out 'persons whose prayers may prove particularly acceptable' to ask God to send him victory.[48]

His messianic vision repeatedly led Philip II to see political issues in religious terms. He justified difficult choices on the grounds that they were necessary not only for the interests of Spain but also for the cause of God; he attributed victories to divine intervention and favour; and he rationalized defeats and failures either as a divine test of Spain's steadfastness and loyalty or else as a punishment for momentary human presumption. When his fortunes received an unexpected boost, he would assure his ministers that 'God has done this'; news of a setback, by contrast, instead of making him reconsider his choices, led him to call on God to provide a miracle. In 1574, for example, as his attempts to suppress the Dutch Revolt bogged down, Philip claimed: 'Unless God performs a miracle, which our sins do not merit, it is no longer possible to maintain ourselves for [more than a few] months, let alone years.' Further reverses simply made him more impatient: 'May God help us with a miracle. I tell you that we need one so much that it seems to me that He *must* choose to give us a miracle, because without one I see everything in the worst situation imaginable.'[49]

Such presumption had far-reaching consequences. Above all, Philip II's conviction that he was doing God's work made him unrealistic in his strategic planning, and inflexible whenever his subordinates complained that his orders seemed impossible. On one occasion, he assured the pope that 'rather than suffer the least damage to the Catholic Church and God's service I will lose all my states, and a hundred lives if I had them'. In 1585, after his commander in the Netherlands (Alexander Farnese, duke of Parma) had persuaded several rebellious cities to surrender in return for limited religious toleration for a period, the king objected because 'I believe it would be better to forfeit all that I have rather than compromise for a moment my constancy where religion is concerned.'[50] Even the failure of the Armada left the king's vision largely intact. In 1590, in order to justify military intervention in support of the French Catholics, he reiterated that 'upholding the faith has been and still is my principal objective in all that has been and is being done'. A few weeks later, he explained to one of his wealthiest subjects (as he requested a hefty donation):

Everybody knows about the great, continuous and unavoidable expenses that I have incurred for many years past to defend our holy Catholic faith and to conserve my kingdoms and lordships, and how they have grown immensely through the war with England and the developments in France; but I have not been able to avoid them, both because I have such a specific obligation to God and the world to act, and also because if the heretics were to prevail (which I hope God will not allow) it might open the door to worse damage and dangers, and to war at home.[51]

It might have been imperialism dictated by sincere religious convictions, but it was imperialism none the less.

At least Philip continued to veto most initiatives for further expansion. Some, like the various projects for the invasion of China, no doubt lacked merit – although the remarkable success of a small combined operation of Spanish and Portuguese soldiers and missionaries in Cambodia between 1596 and 1599 indicates what luck (combined with a total lack of scruple) could do.[52] Others, however, like Portuguese efforts to conquer Sri Lanka after 1594, or the attempts of the Philippines government to occupy Taiwan after 1597, might have succeeded in creating secure profitable new bases had those involved received adequate funding.[53] Within Europe, Philip II's failure to provide substantial and sustained support to the duke of Mercœur's bid for Breton autonomy and to the earl of Tyrone's rebellion in Ireland during the 1590s rank as major lost strategic opportunities.[54]

Worse, the king's decision to devote all his resources against his enemies in Northwest Europe led to grave material losses for his subjects. Direct English assaults on the Iberian peninsula came in 1589 (on Corunna), and in 1596 (on Cadiz) while the English fleet maintained a semipermanent predatory presence off the Atlantic coast. Although the Royal Navy itself scored few spectacular successes – most notably the capture of the India carracks *Madre de Deus* in 1592 and the *São Valentim* in 1601 – English privateers scored far more.[55] In the three years following the Armada, 1589–91, English vessels took at least 299 prizes, worth perhaps £400,000 (equivalent to the government's entire annual revenue) and well over £100,000 annually thereafter. Nine-tenths of the value of this English plunder came from ships sailing from India, Africa and America to the Iberian peninsula, with 'Brazilmen' (vessels carrying sugar and brazilwood from Pernambuco to Portugal) as the commonest prize of all.[56]

The effect of prolonged war with England and the Dutch on Iberian overseas commerce proved devastating. During the first eight decades of direct trade between Portugal and India, between 1498 and 1586, not a single ship fell prey to pirates; but between 1587 and 1596, Philip II's enemies either captured or burnt five fully laden carracks. Furthermore, the constant diversion of shipping and materials to operations in the North Atlantic after 1585 both reduced the number of vessels available for trade with India and complicated the task of preparing the outward voyages, so that the carracks left in smaller numbers and set sail dangerously late. Whereas before the union of crowns only one vessel in ten foundered en route between Lisbon and Goa, between 1580 and 1610 the total soared to one ship in four; moreover, whereas between 1500 and 1579 only six ships sailed from Lisbon too late to catch favourable winds to India, between 1580 and 1608 fourteen 'lost their voyages'. Overall, shipping arriving in Goa from Portugal declined by 25 per cent between 1580 and 1600.[57]

Likewise the trade between Spain and the Americas fell dramatically in 1587–8 and scarcely recovered until the conclusion of peace with England in 1604.[58] In the 1590s the Dutch, too, began to trade and loot in Africa, South America and, eventually, Asia, plunging the colonial administrations of both Castile and Portugal into a frenzy of defence spending – from escorts and convoys to fortresses and garrisons, and from Mombasa and Macao to Manila and Callao. Although the financial state of the *Estado da India* had given some cause for concern before the union of crowns, the detailed fiscal surveys of 1581, 1588, 1607 and 1609 all showed a healthy surplus, despite the almost constant state of war that existed between the Portuguese and some of their neighbours.[59] However, the arrival of the English and Dutch ('os enemigos de Europa', as the viceroys always termed them) both reduced the profits from the various trades on which the Estado thrived and increased the cost of defence, as one outpost after another required expensive new fortifications.[60] By the 1630s, the revenues of Portuguese India fell far short of the costs of administration and defence, while its unsecured debts stood at over four million crowns (£900,000).[61] The evolution of the imperial budget in Spanish America followed a similar path: although remittances to Seville remained high until the 1610s, the cost of defence soared – and the defence not only of the long coastline of the islands and mainland of the Americas but also of the Philippines. Indeed, between 1618 and 1621 the Royal Treasury in Mexico sent more money to the Philippines than to Spain, and by 1640 it spent one-third or more of its revenues on defence.[62]

Fernand Braudel's classic study, *The Mediterranean and the Mediterranean World in the Age of Philip II*, saw the years 1578–83 as 'the turning point of the century', because they marked a decisive shift in Europe's centre of gravity from the Mediterranean to the Atlantic. In political terms, between 1577 and 1581 Philip II disengaged from his long-running struggle with the Ottoman Turks and (although he continued to encourage Safavid Iran to fight on) instead concentrated his resources – both those of the Portuguese empire and the fast-rising remittances from America – in 'a great battle for control of the Atlantic and world domination'.[63] And when that bid foundered, as it did in the 1580s and 90s, those whom the Habsburg monarchy had attacked sought their revenge.

But could one argue that the North Europeans would have tried to overturn the Iberian intercontinental trading monopolies anyway? After all, they had challenged them long before 1580: the French in

Canada, Brazil and Florida; the English in Guinea, the Caribbean and (during Drake's circumnavigation of 1577–80) in the Pacific too. A brief cost-analysis of the ventures that immediately followed the defeat of the Spanish Armada in 1588 sheds some light on this counterfactual question, for while the profits that accrued to Philip II and his subjects from their overseas empires declined, those of their enemies did not soar. Although the capture of individual carracks proved extremely profitable, the expense of fitting out expeditions, and later of maintaining bases overseas, for some time absorbed most of all the gains made from international commerce. The Dutch East India Company – the most profitable overseas enterprise mounted by Philip's enemies – until 1630 landed annually at Amsterdam cargoes well under half the value of those landed at Lisbon, and paid only thirteen dividends in cash.[64] The Dutch West India Company, founded in 1622 to break into the lucrative Iberian trades with Africa and the Americas, despite heavy subsidies from the government had run up debts of 18 million florins (£1.8 million) by 1640 and was declared bankrupt and liquidated by 1674.[65] The financial performance of England's early ventures in Asia and the Americas likewise lacked lustre: even Drake's West India raid of 1585–6 made a loss of 25 per cent; the Virginia Company failed; and the English East India Company (which lacked any fixed capital) experienced constant cash-flow problems until the 1650s.[66]

It therefore seems unlikely that, on commercial grounds alone, merchants from northern Europe would have chosen to make the heavy investment necessary for even modest success in intercontinental trade had they been able to secure the colonial produce they desired within the Iberian peninsula – as they had done until the embargoes of 1585–6. After that, however, in order to secure the spices, silks, silver and other luxuries from the Far East and the Far West, the English and Dutch had no alternative than to sail to the source and get it themselves. In this context, had the embargoes affected Spain but not Portugal – that is to say, had Philip II not been king of Portugal – the financial and the political incentives for the northerners to organize their own trade with Asia would both have been lacking.

In the end, therefore, the annexation of Portugal in 1580 weakened rather than strengthened the monarchy of Philip II: the liabilities ultimately outweighed the assets – principally because the union threatened the prevailing balance of power in Europe. And yet, as Pedro de Ribadeneira had written at the time, what else could the king have done except enforce his claim to the Portuguese succession? The consequences for Philip II's monarchy, had either Dom Antonio (an illegitimate nephew of King Sebastian who enjoyed French and English support) or some other hostile claimant gained control of Portugal, can easily be imagined: the cost of defending the long land frontier and the vital sea lanes would soon have proved crippling. The dilemma bore a curious resemblance to that facing Philip's great-grandson, Louis XIV, in 1700. Carlos II, the last of the Spanish Habsburgs, bequeathed all his territories to Louis's grandson; if he refused the inheritance, it should pass intact and entire to the Austrian Archduke Charles; and if he refused, it should all go to the duke of Savoy. Louis and his ministers, just like Philip II and his advisers, rated the risks attached to allowing the adjacent inheritance to pass to another claimant higher than the likelihood that joining together two great empires would prove unacceptable to the other major powers and so precipitate, sooner or later, a general European war. They therefore accepted the poisoned chalice.[67]

In the event, the union of crowns in 1580, like the Spanish succession in 1700, did unleash an international crisis. It provoked a major conflict with other European states – several of them possessing imperial aspirations of their own – and brought war to almost every corner of Philip II's monarchy, imperilling its integrity and threatening its future. As the duke of Sessa, a senior Spanish diplomat, shrewdly put it shortly after the king's death:

Truly, sir, I believe we are gradually becoming the target at which the whole world wants to shoot its arrows; and you know that no empire, however great, has been able to sustain many wars in different areas for long. If we can think only of defending ourselves, and never manage to contrive a great offensive blow against one of our enemies, so that when that is over we can turn to the others, although I may be mistaken, I doubt whether we can sustain an empire as scattered as ours.[68]

The empire on which the sun never set had become a target on which the sun never set. Worse, the central government always seemed to lack the resources to do more than respond to each attack with half-measures. In the withering assessment of one of Spain's leading naval commanders:

I have been much grieved for some years past to see that, for motives of economy, expeditions are undertaken with such small forces that they principally serve to irritate our enemies, rather than to punish them. The worst of it is that wars thus become chronic, and the expense and trouble resulting from long continued wars are endless.

Or, to quote the duke of Sessa again:

We flit so rapidly from one area to another, without making a major effort in one and then, when that is finished, in another . . . I do not know why we eat so many snacks but never a real meal! I would like to join everything together, so that we could perhaps do something worthwhile – either in Ireland or in North Africa – but I fear that, as usual, we shall do both and thus only lose time, men, money and reputation.[69]

So, thanks to the strategic overstretch caused by the union of the crowns of Portugal and Castile, although Philip II had seemed like David on his coronation day at Tomar in 1581, by the time of his death in 1598 he had begun to resemble Goliath.

2

On Monday 10 April 1989, Jonathan Israel, then Professor of Dutch History and Institutions at University College, London, organized a symposium at the British Academy in London on 'The making of modern British freedom? The English Revolution of 1688–9 and the Dutch'. The programme promised papers by four speakers – Hugh Trevor-Roper, E. H. Kossmann, J. R. Jones and Jonathan Israel – followed by 'A question and answer panel: the Audience may put questions and objections to the four speakers'.

Professor Israel of course meant the question mark in the symposium title to be provocative but his own paper, which portrayed William III's 'Descent on England' as an act of naked aggression, proved more provocative by far. It stressed the size of the Dutch invasion force – over 450 sailing ships, 40,000 men and 5000 horses – and the preponderance of foreign soldiers (Danish, Dutch, French Huguenot and German) among them. William sent Dutch troops ahead to secure London and, although many Londoners turned out to cheer his progress down Knightsbridge to St James's Palace on 18 December 1688, 'putting oranges on the ends of their sticks to show they were for him', William's Dutch guards patrolled the entire route. No English regiments were allowed within twenty miles of London and, for the next eighteen months, Dutch troops occupied all significant buildings in and around the capital. Nevertheless, Professor Israel noted, 'Since the early eighteenth century, a thick wall of silence has descended over the Dutch occupation of London in 1688–90. The whole business came to seem so improbable to later generations that by common consent, scholarly and popular, it was simply erased from the record.'[1]

Some members of 'the Audience' on 10 April 1989 wished it to remain erased, and Israel received numerous questions about and *objections to his evidence, all of which he skilfully addressed. I left the symposium struck by the wealth of comparisons between the success of the 'Dutch armada' in 1688 and the failure of the Spanish Armada's attempt to conquer England just a century before. William's triumph provided an important new perspective on the earlier venture: above all, it proved that England could be conquered in a matter of weeks, just as Philip had expected, because William landed in Devon on 15 November and made his triumphant entry to London one month later. I therefore suggested to Jonathan that we might perhaps write a joint article that compared and contrasted the two invasions, and he graciously agreed. He also offered to include it in the volume of essays he proposed to edit on the subject, incorporating the four presentations at the symposium along with twelve more. We exchanged drafts over the next few weeks and by August 1989 we had a version that we both liked. It appeared in his volume,* The Anglo-Dutch Moment. Essays on the Glorious Revolution and Its World Impact, *two years later.*

Since then, much more work has appeared on both of the campaigns covered in this chapter. The second edition of Colin Martin and Geoffrey Parker, The Spanish Armada *(Manchester, 1999), incorporates most of the new research on 1588. For 1688, the proceedings of a second conference on the Dutch dimension – so often overlooked by earlier historians – sheds much valuable light. Dale Hoak and Mordechai Feingold, eds.,* The World of William and Mary: Anglo-Dutch Perspectives on the Revolution of 1688–89 *(Stanford, 1996), contains fifteen essays based on presentations to a conference held at the College of William and Mary, that examine aesthetic aspects of the 'Dutch connection' such as its impact on English garden design, as well as the more familiar political and religious consequences. Furthermore, John E. Wills has set the 'Descent on England' in an even broader context with his tour de force:* 1688. A Global History *(New York, 2001).*

Although William III quickly became one of the most hated monarchs in British history – variously denounced as the 'new Cromwell', the 'new Herod', the 'new Nero' – his success in 1688 changed the course of British and European history. Above all, it propelled Britain into a major role on the continent almost continuously until 1763: a role that allowed it to acquire, in various treaties with other European powers, a global empire inconceivable before the Revolution. The new regime (and its successors) in London also permitted the development of a remarkable system of representative democracy and encouraged intellectual innovation: cultural hegemony in Europe gradually shifted from the Netherlands to England. Had Providence and the 'Protestant wind' not favoured William in 1688, it is hard to imagine any of these developments taking place. The history of much of the world – for better or worse – would then have been very different.[2]

Of Providence and Protestant Winds: The Spanish Armada of 1588 and the Dutch Armada of 1688

On 30 July 1588 Philip II's 'Invincible Armada', a huge force of 130 ships and some 25,000 men, arrived off the southwest coast of England. It was an awesome sight which struck terror into many of those who observed it, and it has been vividly remembered ever since. But it failed: a devastating attack by the Royal Navy forced the Armada to return to Spain via the North Sea and the Atlantic, where severe storms destroyed at least one-third of the ships and perhaps one half of the men. The English and their Dutch allies were jubilant, and saw the outcome as the direct intervention of Providence: 'God blew and they were scattered' was the message struck on a famous commemorative medal.[3] One hundred years later, on 15 November 1688, another armada, this time assembled by the Dutch Republic, appeared off the same southwest coast of England under the personal command of Prince William III of Orange. This was an even more awesome sight: over 450 ships carrying some 40,000 men and 5000 horses. This time the 'Protestant wind' directed the invaders to a favourable haven – Torbay in Devon – while keeping the pursuing Royal Navy at bay for the crucial three days while the troops, horses and artillery got ashore.[4]

Some obvious points of comparison between the two armadas were noted even before the Dutch fleet set out. In October 1688, the Polish resident at The Hague reported that Europe was about to witness one of the most amazing enterprises in its history, and that:

The Dutch are convinced that they will be as fortunate in their plan to attack England as Philip II was unfortunate, when he sent his fearful fleet against Elizabeth in the month of August in the year 1588. There are few among them who are unaware of this period of history and who do not know by heart the inscriptions on the medals which were struck at that time.[5]

The similarities between the two expeditions were indeed numerous and striking. Both armadas ostensibly set out to reverse England's religious bias (militantly Protestant in 1588; allegedly tending towards Catholic in 1688) and to impose fundamental political changes in the interests of a major foreign power and at the invitation of certain factions in England. Both enjoyed some support from an assortment of European states but had to run the gauntlet of the ships and soldiers of a hostile neighbouring power (the Dutch in 1588; France in 1688) as well as those of England. Both armadas came logistically and mentally prepared to take on the Royal Navy, but both hoped to avoid a battle at sea as far as possible since they carried large invasion armies and had as their essential objective the disembarkation of those armies in England with as little loss and disruption as possible. Both attempted to succeed by stealth, attacking (like the Japanese at Pearl Harbor in 1941) in advance of a formal declaration of war. Above all, both armadas mobilized unprecedented reserves of shipping, supplies, equipment, munitions and manpower so that, to some observers, the invasion fleets appeared almost inconceivably large. That of 1588 seemed, to a foreign diplomat, 'The most numerous that has ever existed in these seas since the creation of the world'. And the English admiral Sir John Hawkins remained equally impressed even after his victory in the Channel: the Armada was, he assured his government, 'The greatest and strongest combination, to my understanding, that ever was gathered in Christendom'.[6] A century later Gregorio Leti, historiographer of the city of Amsterdam, had no doubt that the Dutch armada was 'a fleet the like of which has never been seen'; while the

English ambassador at The Hague claimed that 'such a preparation was never heard of in these parts of the world'.[7]

At least some of these claims were true. Although the battle of Lepanto in 1571 had involved more vessels and more men on the Christian side, the 130 ships (of which about 25 were purpose-built warships), 2431 guns and 26,000 men (19,000 of them soldiers) aboard the Armada certainly formed the largest naval concentration achieved to that date in Atlantic waters. And furthermore, Philip II's fleet was instructed to join forces with an army of 26,000 infantry and 1000 cavalry veterans gathered in the Spanish Netherlands and embarked aboard some 270 barges and small warships.[8] The total size of the invasion force in 1588 was thus 400 ships and 47,000 men, of whom some 37,000 were scheduled to land. The expedition of 1688 was somewhat larger, with 53 warships – 32 medium and small 'capital ships', the rest small escort vessels[9] – some 10 fireships, and about 400 other vessels to transport the troops, supplies and horses.[10] The army numbered 10,692 regular infantry and 3660 regular cavalry: 14,352 men in all. In addition there were the gunners of the artillery train and several thousand volunteers. James II's ambassador in The Hague was probably close to the truth when he put the total strength of William's invasion army at 21,000, including some 5000 volunteers.[11] In addition, the crews of the warships and transports numbered at least a further 20,000. The invasion forces gathered in 1688 thus totalled some 463 ships 40,000 men and 5000 horses.

It was clearly not possible to conceal preparations of this magnitude from the eyes of either domestic or foreign observers. When, in the last week of August 1688, the merchants of the Amsterdam Exchange suddenly grasped that the Republic was intending to attack Britain, frenzied dealing set off the second most catastrophic crash of the entire seventeenth century on the stock market. On 9 September the French ambassador at The Hague, the comte d'Avaux, appeared before the States-General and delivered a blunt warning in the name of his master that the moment the Dutch moved against His Britannic Majesty, Louis XIV would declare war on the Republic. But the preparations continued. In the days preceding d'Avaux's intervention there was still some doubt as to whether the vast armada would be used against France or Britain, but the balance of opinion steadily shifted to the latter view. Thus on 7 September the English consul at Amsterdam reported to London that 'the discourses of, and reasons for, this equipage are very various – one day they say they will demand reason of France another that they will goe and cause a rebellion in England'; while at much the same time the English consul at Hamburg reported that the 'alarm is yet hott here that the Dutch fleet is designed against England'.[12]

The news then spread rapidly: English agents everywhere detected ripples of the Grand Design. ''Tis no wonder that their going for England is no more a secret in these parts,' wrote the English ambassador at The Hague: 'at Berlin the Elector's ministers speak of nothing else'. Ten days later he added: 'these forces, accompanied by many volunteers designe no less than a conquest of the three kingdoms [of England, Scotland and Ireland]: never was an army better furnished with all necessaries'.[13] At Hamburg the residents of the Protestant princes told each other that the 'Prince of Orange is master of Amsterdam and London'; while in Vienna (according to James II's envoy) 'there is nothing more talk'd of here than the quarrel betwixt the Dutch and us'; and in Lisbon 'wee have been here of late extremely alarm'd with the vast preparations that the Dutch have made of sea and land forces, it being the common discourse that their designs are against England'.[14]

The government in London was soon convinced and began to take preventive measures, strengthening the defences of the east coast towns and forts and sending the Royal Navy to Harwich with orders to prevent 'any approach of any fleet or number of ships from Holland upon any of our coasts, or their making any descent upon the same'; and 'to endeavour by all hostile means, to sink, burn, take and otherwise destroy and disable the said fleet'.[15] 'Whoever comes here,' wrote Secretary of State Lord Middleton, 'shall not find us unprovided to receive them, and as the English nation hath been famous for their courage, so I doubt not at all, but on this occasion they will signalize their loyalty.'[16] In fact, of course, the opportunity never arose because James II and his advisers expected the invaders to land in either Essex or Yorkshire, whereas William actually made his descent in the southwest.

It is easy to be wise after the event. Most recent studies have found

James's ministers and commanders guilty of either incompetence or disloyalty, and have praised William for his masterly control of his destiny. They have assumed that all talk of a possible landing by the invaders in the north was an elaborate feint. Thus a report of the English ambassador in The Hague (in late October) that the Dutch 'take all the colliers they can light on [to get experienced pilots and crews], which is a sign that they intend to sayle northwards' has been interpreted as part of an elaborate smokescreen: William ordered these pilots to be seized, some have claimed, simply because he wished the English to think he was aiming for Yorkshire.[17] Likewise the information brought to London by 'a Roman Catholick Pilott come this night from the [Dutch] fleet' that he had heard one of the English exiles with Prince William 'whisper to others . . . that they must steer their course now towards the River Humber' is seen as part of a successful Dutch campaign of disinformation.[18]

But no reliable evidence exists to show that William had decided the matter in advance. The only certain point is that he was determined to avoid the southeast of England at all costs because that was where James had concentrated the bulk of his considerable military and naval strength.[19] The essence of the Dutch strategy was therefore to land at a distance from London. As Hans Willem Bentinck, the prince's chief adviser, wrote sometime in October 1688: 'If the landing be northwards, it is conceived to be very dangerous to land any nearer to London than in some part of Yorkshire; and if the landing be westward, then no nearer to London than some part of Devonshire, the King's forces being all about London.'[20] At that point, therefore, perhaps only a few days before the first invasion attempt, the prince had evidently not made his final choice between the two potential landing zones. And, indeed, when the force finally set out, after one false start sabotaged by storms, it sailed northwards before doubling back. It has usually been argued that this was a feint, largely on the strength of a cogent memorandum written by Admiral Herbert warning the prince of the extreme difficulty of disembarking a large army in winter on the Yorkshire coast.[21] But this point of view ignores a number of considerations. First, the prince and his Dutch advisers normally seem to have paid little heed to Herbert's counsel; second, the minutes of a council of war held aboard the *Leyden* on 11 November displayed a determination to land in the southwest *unless* the wind forced the fleet northwards – in other words, even at that late stage the prince was content to let the wind ('Protestant' or otherwise) make the decision for him. Third, at 1 p.m. the following day William wrote to tell Bentinck (who had been left behind when the fleet sailed) that they had after all taken 'the westerly route' – news that would scarcely have been necessary had that been the Dutch plan all along.[22] Finally, and most telling of all, another letter written by the prince shortly after his descent upon Devon complained about the difficulty of communicating with Holland from the southwest of England and went on to regret that circumstances had forced him to sail west rather than north. 'If we had landed in the north of England,' William remarked, 'we would have found various things easier; but the strong easterly wind that we encountered did not allow it.'[23]

So the unfortunate James II – however good his intelligence – could thus have received no accurate forewarning of the exact place of his enemies' descent since they themselves only made the critical decision at the last moment. The invaders held the initiative until the moment they reached the coast of England.

The same had been true in 1588. The build-up of naval and military forces in Iberian ports had been an open secret for over two years before the Armada finally set sail, with detailed reports on the precise disposition of Philip II's forces available to any spy – whether Catholic or Protestant – willing to pay for the information. But, as in 1688, what the spies all failed to ascertain was the strategy to be followed and, above all, the designated point of disembarkation. Some thought that Plymouth was the target; others feared for the Isle of Wight. Others still remained convinced that the Armada was not destined for England at all but for a direct descent on Holland and Zeeland![24]

Numerous as the similarities between the two invasions may have been, however, they were outweighed by the differences. Most obvious was the outcome: the invasion of 1588 proved an heroic and costly failure, that of 1688 a total and almost bloodless success (although both gave rise to an indecisive, expensive and long-running European war). Since the contrasting outcomes derived largely from the distinct strategies and logistics adopted by the invaders, it is worth examining them in some detail.

To begin with, major fighting took place in 1588, but – rather surprisingly – not in 1688. The contrast stemmed entirely from the different conduct of the Royal Navy, for both invasion fleets were under strict orders to avoid battle if at all possible: as the two orders of battle make clear, the essential element in both armadas was the convoy carrying the army of invasion and its supplies. At all costs, both had to be preserved intact until they could get ashore (Figures 2 and 3).[25] But in 1588 the English warships, although taken by surprise when the Armada hove into view, managed to work their way out of harbour and harry the invaders from the moment they entered English territorial waters. A century later, by contrast, the Royal Navy failed to get to sea until the invaders were two days ahead of them and failed to catch up until the expeditionary force was safely landed and on the way to London. For this striking difference there are two explanations. First, and often forgotten, shipbuilding in Europe advanced markedly during the seventeenth century. The changes occurred less in ships-of-the-line, for the firepower and seaworthiness of, say, Medina Sidonia's Portuguese galleons or of, say, the *Ark Royal* were not so different from that of the third-rates involved in the 1688 campaign; but the quality of the transports was revolutionized. In 1588, both the English and Spanish commanders excoriated the poor performance of the merchantmen in their fleets, which reduced their overall speed (even with a following wind) to that of a rowing-boat; a century later, William of Orange's fleet – larger and thus harder to keep together – covered the distance between the Channel and Torbay (also with a following wind) in one-third of the time.[26] Thus the failure of the English to mount a hot pursuit in 1688 against a fleet travelling at top speed was far more serious than it would have been a century earlier. And some have therefore posed a second question: whether that failure perhaps stemmed from treachery rather than from ill-fortune or incompetence. James II, in retrospect, certainly felt he had been betrayed; and, equally certainly, some captains in his fleet were unsympathetic to his cause. There was none of that enthusiastic, aggressive xenophobia that characterized Elizabeth's commanders against Spain. But, when all the evidence is considered, it would seem that James's admiral, Lord Dartmouth, and at least some of his captains fully intended to intercept and fight the enemy if they could. The two principal obstacles in their path

2 Sailing orders for the Spanish Armada, 1588

The Tuscan ambassador in Madrid made this clandestine copy of the battle plan of the Spanish Armada and sent it to the grand duke on 25 March 1588, four months before the fleet entered the Channel. (The papal nuncio also secured a copy in June and his Venetian colleague did so the following month.) The plan showed the detailed disposition of the 130 ships of the fleet, with the troop transports in the centre (c) – including the vessel contributed by the grand duke (14). The duke of Medina Sidonia, the fleet's commander, sailed in the third rank of the vanguard (7). The ambassador was well informed: the Armada sailed in this exact formation when it first encountered the Royal Navy on 31 July 1588.

were, first, the lateness of the season which made Dartmouth reluctant to take his fleet across to blockade the Dutch coast (as James counselled); and, second, the decision to station the navy at the Gunfleet, which was an excellent position from which to pursue an enemy sailing towards the coast of Yorkshire, but dangerously ineffective against one sailing south for the Channel.[27] The central problem, in 1688 as in 1588, was that (as noted above) the invaders always held the initiative.

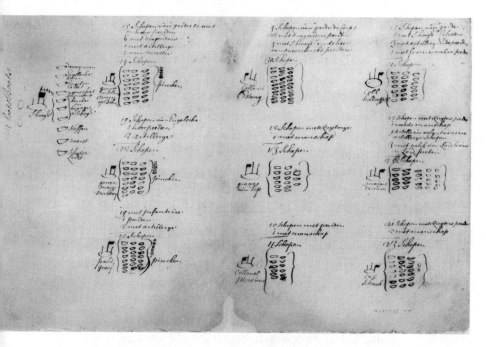

3 Sailing orders for the Dutch armada, 1688

One century after the unsuccessful campaign of the Spanish Armada Hans
Willem Bentinck, principal adviser to Prince William of Orange decided to
deploy the much larger Dutch fleet – almost five hundred vessels – in a very
different way. In a plan drawn up shortly before its departure from Holland
on 13 November 1688, the prince led the way (the ship with two pennants
at the far left) with the various contingents arranged in nine separate
squadrons behind him.

It was, of course, one thing to decide that England must be invaded,
and quite another to make it happen. Nevertheless, nine English
governments had been overthrown or seriously undermined by seaborne invasions in the five centuries since the Norman Conquest, with
at least seven other successful landings of major forces, and many
more lesser raids. Philip II and his ministers studied these various
operations carefully and concluded that three strategies offered a
reasonable prospect of success. The first consisted of a simultaneous
combined operation by a fleet strong enough both to defeat the opposing English navy and to shepherd across the Channel an army sufficient

to accomplish the conquest (as William I had done in 1066 with spectacular success). The second possible strategy involved assembling an army in secret near the Channel while launching a diversionary assault on Ireland which would draw off most of England's defenders, leaving the mainland relatively open to invasion by the main force (a landing at Smerwick in Ireland by papal forces in 1579–80 seemed to show the way). Finally, a surprise assault might be essayed (as Edward of York had done in 1471 and Henry Tudor in 1485).[28] That all these possible strategies received consideration in 1586–8 reflects great credit on the vision and competence of Philip and his 'national security advisers'; that they tried to undertake all three of them at once does not.

In January 1586, in response to English attacks on Spanish possessions in Galicia, the Canaries and the Caribbean, Philip II invited both the duke of Parma (commander of his forces in the Spanish Netherlands) and the marquis of Santa Cruz (admiral of his Atlantic fleet) to formulate a plan of attack on England.[29] Santa Cruz replied first, sending a draft proposal to court in mid-February, followed by a full plan on 22 March. Unfortunately only the lists of necessary resources appear to have survived, but the immense detail of this document – ranging from the number of capital ships down to the last pair of shoes required – makes Santa Cruz's intentions perfectly plain.[30] It clearly corresponded to the second strategy for the invasion of England: a diversionary attack on Ireland followed by a surprise attack on the mainland. Briefly stated, a fleet of some 150 great ships and 400 support vessels would be assembled in Iberian ports in order to transport 55,000 invasion troops – together with their equipment, munitions and supporting artillery – direct to a landing point somewhere in the British Isles. It was to be an operation modelled on such earlier successes as the relief of Malta in 1565 and the conquest of the Azores in 1582 and 1583. Santa Cruz had participated in all three of them.

Early in April 1586, Santa Cruz presented his plans in detail to a meeting of top advisers in the Escorial. Exactly which landing area he designated is not known, for no minutes of the meeting have survived; but it was most probably the port of Waterford in southern Ireland since this was the region mentioned in many subsequent papers.[31] The attack was to be launched in the summer of 1587 and preparations were authorized in three areas: in Lisbon, where ships and men were to be assembled to form a strike force under the personal command of Santa Cruz; in Andalusia, where the duke of Medina Sidonia (who had also been at court for the planning meeting) was dispatched to raise troops and assemble supply vessels which would later be sent to Lisbon; and in Vizcaya, where eight large merchantmen and four pinnaces were embargoed to serve as a new squadron under the command of Spain's most experienced Atlantic seaman, Juan Martínez de Recalde.[32]

However, just as preparations to implement the Santa Cruz plan began, the duke of Parma completed his own strategic assessment. It came in a twenty-eight-page letter dated 20 April 1586, with further details entrusted to the special messenger who brought the letter to court. Parma began by regretting the lack of secrecy concerning the king's intentions. According to him, even ordinary soldiers and civilians in Flanders were openly discussing how England could be invaded. Nevertheless, the duke believed, the enterprise might still be feasible provided certain basic precautions were taken. First, the king of Spain must be in sole charge 'without placing any reliance on either the English themselves, or the assistance of other allies'. Second, some assurance must be obtained that France would not interfere. Third, sufficient troops and resources must be left to defend the reconquered parts of the Netherlands against the Dutch after the assault force had left.

If all this could be achieved, the duke considered that a force of 30,000 foot and 500 horse might safely be detached from the Army of Flanders and ferried across the Channel to launch a surprise attack on England aboard a flotilla of sea-going barges. Provided his precise intentions remained a secret, 'given the number of troops we have to hand here, and the ease with which we can concentrate and embark them in the barges, and considering that we can ascertain, at any moment, the forces which Elizabeth has and can be expected to have, and that the crossing only takes 10 to 12 hours without a following wind (and 8 hours with one)', Parma felt sure the invasion could be undertaken with a fair chance of success. 'The most suitable, close and accessible point of disembarkation [he concluded], is the coast between

Dover and Margate', which would permit a surprise march on London.[33] This was, in essence, the third invasion strategy: a surprise assault.[34]

Philip II was thus confronted by two plausible plans. One was endorsed by his foremost naval commander; the other by his most experienced general. But which was the better?

To some extent, the appeal of Parma's strategy was reduced by the long delay that intervened before it arrived at court. The king had asked for it on 29 December 1585 and yet, despite a reminder on 7 February 1586, it was not sent until 20 April and was not received by the royal cypher clerks until 20 June. Four more days elapsed before the bearer, Giovanni Battista Piatti, was debriefed by the king's ministers: they asked him exactly what shipping was currently available in the ports of Flanders to ferry a major army across the open sea, and about the possible advantage of seeking an alternative landing place in the Thames estuary, closer to London. Then the whole dossier was turned over to the king's leading foreign policy adviser, Don Juan de Zúñiga.

Zúñiga could draw upon a lifetime's experience of political and military affairs. He had fought in the Netherlands in the 1550s, and then rose through the ranks of ambassador to the papal court and viceroy of Naples to become in 1582 a councillor of war and state in Madrid. Now he presided over the Junta de Noche (the 'Night Committee'), formed to coordinate central government policy and advise the king on major affairs of state. He was totally undeterred by the conflict with the Santa Cruz plan already adopted. Instead he sought to amalgamate the two strategies. He proposed that the marquis's fleet should sail from Lisbon, carrying as many troops as could be mustered, together with most of the matérial needed for the land campaign, directly for Ireland. There it would put ashore its assault troops and secure a beach-head. This (Zúñiga anticipated) would threaten and disrupt Elizabeth's naval forces, thereby neutralizing their potential for resistance when, after some two months, the Armada suddenly left Ireland and made for the Channel. The main invasion force of 30,000 veterans would then be led by Parma in a surprise attack, sailing from the ports of Flanders to the beaches of Kent in a flotilla of flat-bottomed craft, while the Armada cruised off the North

Foreland and secured the local command of the Narrow Seas requisite for a safe crossing. It would then offload the siege artillery and supplies necessary for a swift march on London. Finally, once the two beach-heads had been established and the seas made secure, the fleet of supply ships already being concentrated by the duke of Medina Sidonia in the ports of Andalusia would bring up further reinforcements and replenishments.

With significant parts of England and Ireland thus under Spanish occupation, Parma was to create an interim administration in London pending the arrival of the new ruler approved by both pope and king.[35] If, however, Parma proved unable to defeat and capture Elizabeth, he would be instructed to use his presence on English soil to secure three key concessions. First, there was to be complete toleration and freedom of worship for Catholics throughout the kingdom. Second, all English troops were to be withdrawn from the Netherlands, and the places they garrisoned were to be surrendered directly to Spain. Finally, England must pay a war indemnity and the invasion force should remain in Kent until it was paid. With such high stakes, Zúñiga concluded, and with such a complex operation, it would be futile to attempt anything in 1586; so he suggested that the 'Enterprise of England' should be launched in August or September 1587.[36]

One wonders whether Philip II realized the enormity of the proposed change of plan. There was, in retrospect, much to recommend Santa Cruz's strategy. The events of 1588 would prove that, once they got their Armada to sea, the Spaniards experienced little difficulty in moving 60,000 tons of shipping from one end of the Channel to the other, despite repeated assaults upon it, while the Kinsale landing of 1601 showed how easily a beach-head in southern Ireland could be secured and fortified. Likewise, Parma's concept of a Blitzkrieg landing in Kent, without any warning, also had much to recommend it: time and again, his troops had demonstrated their invincibility under his leadership, and it is hard to see how the largely untrained English forces, taken by surprise, could have successfully resisted the Army of Flanders as it marched on London. The Armada's undoing was caused, ultimately, by the decision to unite the fleet from Spain with the army from the Netherlands as the obligatory prelude to launching the invasion.[37]

On 26 July 1586, Giovanni Battista Piatti therefore returned to the Netherlands with details of a masterplan for the conquest of England that embodied, in all essentials, the complex and subtle vision of Don Juan de Zúñiga. A parallel dossier went to Lisbon. But the king invited neither Parma nor Santa Cruz to comment on the orders sent to them; he merely instructed them to carry them out.[38] The king, for his part, instructed all public authorities in Spain, Portugal, Naples and Sicily to prepare troops, munitions and other necessary equipment, while Spanish and Italian reinforcements marched to the Army of Flanders and shipping from all over Europe was lured towards Lisbon and Cadiz.[39]

Then the whole strategic scene changed when in April 1587 Queen Elizabeth, goaded by news of Philip's designs against her, decided to launch Sir Francis Drake with a powerful flotilla on what today would be called 'a pre-emptive strike' (and was then known as 'the singeing of the king of Spain's beard'). It was not the sack of Cadiz and the destruction of stores and ships that proved critical, but rather Drake's subsequent – and well publicized – departure to intercept the returning treasure galleons from the East and West Indies. For that threat forced Santa Cruz to take his powerful fleet to sea, in July, not to Ireland as intended but to await the returning fleets off the Azores. Although he accomplished this feat brilliantly (albeit losing one East Indiaman to Drake) he was unable to return to Iberian waters until October, and by then his ships were storm-damaged and his men sick. There was now no way the Armada could sail against England in 1587. The whole Grand Strategy required rethinking.[40]

Philip worked hard. First, he ordered the auxiliary fleet in Andalusia to sail to Lisbon and join forces with the warships of Santa Cruz (as soon as they returned from the Azores). Then on 4 September he issued a detailed directive for the Armada. There was now no talk of invading Ireland – indeed two whole clauses of the instructions were devoted to explaining that, because of the delays caused by Drake's raid and the need to escort the treasure fleets, there was no time left to secure a base in Ireland before invading England. The purpose of the enterprise, the king emphasized, remained unchanged: to restore England to the Catholic church, to end English attacks on Spain's interests, and to secure an indemnity. Only the strategy had been modified.

Santa Cruz, together with the fleet of auxiliaries from Andalusia and a newly arrived squadron from Guipúzcoa, now received orders to 'sail in the name of God straight to the English Channel and go along it until you have anchored off Margate head, having first warned the duke of Parma of your approach'. Then, the king continued, 'the said duke, according to the orders he has received, on seeing the narrow seas thus made safe by the Armada either being anchored off the said headland or else cruising in the mouth of the Thames, . . . will immediately send across the army that he has prepared in small boats, of which (for transit alone) he has plenty'. The king went on to insist that, until Parma and his men had made their crossing, the Armada 'was to do nothing except make safe the passage, and defeat any enemy ships that may come out to prevent this'. He also loftily asserted that 'from Margate, you can prevent any junction between the enemy warships in the Thames and the eastern ports, with those in the south and west, so that the enemy will not be able to concentrate a fleet which would dare to come out and seek ours'.

It all sounded highly convincing, but certain important questions remained unanswered. To begin with, would the Grand Fleet go across to the ports of Flanders to meet the army, or were the invasion barges expected to put out to meet the fleet in open water? And, in the former event, how would the deep-draught ships of the Armada negotiate the shallows and sandbanks that fringed the Flemish coast; in the latter, how could a fleet cruising some miles offshore protect Parma's vulnerable barges from the heavily gunned Dutch blockade squadron once they left the safety of Dunkirk and Nieuwpoort harbours? These were, to say the least, unfortunate lacunae.[41]

Philip also seems to have devoted little thought to creating a favourable faction in England. Although numerous émigrés at his court, as at the court of William III a century later, clamoured for action, Philip made no effort to disguise his enterprise as a response to the pleas of the English for 'liberation' from religious and political oppression. Instead, propaganda to win local support was entrusted to the Catholic exiles, headed by Cardinal William Allen who in July 1588 published an *Admonition to the People of England*, declaring Elizabeth to be deposed, promising the swift arrival of Parma and his army, and urging English Catholics to rise in arms to support them.[42] After the conquest, the pope and Philip II intended Allen to take charge of the new Catholic state until the arrival of a mutually approved sovereign; but the king's instructions to the duke of Parma in April 1588 made it clear that he expected no uprising by the English Catholics in support of the invaders.[43]

In the event, of course, it did not matter because the invaders never managed to land: the thirty-two heavily armed warships sent by the Dutch to blockade the Flemish coast sufficed to keep Parma's barges confined to port, while the fireships, galleons and guns of the Royal Navy ensured that, although Medina Sidonia might lead his fleet relatively intact to the Narrow Seas, he could not remain there long enough to effect his rendezvous with Parma. But if the proximate cause of the defeat of the Spanish Armada in 1588 was thus tactical, its roots were undoubtedly strategic.

Leaving aside the mistaken decision to place all trust in the union of the fleet from Spain with the army from Flanders before permitting the invasion to proceed, the king's forces were also seriously weakened by the fact that the supreme commander remained at the Escorial, hundreds of miles from the theatre of operations. First, this removed the hot breath of royal urgency from the necks of those preparing the fleet. Where William III and his closest advisers were always on hand to see for themselves, Philip II refused all suggestions that he should move to Lisbon. He therefore had to rely on messengers to convey his orders to the fleet in Lisbon and Brussels, and usually learned only what his commanders chose to tell him.[44] Second, where William in 1688, in conjunction with his closest political advisers and all the relevant military and naval commanders, could take last-minute decisions on the method and direction of attack in the light of changes in the sea and the weather, as well as of up-to-date intelligence from England, Philip imposed upon both Medina Sidonia and Parma strict instructions that were at best ambiguous and at worst incompatible.[45]

The snail's pace at which the necessary ships, men and munitions were assembled also undermined the viability of Philip II's Grand Design. There was, in fact, never the slightest chance of finding all the resources listed in Santa Cruz's original masterplan of March 1586: 150 great ships, 400 support vessels, 55,000 men and all necessary munitions were simply not to be had from a peninsular population of under nine million people. Although the king raised troops all over Spain and Portugal, and brought veterans back from the Spanish garrisons in Naples and Sicily, there were still not nearly enough experienced soldiers. Hence, in part, the decision to involve the duke of Parma's crack Spanish, Italian, Burgundian, Walloon and German regiments (as well as several units raised from British exiles) in the South Netherlands.

Even to concentrate the 130 vessels that finally sailed from Lisbon required constant effort and some illegality, with numerous ships (in effect) hijacked when they entered Iberian ports. Indeed by the time the fleet sailed it was not a 'Spanish' Armada at all, since its ships and crews came from over a score of European ports stretching from Ragusa to Rostock; and when even that did not prove sufficient, in desperation the escort warships of the Indies fleet were commandeered and christened the 'squadron of Castile' in order to bring the Grand Fleet up to strength.[46]

In the end, only the organizational talents of the duke of Medina Sidonia, who had spent most of his professional life overseeing the concentration and dispatch of the convoys sailing from Seville to America, got the Armada to sea at all.[47] But he had to scrape the bottom of the barrel: some of the food accumulated was putrid, several of the ships embargoed sailed barely faster than a rowing-boat, many of the men raised were unserviceable, and a few of the big guns cast early in 1588 'in furious haste' (as the documents themselves state) were seriously defective, having either brittle or misbored barrels.[48]

What a contrast this logistical confusion made with the Dutch armada a century later! Although William III himself worried that the hiring of transports and seamen and the finding of supplies and equipment were not proceeding fast enough, almost everyone else considered the speed breath-taking. According to Gilbert Burnet 'Never was so great a design executed in so short a time . . . All things as soon as they were ordered were got to be so quickly ready that we were amazed at the dispatch' – for, after all, the build-up began only in June and the fleet was ready to sail in October.[49] It seems ironic indeed that a state usually decried for its decentralized federal political structure should have been able to mobilize and deploy its financial, military and naval resources with such efficiency; moreover, the feat was achieved by a relatively small team. Bentinck was involved in every aspect of the operation, assisted by Gaspar Fagel, pensionary of the states of Holland, and other key members of the provincial standing committee. Their chief executive officers were Job de Wildt, secretary of the Amsterdam Admiralty College, and Cornelis Evertsen, the senior Dutch naval commander. Because of the emphasis on speed, secrecy and efficiency, the three outlying Admiralty Colleges (those of Zeeland, Friesland and North Holland) were only marginally involved in preparing the armada; more than half the ships and the total naval manpower were provided by Amsterdam, and the only other major contribution was made by the naval authorities of Rotterdam.[50] The Sephardi Jewish businessman Jacob Pereira, one of the two leading Jews under contract with the States-General to act as 'provisioner-general' of the army at that time, also played a key role in providing the food and fodder sent out to the fleet from Amsterdam.

The major stages in the build-up all took place smoothly and swiftly. In late July the States-General voted to expand the Dutch navy by 9000 men, virtually doubling its strength: these men were recruited in less than a month – thanks in part to the offer of very high wages by the Admiralty Colleges – and (according to James II's consul in the city) the Amsterdam squadron was so well supplied that 'they want no men for them and even runne out some to take on better'.[51] Late in August, however, the same observer noted some shortages: 'the States have taken into their service most of the men that came home with the Smyrna fleet and some off the East India ships'; and, when even that did not suffice, resort was made to impressment: 'Dutch vessels that goe in and out . . . are visited, and such men as they lyke are taken out of them.'[52]

At the same time, manufacture of much special equipment began in Amsterdam, The Hague and Utrecht (a city boasting numerous copper mills and metal workshops). It was reported that the government had ordered 'at Utrecht the making of severall thousand of pairs of pistols and carabins', while Amsterdam 'has undertaken to furnish 3000 saddles in three weekes time' and 'they are also night and day employed at The Hague in making bombs, cuirasses and stinkpotts'.[53] In late August the hiring of transport vessels commenced (the event that seems to have triggered the stock market crash which began on 25 August) and within a month '400 vessels were hired at Amsterdam (at 670 guilders (£67) a month) to transport hay, provisions, etc'.[54]

The range and quantity of specialized equipment loaded on the Dutch fleet in the weeks just before departure were prodigious. To begin with, many vessels were filled with horses (the Spanish Armada had carried virtually none).[55] Although there were only 3660 cavalry troopers in the army of invasion, the prince, his entourage and many officers and gentlemen volunteers brought spares. Furthermore, at least 200 four-horse wagons were required to carry provisions and ammunition for the army, and further draught animals were needed to pull the 50 artillery pieces.[56] Perhaps, as Gilbert Burnet (an eyewitness) asserted, the fleet carried a total of 7000 horses.[57] And then there were 'muskets, pikes of all sorts, bandoliers, swords, pistols, saddles, boots, bridles and other necessaries to mount horsemen; pickaxes, wheel-barrows and other instruments to raise ground' as well as 'a great many . . . boats covered with leather to pass over rivers and lakes'.[58] The fleet also carried a mobile smithy, 10,000 pairs of spare boots, a printing press and a large quantity of printing paper as well as tens of thousands of propaganda leaflets previously printed (in English) at The Hague, Amsterdam and Rotterdam, intended to convince the English and the Scots that the armada had not come to invade and conquer the kingdoms, but merely to accompany the prince of Orange in his proclaimed purpose of rescuing English and Scottish liberty and the Protestant faith.[59]

Finally, in September, the States-General ordered its army to be increased from 41,000 to 70,200 men, and this was achieved in a matter of weeks. But the expeditionary force was no more 'Dutch' than that of 1588 had been 'Spanish'. On the one hand, 3710 men of the invasion army were drawn from the regular Scots and English regiments in the Dutch army, and many soldiers in the 'Dutch' regi-ments embarked were in fact German. On the other, there were the 5000 or so volunteers – mostly discontented English and Scots but also including 600 Huguenot officers and many other French adventurers as well as numerous men from different lands. Finally, English pilots and sailors also sailed on the fleet, including the titular commander Admiral Herbert.[60]

In some cases the cosmetic value of the English and Scots volunteers exceeded their military worth. Even Herbert was regarded as too fiery and rash to be entirely reliable: William only gave him command, over the head of Admiral Evertsen (who actually assembled the fleet and prepared it for action), mainly as a propaganda ploy designed to help encourage parts of the Royal Navy to defect or at least refuse to fight.[61] Moreover, the troops of the British regiments of the States-General's army, though highly trained, were not necessarily as zealous as the British volunteers for combat against their Jacobite compatriots. Agents sent by the marquis d'Albeville, James II's ambassador at The Hague, to the Nijmegen-Arnhem area where many of the troops were assembled before being ferried down the rivers to the fleet, reported that they had 'seen many of the English and Scotch soldiers weep for being forc'd to goe to fight against their own king and country, that many declared they would not fight'; and while the previous assurance that the commander of the British regiments, Major-General Hugh Mackay, had given to d'Albeville that 'always he would retire and never draw sword against the king' may be taken with a pinch of salt (given his unshakeable loyalty to William), there is no reason to doubt that some of these protestations were genuine.[62] Furthermore, some of the British volunteers were radical Whigs subject to strong political passions that clashed with the moderate message (designed to appeal to the Tories) of the prince of Orange's *Declaration*. Yet, while the British volunteers were a diverse, even motley, crew, and many fewer of them were professional military men than was the case with the Huguenots, they displayed no lack of bravado. 'The English and Scotch men who are lately come over and do embark', reported d'Albeville on 28 September, 'boast they will soone graize their horses in St James Park.'[63]

Moreover, the few minor shortcomings in morale and discipline scarcely mattered in such a mighty expedition in which the majority of the invasion army consisted of crack regiments, the finest in the States-General's army (including all the guards regiments), when the troops were equipped with the most modern muskets, 'artillery and that very good ... in abundance' as well as prodigious quantities of supplies of every kind, when the armada carried '100,000 pounds in ready money', and when the men had all been paid in advance. 'One has to admit,' wrote the Polish resident, 'that this undertaking could not have been vaster or better organized.' In fact, before they sailed, the troops were issued with their wages to the year end; and 'for every merchant ship hired to transport soldiers, horse or foot, or ammunition' it was reported 'the Prince pays 1500 florins (£150) a month, a half in hand'.[64] It was a far cry from the financial world of Philip II, who was forced to spend a part of every Saturday morning in 1588 checking and correcting the statements of cash-in-hand forwarded by his Treasury in order to see how many of his bills he could afford to pay. The weekly balance was rarely more than 20,000 crowns (£4500) – less than the cost of the Spanish Armada for one day.[65]

But there is more to Grand Strategy than guns, money, troops and sails. There is also luck or, as contemporaries put it, Providence. One of the Spanish Armada's senior commanders had said – perhaps sardonically – that the Grand Fleet was sailing 'in the confident hope of a miracle'; and Philip II was certainly confident that, whatever shortcomings might exist in his plans, God would intervene directly to ensure the desired outcome. So when the marquis of Santa Cruz complained that it was madness to launch the Armada against England in midwinter, the king replied serenely: 'We are fully aware of the risk that is incurred by sending a major fleet in winter through the Channel without a safe harbour, but . . . since it is all for His cause, God will send good weather.'[66] And in June 1588, after a storm had damaged some of the Armada's ships, driven others into Corunna and scattered the rest, the king remained serene. When Medina Sidonia suggested that these reverses might be a sign from God to desist, the king replied: 'If this were an unjust war, one could indeed take this storm as a sign from Our Lord to cease offending Him; but being as just as it is, one cannot believe that He will disband it, but will rather grant it more favour than we could hope . . . I have dedicated this enterprise to God,' he concluded. 'Pull yourself together, then, and do your part!'[67] A better example of cognitive dissonance would be hard to find.

And yet it almost worked! In the event, a chastened and encouraged Medina Sidonia eventually led the entire Armada – with but few losses – from Corunna to Calais in three weeks. At 4 p.m. on Saturday 6 August 1588, the Grand Fleet anchored only twenty-five miles from Parma, its order unbroken by the English and its strength virtually intact. There they received liberal supplies of victuals and provisions from the benevolent Catholic governor of the port. From their anchorage they could see the designated landing place just south of Ramsgate, where the Romans, Saxons and Danes had all stormed ashore successfully in the past. Had they but known it, the English had absolutely no idea where the Spaniards would strike, and had stationed their main army at Tilbury, in Essex. During the opening weeks of August, the world (with reason) held its breath: a landing at the Downs would have been opposed by only a few untrained militia units, their numbers daily dwindling through desertion. The dramatic success of the fireships on the night of 7 August, which far exceeded expectations, should not be allowed to obscure the fact that Philip II's Grand Strategy came within an ace of success.

A century later it was much the same. At first there was euphoria: in September, at The Hague, according to d'Albeville, 'Here are wagers lay'd that the Prince of Orange will be master of England before two months will be at an end.' Even the Dutch oligarchs with all their *gravitas* seemed unaccountably confident: 'no doubt is made here of a speedy success,' noted d'Albeville on 1 October, 'and of a speedy declaration of war [by England] against France, that if they were not sure of it they would not venture to send into England the flower and best part of their forces'.[68] As the flotillas of flat-bottomed boats specially hired to 'transport the soldiers from Nimighen unto the men-of-war and merchant ships' swept down the Maas and Waal to Rotterdam and Hellevoetsluis, they passed a vast throng of cheering burghers and farmers, the women with tears streaming down their cheeks.[69] A sense of elation filled the country. Yet when all was ready, with the troops, horses and supplies embarked, but with a persistent, strong, westerly wind confining the invasion fleet to port and giving the English time to get their battle fleet ready, the mood began to sour. Correspondingly, at King James's court, spirits began to rise. 'Though we long for your letters,' Lord Middleton wrote to d'Albeville, 'yet we cannot be sorry that they are so long in coming, I mean, that the wind is westerly.'[70] The ambassador replied, on 11 October: 'the [Dutch] Catholics pray ardently for His Majesty's preservation and for the success of his army against his enemies; the wind continuing contrary all this while they call it a "popish wind". God continue it one month longer.'[71] And for that 'month longer' God seemed to listen: 'the continuance of this weather which is very tempestuous,' d'Albeville wrote a week later, 'goes to the heart of the Prince and of all of them. The people begin to say, God does not prosper the design. The soldiers are quite dejected and begin to curse the masters of the design: if they continue embark'd but eight days more, a third part of them will perish.'[72]

A week later the Polish resident at The Hague reported to Warsaw that so many people, Protestants included, were now saying 'the wind is papist' that the magistrates of the Holland towns were obliged to forbid anyone to say those words in public on pain of a heavy fine which was, in fact, exacted from a number of offenders.[73] In Holland during these tense weeks,

[the] common thing every morning, which was most used, was first to go and see how the wind sate, and if there were any probability of a change. When any person came unto a house, in the heart of their city, concerning any manner of businesse, the very first question by all was, Sir, I pray how is the wind to day? Are we likely to get an easterly wind ere long? Pray God send it, and such like. The ministers themselves pray'd that God would be pleas'd for to grant an East Wind.[74]

Meanwhile frenetic activity took place around the Thames estuary. On 8 October, as the Dutch embarked their forces, Lord Middleton wrote to d'Albeville from London: 'I hope our fleet shall be ready in time enough to oppose their landing: all the seamen and soldiers expresse their resolution of dying in doing their duty.'[75] By the end of October all was ready: 'our fleet will be at sea tomorrow,' wrote Middleton on 26 October, 'in a much better condition than theirs'.[76] Nor was his confidence misplaced. Under most conditions, the Gunfleet was a secure anchorage at which to wait and intercept an invasion fleet crossing from the Netherlands and sailing either northwards or to the south. Nor did the English fleet lack firepower, numbering some 41 ships and, according to the *Hollandsche Mercurius*, carrying 11,565 men and 2058 guns.

Furthermore, the bitterest blow to Dutch morale was yet to come. On the first attempt to emerge, the great fleet was driven back in disarray by a severe tempest on 30–31 October. Although actual damage was less than the Dutch propaganda machine pretended (to lull James into a false sense of security), ships, men, and especially horses were badly battered. Moreover, the oligarchs who ran the Dutch Republic now had an additional reason for acute anxiety. Louis XIV had warned them what he would do should they defy him by moving against England. As the Polish resident noted on the day of the storm: 'on attend à tout moment de voir la guerre déclarée entre la France et cet état'.[77] Having been cooped up for weeks in appalling conditions, the Dutch troops became desperate. According to the prince's secretary, William himself now became 'melancholicq'.[78] The English, for their part, considered the Dutch mad. As Lord Dartmouth wrote to the king: 'Sir, we are now at sea before the Dutch with all their boasting, and I can not see much sense in their attempt with the hazard of such a fleet and army at the latter end of October.'[79]

Then, all of a sudden, the picture was transformed. The prayers of the Dutch preachers were answered. The wind veered right round to a strong easterly, the famous 'Protestant wind' that pinned the English fleet helplessly to their anchorage in the Gunfleet and enabled the invaders to reach their disembarkation point swiftly and unmolested. Remarkably, the armada first proceeded northwards right past the Thames estuary and the English fleet, to the most northerly point at which it was still possible for William and his advisers to change their minds.[80] In view of the strong wind and the inadvisability of landing in the northeast under such conditions, the prince gave the order for the entire fleet to turn round. It doubled back, passing Harwich and the estuary within sight of Dartmouth's fleet which was still unable to get out to intercept them. The arrival of the great fleet off Dover caused a sensation in London and a shock at court, where James and his advisers had been convinced that the prince would opt for the northeast.[81] It also caused a sensation at Paris whither couriers sped from Dunkirk, Calais and Boulogne.

The passage of the vast armada through the Narrow Seas presented a stunning spectacle.[82] First, the leading ships paused to enable stragglers to catch up. Then the prince gave the signal 'stretching the whole fleet in a line, from Dover to Calais, twenty-five deep'. The Dutch went through, 'colours flying', the fleet 'in its greatest splendour', a vast mass of sail stretching as far as the eye could see, the warships on either flank simultaneously thundering their guns in salute as they passed in full view of Dover castle on one side and the French garrison at Calais on the other. The Dutch regiments stood in full parade formation on deck, as an English volunteer accompanying the expedition recorded, with the 'trumpets and drums playing various tunes to rejoice our hearts . . . for above three hours'.[83] The boldest enterprise ever undertaken by the Republic of the United Netherlands was stage-managed with exquisite artistry. In all it took six hours for the incomparable mass of shipping to clear the straits. As the great fleet sped down the Channel driven by the strong winds, all available regiments in the London area were ordered to proceed with the utmost haste, some clattering through London in the middle of the night, towards Portsmouth, the Isle of Wight and the south coast. But the amazing luck that had pinned the Royal Navy to the Gunfleet held. The strong easterly wind carried the invaders down to the western reaches of the Channel too fast for James to be able to organize any opposition by sea or land. Then, having dangerously overshot the mark – Torbay being the last suitable and, apart from Teignmouth and Exmouth, the only undefended landing point capable of accommodating such an immense quantity of shipping for any length of time – the wind backed to southerly, sweeping the armada back towards safety, and then dropped to a calm, permitting easy and orderly disembarkation. Ignoring Herbert's advice one last time – Herbert, whose warships stood out to sea to fend off the expected English attack, sent word advising that William disembark at Exmouth[84] – William began landing his troops, horses and supplies in Torbay on the evening of 15 November, the enormous operation continuing until late on the 17th. The English and Scots regiments of the States-General's army came ashore first. Both Dutch regiments and English and foreign volunteers were under the strictest orders to behave civilly towards the inhabitants they encountered and to pay for everything they procured 'without swearing and damning and debauching of women, as is usual in some armies'.

It is ironic that, even in 1988, Britons chose to recall the unsuccessful attack of 1588 rather than the no less complex more imposing and victorious operation which so fundamentally altered the course of

British history exactly a century later. But then peoples, like individuals, often prefer to recall not what is crucial in their past but what best illustrates (and flatters) their own perception of themselves.

3

'Military history is to history,' it has been unkindly claimed, 'what military music is to music – and military intelligence is a contradiction in terms.' With these words, Christopher Andrew welcomed participants to the Sixteenth Military History Symposium held at the Royal Military College of Canada in March 1990. The conference proceedings spanned two millennia, from Roman military intelligence to the reorganization of Canada's 'insecurity services' (as a conference speaker termed them) in the 1970s, and demonstrated that military intelligence usually fails not through defective acquisition but through the inability of governments to analyse and accept what has been found. The failure of Israel's security forces to anticipate danger before the Yom Kippur War of 1973 resembled the blindness of United States intelligence before Pearl Harbor in 1941 or before the attacks on New York and Washington in 2001. In each case, complacency – even contempt for the enemy – played an important part. In the words of the head of the Israeli civilian intelligence agency, Mossad, after the Yom Kippur War: 'We simply did not believe that they [the Arab states] were capable. In effect – that was also my personal problem – we scorned them.'[1]

My own contribution to the Symposium, 'The "worst-kept secret in Europe"? The European intelligence community and the Spanish Armada', examined how Philip II's various plans to invade England in the 1580s all became known to Queen Elizabeth, and why she nevertheless failed to exploit this knowledge – for in August 1588, Philip's Grand Fleet managed to reach the scheduled launch area in good order while Elizabeth deployed her main army to repel an invasion in Essex instead of in Kent.[2] The broad discussions that followed this and other papers forced me to revise my presentation *radically. Above all, Professor Michael Handel (another participant in the Symposium) persuaded me to reorganize my material according to the three basic categories of intelligence-gathering: acquisition, analysis and acceptance. He also encouraged me to look more closely at the history of Sir Edward Stafford, Elizabeth's kinsman and her ambassador in France, who in 1587 and 1588 provided Spain with a stream of classified information.*

I therefore contacted specialists in Tudor history and asked for 'leads' on the ambassador. Naturally, I turned to Sir Geoffrey Elton; preidctably, he gave me the best advice – to contact Mitchell Leimon, who had written a paper on 'The fame of Sir Edward Stafford' for Elton's graduate history seminar at Cambridge University. We duly made contact, exchanged typescripts, met, and got to work. Of course, we were not the first to study the problem. A century ago, in his Calendar of Letters and State Papers relating to English affairs preserved in, or originally belonging to, the Archives of Simancas, 1587– 1603, *Martin Hume drew attention to the information provided to Philip II by a spy based in Paris whom the documents referred to as 'Julio'. Hume speculated that 'Julio' stood for Stafford. Before long, other distinguished Tudor historians weighed in on the issue: A. F. Pollard offered an alternative identification; Conyers Read resurrected the charge against Stafford; Sir John Neale denied it. In 1970, an excellent thesis by R. J. McCue of Brigham Young University concluded, on the basis of numerous English manuscript sources, that Stafford had been a spy – but argued that he had provided Spain with little of value. However, all these scholars made use only of the Spanish materials contained in Hume's* Calendar, *despite the fact that it provided only a précis not a full transcription (still less the original), of the documents.*[3]

Consulting the originals at the archives of Simancas swiftly revealed the scale of Stafford's treason. Part of the confusion arose from the fact that Don Bernardino de Mendoza, the Spanish ambassador in Paris who passed on the intelligence to Spain, used not one but three names for his source; but a close reading of his letters in Simancas established that the 'aliases' all referred to the same person. For example, on the same day, Mendoza requested in identical terms the same reward for his principal source of information in letters to both the king and his secretary of state; but he used a different name in each letter – a distinction omitted by Hume in his Calendar *(see pages 85–6 below). Similar details (including Mendoza's specific statement in an early letter that 'Estafort, ambassador of the queen', was his source) clinched the matter. An analysis of the information passed on by Sir Edward, and the use that the Spanish government made of it, suggested that the ambassador ranked as the intelligence bargain of the century.*

Mitchell Leimon, meanwhile, noted the remarkable 'disinformation' that the ambassador passed back to London. Stafford constantly assured his government in 1587 and 1588 of the pacific intentions of Philip II and successively alleged that the Armada had another destination, had been disbanded, or had been forced back to port by plague! Mitchell also examined the changing factional alignments at Elizabeth's court. He found that Sir Francis Walsingham, English secretary of state, harboured deep suspicions concerning Stafford's loyalty but then was reconciled with Lord Burghley, Stafford's patron, at the precise moment when the ambassador offered to betray secrets to Mendoza: in January 1587. This helped to explain how Stafford managed to stay at his post, his treachery unrevealed, for so long: Walsingham could not pursue his suspicions without alienating his new ally at court.

Putting together the various pieces in the puzzle concerning Stafford's treason was an exciting piece of 'forensic' history, and it proved (if further proof were required) that historians must always consult original sources and not a précis, however convenient. It also demonstrated the limitations of even the best intelligence. For almost two years, Elizabeth's senior diplomat revealed everything he knew about his country's defences to its greatest enemy and also did his best to lull his own government into a false sense of security. Nevertheless, some of his best data either reached Spain too late to be of use (like his warning about the Cadiz raid in April 1587) or else proved to be misleading (such as a detailed survey of the armaments aboard the English fleet in April 1588).[4] Furthermore, in the end, the queen did not accept Stafford's information. Instead, fortunately for the survival of the Tudor state, she trusted those who claimed that the Armada was indeed about to launch an invasion. Sir Edward therefore betrayed his queen and country in vain.

Treason and Plot in Elizabethan Diplomacy: The 'Fame of Sir Edward Stafford' Reconsidered

The political career of Sir Edward Stafford lacked both beginning and end, being composed entirely of middle: serving little apprenticeship, receiving after his service abroad no major office of state, his professional life was dominated by an exceptionally long posting of nearly eight years as Queen Elizabeth's ambassador to the French court. Historical study has been similarly ill proportioned. Stafford has received no biography. He has been studied solely through the prism of the *Calendars of State Papers Foreign*, and *Spanish*, first of all by their respective editors, and subsequently by an apostolic succession of English historians: A. F. Pollard, Conyers Read and Sir John Neale. All these scholars found themselves drawn to passionate advocacy, either in defence or in refutation of the charge that Stafford was a traitor and sold secrets to the Spanish ambassador. This question apart – and the debate petered out half a century ago – Sir Edward has received scant scholarly attention.[5] This is a pity, for he lived in exciting times and his character was dramatic, warm, excitable, sometimes hysterical; his dispatches could be both colourful and witty.[6]

Stafford stood out for his independence of mind: partly brought up in France, he was a Francophile, free of the wary distate that marked most of his predecessors in the embassy. Conversely, entirely at home in the court of the Most Christian King, he lacked the deep sympathy for the Huguenots that so moved most Elizabethan envoys to France. In his prominence while still young, in his exalted court connections, and in his persistent poverty, Stafford somewhat resembled his contemporary Sir Philip Sydney (for whom he professed a fellow-feeling even after a rivalry developed between them). Born in 1552 to Sir William and Lady Dorothy Stafford, Sir Edward boasted noble, indeed royal ancestry: his mother, who became mistress of the robes to Queen Elizabeth in 1564, was the granddaughter both of the last duke of

Buckingham and of George, duke of Clarence; and his stepmother, Mary Boleyn, was the queen's aunt. He moved quickly into government service. In his twenties he undertook continental missions for Lord Treasurer Burghley between 1574 and 1576 (to Emden and to France) and served repeatedly as Elizabeth's confidential envoy to her suitor, Francis Hercules, duke of Anjou, between 1578 and 1581. When Anjou first arrived in London he stayed in Stafford's house.[7] By this means he developed close links with Lord Burghley and the earl of Sussex, the privy councillors who chiefly favoured the Anjou marriage; but he also worked closely with Secretary Walsingham, and foreign observers at this time detected no divergence between the two men. When in 1580 Stafford attempted to profit from a patent 'touching makyng of kerseys', 'the benefits whereof he [was] like to lose by vertue of the late proclamation for revocation of such', the letters of commendation he bore from Burghley were far less forthright than the one from Walsingham: 'for that Mr Stafford is a gentleman I would be glad by any good meanes to please, deal . . . as Mr Stafford may, by the effect and answer to my Lord Treasurer, understand that for my sake he hath been pleasured by you'. The holograph postscript reinforced the point.[8]

Thus Stafford's court favour and obvious talent seem to have made him a prize to be contested for. On the one hand, over the winter of 1582–3 he accompanied the earl of Sussex in a journey to take the waters at Bath (a journey that profited neither man's health); on the other, early in 1583 Walsingham referred a case of fraud alleged by Stafford to two of his close associates. Predictably they appear to have decided in favour of Stafford who, although not entirely satisfied, still acknowledged himself 'more bound as I kanne not be more to Mr Secretarye'.[9] But in the summer of 1583, when he was chosen ambassador to France, Sir Edward decided to put all his eggs into one patron's basket. 'Mr Secretary called me into the presence window,' Stafford wrote to Burghley, 'and asked whether I wolde be content to goe into France.' Stafford 'desired him to provide so for me yff he meant to prefer me thereunto that I mooght do it wyth some abilitie' (that is, to ensure he received adequate funding). But Walsingham 'was called away to come to the Queen withoute speaking' more of it tyll yesterday he called me in the lobbye door, and told me he had presented my name to the Queen among some others, telling me that att the naming of me, and he speaking better of my abilitie than I deserve, she confessed I was fytt but very poore. He asked me yff I liked him to presse her, he would dare yt yff I would.

Walsingham thus seems to have made a determined attempt to have Stafford accept both preferment and enablement at his own hands, and for a while Stafford seems to have hesitated; but in the end he brusquely rejected the secretary's offer. 'I desired, nott by any meanes, and so left,' he told Burghley, 'for I have wholly disposed myself to depend on your good counsell and helpe to doe whatt you think best.'[10]

It may have been significant that between the two conversations with Walsingham Stafford and the court visited Burghley's country house, Theobalds, and that Stafford also met Robert Cecil. But whatever matters were discussed, Stafford had surely been rash: other ambassadors had striven to keep on good terms with all major court figures – most notably Walsingham himself, who had returned from France in 1573 in enhanced credit with both Lord Burghley and the earl of Leicester. Stafford here revealed a factiousness beyond the normal bounds because, travelling to England's only permanent continental embassy as the self-proclaimed 'creature' of Burghley – who secured him a knighthood in September 1583, on the eve of his departure – Stafford represented a clear threat to Walsingham.[11] For although others around the queen may have dominated the formation of foreign policy, the mechanics of diplomacy, the provision of information and the communication of orders abroad all formed part of the secretary's empire; and Paris lay at its heart.

During his long tenure as 'principal secretary', Walsingham had come to regard ambassadors as directly subordinate to him. On occasion he would demand that an ambassador completely alter the tenor of his reports: in 1581 he brusquely ordered his uncle, Thomas Randolph, the queen's ambassador to Scotland, 'to harp no more on that string'. At other times Walsingham dictated the terms on which a government agent should report: also in 1581, Lord Gray was informed not only of the policy he should lay before the Council but also that he should accompany it with a threat of resignation.[12] In addition, as the patron of aspiring diplomats, Walsingham normally managed to provide ambassadors with staff whose first loyalty lay to himself: 'Young Needham' served both Henry Cobham and the earl of Leicester in this way, and his careful reports on Leicester's conduct fully justify Walsingham's care in so placing him.[13] In all this, of course, Walsingham merely emulated the more masterful of his predecessors; in other ways, however, he innovated. In 1568 the last Tudor ambassador to Spain was recalled, leaving only two permanent embassies (in Edinburgh and Paris). Apart from the reports transmitted through these official channels, and by occasional emissaries sent abroad for a specific purpose, previous secretaries of state had relied for news of foreign affairs on the haphazard reports of English merchants, who were seldom well informed about, or welcome in, the courts of the princes in whose countries they traded.[14] Walsingham dramatically expanded this simple machinery. Unlike Burghley, he was a cosmopolitan figure: he could quote Petrarch, and he advised a young emulant never to let a day pass without translating from one foreign language to another. He had practised politics in several European countries and felt able to advise the Ottoman sultan on how best to deal with Iran. He could discuss theology with James VI, mechanics with the Dutch and, apparently, Rabelais with Henry of Navarre. To these far-flung interests he brought a powerful world-view that hinged Europe's security upon a single issue: the struggle of Protestantism against Catholicism.

The need for accurate information stood at the centre of Walsingham's system. 'Knowledge is never too dear' was allegedly his maxim, and Camden called him 'a most subtle searcher out of hidden secrets'.[15] It was this passion that marked out Walsingham for Laurence Humfrey when, in 1596, he celebrated him foremost among the Protestant heroes of a passing age:

> Let Walsingham
> Disperse his riches over every land
> And thus appropriate their destinies
> To his own country; Drake may fly at once
> Across to India, that source of gold,
> Charting his vessels' distant course among

Uncharted seas: Let Sydney make again
For Zeeland, Unton sail for France and Grey
Return to Ireland, reaping great rewards.
These two they'd surely win – Death and a Song:
What else? For, as you see, the present age
Produces nothing more.[16]

Walsingham chose to 'disperse his riches' among both a greater number and a wider variety of correspondents than any of his predecessors. In the Low Countries, where Cecil's ignorance had been particularly noticeable, Walsingham by 1580 probably maintained six or seven regular correspondents in various cities: some were merchants, others soldiers, none of them English. In addition, he communicated with English soldiers in Dutch pay; with several political leaders in the United Provinces; and with spies of whom little is now known. He also drew, probably more fully, on the information traditionally amassed by English merchant sources. Elsewhere he received news from Protestants like Jacob Sturm in Strasbourg, where on occasion he based an agent. Through his shadowy servant, Jacomo Manucci, Walsingham operated a network of Italians, usually soldiers, like Sassetti and Monti in Paris, da Pisa in Milan, and others as far as the Azores. His physician, Geoffroy le Brumen, corresponded with a group of French informants. Among the retinue of Dom Antonio, the pretender to the Portuguese throne exiled in London, Walsingham made contacts and seems to have drawn one Cypryan Figeureido into his private office. Scots in France and in Italy (especially Venice) sent both intelligence and news, and allowed Walsingham to penetrate deep into Scottish as well as continental politics. In addition to William Harborne, a semi-official agent in Constantinople, others of his servants travelled there (including Manucci in 1583) in the hope of mobilizing support against Spain. Finally, Walsingham also recruited agents among English Catholics abroad, both among the exiles who plotted against the queen in Paris and among those who sought refuge in Italy. One of the latter, Anthony Standen, established his own network which relayed detailed and accurate information about the Spanish Armada back to London.[17]

Such a network could not depend on the vagaries of the postal system; instead Walsingham's own servants, acting as couriers, tended it. Thereby they lent the English government a new and widespread presence: in 1586, for example, Sir Horatio Palavicino, an Elizabethan secret service agent, chanced upon a servant of Walsingham's in Dresden, homeward bound; moving on to Frankfurt, Palavicino there encountered Walter Williams, a prominent courier, heading to Geneva with letters for him. Such men led exciting lives. Nicholas Faunt, a Puritan courier, was hunted in Naples in 1581 and then arrested in Rome by the Inquisition; freed, perhaps by a double agent, he soon reappeared in Paris.[18] The French capital served as the clearing house for this network, a crossroads of the diplomatic world where Huguenot, Guise, Spanish, English and Catholic exile interests all coexisted. The English embassy thus offered the ideal holding-post for mail, base for couriers, and receiving point for intelligence destined for London. But where the English ambassador in Paris had previously enjoyed much freedom, he was now only one official, competing with others to provide news and expected to provide services to all manner of agents of whose purposes he was not always informed, and in whose interests he might be ordered to curtail his own activities.[19] Pliancy and trust were required and Walsingham could count himself fortunate that his successors in the embassy down to 1583 were, like him, allied closely with the earl of Leicester.

The irruption of Sir Edward Stafford into such a sensitive yet 'safe' part of Walsingham's territory created trouble almost immediately. Lord Cobham, the outgoing ambassador, departed without offering Stafford more than a handful of documents, and no details of informants whatsoever.[20] Stafford retaliated by sending copies of all his dispatches to Lord Burghley, adding 'I beseech your Lordship [to] seal up this in another paper and to deliver ytt to my mother, sealed, as all coppyes that heereafter I shall send you.'[21] This marked an intrusion of bedchamber influence into foreign affairs not always communicated to the Privy Council and, although Burghley may not always have complied, hence forth Lady Stafford became a diligent and informed participant in all her son's affairs, and his most important advocate with the queen.

In fact the issue of correspondence represented the first battleground between Walsingham and Stafford. However, it is hard to get at the truth because of the uneven survival of the relevant letters. Much of Stafford's correspondence with both Walsingham and Burghley survives, but, not surprisingly, his letters to the former usually reveal less about the distrust between them than do his letters to the latter. By contrast, few letters received by Stafford now exist, except for some from Walsingham which the ambassador copied and sent, sometimes in extract, to Lord Burghley. This imbalance has preserved on many points the views of Stafford alone: his interpretation, his description, his selection of what was relevant for quotation. Some of the problems seem to have been endemic to Elizabeth's system, for all her ambassadors considered themselves underdirected, and all suffered occasional rebukes (on grounds of cost) for sending too many 'special messengers'. True to form, in December 1583, three months after his arrival, Stafford begged Walsingham 'I pray you sometimes to make me partaker of the good or ill haps of our country', to which Walsingham most uncharacteristically replied by suggesting that Stafford should write home less often, because 'her Majesty is many times so offended with the charges of often posting as I dare not make her privy of all the despatches I receive from you'.[22] But three months after that, in March 1584, battle began in earnest when Walsingham's 'searchers' at the port of Rye opened a packet of letters from Stafford and read even items of personal correspondence from both the ambassador and his wife. Walsingham responded disingenuously: 'I am sorry the commissioners so far forgot themselves as to open any of your letters. You will do well to put all your private letters in a packet directed to me . . . and I will do the same with private letters sent to you from hence, if your men may be directed to bring them to me for that purpose.'[23] Stafford immediately saw the trap and complained to Burghley:

I wrote to Mr Secretary to complain of them of Rye that have opened my private letters, and see by his answer that there is half a consent of his in it . . . He tells me to . . . send [my letters] to him and he will have them delivered . . . Truly my Lord it were too much pains for him and therefore I will not trouble him so much for I am sure there is no letter I should write your lordship, or any[one] else, but it should be opened. I write plainly to your Lordship but I am contented Mr Secretary shall think I am [a] child and cannot find the bondage he would bring me in; and therefore I pray your lordship say nothing to him of it.

Scarcely had the ink dried on this dispatch than Walsingham wrote privately to Stafford that 'there is great fault found with the charge of [your] often sending, and therefore I cannot but once again advise you not to write but upon causes of very great importance', urging Stafford to inform him privately 'of such occurrences as shall daily happen there, wherein, as you shall do me a pleasure, I shall not fail to keep the same to myself, lest her Majesty think she is still at the charge thereof'. Once more Stafford complained to Burghley: 'I have been served but very evil touches since I came here ... I know that by his [Walsingham's] means the queen has had false advertisements of preparations here from his factors and has been incensed that news of importance should come from others; but some have come from me and he has kept them a day and delivered his first.' Nor did Stafford consider the cost of his letters excessive, since they were most often given to Walsingham's men (who thereafter headed home and claimed travel expenses!).[24] In addition, Stafford began to feel bypassed by the mysterious activities of Henry Unton, a gentleman close to Walsingham (and many years later Stafford's replacement in Paris), and also by the close friendship developed by Walsingham with the French ambassador in London, Mauvissière, by whose means business was often channelled directly to Henry III, only reaching Stafford later. Walsingham defended this practice, somewhat ironically, 'because if ambassadors resident are not made acquainted with matters, they seek to cross them'.[25]

Stafford was surely correct to guess that pressure was being applied to bring him into Walsingham's orbit. The authorities of the port of Rye who opened and read the ambassador's letters were both the most efficient in England and the most obedient to the secretary; and Walsingham's office had developed sophisticated methods of undetectable letter-opening. Taken together, the steps Walsingham urged upon Stafford would have led to an ambassadorial correspondence that was slender, narrowly channelled, and entirely open to the secretary's manipulation.

Intelligence formed the second battleground between the two men. Stafford, perhaps to prove his value and his independence, began himself to seek intelligence in ways that Walsingham (and on occasion the queen) thought rash and ill considered. Stafford itched to mimic disloyalty, and proposed a charade of distrust in which the queen too should join. Realizing that some communications with his home government might be intercepted, in November 1583 he proposed to include in them seemingly classified information that he knew to be false. He warned the queen that such passages would be indicated by a special mark in his letters so that she would know they were 'wrytten for a pourpose and nott for a truthe'.[26] Six months later Stafford was equally frank about the fact that he had deliberately written a letter full of false information because he knew it would be intercepted, so it 'caryed both matters which the Spanishe imbassador knew to be trewe, and also introductions owte of cypher to help [him] to discover partlye that which was in cypher'.[27] He further suggested that his wife, by feigning Catholicism, enter into a French court intrigue – but this the queen expressly forbade.[28]

Besides thus leading some to question the extent to which his enthusiasm was tempered with common sense, Stafford shamelessly entered areas already infiltrated by Walsingham, regardless of the damage this might do, and interpreted the refusals from London with which he met, even when originating with the queen herself, as merely a product of the secretary's monopolistic urge. 'Perchance,' wrote Stafford, Walsingham objected because he 'can send nobody secretly hither without my being advertised of it', and added tartly, 'I never heard of any ambassador being blamed for seeking intelligence any way he could.'[29] Frustrated by such treatment, Stafford at first tried either to deal directly with the queen (difficult, since she always lost his cyphers), or to bypass Walsingham via Burghley; but on every occasion Elizabeth seems to have backed her secretary's judgement.[30] So the ambassador began to take matters into his own hands, seizing the kind of discretionary powers that his predecessors had been granted only after several years' display of sober judgement. 'Which way I deal,' he informed Lord Burghley, 'is not reason anybody should know but them that I may trust well, which truly is not [Mr Secretary].'[31] So Stafford began to take more risks, slipping into unorthodox dependencies in order to obtain information with which to restore his credit at home. In particular he made contact with two of the duke of Anjou's former advisers, Marchaumont and Simier (who were later said 'wholly to govern him'), using them (for example) to develop a connection in the spring of 1584 with the Catholic exile and conspirator Charles Arundel.[32] The liaison with Arundel coincided with, and may well have caused, Walsingham's change of mind, from a desire to control Stafford towards an attempt to discredit him; for Arundel was no ordinary plotter.

Although Robert Parsons is now thought to have been the final author of the libel known as *Leycester's Commonwealth*, published in September 1584, the essential material in the book was probably provided by Arundel.[33] It is highly significant that, at precisely this time, Arundel should have been in close contact with Stafford, an avowed opponent of the earl, and the ambassador's wife, who as Lady Douglas Sheffield had dallied so embarrassingly with the earl until ousted by Lettice Knollys.[34] Walsingham's harsher attitude became evident as soon as the book reached him: in October 1584 Michael Moody, one of Stafford's servants, at court to receive letters for his master, was detained at Walsingham's command on the grounds that he was conveying letters to and from Catholics. Stafford was not informed of this development for four months and immediately saw it as part of a campaign to denude him of servants, to force him to 'seek new fellows to trust to, that may serve other men's humours more than [mine]'. Then in the autumn of 1585 Walsingham detained William Lilly, another of Stafford's personal servants, on the grounds that he had read *Leycester's Commonwealth*: he was to be sent to the earl, then in the Netherlands, to clear himself.[35]

Leycester's Commonwealth, it should be remembered, was a 'Marian' tract. In the aftermath of the failure of the Anjou marriage project, English politicians turned their thoughts once more to the succession question. Scarcely a month after the publication of *Leycester's Commonwealth*, the Privy Council drafted for the consideration of Parliament various papers concerning arrangements for an 'interregnum' should the queen die a violent death, including the summoning of a Great Council of the Realm which would convene a Parliament to examine the credentials of the various claimants to the throne and choose a new monarch.[36] Although he never declared himself openly, Burghley was suspected of favouring the claim of Mary Stuart, whereas Leicester and Walsingham, whose candidate for the succession was not so easily discovered, girded themselves for her destruction.[37]

Stafford was, characteristically, less ambiguous: he may have begun to move towards support for Mary as early as June 1583, and was certainly in contact with her agents by December. When Elizabeth heard of the links, she ordered them to cease. Stafford agreed, while protesting that they served only to gain intelligence about Mary and her supporters. Nevertheless, by January 1585 he and his wife were still described as Mary's 'friends'.[38]

The campaign against Mary gained in drama towards the end of 1584 with the public theatricality of the Bond of Association. More Catholic notables came under scrutiny, in addition to those who had fled in 1583, and the earl of Arundel joined the earl of Northumberland in the Tower. All this coincided with acrimonious debates among the queen's councillors over whether or not England should enter the Netherlands war – an issue that aroused such passions that Burghley suspected Walsingham of setting spies on him, an accusation that Walsingham found it hard to deny. Then in January 1585 the folly of Dr William Parry, a prominent member of Burghley's entourage and a man whom Stafford had warmly commended to the queen, led to his dramatic unmasking as a spy and would-be assassin. Walsingham's denunciation of Parry while Parliament sat provided a well timed revelation both of the malice of the Catholic enemy and of the unreliability of Lord Burghley's followers.[39] Later in the year the correspondence of Mary Stuart, to which Walsingham was now privy, served to embarrass both Burghley and Stafford still further.[40]

By spring 1586, thanks in part to the damaging detention of his servants, Stafford was widely seen as a lame-duck ambassador. His conciliatory moves evoked no response and in a heated argument with Stafford's mother, Walsingham refused either to let the men go or to reveal the evidence against them. News of his weak position spread to Paris, where the Abbot Delbene dismissed Stafford as an 'honest man but he confides in too many men', while from London the French agent Buzenval replied that the ambassador 'depends only upon [Lord Burghley]; but it may cost him dear, and he may be sure that the greatest advancement he will ever have is where he is: I am astonished that he does not see that this one [Walsingham] is better, and at the end of his days begin to depend on him, which he had never done'. Buzenval, who was intimate with Walsingham, had by May

1586 become convinced that the secretary intended to replace Stafford.[41]

But the political ground was shifting. Having achieved the necessary dominance at court to secure Elizabeth's commitment to assist the Dutch against Spain in August 1585, the earl of Leicester's departure for the Netherlands the following December separated him from Walsingham. Although Burghley seems to have maintained steady support for Leicester, he also exploited the earl's absence to set in train a peace process surely designed to reduce English support for the Dutch. As the negotiations inched forward, however, Walsingham worked hard to undermine them, both by making contacts of his own and by seeking to compromise the emissaries employed by Burghley. Even so, by the autumn of 1586 Burghley's peace initiative had won the support of a coalition of courtiers that included Lord Cobham, Sir Walter Mildmay and Sir James Croft, the original proponent of the negotiations.[42] Walsingham remained Leicester's principal pillar at court, but one that temporarily stood alone.[43]

Nevertheless, the secretary's determination to have Stafford recalled never faltered. In July 1586 he solicited from Thomas Rogers (alias Nicholas Berden) a full statement of the allegations against Stafford current in Paris. Rogers had spied in Paris during 1585 and communicated with Walsingham by means of Burghley's servant Horatio Palavacino. Several times he (and Palavacino) reported doubts concerning Stafford's loyalty; but Burghley, it appears, suppressed them.[44] Therefore Rogers's testimony became available to Walsingham only on his return to England in the spring of 1586, and even then only in secret, since Rogers remained deep in the confidence of the London Catholic underground. At the request of Walsingham's private secretary, however, Rogers now stated the charges against Stafford. Four of them seemed especially serious: that Stafford, for 6000 crowns (£1350), had shown his intelligence and letters to the duke of Guise and to Charles Arundel; that 'Arundel can send any man into England by the ambassador's means' (Rogers cited as evidence his own case); that, in return, 'the better to increase his credit they would deliver him from time to time such intelligences or the first fruits of the new books or libels as should first come forth . . . but for other matters they never troubled his head withal'; and, finally, that Stafford had betrayed English informants, in particular a highly placed diplomat whose loyalty Walsingham had bought, and who in consequence had since been recalled.[45]

Then as now, this evidence may be read in two ways: either that under financial and political pressure Stafford had played dangerously and for diminishing returns; or that he was a traitor. Burghley, for one, seems to have harboured no suspicions and his confidence apparently remained unshaken. In October 1586 he warned Stafford:

Here is secret whispering that you are in dett by unmeasurable playing; that Marchaumont and Simier do wholly rule you; and that you do lodge another Frenchman of no known honesty ... These I hear of you but yet in great secrecy, collored with speeches of pytteying of you. But I find the inwardness of these collorable speeches to tend to another end.

Burghley underlined the gravity of the charges and appealed for counter-evidence to use in Stafford's defence, for Walsingham 'speketh often time afor the Queen to have one sought to succeed you. But without your own privitie and lykyng, I mynde not to further it.'[46] Nevertheless, the bearer of this letter was the queen's special envoy to the French court, sent to justify her proceedings against Mary Stuart, Edward Wotton – precisely the man whom Walsingham 'sought to succeed' Stafford.[47] Having a replacement *in situ* was a favourite way of overcoming the queen's reluctance to contemplate administrative change. Stafford thus stood on the edge of disaster, and his reply to Burghley can have offered little satisfaction, for he admitted to being heavily in debt to Marchaumont, now a member of the Catholic League, and to others (although he swore that he had given up gaming since Anjou's death).[48] All this was deeply compromising, as Stafford painfully accepted – although to the queen, Marchaumont and Simier might still have counted as Anjou's men, and therefore her 'friends', rather than enemies of the realm (as they seemed to Leicester and Walsingham).[49]

However, Stafford's recall formed only one of four linked political battles in which Walsingham was engaged: he also strove to secure the execution of Mary queen of Scots, to support Leicester in the Netherlands, and to scotch the peace negotiations with Spain. With regard to the ambassador, a damaging body of evidence had been amassed, and by October 1586 a replacement dispatched, who to Stafford showed every sign of awaiting a permanent commission by the next post. Yet Stafford survived, Wotton departed for home in November, and within three months Walsingham and Stafford had settled their differences.[50] Why?

On the one hand, given his isolation at court, perhaps Walsingham feared that Stafford's recall might sooner or later recoil against him. Returning ambassadors had in the past proved natural candidates for the secretaryship of state – Sir Thomas Smith and Walsingham himself had served in Paris, while Sir Thomas Wilson had resided in Brussels. On the other hand, Walsingham seems to have lost all zest for public affairs when, at the end of October 1586, he received news of the death of Sir Philip Sydney, his son-in-law, his heir, and in politics his great hope. Gone was the living bond of his relationship with Leicester (to whom Sydney was also heir). But the distraught secretary, deep in debt as a result of Sydney's death, soon received an offer of help, amid lugubrious soliloquizing, from Lord Burghley. According to William Davison, on 20 December

it was my fortune to come into the Privy Chamber as my Lord Treasurer was dealing with her Majesty in your particular causes in most honourable sort, as one to whom she should acknowledge her life . . . alleging that, for that hard estate you stand in the dishonour must fall upon herself if such a servant should be suffered to quail . . . Her answer in general . . . was good . . . [although] the Lord Treasurer thinketh that as she is not sudden in her resolutions . . . so this must endure a little.[51]

Six days later, in a manoeuvre that Lord Burghley may have suggested, Walsingham left court professing disgust with the queen, but acknowledging himself 'infinitely bound' to Burghley, 'which I will never forget'. Some months later Walsingham's suit appears to have been granted.[52]

Amid such renewed friendship with Stafford's patron, Walsingham's hostility towards the ambassador could hardly be allowed to continue – if indeed its cessation was not a condition of Burghley's aid. Stafford swiftly took advantage of the changed climate. In January 1587 he wrote coyly to the secretary: 'A friend of yours here would be glad if you would send over with the next packet some trusty body belonging to you to whom he might speak freely.' Within a month Nicholas Faunt returned to Paris, where Stafford conveyed his griefs to him. Shortly afterwards Walsingham received William Lilly and Edward Grimstone (another of Stafford's servants) into his good graces and assured Stafford he would 'have his goodwill unfeignedly and that he will satisfy me by the first opportunity of all things and jealousies past'. Stafford reciprocated these sentiments in April, adding to Burghley 'I hope that I have a friend more now than I had.'[53] From then on Walsingham never openly swerved from the support he had promised the ambassador; however, unfortunately for the security of Tudor England, this reconciliation came at precisely the moment when Sir Edward Stafford agreed to become a spy for Philip II of Spain.[54]

In January 1587 Don Bernardino de Mendoza, Spanish ambassador in London (1578–84) and subsequently in Paris, informed his master that Charles Arundel had just delivered a most interesting message from his English counterpart, 'Estafort'. In the first place, Elizabeth's envoy complained about the implacable hostility shown towards him and his patron Lord Burghley by Walsingham and Leicester, and swore

that he would not be happy until he had revenged himself . . . by whatever means; and that now was the time for Your Majesty to make use of him, if it suited you . . . He told Arundel to write to assure Your Majesty on his word of honour that . . . not a single warship would be fitted out [in England] without him giving good advanced warning.

Mendoza went on to reveal that he had been in pursuit of Stafford for some time (presumably on the grounds that a resident ambassador known to have betrayed secrets to the duke of Guise – who had been clearly implicated in several plots to remove Elizabeth – might also betray them to the king of Spain). Although Stafford had been reluctant to deal directly with Mendoza, he had placed his trust in Arundel (a relative of Lady Stafford), who claimed, on Mendoza's instructions, to possess a special cypher which enabled him to pass Stafford's information on to Madrid directly, without going through Mendoza.[55]

All this perplexed the Spanish ambassador. For the time being the charade with Arundel could be continued – indeed, even as he was writing to the king, Arundel called again to say that Elizabeth was putting together a fleet to convey Dom Antonio and an army to Portugal: the source was Stafford, who had just heard it from a secretary of Admiral Lord Howard of Effingham, Stafford's brother-in-law. But, Mendoza continued, a more regular channel for communications was advisable, since Stafford seemed prepared to do anything for money: 'The said ambassador is very short of money, and even if he had not made such an offer, his poverty would be enough to expect from him any service if he saw he was going to be paid for it.' Mendoza advised the king to provide 2000 crowns (£450) as a down payment, 'offering to reward him [further] as his services merit'.

Philip quickly accepted the suggestion that 2000 crowns be given to someone the king called 'the new correspondent', and he congratulated both Mendoza and 'the intermediary' (Arundel) on their outstanding intelligence coup.[56] For the next eighteen months Mendoza's dispatches bristled with detailed information concerning English policy provided alternately by 'the new correspondent', 'the new friend' and the 'new confidant', as well as by someone referred to as 'Julio'. Often two or three of these terms appeared in the same letter, implying that Mendoza drew on data supplied by several spies, while the 'English ambassador' was also often mentioned, as if he were a quite different person. Some historians have therefore argued that Stafford was only one of Mendoza's sources.[57] Admittedly on one occasion even the king became confused, because he wrote in the margin of a dispatch in which Mendoza spoke of letters from Burghley shown to him by 'Julio', 'I think that he calls the "new confidant" "Julio" because that is the man to whom Cecil [i.e., Lord Burghley] writes.'[58] But the confusion was deliberate: like all good spy-masters, Mendoza deliberately used several names, and indeed mixed in news derived from others, in order to protect his source in case his letters were intercepted. Abundant evidence exists to prove, first, that the king had correctly identified both pseudonyms with the same person; and, second, that both referred to Sir Edward Stafford.

To begin with, in January 1588, Mendoza wrote to both Philip and the secretary of state, Don Juan de Idiáquez, reminding them in almost identical terms that it was about a year since 2000 crowns had been paid to their prime source, but to the king Mendoza used the phrase 'the new confidant' while to Idiáquez he spoke of 'Julio'. So these two aliases clearly referred to the same person.[59] And, equally clearly, that person must have been a very senior minister of the English crown resident in Paris because (as Philip II remarked) 'Cecil' – as well as Walsingham, Howard and the queen – corresponded with him directly and frequently. Moreover, 'Julio' also often stated that Burghley was his patron and Walsingham and Leicester his enemies.[60] Furthermore, 'Julio' and 'the new correspondent' not only displayed intimate knowledge about affairs in England: they also conveyed a wealth of information about English diplomatic relations with France, the Dutch, and the Spanish Netherlands – for example, revealing in advance to Mendoza, and thus to the Spanish negotiators, every gambit of the commissioners sent by Queen Elizabeth to meet with the duke of Parma at the Bourbourg conference in 1588.[61] In May 1587, the 'new friend' claimed to have been offered the post of lord deputy of Ireland, and the next month 'another office which carries with it membership of the [Privy] Council' – which almost certainly meant the post of secretary of state.[62] The only Englishman in Paris at this time to whom either of these offers could plausibly apply was Stafford. Finally, in June 1588, Mendoza reported that 'Julio' was 15,000 crowns (£3 500) in debt 'in his account with the queen', that Walsingham was pressing him for immediate repayment, and that until he discharged this debt 'his salary [*sueldo*]' was not being paid from England.[63] Once again, the only person in Paris drawing a salary from the queen, and the only person who owed her such a large sum of money, was Sir Edward Stafford.

Now the fact that Elizabeth's resident ambassador should offer his services to Mendoza, of all people, seems remarkable in itself, for Don Bernardino had been clearly implicated in more than one plot to assassinate the queen. It has therefore been suggested that Stafford actually served as a 'double agent', passing only false, outdated or insignificant information to Spain with the full knowledge of his government. And some data provided by 'Julio' were indeed false – such as the statistics on the strength of the Royal Navy, communicated to Mendoza in April 1588, which exaggerated the fleet's firepower by almost 40 per cent. One could argue that this aimed to alarm, and perhaps deter, Philip II; but equally Stafford may have believed the information to be true, since it came directly from his brother-in-law, Admiral Howard.[64] Even more tantalizing was the ambassador's role in Drake's 1587 raid on Cadiz to 'singe the king of Spain's beard'. Stafford began to supply information on Drake's preparations in December 1586, first via Arundel and then directly through Mendoza.[65] Early in April 1587 Stafford sent Mendoza as a matter of urgency information just received from Walsingham that 'the queen had not yet taken any decisions about sending the [Drake's] fleet because she had been discouraged by the news sent by her ambassador here that the warships promised by the Dutch were not as ready as they thought'. Interestingly enough, this news was not sent directly to Stafford but rather to another English envoy staying at the Paris embassy, but it was written in the cypher used by Stafford so that he could read it undetected.[66] Indeed it was almost as if Walsingham had *wanted* Stafford to read and pass on this information – which, significantly, was entirely false, for Drake received orders from the queen on 25 March to sail forthwith and destroy all the Spanish shipping and property that he could.

Stafford, however, had other sources of information besides the secretary of state, and as soon as they revealed the deception he sent another urgent message to Mendoza. Although, he regretted, only the queen and Burghley knew Drake's precise orders, he believed that Drake had been commanded to

prevent the joining together of Your Majesty's fleet, which of necessity was being prepared in different regions and ports. And if he succeeded in destroying some part of the Armada, he would go on to find the Indies fleet. In this connection someone had suggested to Drake that Cadiz was a suitable port, in which anyone who arrived in force might burn any ships that were there.

Subsequent events proved this intelligence to be extremely accurate, and Stafford claimed to have received it in letters from England dated 7 April.[67] Mendoza sent the warning about Cadiz from Paris on 19 April by express courier, and it reached Madrid in record time on the 30th – only one day after the English attack! It was a very close call:

Drake's fleet left Plymouth on 12 April, but ran into a storm off Cape Finisterre and only managed to regroup off Lisbon on the 26th. Had Drake taken but a few days longer, thanks to Stafford's intelligence his reception at Cadiz might have been very different.[68]

It is highly significant that Stafford's 'early warning' did not come from Walsingham; on the contrary, the secretary ordered all English ports to be closed for some weeks specifically to prevent news about Drake's expedition from getting abroad.[69] He also delayed writing to Stafford until 1 May, rather disingenuously concluding his letter 'Sir Francis Drake, as I doubt not but you have heard, is gone forth to the seas', providing some details on his instructions but none on his destination. And even then Walsingham held back this news for eight days, explaining in a cover note that the letter had been held 'by her Majesty's express commandment' while she composed a personal letter for Henry III to go along with it.[70] This sequence of events does indeed strongly suggest that Walsingham knew of Stafford's treason and sought to exploit it, sending him a stream of lies to pass on to the enemy (such as the superior power of the Royal Navy), but surrounding such deception with a bodyguard of truth that was either trivial or outdated (such as full details on the Cadiz raid once they were too late to be of any use) – both classic intelligence procedures.[71] But on other occasions Stafford provided Mendoza with extremely valuable operational intelligence well in advance, which Walsingham surely had not intended. Thus a letter from Mendoza to Philip II dated 16 January 1588 bristled with details on the operational directive given by Elizabeth to her navy, derived from the 'designio' (plan) sent to 'Julio' by Howard on 4 January. Its authenticity emerges by comparing it with the actual instructions, couched in almost identical terms, issued by Elizabeth to Howard on 30 December 1587. This news had reached the king by 29 January, in plenty of time to be of use, for the Armada did not set sail from Lisbon until May.[72] Stafford had indeed kept his 'word of honour' that 'not a single warship would be fitted out [in England] without him giving good advanced warning' to Philip.

An analysis of the information about Spain's preparations and intentions sent back to London by Stafford dispels any remaining doubts about his treasonable intentions. For a man who was in almost constant contact with Mendoza (as well as with the rest of the *corps diplo-*

matique in Paris), Stafford should have been able to transmit a constant stream of high-grade intelligence on Philip's plans to his government, just as other ambassadors did.[73] But, curious to relate, such information figured only rarely in his dispatches. Instead, he played up the hostility of the French to England, especially after Mary Stuart's execution, making the French Catholics seem to be Elizabeth's principal enemy.[74] On the relatively few occasions when he did mention Spain, he went out of his way to stress (on the one hand) the unpreparedness of the Spanish Armada, and (on the other) the restraint, the pacific intentions and the moral rectitude of Philip II. A good example of the former occurred in spring 1587, when Elizabeth made up her mind to respond to the reports of Spanish military and naval preparations against her by sending Drake against Cadiz. At first she instructed him to use maximum force; but then, on 29 April, 'Her Majesty being otherwise advertised that neither the said preparations were so great as was reported, and further that they are of late dissolved', she ordered Drake only to attack shipping on the high seas and on no account to enter harbours or to land. The chief of those who 'otherwise advertised' Elizabeth was Sir Edward Stafford.[75]

As an example of the ambassador's reassurances regarding Philip II's character, consider his account in January 1587 of a curious conversation with a Spaniard passing through Paris who (Stafford alleged) had stopped by the embassy in order to report an interview with Philip's foreign secretary, Don Juan de Idiáquez, to whom he claimed to have made an offer to kill Queen Elizabeth in return for a payment of 4000 crowns (£900). Idiáquez, according to the Spaniard, had graciously declined, remarking that although King Philip would 'be contented that Her Majesty were under the ground by God's hand, his conscience was too good to seek it that way'.[76] This is a suspicious tale on two scores. First, it seems unlikely that any would-be assassin would visit the residence of the official representative of the queen in Paris simply to volunteer a confession; and, second, it was well known that Philip II's conscience had recently allowed him to support several plots aimed at killing Elizabeth, to offer 25,000 crowns (£5500) for the assassination of William of Orange (a sum duly paid when the deed was done in 1584), and to place a price of 30,000 crowns on the head of Dom Antonio.[77]

Stafford continued to deceive his own government in 1588 by repeatedly assuring Elizabeth that the Spanish Armada had been disbanded. A copy of one letter, in January 1588, was forwarded to Admiral Howard, who expressed incredulity: 'I cannot tell what to think of my brother[-in-law] Stafford's advertisement; for if it be true that the King of Spain's forces be dissolved, I would not wish the Queen's Majesty to be at this charge that she is at; but if it be a device, knowing that a little thing makes us too careless, then I know not what may come of it.'[78]

If Stafford had made a special mark in the margin of this 'advertisement' to indicate it was false (page 78 above), clearly Elizabeth and her ministers had forgotten its significance. Otherwise, to advise his government that Spain no longer intended to launch an invasion, at a time when every effort was being made to get the Armada to sea, clearly amounted to treason. But Stafford persisted: on 3 May 1588 he suggested that the Armada was intended for Algiers; the next day he at last referred to a letter he had seen in Mendoza's study mentioning an enterprise against England, but speculated that anything left out in the open there would clearly be meant only to deceive, thus providing one more indication that the Armada was intended for some other purpose. On 16 June he told Walsingham that he thought the Armada was bound for the Indies; on 8 July he claimed that an outbreak of plague had driven it back to Spain; and on 13 July he asserted that bets of 6:1 were being made in Paris against it ever reaching the Channel.[79]

It seems inconceivable that the English government believed all these blatant lies. After all, Elizabeth and her ministers did not depend totally on Stafford for their news: many independent agents also reported directly to Walsingham and Burghley, and many of them transmitted copious and accurate detail on the 'Enterprise of England'.[80] Nevertheless, Burghley's support for his man seems to have remained strong and, with Leicester absent in the Netherlands for much of the time and the kingdom in danger of invasion, Walsingham apparently did not wish to disrupt things at court. Thus in September 1587, perhaps on Burghley's birthday, Walsingham wrote to him that 'this bearer havyng made me a very rare cooche for ease strength and lyghtness, wherof I have made this day trial on London stones: I am bold to present the same to your Lordship . . . Yt hath many artificiall points that wythout his demonstration wyll not easily be discerned.'[81]

Walsingham also remained civil towards Stafford. In January 1587 Sir Edward's younger brother William tried unsuccessfully to blackmail the French ambassador in London by proposing to him a plot to murder the queen; this would have afforded a golden opportunity to recall Stafford without raising suspicion abroad, but Walsingham let it pass.[82] To be sure a minor crisis occurred in December 1587 following the arrest in Paris of Gilbert Gifford, an English Catholic double agent, for he carried letters from Thomas Phelippes, a servant of the secretary, encouraging him to spy on Stafford. Although almost certainly written a year earlier, they were published in Paris and were read at the French court to Stafford's considerable (and understandable) embarrassment; but he managed to turn them to his advantage in London. He was scathing about the search for information against him by Phelippes: 'I take all this to come of his curiousity to show that he was a man of service.' And he gloated over the fact that the captured correspondence revealed the identity of several of Walsingham's other agents, and their business: 'Mr Phelippes must pardon me, being such a statesman as he would fain be, for saying that to hazard to write to such a knave as this is, things that may be scanned as these are, is not the greatest discretion in the world.'[83] Walsingham quickly repaired the breach, apologizing deeply for Phelippes's conduct (while assuring Stafford of his good character and loyalty). The ambassador's renewed wariness lingered, having found 'so many protestations and oaths one way, and so much double, hard dealing in effect'; but Walsingham eased his mind, largely by providing the financial help he so badly needed.[84]

And so Stafford survived. He pocketed further subsidies from Mendoza – 2000 crowns in February 1588 and 1000 more in August – but subsequently his ardour cooled. For about three months after the failure of the Spanish Armada, Mendoza complained that 'the new confidant' provided no more useful information.[85] Then in November Stafford resumed contact, and received another small payment; but he still reported little news about England and, although for a while he supplied helpful information about France, that too gradually dried up.[86] Several reasons explain this change. First, the collapse of royal authority and the onset of civil war in France caused the physical separation of the two ambassadors, with Stafford attending first on Henry III and then (after that king's assassination in September 1589) on Henry IV while Mendoza continued to reside in Paris, the capital of the Catholic League. Second, Stafford seems to have improved his standing in London: he returned to England twice in 1589 and twice more in 1590 before his final recall in November that year. It seems likely that on one of these visits the queen cancelled his debt to her and paid his salary arrears, thus redressing one of his principal grievances.[87] Third, the death of Leicester late in 1588 and of Walsingham early in 1590 removed a major bone of contention and fear. Should Elizabeth die, Burghley's influence seemed assured and therefore Stafford had less to fear. Above all, the failure of the Spanish Armada reduced the prospect of Philip II's succession to the throne of England. And so 'Julio' faded out of Mendoza's correspondence.

What had Spain gained for the money given to Stafford? At the very least, his Spanish connection seems to have inhibited the ambassador from revealing to London what he knew about Philip's 'Enterprise of England'; instead he took every opportunity to deny the existence of any hostile intention. Furthermore, and no less valuable, Stafford hastened to pass on to Spain every piece of information that came his way on the diplomatic, political and naval moves made by his own government: the various instructions issued to himself and to the queen's envoys at Bourbourg and in the Netherlands; the policies favoured by Elizabeth's various councillors and the differences between them; the strength and intentions of the English fleet. All in all, at 5200 crowns (£1155), Stafford surely represented the intelligence bargain of the century.

And what motivated Stafford? Why had he lived so dangerously? At his first personal meeting with Mendoza in April 1587, after Mary Stuart's execution, he promised to do everything he could to serve Spain 'except as it affected the person of the queen'. The following month, when he claimed to have been offered the post of lord deputy of Ireland, he declared himself prepared to accept (if it suited Philip II) 'with the resolve to deliver the kingdom to Your Majesty on the day his mistress dies and, until then, to keep it at your service, as he will do in any other area to which he is sent'.[88] In December 1587 he told Mendoza that he 'did not think Your Majesty was so ill-advised as to incur all this expense for the benefit of someone who was so far from being a Catholic as the king of Scotland, forgetting your own rights [to the English throne]'.[89] Clearly Stafford had his eye on the succession to Elizabeth – as no doubt he had done earlier, during his enthusiastic support of the Anjou match – and hoped to assure himself a leading role in the post-Elizabethan order. He therefore took care to keep on good terms with Mary Stuart, while she lived, and thereafter with Philip II, for both represented the 'reversionary interest' to the English crown: had Elizabeth died and Mary lived, the Scottish queen would probably have succeeded, just as Mary Tudor had replaced her Protestant half-brother in 1553; and while Philip II's title after Mary Stuart's execution was less clear, it remained in Catholic eyes as good as anyone else's.[90] Stafford, of course, was not alone in hedging his bets: Burghley and Leicester both made clear on several occasions that, although they were totally committed to Elizabeth, they had no personal hatred of Mary. Indeed Leicester even met the exiled Mary twice (while both took the waters at Buxton).[91] Nor was Stafford alone in accepting money from Spain: Sir James Croft, one of Elizabeth's longest-serving officials, received a pension from Philip II after 1579 and, having secured a place as commissioner at the Bourbourg conference, undertook talks on his own initiative to try and induce the queen to make peace.[92] In addition, immediately after the conclusion of peace with Spain in 1604, the Spanish ambassador in London began to pay pensions totalling over 30,000 crowns (£7000), a year to English courtiers, led by Robert Cecil and Howard of Effingham.[93]

The motives of such men in accepting money from a foreign prince are hard to judge. On the one hand, at least until the Armada entered the English Channel, Philip II was technically at peace with England, so that the transactions did not necessarily rank as treason. On the other hand, Stafford, at least, needed cash desperately: by the beginning of 1587 he owed the queen perhaps 15,000 crowns (£3500) and his total debts probably amounted to double that. Although he received only just over 5000 crowns from Spain, mainly because Philip did not want to let him off the financial hook, the ambassador no doubt hoped to receive more in due course and must have expected a major reward when Spain 'won'.[94] In addition, and no less important, Sir Edward seems to have harboured genuine fears of disgrace or punishment at the hands of Walsingham and Leicester. In October 1587 he assured Mendoza that he wanted 'the tables to be turned in England so that he may be avenged on Walsingham'.[95]

The role of 'factions' at the court of Elizabeth remains the focus of much debate. They were clearly not the embryonic political parties sometimes implied by Conyers Read and Sir John Neale: Simon Adams is surely right to point out that leading ministers 'were all recipients of the queen's favour, and, however much they may have disagreed, they had too much in common for permanent antagonisms to be established'.[96] Queen Elizabeth's style of government promoted caution and consensus: she trained her ministers and favourites to see that they had much in common, in patronage as in policy. Her politicians and courtiers came to learn that a balanced network of graduated contacts to earn the goodwill – or at least to avert the enmity – of each major patron was the surest way to prosper, although only a close personal link of explicit loyalty would fend off a major crisis. Yet it is important not to lose sight of the reality of Elizabethan politics in one of its most tense and exciting decades. Choosing war with Spain was a traumatic decision, while adjusting to the fact, inevitable since 1581, that the open succession to the barren queen laid bare all the questions of religion and allegiance that underlay the Elizabethan polity. Together they unsettled the politics of the period and accentuated political divisions to unusual levels. Stafford's story demonstrates the existence of acute political tensions and some sharp group allegiances. Nevertheless, his behaviour is too idiosyncratic to be taken as typical. Sir Edward was indeed 'factional'. He sought only Burghley's support; increasingly he spurned all others; and, as a result, he found himself isolated, endangered and embittered. He is one of those who, like William Davison, proves by exception the greater sophistication of most other practitioners of Elizabethan court politics.

Ironically, however, as Stafford's factionalism contributed to his isolation, so it assisted his survival. Walsingham had to let Stafford be, probably because Burghley proved unchallengeable, although also perhaps because Sir Edward, as the queen's relative, possessed some sort of immunity in her eyes. Why Burghley remained committed to

Stafford is less clear: perhaps he hesitated to admit an error of judgement; perhaps he wished to demonstrate that his power had withstood the struggles of 1584–5; perhaps Stafford represented one of Burghley's own 'hedges' against the uncertain succession. But whatever the reason, the secretary secured his revenge posthumously because, despite Stafford's remarkably long period of service in the foremost posting of the Elizabethan diplomatic service, and although he lived until 1605, he never received the office of principal secretary or any other position appropriate to his standing and experience. As Buzenval had predicted in 1585, by the age of thirty-three Sir Edward Stafford had already passed the summit of his career.

4

I have always loved maps. At primary school I enjoyed drawing maps; at secondary school geography was one of my favourite subjects. In my doctoral thesis, I drew all the maps with indian ink and coloured them with crayon. I also studied contemporary maps. One of my happiest days while researching The Army of Flanders and the Spanish Road came when I found a map of the frontier between France and Savoy, drawn in 1606, which picked out the Spaniards' itinerary between Lombardy and the Low Countries in red, with the label 'Chemin des Espagnolz': the Spanish Road (see Figure 11, page 135).

My attention was drawn to this item by David Buisseret's biography of the duke of Sully, the minister who coordinated the mapping of France's frontier. In 1985, as director of the Hermon Dunlap Smith Center for the History of Cartography at the Newberry Library in Chicago, he organized a conference called 'Monarchs, ministers and maps: the emergence of cartography as a tool of government in early modern Europe', and invited me to survey the use of maps by the Spanish Habsburgs. I worked on the subject in the map room of the National Library of Scotland in Edinburgh, which seemed to possess every relevant reference tool, and in the map collections of Madrid and Simancas.

The conference brought together an outstanding team of historians interested in maps, and exposed us to the Newberry's own formidable cartographic resources. I received much useful feedback at the conference, and also afterwards from other participants, especially from Peter Barber, curator of maps at the British Library, who let me browse through the collections in his care and taught me new ways to study early modern cartography. I also visited other repositories and corresponded with other historians familiar with early modern maps.

I recall with special gratitude the assistance of the late Richard Boulind, who had worked in many cartographic collections and seemed to have a photographic memory for striking details. In 1992, my essay appeared in the conference proceedings and it covered the period from the 1450s, when the first 'modern' map of Spain appeared, to the 1650s, when the Spanish government apparently lost its capacity to meet its own cartographic needs.

Since then, much new work on the maps commissioned by the Spanish Habsburgs, and particularly by Philip II, has appeared. For example, two monographs appeared at virtually the same time on the king's cartographic study of New Spain; while Jacob van Deventer's maps of the North Netherlands have appeared in a magnificent fac-simile edition (see pages 101–2 and 116 below). I therefore decided to confine this essay to the use of maps by Philip II and his ministers. Although they built up the best cartographic resources in Europe, they failed to make full use of their investment: some projects, like the 'map of Spain', they allowed to atrophy; others, such as the sailing directions for the Spanish Armada, they failed to update; others still they mislaid. As with intelligence, it is not enough simply to acquire maps: before they can produce an advantage they require analysis, acceptance and action.

Philip II, Maps and Power

In the summer of 1566 Philip II wished to evaluate a report from the council of the Indies about the voyage of Miguel López de Legazpi to the Philippines, but he could not find any maps to show him where the islands were. 'Tell the councillors,' he irritably instructed his secretary, Francisco de Erasso,

That they are to make every effort to find all the papers and charts which exist on this, and to keep them safe in the council offices; indeed the originals should be put in the archives at Simancas, and authenticated copies taken to the Council. I think that I have some [maps of the area] myself, and I tried to find them when I was in Madrid the other day – because if I do have them, that is where they will be. When I get back there, if I remember and if I have time (which I don't just now), I shall look again. Do you think you could find something on this, Erasso? I would like you to search, and make sure that anything you find is looked after as I have just said, with the Council always in possession of the copies.[1]

Did Erasso ever find them? The posthumous inventory of Philip II's possessions, drawn up in 1607, which listed in meticulous detail every-thing from toothbrushes to bone rings for the treatment of the king's haemorrhoids, scarcely mentioned cartographic items: a few charts and maps (all of either America or the Atlantic; none of the Pacific), four globes, and three copies of Ortelius's *Theatrum Orbis Terrarum*. But this is misleading: many items from the king's extensive carto-graphic collections have in fact survived, although they are not listed among his worldly goods.[2]

During Philip II's reign maps became for the first time a standard instrument of government – a vital tool both for mobilizing the state's resources at home and for projecting its power abroad – but the loss of many cartographic materials has obscured this crucial development. Three separate causes are responsible. First, by their very nature all maps testify to matters of only *temporary* interest: they are most useful when new, and outdated ones tend to be discarded, if not destroyed, in favour of a more current version. Second, maps – especially parchment maps – share the risks that threaten any ancient document: of being reused as binding for a book; scraped off to become a palimpsest for some later information deemed to be more important; destroyed by fire or some other disaster; or, like Philip's maps of the Pacific, simply getting lost. Third, and most important, many early modern govern-ments deliberately destroyed or 'classified' their maps through fear that the information they contained might compromise national secur-ity and should therefore be concealed from hostile eyes. Thus in 1573 the Spanish government paid a considerable sum to purchase a copper engraving of a map of Hainaut in the South Netherlands 'to be locked away in order to suppress it and ensure that it should not become public (a thing contrary to the service of His Majesty)'.[3] The principal problem facing students of Spanish cartography is therefore to repair the ravages of time, secrecy and Philip II's filing system in order to establish the true extent and the nature of his cartographic resources, and the uses to which they were put.

The surviving maps fall into two main categories. First come general surveys – covering both Philip's own states and those of his neighbours – which allowed him to locate and visualize geographically a place that was in the news and thus to cope with the unforeseen. The rest relate to a specific problem, often involving the use of armed force and prepared in order to facilitate a specific course of action. Given the considerable variety within these two categories, each will be examined separately.

Philip commissioned his first important map in 1555: the *Nova descriptio Hispaniae* published in London by Thomas Geminus to provide the king's new English subjects with a more accurate delineation of Spain. Since this map enjoyed official approval, it probably drew upon government sources, and later cartographers made heavy use of it – even though the interior of the peninsula still contained little more than an idiosyncratic selection of half-known place-names and features.[4]

The next landmark in mapping Spain came with the *Theatrum Orbis Terrarum* of Abraham Ortelius, dedicated to the king and published at Antwerp in 1570. Although some thirty of the thirty-eight maps in the *Theatrum* were of Italian origin, 'Spain' formed an exception. Ortelius chose the *Hispaniae nova descriptio* of the French botanist Charles de l'Écluse (or Carolus Clusius), recently printed at Antwerp in large format as a separate wall-map. This work reflected careful study and some personal reconnaissance, and included almost 1200 place-names – although Ortelius changed some of them in subsequent editions. Thus in 1571 he received a communication from Philip II's chief minister in Spain, Cardinal Diego de Espinosa, expressing general satisfaction with the Clusius map, but regretting that it omitted his own birthplace, Martín Muñoz de las Posadas. Since the place was small, not to say obscure, the cardinal graciously described exactly where it was and suggested a place-name that could be deleted in order to make way for the new entry. Ortelius took the point: the 1573 edition of the *Theatrum* included 'Martimuñoz', about halfway between Ávila and Medina del Campo.[5] Rather more usefully, throughout the 1570s Benito Arias Montano, librarian of the Escorial and a noted humanist who had resided in Antwerp for several years, sent Ortelius various maps of Spain and Portugal, and of their overseas colonies, for future editions. Best of all, agents of the Antwerp cartographer received permission to visit Spain and make their own maps. Ortelius had not dedicated his *Theatrum Orbis Terrarum* to Philip II in vain!

Other foreign compilers of maps in the later sixteenth century knew less about the peninsula. Gerard Mercator could not find reliable maps of Spain to include in his original *Atlas* of 1585; and none adorned the editions of 1595 or 1602. Only after the Amsterdam map-maker Hondius acquired Mercator's plates was this anomaly rectified: the 1606 edition of the *Atlas* included seven maps of the peninsula (admittedly, six of them plagiarized from inferior earlier works), while the 1611 edition contained nine and the 1638 edition had fourteen.[6] Yet none of Mercator's Spanish maps were particularly good – few compared favourably with those available at the time for France, Italy or the Netherlands – and historians must wonder why. An initial explanation is that, after Geminus, all the published maps of Spain were made by outsiders: they were neither commissioned by the government nor compiled from official resources. Thus the *Hispaniae nova delineatio* of 1581, the only map of the peninsula ever printed in Habsburg Spain, was prepared by Enrique Cock from Gorinchem largely on the basis of the Ortelius map. Nevertheless, Cock made some changes: on the one hand he omitted more than half the place-names included by Ortelius; on the other, he added a score of new names, including the Escorial. These additions did not come from cartographic study, however, but from his travels with the court and from reading the *General Chronicle of Spain* published a few years before by Ambrosio de Morales![7] Few sixteenth-century map-makers showed any interest in personal reconnaissance (let alone in measuring or surveying for themselves); instead, they preferred to use second-hand cartographic data, often combining a number of small-scale maps to create a sort of mosaic to represent larger areas. Admittedly, they strove diligently to select only the best of the second-hand data; but that was still no substitute for personal reconnaissance.[8]

Paradoxically, those who collected data on Spanish topography in person seldom seemed interested in maps. Thus Pedro de Medina's *Grandezas y cosas notables de España*, published in 1548 to help the young Philip II learn about 'the things of this, your Spain', included descriptions of over four hundred settlements, and included a woodcut view of about one-quarter of them. However, the woodcuts differed little: one, depicting a building surrounded by walls, served for most small towns; another, with a castle at the centre, represented almost all the cities. Even the map of Spain that served as a frontispiece merely reproduced one created about a century before to illustrate early printed editions of Ptolemy's *Geography*. A second edition of Medina's *Grandezas* in 1595 also unashamedly reproduced the Ptolemaic map, although it did offer some slight improvement in the cityscapes. For example, a recognizable likeness of Seville (clearly showing the Arenal, the Giralda and the Golden Tower) now accompanied the city's description; but it also adorned the entries on Gibraltar and Aragon; while the woodcut for Madrid, which also served for Lisbon and Valencia, looked like none of them.[9]

Philip II, to whom Medina dedicated his work, strove to promote better city plans. In May 1559, shortly before he returned to Spain, he commissioned the cartographer Jacob van Deventer, who had already produced a series of detailed maps of each province of the Habsburg Netherlands, 'to visit, measure and draw all the towns of these provinces, with the rivers and villages adjoining, likewise the frontier crossings and passes. The whole work is to be made into a book containing a panorama of each province, followed by a representation of each individual town.' At the outbreak of war in the Netherlands in 1572, van Deventer fled to Cologne; and by the time of his death there, three years later, he had completed over 250 bird's-eye plans, of which 222 have survived (119 of them in two copies).[10]

Van Deventer's survey constitutes a unique cartographic achievement: no other region in the sixteenth century can boast a series of town plans of similar accuracy, uniformity and precision. The 'fair copy', now preserved in two handsome volumes in the Biblioteca Nacional in Madrid, includes not only a fine coloured view of each city, but often also an inset showing in greater detail its streets, fortifications and principal structures. All are oriented towards magnetic north; all but two are drawn on a scale of between 1:7400 and 1:8400, making it possible to depict urban areas of up to three-quarters of a square mile (2 square km) on a single sheet of paper measuring approximately 9 × 12 inches (24 by 30 cm).[11]

Two years after setting van Deventer to work, Philip II asked Anton van den Wyngaerde to come to Spain and undertake a similar survey there. Wyngaerde's technique was somewhat different, for he worked from a slight elevation and in panoramic format, rather than from bird's-eye perspective; but the record was just as impressive. Finished views of fifty-six Spanish cities by Wyngaerde exist, together with preparatory sketches for several more. After the artist's death in 1571, Philip decided to send his œuvre to the Netherlands to be engraved but (as with van Deventer's project) the outbreak of the Dutch Revolt the following year made this impossible. In 1587, Enrique Cock tried again. He sent to the Plantin Press in Antwerp a full Latin description of fifty-one of the places painted by Wyngaerde, calibrated with his 'views'. The press responded enthusiastically and Cock was still at work on the project in 1596, two years before his death, but once again the views never left Spain. Instead, the king displayed them in his palaces, along with other urban images, so that he and his advisers could view the salient cities of the monarchy at a glance.[12]

Wyngaerde's series of topographic plans formed one of three simultaneous geographic projects for Spain commissioned by Philip II. The second was a set of government questionnaires, later called the *Relaciones topográficas*, sent out to various communities of Castile in the 1570s. The idea seems to have originated with the royal chronicler Juan Páez de Castro, who prepared a questionnaire to be sent to each village in Spain requesting information about its geography, history, economy, population and 'antiquities' as a prelude to writing a detailed history and description of the kingdom. Páez died in 1570, however, before it could be distributed. Then, five years later, Juan de Ovando, president of the council of finance and of the council of the Indies, and one of Philip's most energetic ministers, sent a fifty-seven point questionnaire to all communities in Castile. The king apologized for this unusual initiative, but explained that 'if we were to send a person to compile the descriptions required, it could not be done with the speed we desire'. Returns for some six hundred villages of New Castile, and for the city of Toledo, have survived in eight vast manuscript volumes (at least five more of them once existed).[13] In 1583, ministers discussed extending the survey to Aragon and Portugal, but nothing happened; indeed the government seems to have made little use even of the returns from Castile.[14]

The same is true of the third, simultaneous, geographical project: a complete and detailed cartographic survey of the Iberian peninsula directed by Pedro de Esquivel, professor of mathematics at the University of Alcalá de Henares and an expert in surveying. According to his friend Ambrosio de Morales, the king commissioned Esquivel 'to travel throughout his kingdoms, seeking out with his own eyes all the villages, rivers and mountains – both large and small – so that a description of Spain could be made as certain and as complete, as detailed and as perfect, as His Majesty desired and Professor Esquivel could execute'. Felipe de Guevara (whose son served as one of Esquivel's assistants) claimed that:

Without exaggeration, it was the most careful, diligent and accurate description ever to be undertaken for any province since the creation of the world ... There is not an inch of ground in all of Spain that [Esquivel] did not see, walk over or tread on, checking the accuracy of everything (insofar as mathematical instruments make it possible) with his own hands and eyes.

In 1575, just after Esquivel's death, Morales added further tantalizing details on his late colleague's cartographic achievement:

He located places in the map or picture he was making by means of the tables of Ptolemy, covering the paper with squares and calibrating the sides by longitude and latitude. But he also worked with elegant devices so that everything would be as accurate and fine as possible. His friends and I admired these devices in his room and I would say something about them here except for the fact that they can only be understood by looking with one's own eyes, not by writing.

According to Morales, Esquivel left his work largely 'completed when he died, and His Majesty has it in his Chamber'. The surviving data suggest that Esquivel and his team established coordinates by personal survey for some six thousand locations.[15]

Nevertheless, the 'map of Spain' remained incomplete and when Philip II heard of the death of another member of the team in 1577 he wrote to his secretary: 'I am reminded that he possessed the instruments and other papers of Esquivel. If this is so, I would like them to be collected ... so that they should not be lost and so that the map of Spain, which he was making, should be continued.' It seems likely that his work eventually formed part of the remarkable atlas of twenty-one maps now in the Escorial library.[16] The first (and most complete) map in the collection covers the whole peninsula (Figure 4); the rest form a series of sectional surveys done to the same scale in which Portugal is the best covered and Aragon and Catalonia the worst. It is worth lingering over this achievement because, at a scale of 1:430,000 (the same as standard aeronautical charts today), the Escorial Atlas contains by far the largest European maps of their day to be based on a detailed ground survey. No other major Western state of the sixteenth century possessed anything like it. Where Apian's celebrated map of Bavaria, based on a survey carried out between 1554 and 1561, covered under 17,000 square miles (45,000 square km), and Seco's map of Portugal (printed in 1560) covered almost 34,000 square miles (90,000 square km), the Escorial Atlas covered almost 193,000 square miles (500,000 square km).[17]

How was it made? One important clue comes from the existence in Stockholm of a codex from the second half of the sixteenth century containing the coordinates of some 3000 locations in Spain – about half of those covered in the Escorial Atlas. Each set of data consists of bearings from two separate observation stations, with a rough estimate of distances: on such a scale, they can only be the work of Esquivel and his team. However, these initial entries do not stand alone: they also bear a host of annotations in the hands of the royal cosmographers João Baptista de Lavanha (whose name is on the flyleaf of the volume) and Juan López de Velasco.[18] Lavanha's comments largely took the form of corrections to coordinates and geographical data: 'This can't be right' (book I, fo. 28); 'Our informant was wrong' (book I, fo. 15); 'This observation coincides with mine' (book IV, unfoliated); and so on. Velasco, by contrast, attempted to improve the accuracy of the whole work by adding several pages of stellar observations and declinations for various different latitudes, as well as the longitudes of a

4 The Escorial Atlas: map of Spain and Portugal, c. 1585
In the 1570s and 80s a team of cartographers, led first by Pedro de Esquivel
and then by João Bautista de Lavanha and Juan López de Velasco, surveyed
the entire Iberian peninsula – over 190,000 square miles (almost 500,000
square kilometres) – and portrayed the results in an atlas of twenty-one
sheets. The first map (shown here), although slightly skewed because the
surveyors made no allowance for the curvature of the earth's surface,
provided a remarkably accurate overview of the physical and urban
geography of both Spain and Portugal. The rest of the atlas contained the
largest European maps of their day to be based on a detailed ground survey.

number of cities – Toledo, Madrid, Valladolid, Seville – calculated from the time recorded at different locations for lunar eclipses in 1577 and 1584. This is important, because Velasco's hand also appears on the maps in the Escorial Atlas, probably precisely to add the longitude of (at least) some places, without which accurate maps on this scale could scarcely have been completed.

Another obvious consideration suggests that the maps were not finalized until the 1580s: Portugal, which forms a fully integrated part of the Escorial Atlas, remained until 1580 an independent state into which Esquivel and his team could not go. Indeed, it seems likely that the maps covering Portugal in the Escorial Atlas derived from a separate and far superior survey, for there is a clear disparity in standard. Thus the rivers that cross the frontier are shown in far more detail on the Portuguese than on the Spanish side, which suggests that the Escorial cartographers incorporated the results of a prior survey for areas across the border. At first sight, the progenitor seems obvious: Pedro Alvares Seco's fine map of Portugal engraved and published in Italy in 1560 by Aquileo Estau, a Portuguese resident in Rome, with a dedication to a munificent prince of the church, Cardinal Sforza. But Seco's map is not as straightforward as it looks. In the first place, it was so accurate that it clearly stemmed from a detailed ground survey that would have taken several years to complete (if Apian took seven years to survey Bavaria, it must have taken at least ten to cover Portugal). Such a protracted exercise could only have taken place under government licence, almost certainly as part of a state enterprise. And yet, if Seco's work was official, why was it published in Rome instead of in Lisbon, with a dedication to an Italian cleric rather than to the Portuguese king? All the evidence suggests that the published map of 1560 was, in fact, a pirated edition of some master-map based on a geometrical survey made for the Portuguese government.[19]

Given this chronology, and given the similarity in scale, calligraphy and technique employed for both Castile and Portugal, it seems likely that the sectional maps of the Escorial Atlas were plotted only after the Spanish conquest of Portugal in 1580 which gave Philip II and his ministers full access to the rich cartographic materials in Lisbon. Perhaps the key lies in the addition of three cartographers to the royal payroll in December 1582: Luis Georgio, 'an expert in making cosmographical, geographical, and nautical charts'; Pedro Ambrosio de Onderiz, an assistant; and João Baptista de Lavanha. Philip charged Lavanha, a Portuguese map-maker, to reside 'in our court, and wherever we decree, to work on cosmographical, geographical and topographical matters': presumably, the 'topographical matters' included the 'map of Spain' project.[20] The Escorial Atlas was probably then finalized by a team of cartographers who plotted the thousands of observations made by Esquivel in Spain and by an anonymous team in Portugal into a framework laid down by López de Velasco, with Lavanha checking the information as it was mapped. Unfortunately, the work was apparently abandoned with several of the maps still unfinished, perhaps when Lavanha returned to Portugal in 1591; nevertheless, by the end of Philip II's reign the Iberian peninsula was better represented in maps than any other European area of comparable size.[21]

Philip II displayed the same mapping impulse towards his other possessions. In 1566, for example, he wrote to his viceroy of Naples: 'Since things crop up every day which can only be clearly and properly understood by knowing the distances, the rivers and the borders of that kingdom, we have resolved that it would be useful to have here a map and description of it.' If the viceroy did not have one to hand, he was to commission and send one. Nine years later, the king asked again and added that he would like one 'similar to the one by Paulo Juano Cano of Genoa that is said to exist in the Treasury there'. In the 1570s, he commissioned a survey of the coasts of Sicily from Tiburcio Spanocchi, and in the 1590s a splendid atlas of the Canaries from Leonardo Turriano, who filled it with views, plans and maps.[22] The most ambitious overseas cartographic venture of the reign concerned the viceroyalty of New Spain (Mexico). Juan de Ovando prepared questionnaires for the various communities of Spanish America some years before he issued them for Castile: 37 questions in 1569, 200 in 1571, and 135 in 1573. He also dispatched scientists – botanists, zoologists, herbalists and cartographers (notably Francisco Domínguez) – to gather specimens, make drawings of the flora and fauna, and prepare maps of Philip's overseas possessions. Meanwhile, Philip commissioned Juan López de Velasco, formerly Ovando's secretary and now 'royal cosmographer and chronicler of the Indies', to compile two works – 'A geography and general description of the Indies' and 'A demarcation and division of the Indies' – which displayed, in cartographic as well as written form, all data known about the western hemisphere. The two works, presented to the council of the Indies in 1574–5, contained surprisingly accurate maps of the Americas and the Caribbean, as well as the first map ever drawn of the western Pacific.[23]

The results of the questionnaires and surveys commissioned by Ovando proved disappointing, and so in 1577 López de Velasco sent a simpler printed list of fifty-five questions to each community in New Spain accompanied by a request for a map, a description and – most ambitious of all – a calculation of longitude based on simultaneous observations of two predicted lunar eclipses.[24] A great deal of data again flowed in, with numerous detailed descriptions, and almost one hundred maps of individual communities. No one, however, succeeded in calculating longitude and so the king's new Academy of Mathematics in Madrid organized another attempt. Over the winter of 1582–3, its professors prepared a package of materials for observing the lunar eclipse forecast for 17 November 1584, including instructions on how to prepare recording disks of the same size, and sent them in advance not only to Antwerp, Toledo and Seville, but also to Mexico City, Manila and perhaps even Macao. To assure the accuracy of the observations they also sent the noted Valencian astronomer Jaume Juan to Mexico well ahead of time in order to assemble the necessary instruments and liaise with local experts. On 17 November 1584, right on schedule and with two clocks and a barrage of other instruments beside them, Jaume Juan and his associates recorded their observations of the eclipse on the roof of the archbishop's palace in Mexico City.[25]

These various ventures all failed to achieve the goals anticipated. In 1583 Francisco Domínguez had still not finished his maps of Mexico. The following year, Jaume Juan could not make the accurate observations he sought because, when the moon first became visible in Mexico, the eclipse had already begun and so he could only record its end (furthermore, given the inaccuracy of the clocks available, he could not be sure of the exact time anyway). Finally, most of the maps sent from America in response to Velasco's questionnaire proved unintelligible because most of them came from Nahua cartographers who used conventions totally unfamiliar to their European colleagues.[26]

Nevertheless, Philip persisted in collecting maps. Some he commissioned; others arrived from government agents stationed in foreign cartographic centres (above all Venice and Antwerp) who possessed standing orders to acquire all the latest maps and plans; while others still came as the result of espionage. The king occasionally sent agents specifically to steal maps from his neighbours, as Giovanni Battista Gesio did in Portugal in the 1570s, but most spies provided their services spontaneously. Thus in 1594 Robert Parsons, SJ, forwarded to the king a set of detailed charts of the approaches to the main ports of southern England and Wales (Milford Haven, Falmouth, Plymouth and Dartmouth, and the Solent), together with a detailed description. One 'Mr Lambert', an English Catholic pilot, had supplied them, obviously with a view to assisting a Spanish invasion. They offered the best charts of the area available at the time.[27]

In fact, the majority of the maps commissioned by Philip II and his ministers originated with a specific issue. A few concerned social problems – the progress of the plague in Galicia in 1598, for example – but the majority related to war: the disposition of enemy forces; the progress of a siege; the possible itineraries for troops.[28] The surviving maps and sketches prepared for Philip's various projects to invade England offer an interesting case study. Some he acquired on the open market. Thus the king (and some of his ministers) purchased a map of England published by Gerard Mercator in 1570, probably in conjunction with the invasion plans under discussion at that time; somewhat later, he also acquired a copy of Saxton's (Latin) *Atlas of England and Wales*. In 1574, when Philip planned to send an invasion force from Spain, the count of Olivares, a prominent minister, called for the preparation of two copies of a map of the coast beyond Calais 'in which the sandbanks there, and in Holland and Zeeland, should be shown, and the buoys and leading marks that used to be there, and the depths of all areas are all shown very clearly'. This seemed promising but, Olivares continued, 'one copy of the two charts should be carried by the fleet commander, and the other should remain here in the Council'. The needs of vessels separated from the flagship do not seem to have occurred to him.[29]

In 1583, when Philip II again contemplated a descent on England, the duke of Parma sent him a 'careful account' of all the ports around the British Isles by Robert Heighington, a Catholic exile, together with his own assessment of the data. The king annotated his copy and in 1587 sent it to Santa Cruz in Lisbon, when the Armada was (he thought) about to depart.[30] A volume of superb sea views of the European coast from Poland to Brittany came into the king's possession at this time (Figure 5), as did a less helpful atlas of portolan charts supplied by the Oliva family in Naples, and a rudimentary sketch of the theatre of operations drawn by Bernardino de Escalante (Figure 6).[31] Although a priest when he forwarded his project for the conquest of England, Escalante had served as a soldier in Flanders and spent eighteen months in England during the 1550s; he had also composed an excellent manual of military practice and a treatise on navigation. His map showed three possible invasion strategies. The first (on the left of the map) required a daring voyage into the North Atlantic directly to Scotland, where the invasion fleet would regroup before launching its main attack ('The seas are high and dangerous,' Escalante observed, 'but through Jesus Christ crucified everything is possible'). The second was a direct attack into the Irish Sea, a route 'which the Armada could well have undertaken but for the danger' (presumably of 'the enemy' whose forces are shown at the entrance to the English Channel). The third route involved a direct attack from Flanders to Dover, and on to London. In the event, Philip decided to adopt a combination of these suggestions, with the Armada leaving Lisbon for the Channel in order to rendezvous with a second expeditionary force assembled in the Spanish Netherlands (see pages 52–6 above).

This was easier said than done. To begin with, to ensure success, the 130 vessels of the Grand Fleet assembled in Lisbon each required appropriate charts, sailing directions, and competent pilots to be sure of reaching the rendezvous. In September 1587, the king sent to the commander of the Armada Robert Heighington's 'careful account' of the coasts of England prepared four years earlier, which recorded the depth and size of the harbours and the condition of the roads leading to London. He also commissioned Luis Teixeira, a Lisbon cartographer, to prepare new charts of England, Scotland and Ireland. The duke of Medina Sidonia, who arrived in Lisbon to take command of

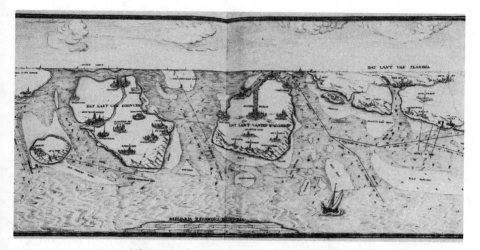

5 The coastline of Atlantic Europe, 1586

This striking view of the Scheldt and Maas estuaries comes from an 'atlas' of
1586 containing twenty-four charts of the coast of Europe from Reval in the
Baltic to La Rochelle. All views are done from an imaginary 'crow's nest'
position out to sea and show the 'leading marks' before each port, together
with sandbanks and other hazards. The atlas was probably prepared by the
Dutch cartographer Aelbert Haeyen; however, the publication of
Waghenaer's *Mariner's Mirror* in 1585, with a licence that prevented
anyone from bringing out a rival product for ten years, forced Haeyen to
look elsewhere. He therefore sent – or, more likely, sold – his work to Spain.

the fleet in March 1588, found this inadequate. He immediately
ordered his nautical advisers to put together some sailing instructions,
and the result (published as a pamphlet of ten folios by a local printer)
was the *Derrotero de las costas de Bretaña, Normandia, Picardia hasta
Flandes*.[32] He sent an advance copy to the king, who took a personal
interest in its accuracy, checking its information against his own collection of maps. He worried that he could not find a particular place
noted in the *Derrotero* on his maps and sent a secretary to check its
location on the map of France included in Ortelius's *Theatrum*. He
also noted that another place was spelled differently in the *Derrotero*
and on one of his maps ('but they must be the same place, which is
very close to Usshant'). More ominously, the king fretted that one of
his maps showed Dunkirk to be '35 to 40 leagues' from the Isle of

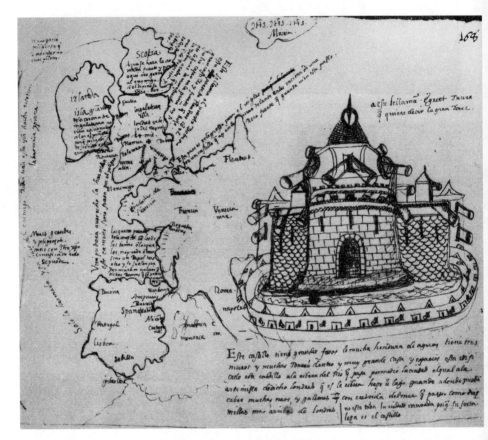

6 Bernardino de Escalante's campaign plan against England, 1586
The only surviving 'campaign map' for the Enterprise of England was drawn
up in June 1586 by Bernardino de Escalante, to illustrate the invasion
strategies discussed in a memorial he sent to court. Dismissing expeditions
via either Scotland or the Irish Sea, Escalante favoured a landing in southern
Ireland to draw off the Royal Navy while Philip's troops in the Netherlands
made a surprise landing in Kent and marched on London, defended only by
'E Greet Tuura' – (which Escalante remembered only imperfectly from his
brief sojourn in England during the 1550s).

Wight, whereas another showed the distance as fifty, 'and I think this
conforms more to the *Derrotero*'.[33]

Nevertheless, the Armada's *Derrotero* was not what it seemed. It
was not a guide specially made for the Grand Fleet (which, given that

it was put together in less than a fortnight, was hardly to be expected) but rather a hybrid compilation of information from the 'rutters' normally used by merchants travelling between the Iberian peninsula and the North Sea. Thus it assured the Armada captains that, once they reached the anchorage bounded by the Goodwin Sands, 'There you will wait for a pilot to take you either to London or Dover.' If, on the other hand, they wished to sail from Dover to Flushing, they should cross the Channel to the Flemish coast 'and when you are off Blankenburgh you will fire a gun and a pilot will come out to take you to Flushing'. At a time when Spain was at war with both England and the Dutch Republic such counsel was clearly worse than useless. The true value of the *Derrotero* lay in the detailed information it provided on the different depths and 'bottoms' to be found in various parts of the Channel, and on how to recognize different landmarks ashore, so that pilots without direct experience of the area (and ships without pilots at all) might have a chance of fixing their position as the fleet advanced.[34]

Together with the *Derrotero*, in April 1588 Medina Sidonia also sent the king some kind of map (*un cartón*). Perhaps it was one of the 'mounted sea charts, with soundings around the coasts of Spain, England and Flanders' which the duke commissioned from Ciprián Sánchez, a Lisbon chart-maker. Eighty-five of them were delivered just two weeks before the Armada sailed.[35] Two of these charts seem to have survived. Both look like Portuguese manuscript copies of the corresponding maps printed in Lucas Waghenaer's *Mariner's Mirror* (of which a Latin edition appeared in October 1586), but as such they represented the most up-to-date aid to navigation available at the time.[36]

The cartographic care with which Philip II's ministers and generals prepared for war on land can best be appreciated by considering the use of maps made by the king's most successful military commander: Don Fernando Álvarez de Toledo, third duke of Alba. A large number of maps connected with his campaigns in northern Europe between 1567 and 1573 have survived, including two striking items now among the records of the government of Franche-Comté at Besançon. The duke had himself marched through the province along the 'Spanish Road' from Lombardy to the Low Countries in 1567 at the head of ten thousand troops, and he made use of a newly completed map of the area. Alba considered it so accurate and useful that he forbade its publication and it was only printed twelve years later, in the third edition of Ortelius's *Theatrum*.[37] However, the duke evidently felt that something more specific would have been useful, and so for the next major military expedition up the 'Spanish Road' in 1573 he commissioned two special maps of Franche-Comté, showing everything that an army on the march needed to know: the route it should follow, in a numbered sequence; the major rivers and forests, and the ways to traverse them; the alternative itineraries, in case of need; and the position of the nearest towns. It is difficult to see how, in the sixteenth century, better summary guides could have been produced at short notice (Figure 7).[38] Interestingly, the infantry column moved up the Spanish Road with unusual speed in 1573, covering the 600-odd miles (1000 kilometres) between Milan and Brussels in forty-two days.

Shortly after he arrived in the Netherlands, Alba faced an armed invasion. He confronted it in person, moving slowly but inexorably against his enemies, first in Friesland in spring 1568, then in Brabant and Limburg in the autumn. Again the duke commissioned maps in order to improve his understanding of the military situation. This proved particularly important in the autumn campaign, against the prince of Orange in person, for the duke (as usual) adopted a Fabian strategy designed to avoid a battle that might go against him; instead he sought to harass the invasion forces constantly and thus wear them down through attrition. In the words of one of his field commanders, Don Sancho de Londoño:

The duke has laboured specifically to avoid fighting a battle, despite pressure from those who forget that victory is a gift of Fortune, which can favour the Bad as well as the Good. If Orange were a powerful monarch who could maintain a mighty army for longer, I would be in favour of fighting a battle; but since it is certain that shortage of money will cause his forces to crumble, and that he will not then be able to regroup, I am against it.

In the event, the duke's men skirmished for twenty-nine days continuously in order to keep Orange away from the heart of the Netherlands. Such a strategy required an intimate knowledge of local topography

7 The itinerary for troops marching through Franche-Comté, 1573
This map, one of two prepared for the passage of some 5000 Spanish troops
through Franche-Comté in 1573, shows the eleven *étapes* (food magazines)
prepared in advance to supply them. Most lay just beyond a bridge over a
river: at Montfleur and Chavannes across the Ain in the south (number 1, at
the top of the map); at Ranchot across the Doubs (number 6, between
Besançon and Dôle); and so on. Though schematic, the map thus provided
vital data for an army moving through unfamiliar territory.

and so his scoutmasters prepared a detailed series of maps and descriptions of the Maas valley. Like the later Besançon maps, their dossier
shows everything a local commander would need to know: each map
and text described how easy (or otherwise) it was to cross the Maas at
any given point (in case an opportunity suddenly arose to take the
enemy in the flank by surprise) and which features could be seen from
each location (Figure 8).[39]

Once the invaders had been defeated. Alba set about reorganizing
the government of the Netherlands in order to prevent such troubles

8 The duke of Alba reconnoitres the Maas, 1568

As part of his campaign to expel the prince of Orange and his army from the
Netherlands, the duke of Alba sent forward scouts to prepare a detailed
account of the Maas valley. Here, they have sketched and described the river
above Roermond, with special attention to places where troops might cross.
On the left, the authors noted that their guide claimed thirty horses could
cross when the river was low, 'but it seems to me that at present not even
two could cross without great risk'. On the right, they observed that
although horses could cross to the island (marked xi) with the water
up to their stomachs, they would have to swim the rest of the way
across.

recurring, including the preparation of a series of maps and plans
covering every province and all major towns. The work of van Deventer (pages 101–2 above) was continued and intensified; while in 1569
experienced engineers carried out a special topographical survey of
military installations in Holland and Zeeland. At the same time, Bruges
painter Pieter Pourbus surveyed the northwest coast of Flanders and
in 1571 completed a map of the Brugse Vrij of extraordinary accuracy
and measuring a massive 130 by 245 inches (335 by 620 cm).[40] Alba
also accumulated plans of urban and other fortifications. Above all,

he commissioned a set of strategic maps of the provinces: between 1568 and 1573, the noted cartographer Christopher 'Sgrooten prepared a series of thirty-eight large maps of the Low Countries and adjacent areas of Germany showing roads, river-crossings and sea-routes (Figure 9). Spain herself would have nothing as good until the nineteenth century.[41]

Some of Alba's subordinates also formed their own collections of military maps. Gaspar de Robles, governor of Friesland, not only possessed fifty plans of urban fortifications in the Netherlands and northern France but also commissioned a series of pen-and-ink 'news maps' that showed in cartographic form his various military successes in the 1572 campaign (Figure 10).[42] At much the same time Gilles de Berlaymont, lord of Hierges and another provincial governor who commanded Spanish armies in the Netherlands, collected about fifty manuscript sketches of sieges (especially those in which he participated), town plans and fortress designs from the Netherlands, central Europe and the Mediterranean. Like Robles, Hierges used Italian draftsmen (as yet unidentified) who may have made copies from Alba's collection in Brussels. Finally, the duke's senior civilian adviser, Viglius van Aytta, also accumulated an impressive collection of maps – almost two hundred of them – but with less of a military focus. Although these various cartographic collections did not suffice to produce victory for Philip II in the Low Countries' Wars, they surely assisted Alba's remarkably successful reconquest of most areas in rebellion in 1572–3 and Hierges's successful invasion of Holland in 1575.[43]

Alba's regime probably marked the high point of Spanish military cartography. Neither of the duke's immediate successors as governors of the Netherlands possessed much in the way of cartographic aids. It is true that the duke of Medina Celi, appointed in 1571, owned provincial maps of Holland, Brabant, Flanders and Zeeland and one of France, an Ortelius 'World Map', and a 'map on which to make compass measurements' when he died four years later; but Don Luis de Requesens, appointed in 1573, apparently possessed only 'a pair of compasses to make measurements on maps'.[44] Matters improved under Alexander Farnese, duke of Parma, who governed the Netherlands between 1578 and 1592. In his youth he received personal instruction

9 A map of the Low Countries by Christopher 'Sgrooten, 1572–3
This remarkably accurate view of Holland between Haarlem and Delft
forms part of an atlas of thirty-eight maps of the Holy Roman Empire, but
with special attention to the Low Countries. The archivist Louis-Prosper
Gachard acquired it in Spain from someone who claimed to have got it from
the king of Spain's library and sold it in 1859 to the Royal Library in Brussels.
Almost certainly the duke of Alba commissioned the atlas in the years before
the revolt of 1572, for 'Sgrooten devoted little attention to military details
(such as walls and bastions) but included items of archaeological interest (such
as the ruins of a Roman camp off the coast at Katwijk).

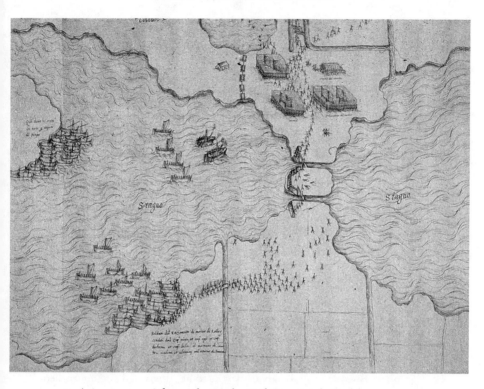

10 A 'news map' from the 'Atlas' of Gaspar de Robles, 1572–3
Gaspar de Robles (1527–85), from a Portuguese family, served both Charles
V and Philip II in the Netherlands, rising to become governor of Friesland and
Groningen in 1569. He opposed supporters of the prince of Orange in these
provinces after 1572, commissioning from an unknown Italian draftsman a
series of 'news maps' about the leading military actions in which he took part.
Here, Robles leads his musketeers ashore at 'Coldam' (Koudam).

from one of the foremost military engineers of his day and copied
drawings of (and texts on) fortifications into a special notebook.
In the Netherlands, like Alba he assembled a corpus of plans and
commissioned a special atlas of regional maps from Christopher
'Sgrooten; like Robles and Hierges, he also collected special plans of
his principal campaigns. Although the dispersal of the papers of Parma
and his successors makes it hazardous to generalize, it seems unlikely
that any subsequent commander of the Spanish Army of Flanders
could match these cartographic resources.[45]

Much the same decline occurred in Spain. Although some spectacular maps appeared – for example, the meticulous drawings and designs of Tiburcio Spanocchi for the fortifications in Aragon following the unsuccessful revolt of 1590–1, or the detailed map of Aragon by João Baptista de Lavanha (after a personal survey) published in 1620 – they were all the work of foreigners.[46] After the death of Esquivel, map-making in Spain became dependent upon the imported skills of other nations: at first on the Portuguese, then increasingly on the Italians, and finally on the Dutch. The prizes offered in a poetry competition held at the University of Salamanca in 1598 provide an interesting reflection of the value placed on cartography by Spaniards in the year of Philip II's death. The first prize for a sonnet written in Spanish was 'a Bible, beautifully bound' and the second 'a silk vest'; the third prize was 'a map'.[47]

As Richard Kagan has observed, in most parts of early modern Europe, map-making remained

primarily a private affair, although it was generally subject to some form of state oversight and control. The Spanish Habsburgs, however, sought to make cartography a royal monopoly, an enterprise to be supervised and controlled by crown officials. This policy of favoring 'official' cartography offered certain advantages, among them the ability to embark on large-scale enterprises . . . Yet centralization also meant that the only cartographic projects to be realized were those that received official encouragement and support.

This policy, although rooted in defensive concerns, eventually produced a shortage of both maps and map-makers that seriously compromised Spain's national security. Just as Philip II tried to finalize the itinerary of the Armada with the aid of Ortelius's *Theatrum* – a work compiled from secondary sources, many of them unreliable (pages 99–100 above) – so in 1642, two years after the outbreak of the Catalan and Portuguese revolts against the Habsburgs, the Royal Cosmographer of Spain asked a colleague in the Spanish Netherlands:

Is it possible to find in Flanders some map of Portugal or Catalonia? I would be awfully grateful if you would tell me, so that I can have it brought here, because here we know very little about this country. I can see that the maps of Ortelius are highly erroneous on Portugal and its frontiers so I am not surprised that our enemies, with smaller forces, are getting the better of us.[48]

Although his colleague's reply has not survived, it seems unlikely that he could have obliged: the previous decade, when trying to convince the king to flood the province of Holland into submission, he relied upon Mercator's *Atlas*![49]

Clearly the ravages of time, secrecy, and Philip II's filing system had already left their mark on Spanish government cartography, for (as we have seen) excellent maps had once existed in both Brussels and Madrid. By the seventeenth century, however, ministers could evidently neither find them nor generate replacements locally. Some might see this failure as a reflection of the decline in Spain's international standing between the reigns of Philip II and Philip IV; but this understates the problem. The lack of suitable maps to prepare the campaigns on which the survival of the monarchy depended was not a *reflection* but a *precipitant* of that decline. A government that lacked the cartographic tools required to organize its resources or to project its power, and instead resorted to outdated general atlases for strategic planning, was no longer a convincing imperial power.

PART II
THE CENTURY OF
THE SOLDIER

Fulvio Testi, an Italian warrior and man of letters, claimed in 1641 that 'This is the century of the soldiers', while Thomas Hobbes's On the Citizen, *published in the same year, asserted that 'It cannot be denied that man's natural state, before they came together into society, was war; and not simply war, but the war of every man against every man.' It is easy to see why Hobbes and his contemporaries saw war rather than peace as the norm. According to a recent study, the years between 1500 and 1700 were 'the most warlike in terms of years of war under way (95 per cent), the frequency of war (nearly one in every three years), and the average yearly duration, extent and magnitude of war'.[1]*

The study of war has always fascinated me. At school, I joined the naval section of the Cadet Force and for several summers I spent a week or more at various naval barracks. This gave me some understanding of the difficulties involved in making complex organisms work; it also taught me respect for those who have endured combat. I took both these lessons with me to the study of military history. In part, the logistics of the Spanish Road interested me so much because I felt sympathy with those who dealt with the 'friction' generated by moving thousands of troops at a time across the 600 or more miles (1000 km) (including the Alps, the Vosges and numerous rivers) that separated Lombardy from the Low Countries. Viewing early modern fortifications, by contrast, brought to mind the desperate struggles that took place between besiegers and defenders, leaving hundreds of dead and maimed on either side. The first chapter in Part II reflects my first interest; the other three correspond to my second. All four case studies suggest that superior logistics, morale and siegecraft decided the outcome of the wars of early modern Europe far more often than battles, and demonstrate how eaily neglect of these aspects could snatch defeat from the jaws of victory.

5

John Elliott first awoke my interest in Habsburg Spain in 1964 when, as an undergraduate, I attended his lectures at Cambridge University. Although his course covered the early modern history of all Europe, Elliott clearly had a passionate interest in the Spanish empire. In the middle of a lecture on Philip II, he turned to a map of Europe hanging on the wall behind him and said:

One of the great mysteries concerning the power of the Habsburgs is how Spain managed to send so much treasure and so many soldiers to the war in the Low Countries. They could not go by sea, due to the threat from the English and the Dutch fleets, and so Philip II created an alternative overland route from Milan to Brussels, called by contemporaries 'the Spanish Road'.

This problem of logistics fascinated me and I decided there and then to try and solve the 'mystery'. Under Elliott's genial, erudite and firm guidance, I carried out research on the Spanish Road in Spain, Italy, France, Belgium and the Netherlands and completed my doctoral dissertation on the subject in 1968.

In 1969, I travelled along the Spanish Road again, this time stopping at the archives of places through which the Spaniards had passed. By then, most communities had transferred their archives to a regional repository, although some remained in the towns and villages along the troops' itineraries. In any case, all documents in public archives within the borders of France boast a remarkable and very useful characteristic in common: they share the same classification system. In the mid-nineteenth century, Napoleon III's ministers decreed that all local archives should be divided at the Revolution of 1789, and that all Archives anciennes be organized according to a simple letter *classification. Thus all documents concerning military affairs went into series 'E' in departmental archives and series 'EE' in communal archives. Since the passage of the Spanish troops after 1567 generated much paperwork – above all records of the food, drink and lodging supplied and of the damage caused – even in communal archives for which no detailed inventory existed, I could usually ask to see 'EE1' and find documents about the troops who used the Spanish Road.*

After publishing The Army of Flanders and the Spanish Road *in 1972, I moved on to other historical issues, although still taking note of further publications on the subject (duly reflected in new editions of the book). Then, in 2000, Denise Turrel of Tours University asked me to write an article for a special issue of the journal* Cahiers d'histoire *commemorating the treaty of Lyon in 1601. I agreed, thinking I could build something around the relevant passages of* The Army of Flanders, *since it had never been translated into French, but the scope and scale of work published on the subject since 1972 deterred me. So I revisited my notes, and relived those days working in quiet provincial archives (while living in youth hostels or in the back of a camper). The resilience of the Spanish Road continued to impress me: Philip II's empire seemed so vulnerable, with its main components separated by hundreds of miles, that his ability to create and maintain military corridors between them must rank as a major success. On its survival, indeed, the Grand Strategy of the Spanish monarchy came to depend; inevitably, however, it could not endure for ever.*

The Treaty of Lyon (1601) and the Spanish Road

When Charles of Habsburg began to rule in 1515, he governed only the western and southern provinces of the Netherlands. The following year, however, he succeeded to the crowns of Spain, Sicily and Naples and in 1519 he was elected Holy Roman Emperor, taking the title

Charles V. In 1530 he gained control of Franche-Comté upon the death of his aunt Margaret of Savoy and in 1535 his forces occupied the duchy of Milan upon the death of the last native duke. That same year, as he entered the city of Messina in Sicily after his triumphant conquest of Tunis, for the first time the emperor saw his possessions described in a phrase used by the Roman poet Virgil for the possessions of Augustus Caesar: A SOLIS ORTU AD OCCASUM, 'from the rising to the setting of the sun'. Contemporaries soon boasted that Charles ruled an empire on which the sun never set.[1]

His extensive possessions nevertheless suffered from a major logistical problem: messages, men and money had to travel large distances between the various component parts, which often made it difficult to respond swiftly and effectively to a sudden crisis. These difficulties intensified after 1555–6 when Charles passed on to his son Philip II the Netherlands, Franche-Comté, Spain, and the extensive Spanish outposts in Italy and America – but not the Holy Roman Empire, which went to Philip's uncle Ferdinand. For the rest of the sixteenth century, Ferdinand and his successors forbade the passage of Spanish troops through Germany in case it upset the delicate equilibrium between Catholics and Protestants there.

Philip II and his ministers therefore needed to create alternative itineraries to connect the far-flung monarchy, especially after 1566, when disorders broke out in the Netherlands. In May 1566, Cardinal Antoine Perrenot de Granvelle, an experienced minister of Charles V, urged the king to travel from Spain to the Low Countries immediately in order to nip the problem in the bud, and reviewed the various routes available. He conceded at once that religious tensions ruled out a passage through the Empire. He next briefly considered a royal progress via Milan, Innsbruck and Alsace (ruled by a Habsburg archduke favourable to Spain) to Franche-Comté; but this too he rejected as too uncertain. Instead, he argued, 'The shortest route would be from Genoa through Piedmont and Savoy, crossing the Mont Cenis. In fact, it would be more than one-third shorter. The route runs between the mountains between Piedmont and Franche-Comté, which borders on Savoy [on one side] and Lorraine on the other. You can cross Lorraine in four days and reach the duchy of Luxembourg.'[2] Six months later, with Philip still in Spain and the Netherlands in open revolt, Granvelle returned to his theme and pointed out that the same Mont Cenis itinerary would also be suitable for an army, because 'I recall that King Francis I travelled this way with his army and court when he went to relieve Turin in 1527. It is not as hard a road as people claim: I travelled it myself thirty years ago.'[3] The king immediately sent out agents to examine the route and provide a full report (plus, if possible, a map or panorama). They confirmed everything Granvelle had claimed and, in the summer of 1567, 10,000 Spanish and Italian troops crossed the Mont Cenis safely and marched to Luxemburg.[4]

Between 1567 and 1620, almost 100,000 troops travelled from Milan to reinforce the Spanish army in the Low Countries along the itinerary that contemporaries came to call 'le chemin des espagnols': the Spanish Road. Countless couriers carrying messages and orders travelled the same route, as did convoys of carts and mules carrying gold and silver coins. Each group of users had their own rationale.

The troops marched along the Spanish Road because the Habsburgs firmly believed that their soldiers fought better away from home. In the words of the commander-in-chief in Brussels in 1595, 'The main strength of this army consists in its foreign soldiers' – that is, in those who came from Spain, Italy, Germany, Franche-Comté and the British Isles. The same principle held true for Habsburg armies elsewhere. As an experienced commander observed in 1630: 'If there should be war in Italy, it would be better to send Walloons there and to bring Italians here [to the Netherlands], because the troops raised in the country where the war is being fought disband very rapidly and there is no surer strength than that of foreign soldiers.'[5] Half (or more than half) of the Spanish Army of Flanders, whose wartime strength oscillated between 50,000 and 80,000 men, came from outside the Netherlands; and the thousands of men required to maintain this proportion had to march overland by a network of secure military corridors, including the Spanish Road.

Couriers also travelled along the Spanish Road whenever it proved impossible to send messages safely through France. In 1567, as he advanced from Milan to Brussels, the duke of Alba established a new postal chain, with two horses at each relay station. After 1572, when the Dutch Revolt began in earnest, he sent two copies of all his letters to the king: one through France and the other down the Spanish Road to Italy and from there to Barcelona by sea.[6] Whenever France went to war with Spain, the new itinerary provided a vital postal artery, but it took far longer. Whereas an express courier travelling from Brussels through France could reach the court in eleven, ten or (in at least one case) nine days, the same message sent by the alternative route could take two months. In 1586 the duke of Parma prepared a strategy for the conquest of England: given the sensitivity of the subject, he sent his special messenger from Brussels on 20 April via Besançon, Chambéry and Turin to Genoa, whence he sailed to Barcelona. He arrived in Madrid only on 20 June.[7]

Large quantities of bullion took the same route from Lombardy to the Low Countries because of the limitations of Europe's international banking system. Maintaining the Spanish Army of Flanders cost at least five million crowns (£1.11 million) every year, some of it paid by the Netherlands but much of it supplied by Spain and, to a lesser extent, the Spanish territories in Italy. Normally, letters of exchange drawn in Spain or Italy and payable in Antwerp transferred these funds; however, the Dutch Revolt so damaged the economy of the Spanish Netherlands that the bankers' correspondents in Antwerp could not find sufficient cash locally to make their payments. The crown therefore granted bankers export licences to transfer specie from Spain to the Netherlands. In addition, the king sometimes sent convoys of money on his own account for particularly sensitive issues. In the 1580s and 1590s, most shipments – whether for the king or for his bankers – travelled from Spain to Italy aboard royal galleys, and from there through Savoy, Franche-Comté and Lorraine to the Netherlands.[8]

Naturally, the Dutch and their allies devoted much thought to blocking this vital artery. In April 1584, an adviser to the French Huguenot leader Henry of Navarre noted that the capture of a single stronghold in Franche-Comté would mean 'no more communication between the Netherlands and Italy or Spain, except with great difficulty'.[9] Equally naturally, Spain began to search for alternative itineraries in case this happened. Later in 1584, the governor of Milan pointed out that it would be possible to send troops and treasure to the Netherlands through the Catholic Swiss cantons. Cardinal Granvelle, now the king's principal adviser on Italian affairs, disagreed. Again, he spoke as an eyewitness: 'I have travelled the route and seen all that area. The pass is narrow for troops and horses, and before reaching Franche-Comté one must travel close to Lausanne, through the lands of Bern and Geneva. Although that route is shorter, I do not believe it is as convenient or as safe as the one through Savoy.'[10] The cardinal did favour closer relations with the Catholic cantons, however, and three years later Philip II secured an alliance that provided customs privileges, pensions and scholarships for the Swiss in return for permission for unarmed Spanish troops to pass through the area.[11]

In the 1590s, pressure on the Spanish Road mounted. In 1592, the governor-general of the Spanish Netherlands reported the first concrete attempt by Dutch and French Huguenot troops to capture strategic positions in Lorraine to create 'A sort of barrier [barrière] across the said duchy in order to close the routes to Italy, Burgundy and Lorraine, and from Germany to the Low Countries, and thus to prevent all access here by land from Spain, Italy, Savoy, Franche-Comté and Lorraine'.[12] Later that year, the governor of Milan secured a treaty with the Grisons, overlords of the Valtelline in the eastern Alps, that allowed 'free passage through their lands for all the goods, money, weapons and troops that His Majesty may send to the Netherlands, Franche-Comté or elsewhere, provided the soldiers travel in small groups'.[13]

Neither agreement entirely solved the problem, however, because each of the allies controlled only one Alpine pass – the St Gotthard and the Stelvio respectively.[14] Moreover, all these itineraries depended upon the security of Franche-Comté, and in 1595 Henry of Navarre, now Henry IV of France, declared war on Spain and invaded the Comté, where he defeated an army marching north from Milan. This development did not actually cut the Spanish Road, but it did force Philip II's troops, couriers and bullion convoys to travel further east, even via Saarbrücken, in order to reach the Low Countries in safety. In 1597, Henry IV attacked the Spanish Road again. His lieutenant in Dauphiné invaded Savoy and occupied the Maurienne valley, forcing a Spanish army en route to the Netherlands to retire beyond the Mont Cenis. Although a second army of 4000 Italians managed to get through the Tarantaise, no more soldiers or specie passed through Savoy until France withdrew its troops after the peace of Vervins (2 May 1598).

In theory, Vervins restored safety to the Spanish Road, but it left unsettled the possession of Saluzzo, a small French enclave in the Piedmontese Alps occupied by the duke of Savoy ten years earlier. At Vervins, Henry IV demanded the restitution of Saluzzo but referred the question to papal arbitration since, although France possessed a clear claim to the territory, the duke of Savoy occupied the enclave and vigorously opposed the return of a powerful French garrison to the heart of his lands. He eventually offered to cede to France the territory of Bresse on his western frontier if, in return, he could retain Saluzzo. Philip III of Spain now objected that the surrender of Bresse would block the Spanish Road and promised the duke of Savoy (his brother-in-law) full military support if he rejected the agreement with France. Foolishly, the duke did so in August 1600.

Anticipating this, Henry IV had already moved to Lyon and mobilized an army. He now declared war on Savoy and his men reached the Alpine passes before a single Spanish soldier could cross. Papal negotiators again offered an alternative to the duke of Savoy: either to return Saluzzo to France, or else to retain Saluzzo and surrender to France all the territories of Savoy (already under French occupation) west of the river Rhône. This choice involved Spain because if France annexed all the land between the Rhône and the border of Franche-Comté (over twenty miles (30 km) from the river at its closest point) the Spanish Road was lost. The duke of Savoy, although humiliated, refused to restore Saluzzo. The delegates at Lyon, in an attempt to meet Spain's demand for a secure military highway, proposed one that ran from Milan through the Swiss cantons via the Simplon pass, Martigny and Lausanne to Pontarlier in Franche-Comté.

This plan was on the point of acceptance when the representative of the republic of Geneva at the conference protested that such a plan would expose his city to attack by the Spanish troops on its exposed eastern side. According to François de Chapeaurouge's own account, later given to the magistrates of Geneva:

At Lyon, he found a way to avoid an injury that threatened us through the passage of Spanish troops. While he was speaking with M. de Rosne [later duke of Sully] and M. de Sillery [Nicholas Brûlart de Sillery], they showed

him two excellent maps of the area and said: 'Show us if we can get to
Franche-Comté without crossing the lands of Bern.' He said 'Yes', and begged
them to listen because he knew they wanted to establish an itinerary for the
Spaniards: 'Please consider the damage that you will do us, and Bern, if you
bring them to our gates.' They said: 'Show us another, better route.' He then
showed them [the route] by the bridge at Grésin, and convinced them, causing
the Spaniards to complain.[15]

The treaty of Lyon in January 1601 incorporated Chapeaurouge's
ingenious proposal: Savoy retained Saluzzo and the Val de Chézery
but ceded all other territories west of the Rhône to France.[16]

The treaty thus confined the Spanish Road to one narrow valley,
lying between a high pass and a single two-span bridge over the Rhône
at Grésin. In May 1601 a Spanish engineer surveyed the new itinerary
and reported several serious problems. First, the bridge at Grésin
required strengthening and the road leading to Franche-Comté needed
improvement at several points before large formations of troops could
use it. Even then, a hostile party of only twenty could block the bridge
and, the engineer noted grimly, France maintained powerful garrisons
only a few miles from Grésin.[17]

Nevertheless, Philip III determined to send 8000 Spanish and Italian
troops, commanded by Ambrogio Spinola, along the new itinerary.
Engineers therefore arrived at St Claude, the first town in Franche-
Comté, 'From the direction of Chézery to restore and prepare the
roads for the crossing of the said troops. They spent about eight days
on this, and repaired the said roads from the border of Savoy and the
land of Chézery up to our town limits.' Spinola and his men reached
the Netherlands safely a few months later.[18] In July 1602, Spinola led
a further 9000 Italian troops marching from Lombardy but Henry IV
feared that they planned to aid the conspiracy against him led by
Marshal Biron. He therefore ordered his commander in Dauphiné to
close the bridge at Grésin. The Italians had to wait impotently while
Philip's agents protested to the pope, guarantor of the treaty of Lyon,
that 'Their troops could only pass through the territories that had been
left expressly for that purpose to the duke of Savoy by the treaty of
Lyon, and that no one could stand in the way of their passage without
revealing openly the desire to break the peace.' The papal mediator

did his best to make the French withdraw, but Henry refused until after the execution of Biron. Even then, French troops shadowed the Spaniards until they reached Luxembourg.[19]

The Spanish Road never recovered from the treaty of Lyon. After 1601 it depended absolutely on French goodwill, an advantage that France never forgot. In the detailed map of Savoy drawn up in 1606 for Henry's chief minister, the duke of Sully, the cartographer labelled 'le chemin des espaignolz' and picked it out in red (Figure 11). The principal supply route of the Army of Flanders lay at France's mercy.

This situation was clearly unsatisfactory for Spain. From Brussels, Don Balthasar de Zúñiga (who later became Philip III's chief minister) warned the king that, 'if all the troops whom Your Majesty sends here have to pass through that gorge', he could never win the war against the Dutch.[20] Nevertheless, Henry IV's belligerence at first strengthened the alliance between Spain and Savoy and a regiment of Spanish infantry moved in to garrison the major towns in the Maurienne and Tarantaise valleys: four companies in Annecy and Montmélian, three in Rumilly, two in St Jean de Maurienne, and so on. Under their aegis, Spanish and Italian troops regularly marched through the duchy, crossed the bridge at Grésin and reached the Netherlands: 4000 in 1603, 6000 in 1605 and 3000 in 1606.[21]

The precariousness of the route nevertheless obliged Spain's ministers and allies to continue their search for alternatives. In January 1602 the governor of Besançon, an imperial enclave in Franche-Comté, suggested the acquisition of Neuchâtel in order to create a military corridor through the Pays de Vaud.[22] In December 1602, the duke of Savoy attempted a surprise attack on Geneva – the 'Escalade' – which would have opened another link with Franche-Comté. In spring 1604 the count of Fuentes, governor of Milan, persuaded the Catholic Swiss cantons to renegotiate the terms of the 1587 treaty, increasing the size of the units allowed to cross 'between the various states of His Majesty for their defence', in return for directing merchant convoys from the Netherlands to take the same route. 'Self-interest,' observed Fuentes, 'is the best hold one can have over the [Swiss].' In September 1604, the first Spanish troops – 2000 infantry – crossed the St Gotthard and marched through the heart of Catholic Switzerland to the Netherlands. Admittedly, the troops could carry only their swords with them – all

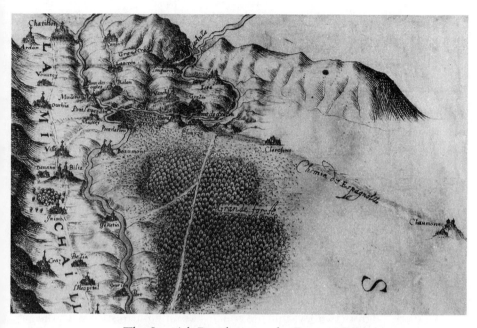

11 The Spanish Road as seen by France, 1606
After 1600, Henry IV commissioned a series of maps of France's frontier
regions from his engineer, Jean de Beins. One showed in detail the area
through which Spanish troops passed on their march from Lombardy to the
Netherlands, across the bridge at Grésin. Beins coloured their itinerary in
red and labelled it 'Chemin des Espagnolz': the Spanish Road.

other weapons had to be packaged and sent ahead – but Fuentes felt
justifiably proud of

> The new route through Switzerland, which (as I have said) will save many
> days. It is important to draw attention to this route, and make it known, for
> all eventualities and [in particular] so that no one should think that they can
> stop the passage of Your Majesty's troops. Instead this will show them that,
> with greater ease and less cost, Your Majesty can make use of it whenever he
> likes, not only for the Netherlands but also for the House of Habsburg if we
> ever need to send Spaniards to Germany.[23]

In 1605, Fuentes underscored the point by sending two columns of
reinforcements to the Netherlands simultaneously via the two different

routes – 6000 Italians over the bridge at Grésin and almost 3000 Spaniards over the St Gotthard – 'so that everyone can see Your Majesty's troops going to the Netherlands at the same time'.[24]

Fuentes's recognition that Spanish troops might need to enter Germany or Austria one day also renewed interest in the Valtelline. In December 1601, France secured a treaty with the Grisons that reserved the valleys 'for her alone' in military matters; two years later, despite the apparently exclusive nature of this concession, Venice secured a similar agreement. In October 1603, after the Grisons rebuffed Spain's request for the same rights of transit, Fuentes suddenly sent engineers to the commanding hill of Montecchio, at the mouth of the valley, where in two months they built a powerful fortress: the Fuentes fortress.[25] In 1607, a Venetian attempt to send troops through the valley, according to their treaty with the Grisons, provoked a popular uprising by the Catholics of the Valtelline. Fuentes hoped to exploit this unrest by sending 8000 Spanish and Italian troops destined for the Netherlands through the valley, but the conclusion of an armistice with the Dutch prevented this taking place. The Protestants therefore regained control, executing the Catholic leaders and brutally restoring order.[26]

Fuentes's resolve to send troops through the Valtelline reflected growing tension between Spain and Charles Emanuel of Savoy. In 1605, the duke refused to allow Italian regiments bound for Flanders to cross his territories until the governor of Milan paid for the cost of lodging them in advance; in 1607, he flatly refused to allow another detachment of Philip III's troops to enter his duchies; and in 1609, he expelled the Spanish garrisons from Savoy. In 1610, he signed a mutual defence pact with his former adversary, Henry IV.[27] Although the king's death later that year restrained Charles Emanuel, in 1613–15 and again in 1616–17 he went to war with Philip III over the succession to the duchy of Monferrat. Now the flow of Habsburg troops reversed: Austrian regiments crossed through the Catholic cantons to Lombardy in 1614 and 1616, followed the next year by troops from the Netherlands. Savoy and Spain made peace at Pavia in October 1617.[28]

Then the situation changed again. In 1618, the Protestant Grisons lent clandestine aid to Venice in its struggle against Archduke Ferdinand of Styria, to which the Catholics of the Valtelline objected. The Grisons reacted with unexpected violence: their troops marched into the valley and arrested, tried, tortured and executed two Catholic leaders. At just this time, however, the revolt of Bohemia increased the Habsburgs' need to find a reliable military corridor to convey men and money from Lombardy. In 1619, although the Grisons' occupation prevented Spain from sending aid to Ferdinand through the Valtelline, 7000 Italian troops marched north through the Catholic cantons. The Swiss insisted, however, that they would allow only the passage of troops destined for Austria, not for the Netherlands; and the Madrid government – now led by Don Balthasar de Zúñiga, who had served as ambassador in Brussels and Vienna and thus had direct experience of the areas in question – searched yet again for alternative routes.[29]

The peace of Pavia expressly required the duke of Savoy to allow free passage to Spanish troops bound for Germany or the Netherlands and in 1620, with war in the former and the armistice about to expire in the latter, Zúñiga arranged for almost 9000 Spanish and Italian troops to use the Spanish Road. Despite protests from the republic of Geneva, which feared another Escalade, they did so (even holding a muster as they filed across the bridge at Grésin). Despite this apparent return to normal relations, however, no troops in Spanish service ever crossed the bridge at Grésin again – even though it, and the Chézery valley, remained under Savoyard control until 1760.[30]

Meanwhile, even as the Spanish troops marched through Savoy, the Habsburgs decided to support a rising by the Catholics of the Valtelline against their Grison overlords. In July 1620, troops from Milan blocked the mouth of the valley while imperial forces sealed its northern end, preventing any possible counterattack by the Grisons while the Catholics in the valley massacred some six hundred Protestants. Four thousand Habsburg soldiers thereupon garrisoned all the Grison lands, while engineers worked on building a fortress at Bormio in the Valtelline and on widening the existing roads so that they could accommodate large numbers of troops and pack animals.[31]

Although providing an ideal connection between Milan and Vienna, the Valtelline was less attractive for troops marching to the Netherlands; but the Brussels government had already begun to plan another alternative to the bridge at Grésin. In May 1621, the Antwerp newspaper *Nieuwe Tijdinghe* announced a new itinerary for merchants and merchandise travelling between the Netherlands and Milan that was 'ten or twelve days shorter than ever before, and without danger'. The newspaper advertisement called the route the *Prince conduitte* because it lay under the protection of the Archdukes Albert and Isabella, and urged readers to acquire a copy at the shop of Abraham Verhoeven (publisher of the newspaper).[32] The map itself, drawn by the Antwerp engineer Michel Coignet, has survived in only two copies – probably because hostilities spread so fast in the decade after 1621 that it soon became outdated – but it clearly shows a 'road' from Antwerp, via Verdun, Besançon and Lausanne, over the Simplon pass to Domodossola and down to Milan ('Mediolanum': see Figure 12).[33] In the words of the English ambassador to Venice, Sir Henry Wotton, the Spaniards were 'now able to walk (while they keep a foot in the Lower Palatinate) from Milan to Dunkirk upon their own inheritances and purchases, a connection of terrible moment in my opinion'. By then, 4300 Spanish and Italian troops garrisoned the Grisons, with 3600 more in Alsace and 5000 in the Rhine Palatinate.[34]

Almost immediately, however, the war in Germany cut all the military corridors between Italy and the Netherlands: early in 1622, the Protestant general Ernest of Mansfelt built up an army of 50,000 men in Alsace. When the Brussels government, now at war with the Dutch, pleaded for the dispatch of reinforcements for the Army of Flanders from Spain, the council of state in Madrid unanimously favoured sending them by sea in small vessels. In the summer, however, the combined forces of the Austrian and Spanish Habsburgs defeated Mansfelt and his allies, and in October 1623 7000 men crossed through the Grison lands and South Germany to the Netherlands.[35]

The Habsburgs' success did not go unchallenged for long. As Philip III's envoy to the Catholic Swiss cantons observed in 1613, granting permission for troops to cross through the Alpine valleys 'is what most irritates the French . . . because it goes right against the goal they have always had of closing to Your Majesty the passes between Italy and the Netherlands and between Germany and Italy'.[36] Accordingly, in February 1623, after long discussion, France, Venice and Savoy signed the league of Lyon: an alliance pledged to expel the Habsburgs from the lands of the Grisons and to support Savoy's claims over both Monferrat and Genoa. Zúñiga had died in October 1622 and his successor, the count (later the count-duke) of Olivares, did not intend

12 The 'New Route' between Antwerp and Milan, 1621
Michel Coignet (1549–1623) published a map of the 'new route' for
commercial travel between Antwerp and Milan in 1621 which, he stated, lay
under the 'name, protection and blazon' of the Archdukes Albert and
Isabella, rulers of the South Netherlands. The route had been 'carefully
measured by the compass', and Coignet provided the names of factors along
the way prepared to receive and store customers' goods. The map went on
sale in May 1621 and Abraham Verhoeven, its publisher, advertised it in his
Antwerp weekly newspaper.

to fight France for a distant Alpine valley. Spain therefore surrendered
the Valtelline to the papacy, which sent in its own forces; but this still
left the Austrians in possession of the other valleys, and allowed
Olivares to continue sending forces through the eastern Alps. France
thereupon sent its own army, which in the course of 1624 occupied all
the lands of the Grisons. Two years later, the conquerors returned the
Valtelline to papal control, which allowed Spain to send more armies
to Germany: 11,000 men marched through the Catholic cantons in

1631 and as many again went through the Valtelline in 1633.[37] It also allowed Ferdinand of Styria, now Holy Roman Emperor, to send almost 50,000 German soldiers to take part in the third and final war over Monferrat between 1629 and 1631.

In 1633, however, the French occupied Lorraine, whose duke had repeatedly defied his powerful neighbour. This cut all the overland military supply routes to the Spanish army in the Netherlands. In April, a regiment of troops raised in Franche-Comté attempted to cross Lorraine – as others had done in previous years – but the advance of Louis XIII and his main army forced them to withdraw. 'This totally unexpected event,' the governor-general of the Spanish Netherlands warned Philip IV, 'has obvious significance for Your Majesty's service. Luxembourg is so close [to Lorraine] and our communications with Franche-Comté and our links with Italy and Germany are severed and at the mercy of the French, placing everything here in the greatest danger.'[38] In Spain, the king's advisers fully agreed. As Olivares put it:

The king of France has entirely closed the Italy-Flanders route. France lies between Spain and Flanders, so that no help from Germany can reach either Flanders or Italy; none from Italy can reach Flanders; and none can reach Spain from Flanders or Flanders from Spain except by way of the Channel, bordered by French ports on one side and English ports on the other, and swarming with Dutch [ships].[39]

Olivares had already assembled a large army in Milan, under the command of the king's younger brother, the Cardinal-Infante Fernando. He now recommended that Fernando should go to Germany where, in combination with the forces of Emperor Ferdinand, his army would defeat the German Protestants. It would then march to the Netherlands, forcing the French to evacuate Lorraine – which would reopen the blocked military supply routes – and intimidating the Dutch so that they would make peace. The cardinal-infante achieved almost all these ambitious goals. In July 1634, at the head of almost 12,000 Italian and Spanish soldiers – the largest army ever to leave Milan for northern Europe, and the only one to do so under the command of a prince of the blood royal – he entered the Valtelline and in three weeks reached Innsbruck. After a pause for recovery, the army marched west and in September, having joined forces with the army of the Austrian Habsburgs, routed the Protestants at the battle of Nördlingen, recovering most of southern Germany for the Catholic cause. The cardinal-infante then moved northwestwards, reaching Brussels just four months after leaving Milan.[40]

The odyssey of the cardinal-infante nevertheless proved to be the last overland expedition of Spanish and Italian troops to the Netherlands. Frustrated that the expedition had failed to dislodge the French from Lorraine, in March 1635 Olivares authorized the invasion of the electorate of Trier, a territory under French protection, in order to create an alternative link between the Spanish Netherlands and both Germany and Italy. Spanish troops arrested and imprisoned the Elector, as well as occupying the principal strongholds of his territory. The seizure of a ruler and his capital while under French protection was a challenge that Louis XIII could not afford to overlook, and a French herald duly delivered a declaration of war on Spain in May 1635. The cardinal-infante's government now faced war on two fronts – against the Dutch as well as the French – which increased its need for Spanish troops and treasure; yet now these could only arrive by sea. Some 27,000 troops reached the Low Countries from Spain by sea between 1631 and 1639, but each troop convoy had to run the gauntlet of the Dutch and French squadrons that lay in wait. In 1639 Olivares decided to send a far larger fleet of 60 warships carrying 14,000 troops which, he hoped, would overwhelm all opposition. It failed: instead, a Dutch fleet commanded by Maarten Tromp outmanoeuvred the count-duke's armada and virtually annihilated it at the battle of the Downs. It was, as Olivares realized, a calamity that 'strikes to the heart', and thereafter Spanish troops only reached the Army of Flanders in small numbers aboard relatively small ships.[41]

Although substantial reinforcements from southern Europe continued to reach the Army of Flanders for another four decades, each expedition involved extensive diplomatic and logistical preparation, and a high degree of risk. The last major contingents to travel by both land (in 1634) and sea (in 1639) had to fight a major battle. The Army of Flanders' defeat at Rocroi in 1643 proved so disastrous in part because Philip IV no longer possessed the means to send replacements for the Spanish and Italian troops who perished in the battle, yet without these 'foreign' veterans the Army of Flanders could no longer withstand the French and the Dutch. In 1645 alone, the French captured ten major towns; the following year they captured the port of Dunkirk. Philip IV soon agreed 'to give in on every point that might lead to the conclusion of a settlement'; indeed, according to an unsympathetic observer, he was so desperate for peace that 'if necessary he would crucify Christ again in order to achieve it'.[42] The Dutch States-General approved a final peace treaty in January 1648 – the forty-seventh anniversary of the treaty of Lyon which, by compromising the security of the Spanish Road, initiated the decline of Spain as a Great Power.

6

The business of the armed forces in wartime is to kill people and break things, and in the early modern period most Europeans believed that Spanish soldiers applied themselves to both activities with special enthusiasm. Some started to catalogue Spanish atrocities in Europe and the Americas and created from it a 'Black Legend'. It was a legend, not a myth: many egregious acts of brutality occurred. Thus in 1576, when the Spanish veterans in the Netherlands tired of waiting for payment of their wages, they seized and sacked Antwerp, destroying 1000 buildings (including the new town hall) and leaving 8000 inhabitants dead. The survivors were beaten, raped and robbed; according to one victim, the Spaniards even broke open the children's spaerpotkens *(piggy-banks). News of these excesses soon spread. George Gascoigne, an eyewitness, immediately published a blood-curdling pamphlet,* The Spoyle of Antwerp, *which in the 1590s inspired a play entitled* A Larum for London or the Siedge of Antwerp, *its fifteen scenes crammed with rape, murder and theft as a warning to Londoners of what would happen if ever the Spaniards landed in England. In the Netherlands, prints of the sack of Antwerp swiftly circulated, and in time adorned the basic school history textbook of the Dutch Republic, the* Spiegel der jeugd van de Nederlandse Oorlogen *(Mirror of the Low Countries' Wars for Young People) – appropriately nicknamed the* Spaanse tirannie – *first published in 1614 and reprinted more than twenty times in sixty years.*[1]

In April 1991, I welcomed an invitation from Paul Kennedy to participate in a course of lectures for Yale University History Majors on 'The Laws of War: constraints on warfare in the western world', because it provided an opportunity to set the Black Legend in the context of how the troops of other early modern states behaved. The lecture, on early modern Europe, was due the following September. As I worked on my presentation over the summer, however, the Yugoslav Civil War broke out: first in Croatia and then in Bosnia atrocities occurred that rivalled those in Antwerp four centuries before. The aftermath of the Gulf War of 1991 also provoked much discussion of the current 'Laws of War', and the list of topics I wanted to include in my paper expanded rapidly.

Too rapidly: I tried to show that the conventions – and the breaches of those conventions – in the Yugoslav Civil War closely paralleled those of the early modern wars. I also sought to demonstrate that 'atrocity does not pay': that the selective use of brutality – whether by the duke of Alba in the Netherlands in the 1570s, by Oliver Cromwell in Ireland in the 1640s, or by the Serbs in Bosnia in the 1990s – brought short-term success but long-term failure. A discussion with the students after the lecture revealed several shortcomings in my analysis; so did comments from colleagues to whom I subsequently sent the paper. In some confusion, I turned to John Lynn, an expert in early modern military history at Illinois (where I then taught), and to Jeff McMahon, a philosopher at Illinois who specializes in 'the just war'. With great generosity, they helped me to distinguish what has changed in the conventions governing restraint in war over the past four centuries, and what has stayed the same. The chapter that follows owes much to them.

The Etiquette of Atrocity: The Laws of War in Early Modern Europe

In a provocative article published in 1991 entitled 'The Gulf crisis and the rules of war', Martin van Creveld highlighted numerous contrasts between the ancient and modern Laws of War. On the one hand he noted a transformation in the *jus ad bellum* (rules concerning the legitimacy of war), since the use of force to alter national boundaries is now prohibited by the United Nations Charter, whereas formerly it was the commonest single cause of conflict. On the other hand, van Creveld pointed to significant changes in the *jus in bello* (rules concerning the conduct of war), with widespread condemnation of Iraq's use, or threatened use, of hostages, terrorism and prohibited weapons during the Gulf War of 1991, despite the fact that all of them had long formed a part of the West's military repertoire. On the basis of these continuities he concluded that 'what is and is not considered acceptable behaviour in war is historically determined, neither self-evident nor unalterable'.[2]

Van Creveld's argument is misleading in two respects. First, many of his contrasts are more apparent than real since they juxtapose principle, which always tries to set standards, however exalted, and practice, which often, for one reason or another, falls short of the ideal. Thus, despite the United Nations Charter, Israel, Korea, Vietnam and Iraq have in fact used force with varying success to extend their national boundaries since 1945. Second, some of the greater restraint in the conduct of war stems from changes in technology, logistics and the power of the state rather than from improved morality on the part of troops. Thus the fate of the civilians killed or mutilated by the aerial bombardment of Dresden or Hiroshima in 1945 or of Baghdad and Basra in 1991 was no more humane than that of the equally defenceless victims of My Lai or Bosnia who actually saw, however briefly, the soldiers who terminated or ruined their lives. Yet, in general, only those who kill or maim innocent civilians face-to-face risk citation before a war crimes tribunal; those who act from a distance, although they do far more damage, rarely go to trial. On the positive side, the growing power of the state in most parts of Europe notably reduced military mistreatment of the civilian population by removing one of its underlying causes: with regular pay and food, soldiers no longer needed to plunder in order to survive.[3]

This is not to deny that important changes have occurred over time in Europe's prevailing Laws of War. Thus in the mid-sixteenth century hostages were regularly taken from hostile, or potentially hostile, communities and were frequently executed if need arose; at least twenty attempts were made by Catholic fanatics sponsored by foreign powers to assassinate Queen Elizabeth I of England in the 1570s and

1580s, while the queen herself made widespread use of hired assassins in Ireland to rid herself of tiresome opponents; and in 1566 enemies of Philip II of Spain allegedly entered areas through which his army was about to pass 'with ointments to spread the plague'.[4] All of these practices would now, as van Creveld correctly observed, be condemned as contrary to the current Laws of War, yet at the time they were almost universally accepted as legitimate. So when did this critical change occur?

The Laws of War in Europe have rested since the Middle Ages upon the same five foundations. First come a series of prescriptive texts: the Bible (above all Deuteronomy 20:10–20), Roman law, canon law (especially the *Decretum* of Gratian), the writings of Augustine and the *Summa* of Thomas Aquinas. All these works laid down the permissions and prohibitions that should obtain in war, and as time passed their findings were collected, codified and developed by writers interested in the law of nature and, later, the law of nations.[5] Second, from the eleventh century in France and slightly later elsewhere, the Peace of God movement pioneered by the Roman church laid down the principle that the weak who could do no harm should not themselves be harmed, while the Truce of God simultaneously attempted to restrict armed conflict between Christians to certain days of the week.[6] Third, at much the same time armies began to enact their own legal codes, the Articles of War, that determined the rules of tolerable and intolerable conduct for all troops: duty to God, obedience to all superiors, vigilance and loyalty in camp and in action, humanity towards civilians (unless ordered otherwise), and so on. Most codes consciously emulated earlier ones, creating an impressive continuity and leaving any offences not specifically mentioned to 'be punished according to the general customs and laws of war'.[7] These customs – the fourth foundation of Western military practice – consisted largely of precedents created by the conduct of war itself, to which both theorists and practitioners referred when considering or justifying their military choices. 'The general sense and practice in all Wars', in the phrase of Sir Thomas Fairfax, parliamentary commander during the English Civil Wars, was already the touchstone of acceptable and unacceptable behaviour by the 1640s.[8] Fifth and finally, participants in armed conflict almost always came to appreciate, sooner or later, the advantages of mutual restraint. Honouring surrenders, sparing the wounded and respecting flags of truce reduced the danger and chaos of conflict for all combatants because creating a contractual etiquette of belligerence provided each party with a vital framework of expectations concerning the conduct of others. However, this powerful combination of natural and divine law, ecclesiastical precept, military law, common custom and self-interest only coalesced to impart a new and enduring consistency to both the *jus ad bellum* and the *jus in bello* in the period between 1550 and 1700.

Few Europeans before the eighteenth century seem to have questioned the legitimacy of war itself. Although most Anabaptists, and later most Quakers, argued that violence was incompatible with the teaching of Christ, their numbers remained low. The majority of Christians, Protestant as well as Catholic, saw their God as the Lord of Battles and had little time for pacifism. Instead, they concentrated on establishing whether a war was just or not. In the Middle Ages, cities, nobles and even ordinary knights exercised the same freedom as their rulers to redress a grievance or avenge a wrong by declaring war on an enemy and seeking to inflict maximum damage on his or her dependants and property. However, the combined pressure of continued church censure, the spread of Roman law and the growing power of the state gradually redefined the issue so that by the sixteenth century wars were only deemed just when waged by a legitimate government. Of course, in some parts of Europe the earlier norms survived: thus the memoirs of Götz von Berlichingen 'of the iron claw' (dictated in the 1540s and entitled, significantly, *My Feuds and Disputes*) boasted of the thirty private wars he had waged in Germany since the turn of the century, either in his own name or by proxy; while in Scotland the blood feud long continued to be big business (at least in Scottish terms) with almost four hundred feuds recorded between 1573 and 1625.[9] But by then, in most parts of Europe, ordinary subjects – whether knights, nobles or cities – who went to war without government warrant faced condemnation as rebels, traitors or enemies of the public peace and, when defeated, suffered draconian penalties.

Conversely, few now questioned the absolute right of sovereigns to wage war – with the brief and remarkable exception of Britain in the mid-seventeenth century when King Charles I was tried and executed for war crimes. In April 1648, after a three-day marathon of fasting and prayer, the assembled officer corps of England's New Model Army declared that after they had defeated the royalists they would call 'Charles Stuart, that man of blood, to an account for that blood he had shed, and mischief he had done . . . against the Lord's cause and [the] people in these poor nations'. In November of that year the council of officers agreed to put this demand to Parliament and, when that body proved recalcitrant, the following month they purged its members ('Pride's purge') until a majority in favour of trial was secured. A high court of justice was then set up, with 135 commissioners, 57 of whom agreed to sign the king's death warrant. He was beheaded in London on 30 January 1649.[10]

Charles I was unlucky. Almost all of his contemporaries accepted the absolute right of legitimate rulers to use war as an instrument of policy, as and when they chose. The debate on the *jus ad bellum* from the sixteenth century onwards focused not on who had the right to make war, but on the conditions upon which sovereigns (and only sovereigns) might justly do so. The formula laid down in the treatise *De iure et officiis bellicis*, published in the Netherlands in 1582 by Balthasar de Ayala, represented the prevailing orthodoxy on this question. Ayala acknowledged several grounds for a just war: 'for defence of ourselves or our allies'; 'to regain from the enemy something which he is forcibly and unjustly detaining'; 'to take vengeance for some wrong which has been unjustifiably inflicted'; when a neighbour denies to our forces permission to cross his territory peacefully; and to repress heresy and rebellion.[11]

Scarcely surprisingly, since he wrote in the midst of Spain's bitter struggle to suppress the Protestant-led Dutch Revolt, Ayala devoted much space to his last category. Heresy, he argued, should be met according to God's direct command in Deuteronomy 20 with 'wars of fire and blood' in which no quarter was either given or expected. Survivors, if any, should be deprived of all their possessions and enslaved. It is true that other writers of the day (such as Matthew Sutcliffe, Richard Bernard and William Gouge) condoned only wars in defence of a given faith, while others still (Francisco de Vitoria, Francisco Suárez and Francis Bacon) denied the legitimacy of any

religious war among Christians; but in practice many European states-
men proclaimed with pride that they fought principally to advance the
cause of their church.[12] Thus in 1586 King Philip welcomed a papal
suggestion that he undertake either the invasion of Protestant England
or the conquest of Muslim Algiers, because 'the destruction of the
infidels and heretics, extending the bounds of Christendom, is also the
desire of His Majesty'. Having consulted (as was his custom) a team
of theologians concerning the legitimacy of the two ventures, the king
opted for the 'Enterprise of England'. Somewhat later, when the pope
rather unfairly accused Philip of wishing to attack England solely for
political reasons, the king retorted that there were many other ways
for him to solve his differences with Elizabeth Tudor (negotiation, for
example), and that 'I was only persuaded to listen to His Holiness's
proposal for the sake of God's service.'[13] A similar 'messianic imperialism' coloured the political rhetoric of many Protestant countries –
particularly England, Sweden and the Dutch Republic – whose leaders
between 1550 and 1650, despite the censure of the theorists, were
usually prepared to wage war for the Protestant cause.[14]

Ayala likewise argued that 'disobedience in the part of subjects and
rebellion against the prince is treated as a heinous offence and put on
a par with heresy'.[15] He denied rebels the right to make war, however
intolerable their situation, and claimed that if they did so they 'ought
not to be classed as enemies, the two being quite distinct, and so it is
more correct to term the armed contention with rebel subjects
execution of legal process, or prosecution, not war . . . For the same
reason the laws of war, and of captivity, and of postliminy, which
apply to enemies, do not apply to rebels.' It followed that 'a war waged
by a prince with rebels is a most just one, and that all measures allowed
in war are available against them, such as killing them as enemies,
enslaving them as prisoners, and, much more, confiscating their property as booty'.[16]

Alberico Gentili, a noted legal theorist who taught in Tudor England,
proved tragically right when he wrote in 1589 that the 'chief incentive
to cruelty [in war] is rebellion'. Thus during the Spanish campaign to
annex the Azores seven years before, Philip II's commander justified
the summary execution of all his captured opponents because he did
not consider it a war but rather a police action against rebels. Later

revolts such as the Jacobite rising in Britain (1745) were repressed with exemplary brutality. In 1774–5 some British officers viewed the American colonists' defiance in the same light as the Jacobite insurrection and advocated the same treatment; while in 1777 the Howe brothers received orders from the British government to consider the systematic destruction of the New England ports used by American cruisers attacking Britain's maritime communications.[17] Even the repression of more recent rebellions confirms Gentili's dictum, with levels of brutality rarely replicated in conventional wars: the Paris Commune (1871), Warsaw (1944) and Hungary (1956) in Europe; the Congo and Biafra in Africa during the 1960s; Nicaragua and El Salvador in Central America during the 1980s; and so on.

A certain amount of brutality is inevitable in all conflicts since, to quote Francisco de Valdés, a prominent Spanish soldier of the sixteenth century, 'The day a man picks up his pike to become a soldier is the day he ceases to be a Christian.'[18] Moreover, many atrocities take place in situations that have produced similar results in almost all societies: when the sudden collapse of an enemy force turns one army into a cowardly mob and the other into a murderous crowd. This could easily happen after an adversary was completely broken in battle; for whereas in close combat, in the midst of a press of men, it might be difficult to deal deadly blows, it was very different when the victors could ride down individual fugitives. In 1586, reporting the massacre of a Scottish expeditionary force in Ireland, Captain Thomas Wood-house wrote, 'Truly I was never, since I was a man of war, so weary with killing of men, for I protest to God, . . . as fast as I could I did but hough [hew] at them and paunch [stab] them, sometimes on horseback, because they did run as we did break them, and sometimes on foot.' Some two thousand men were slain. And in 1643, after the rout of the parliamentary infantry at the battle of Torrington, the royalist cavalry pursued them 'until their swords were blunted with the slaughter' and, of the survivors, there was 'scarce a man without a cut over the head or face'.[19]

Carnage was even more common when a town was taken by storm, for sieges have always been treated as total war. Soldiers who sought a civilian shelter and civilians who militarized their homes by accepting a garrison in effect presented an undifferentiated target to the besiegers: military and civilian personnel and property were hard to distinguish during the battery, the assault, or the sack that normally followed a successful storm.[20] Moreover, the catharsis of passing through the killing ground of the breach and emerging unscathed spurred many victors on to indiscriminate violence, while the panic and even paralysis that often gripped defeated defenders seem to have whipped up a blood lust, much as a frightened and cornered animal may provoke rather than pacify its hunters. Thus, during the English Civil War, when Cirencester fell to the royalists in 1643 the parliamentary garrison 'were at their wits' end and stood like men amazed, fear bereft them of understanding and memory' as they were cut down; while at the storm of Lincoln, the following year, the royalists within threw down their arms and 'cried out for quarter, saying they were poor Array Men [conscripts]. We slew fifty of them.'[21]

Similar examples of brutality can be found in almost any conflict. At Jericho around 1350 BC Joshua and the Israelites 'utterly destroyed all that was in the city, both man and woman, young and old, and ox, and sheep, and ass, with the edge of the sword . . . And they burnt the city with fire, and all that was therein.'[22] Much the same fate befell captured cities on the European eastern front during the Second World War, and the intervening 3300 years bristle with similar instances of barbarism. But did such terrible examples of blood lust occur more frequently in certain periods? At first sight the sixteenth and seventeenth centuries stand out. On the one hand a rapid growth in army size – tenfold in some states – created logistical problems that few governments seemed able to solve directly. Plunder and wanton exploitation of civilian resources took place more frequently in part because, until the emergence of an adequate tax base and administrative structure, the larger armies could not be fed in any other way. Thus, although they deprecated unrestrained looting (which had been central to the feud), most early modern writers accepted that it was lawful to take away from innocent parties goods that an enemy could also use (for example, their weapons and their ships), and to destroy any assets (crops, merchandise and so on) that might nourish enemy forces. On the other hand the fragmentation of religious unity in the West in the wake of the Reformation weakened some other restraints on war derived from the Middle Ages: although women and children were still normally spared (except during a sack), and mutilation of the dead and wounded remained rare, the protection of priests and pilgrims now usually extended only to those of the same creed, while foreigners, merchants and the poor (formerly covered by the Peace of God) became fair game.[23]

Nevertheless, some striking examples of restraint still occurred during this period. Thus in 1574 during Spain's desperate struggle to crush the Dutch Revolt following the failure of the Spanish army's siege of Leiden, serious consideration was given to the systematic inundation of the rebel provinces. The opportunity seemed perfect: the fact that most of Holland and Zeeland lay below sea level was self-evident – everyone could see the drainage mills on the dikes, ceaselessly keeping the water at bay; and memories of previous catastrophes which had inundated large areas of the province remained vivid. Furthermore, the rebels themselves had broken several dikes, first in order to blockade the royalist garrison in Middelburg (1572) and then to impede the Spanish siege of Alkmaar in North Holland (1573).[24] More dramatically, in August 1574 they began to break the dikes and open the sluices along the rivers to the south of Leiden. It was a controlled operation, designed to let in only enough water for a fleet of flatbottomed barges to sail provisions into Leiden and thus raise the siege; but it gave the frustrated Spaniards in the trenches pause. As Francisco de Valdés, the Spanish commander before Leiden, wrote to his commander in chief:

When I first entered Holland with the army, I intercepted a letter written by the prince of Orange [the Dutch leader] in his own hand [to one of his officials] . . . in which he wrote the following words: 'I had given orders that you should break the sluice at Maaslandsluis in order to flood the area, but we have gathered together here . . . some learned men, and they find that if these sluices are broken, the whole countryside will be flooded without it being possible ever to reclaim it. So it would be better not to break them.' I thought I should let Your Excellency know this so that you will be aware that if at any time you might wish to flood this country, it is in your power. And since our enemies have taken the initiative in doing so, if they continue in their obstinate rebellion they indeed deserve to be flooded out.[25]

This suggestion, which bears a striking resemblance to the proposed United States air strikes against the dams and dikes of the Red River delta during the Vietnam War (the Rolling Thunder and Linebacker campaigns), was duly approved by the high command in Brussels and forwarded to the king for authorization. But, to the disgust of all the military men, Philip II – like President Johnson four hundred years later in remarkably similar terms – forbade the operation:[26]

It is very clear that the severity, wickedness and obstinacy of the rebels have reached the level where no one can doubt that they are worthy of a harsh and exemplary punishment . . . And [we know that] we can easily flood Holland by breaking the dikes. But this strategy would give rise to a great disadvantage: that once broken, the province would be lost and ruined for ever, to the evident detriment of the neighbouring provinces which would have to build new dikes of their own . . . So that, in effect, it would not be wise to adopt this strategy, nor must we do so because (apart from the disadvantages already mentioned, great and manifest as they are) we should also recognize that it would earn for us a reputation for cruelty which would be better avoided, especially against our vassals, even though their guilt is notorious and the punishment justified.[27]

However, such restraint by a sovereign against rebellious subjects, especially when many of them professed a different faith, proved rare in the century following 1550. François de La Noue, like other military writers of the later sixteenth century, believed that war had grown far more brutal during his own lifetime, with virtually no holds barred in conflict; and he ascribed this development to the prevalence of both rebellion and religious schism which multiplied the number of those to whom no quarter should be given.[28] The argument is highly plausible: both political and social uprisings, many of them aiming at religious change, occurred with remarkable frequency in early modern Europe, with peaks in the 1560s, the 1590s and the 1640s.[29] Moreover, some of the worst recorded excesses involved soldiers of one creed butchering those of another: the massacres perpetrated by the Catholic forces of Spain in the Netherlands during the 1570s; the destruction of Protestant Magdeburg in Germany by the Catholic imperial army in 1631; or the sack of Drogheda in Ireland by the Protestant New

Model Army in 1649. Furthermore, the victors normally justified these and other similar deeds with the rhetoric of messianic imperialism buttressed by the examples of severe chastisement of unbelievers to be found in the Old Testament. Thus a sermon preached in 1645 to the parliamentary forces just before they stormed Basing House (the stronghold of a Catholic peer) condemned those within as 'open enemies of God', 'bloody papists' and 'vermin', and called for their extermination. Not surprisingly, few of the defeated defenders received quarter.[30]

But there is less to all this than meets the eye. In the first place, it may well be that atrocities seemed more numerous simply because wars were more numerous: scarcely a year in the period 1520–1650 saw the continent entirely at peace. Second, the age abounded in brutality: the soldiers themselves were normally subjected to draconian and sometimes arbitrary penalties by their officers. The Articles of War promulgated for the English parliamentary army in 1642 contained forty-five offences punishable by death. Collective misdemeanours in most armies were castigated by drawing lots or by decimation to determine who would be shot; several mutinies by the Spanish Army of Flanders in the 1570s were provoked by punishments deemed by the soldiers to be arbitrary or degrading.[31] Third and most important, in most parts of Western Europe battles became relatively rare and sieges constituted the hinge of success and failure.

According to the Laws of War, a town which rejected a summons to surrender from someone who claimed it as a right offered an insult to his authority which he was honour bound to avenge; and the longer it held out, the worse the penalty. In the early stages this might merely be pecuniary. Thus in 1650 during the English conquest of Scotland the city of St Andrews in Fife surrendered only at the second summons and therefore had to pay £500 to the soldiery.[32] Far more serious was refusal to surrender until the battery was brought up, for then the inhabitants had no right to quarter if the town was taken by storm. Henry V's brutal speech to the besieged burghers of Harfleur, written by Shakespeare in the 1590s, reflected the contemporary situation well:

If I begin the batt'ry once again,
I will not leave the half-achieved Harfleur
Till in her ashes she lie buried.
The gates of mercy shall be all shut up
And the flesh'd soldier, rough and hard of heart,
In liberty of bloody hand shall range
With conscience wide as hell, mowing like grass
Your fresh fair virgins and your flow'ring infants.
What is't then to me if impious war,
Array'd in flames, like to the prince of fiends,
Do, with his smirch'd complexion, all fell feats
Enlink'd to waste and desolation?

Attitudes remained the same throughout the eighteenth century, of which the duke of Wellington later wrote: 'I believe that it has always been understood that the defenders of a fortress stormed have no claim to quarter.'[33]

Even so, the degree of violence permitted during a sack was limited. Public opinion normally tolerated actions committed in the sudden flush of total victory when, as Lucy Hutchinson observed in her memoirs of the English Civil War, 'the brave turn cowards, fear unnerves the most mighty, [and] makes the generous base, and great men do those things that they blush to think on'.[34] Afterwards it was different. Thus when Mechelen (Malines) in the Netherlands fell by storm in 1580 a group of nuns begged the Protestant soldiers who had invaded their convent for a swift death, but the troops rather surprisingly spared them on the grounds that 'the fury was over and they no longer had licence'; while in 1644 an English royalist preacher enjoined the king's soldiers that 'you neither do, nor . . . suffer to be done, in coole blood, to the most impious rebells [i.e., supporters of Parliament], any thing that savours of immodesty, barbarousnesse, or inhumanity'.[35]

Nevertheless, even armchair theorists of this period, while calling in general terms for restraint, acknowledged that sound military reasons might justify unbridled brutality. Thus Francisco de Vitoria, in his seminal work on international law composed in the 1540s, recognized three reasons for the exemplary punishment of an obdurate town and its population: first, on grounds of overall strategy (for example, to prevent the provision of assistance to the enemy at a later stage); second, to keep up the morale of one's own army (especially if pay had been in short supply during the siege); and third, to scare other enemy towns into surrender.[36] These considerations became particularly important when the towns concerned were engaged in rebellion for, as the duke of Alba (commander of the government's forces in the Netherlands) acutely observed soon after the outbreak of the Dutch Revolt in 1572, not all towns that fell into an enemy's hands were equally guilty: they should therefore not all be treated alike. He discerned six distinct types. First, those that had been taken by the enemy after a siege; second, those that had held out until the enemy brought up its artillery and could therefore resist with impunity no longer; third, those that had admitted the enemy because they had no alternative; and fourth, those that had requested a royalist garrison but had been threatened by the enemy before help could arrive. All such towns, according to Alba, deserved leniency when recaptured. Quite different were his fifth category – those that had surrendered before need arose – and his sixth – those that had refused government troops when offered them, choosing instead to admit the enemy.[37]

An analysis of the conduct of the Spanish Army in the Netherlands during the first stage of the Dutch Revolt shows that the duke adhered meticulously to his own formula. Thus the first town to be sacked in 1572 was Mechelen, which undoubtedly belonged to Alba's sixth category. It had refused his offer of a garrison in June but had freely admitted – and had paid – the troops sent by the prince of Orange in August. To make matters worse, as the Spanish troops approached, the Orangist garrison fired warning shots (before abandoning the town at midnight).[38] Mechelen nevertheless refused the duke's demand for unconditional surrender and was taken by storm almost immediately: the ensuing orgy of sack and plunder lasted three entire days, with the duke and his senior commanders grimly looking on. According to an eyewitness, 'the soldiers behaved as if this religious capital of the country were a Muslim city and all the inhabitants barbarians. The desolation was so complete that not a nail was left in a wall.' Even four years later another eyewitness remained unable to describe what he had seen: 'One could say a lot more,' he wrote to a friend, 'if the horror of it did not make one's hair stand on end – not at recounting it but at remembering it!'[39] But these men were civilians: most soldiers recognized that Francisco de Vitoria's three justifications for exemplary punishment all came into play at Mechelen. First, as already noted, the town was unquestionably guilty, yet it refused to surrender when summoned: therefore a full sack was entirely legitimate under the prevailing Laws of War. Second, the Spanish army was suffering from chronic lack of pay: the Spaniards themselves were owed eighteen months' wage arrears and the Walloon troops almost three, while the German regiments had received nothing at all since they enlisted.[40] Alba may well have felt that he could not afford clemency for fear his unpaid troops would mutiny unless they were allowed some plunder.[41] Third, and no less important, the duke calculated that exemplary brutality against one town in revolt would persuade others to surrender swiftly.[42] And so it proved: the sack of Mechelen seems to have satisfied the victorious troops both psychologically and financially; and it provoked within a matter of days the submission of the other rebellious towns in Flanders and Brabant.[43] All of them received an immediate pardon. Alba and his troops thus did no more than put Francisco de Vitoria's stern views on the *jus in bello* into practice: it was a classic 'hard war' combination of terror and discipline.

A similar explanation can be advanced for the sack of Magdeburg in 1631, an event condemned by Protestants at the time as a 'memorable catastrophe' to be ranked alongside the fall of Troy and Noah's flood.[44] Yet the city had refused to admit an imperial garrison since the summer of 1629; it made an alliance with Gustavus Adolphus of Sweden, a declared enemy of the emperor, in the summer of 1630; and it repeatedly rejected the demands for surrender received from an imperial siege army commanded by Count Tilly. Even after some of the outer defences fell, trusting in Gustavus's rash promises of immediate assistance, the city repudiated a final ultimatum on 18 May 1631. Tilly, fearing the arrival of a Swedish relief column, launched a general storm at dawn two days later. His forces burst through the walls in three places and vented their fury on all who crossed their path. Thousands perished but, contrary to the assertions of Protestant polemicists, not through sectarian passion but according to the Laws of War reinforced by strategic necessity.[45]

Much the same story can be told of the equally reviled sack of Drogheda in 1649. A relatively small English army commanded by Oliver Cromwell brought up a powerful siege train on 9 September and summoned the town the following day but was rebuffed. Thereupon battery began in earnest and by the afternoon of the 11th two breaches had been made and a general assault took place. It is true that Cromwell later claimed that he was moved by a spirit of confessional vengeance: 'I am persuaded that this is a righteous judgement of God upon these barbarous [Catholic] wretches, who have imbrued their hands in so much innocent [Protestant] blood'; and that accordingly, 'in the heat of the action' he forbade his troops 'to spare any that were in arms in the town'. But that statement scarcely does justice to events. First, the defenders of Drogheda included English Catholics, English Protestants and Irish Protestants as well as Irish Catholics; second, English and French Catholics previously encountered by Cromwell's army had been decently treated; third, a number of noncombatants in the town (including all Catholic clergy) were also killed; and fourth, much of the slaughter took place some time after the 'heat of the action' was past. Thus several parties of defenders (including the one-legged governor, Sir Arthur Aston, and his entourage) were first allowed to surrender and then butchered an hour after quarter was given them. Indeed, according to one source, Aston's brains were beaten out with his own wooden leg, and what remained of his head was then sent to Dublin along with those of fifteen other senior officers to be set on poles. In all, perhaps 1000 civilians and 2500 soldiers were killed by the New Model Army at Drogheda on or immediately after 11 September 1649.[46]

As at Mechelen and Magdeburg, however, this appalling brutality was intended to secure important strategic goals. According to Cromwell's lieutenants, sometimes less addicted to religious rhetoric than their leader, 'the extraordinary severity was designed to discourage others from making opposition' and thus 'tend to prevent the effusion of blood for the future'. In this it succeeded splendidly. According to the marquis of Ormond, the leader of the Irish forces,

It is not to be imagined how great the terror is that those successes and the power of the rebels [Cromwell and his troops] have struck into this people, who though they know themselves resigned, at best, to the loss of all they have and to irrecoverable slavery, and have yet numbers enough and other competent means to oppose ... are yet so stupefied that it is with great difficulty I can persuade them to act anything like men towards their own preservation.[47]

Sure enough, news of the sack of Drogheda swiftly produced the surrender of other neighbouring garrisons. Its fate, like the others discussed above, was thus no sectarian massacre – let us recall once more that many of the defenders and townsfolk were Protestant – but an action carried out for strategic (not confessional) reasons and, as such, largely sanctioned by the contemporary Laws of War.

Before long, such orgies of destruction began to seem exceptional. On the one hand, fewer places chose to resist until an assault became inevitable, thus permitting a negotiated surrender: in the concise formula of Alberico Gentili, 'Cities are sacked when taken; they are not sacked when surrendered.' Admittedly the terms might be harsh, even unconditional, which could lead to the execution of some of the defenders after they had laid down their arms; but the loss of life and property was still less.[48] On the other hand, as time passed, the range of misconduct condoned by military authorities and by public opinion steadily narrowed. Taking and killing hostages or perpetrating exemplary atrocities, which Vitoria and Gentili had tolerated in the sixteenth century, came to be execrated by writers such as Johann Justus Moser and Emerich de Vattel in the eighteenth; while today some theorists condemn even sieges and economic blockades as a species of terrorism because they intentionally inflict harm on innocent civilians in order to force governments to capitulate.

Moreover, in most of the wars waged in Europe since the sixteenth century, breaches of the norms for military conduct laid down in treatises (and more recently in treaties) have been condemned and chastised with increasing rigour. Individual soldiers faced trial and punishment by special military tribunals for crimes committed against either fellow soldiers or civilians.[49] Thus in 1574 Philip II ordered a judicial inquiry into accusations that the duke of Alba had used disproportionate force in his conduct of the war against the Dutch rebels, and although Alba himself was acquitted, several of his senior officials were banished from court.[50] After the brutal sack of Antwerp by the Spanish army in 1576, a full judicial inquiry was held to determine responsibility for the atrocities which left eight thousand citizens dead and one thousand houses destroyed; and in Ireland after the trauma of the Civil War and the Cromwellian occupation, a court of claims was established in 1662 specifically to examine charges against those accused of war crimes.[51]

This development constituted a significant and lasting extension in the application of the Laws of War and it was paralleled by another: conventions previously applied selectively during the early modern period gradually came to be enforced almost universally. In a sense this process merely represented a stage in a longer evolution. Many tribal societies equated humankind with members of their own tribe and regarded all others as nonhumans to be treated – or, rather, mistreated – as animals. Even in medieval Europe the Laws of War governed only 'the conduct of men who fought to settle by arms quarrels which were in nature private, and whose importance was judged by the social status of the principals involved'. They therefore affected only equals.[52] In the sixteenth century, however, starting with Spain's war against the Dutch, the same rules began to be applied to all combatants, whatever their social status.

Even as Balthasar de Ayala composed his uncompromising treatise on the need to wage a war to the death against all rebels, his commanding officer (Alexander Farnese, duke of Parma) negotiated generous terms for the return of rebellious cities to the king's obedience and for the exchange and ransom of captured soldiers in enemy hands.[53] Soon afterwards the regular exchange of prisoners of war became standard practice: by 1599, if not before, Spain and the Dutch Republic had concluded a formal convention – the *cuartel general* – stipulating that every captain should ransom all his captured men within twenty-five days. First, prisoners of equal rank on each side were to be exchanged free of charge; thereafter, a ransom appropriate to the soldier's rank (usually the equivalent of one month's pay) was due, plus an agreed per diem 'entertainment' for time spent in captivity. The convention was reissued every few years, with the schedule of payments revised upwards to take account of inflation. In 1637 and again in 1643 the Dutch-Spanish protocol was translated and published in English; and from 1639 the same system was introduced into the war between Spain and France.[54] Likewise, agreement was reached that sick and injured soldiers who fell into enemy hands should be placed under a special safeguard and repatriated with a minimum of formality.[55] Thus matters that had previously been subject to private contract now came under state regulation; and the available evidence suggests that exchanges were effected fairly and fast – even if the prisoners were released 'from the most remote parts, as usual, so that they will not find it easy to return home'.[56]

Simultaneously, new regulations began to limit the violence and plunder of unpaid soldiery at the expense of noncombatants. Both sides in the Low Countries' Wars began to accept prearranged sums of protection money from individual communities based on mutual guarantees that they would neither engage in hostilities nor be subjected to further extortions from those whom they paid. Parties of troops took up station specifically to enforce the agreements. Once again, the idea was not new: during the Hundred Years' War most local commanders had issued letters of protection to a community in return for financial contributions, but each safeguard only bound the party that issued it – a community was still liable to depredations from the troops of other commanders even when they were on the same side. In the Low Countries' Wars, however, the growing power of the state made the system binding on all troops, and its effectiveness may be judged from a letter written by a Spanish field officer to his superiors in 1640:

The majority of the villages [near the enemy frontier] . . . contain enemy 'protection troops.' . . . [This] gives rise to many inconveniences for His Majesty's service. One is that our own men cannot go there to collect information about the enemy, because they are immediately arrested as spies by the protection troops. And, thanks to their presence, the peasants are able to bring in their crops safely and provide full aid and assistance to the enemy.[57]

Four factors explain the new restraint in war. First, the composition of armies underwent a major change: the contingents hired and maintained via military contractors gave way to units raised and sustained directly by the state. The significance of this transition for the conduct of war was illuminated by an exchange between two royalists – Lord Glamorgan, an aristocrat, and Lord Ruthven, a professional soldier – during the English Civil War. Glamorgan (admittedly a very rich man) had kept his own troops under tight control at the siege of Gloucester in 1643, 'without so much as making use of free quarter, but all uppon the penny'. Ruthven (a veteran of the Thirty Years' War) objected that this created problems for other commanders who lacked the money to pay their troops, and complained to King Charles I; but Glamorgan boldly replied:

I yielded to His Excellencie to be a better soldier, but still to be a soldier of fortune, here today and God knows where tomorrow, and therefore needed not care for the love of the people; but though I were killed myselfe I should leave my posteritie behind me, towards whom I would not leave a grudge in the people, but whilst I could serve His Majestie upon my owne purse and creditt I would readdyly doe it, and afterward leave it to such as his Lordship.[58]

As the seventeenth century advanced, less and less was left 'to such as his Lordship' and troops raised by private contractors. Instead, governments created supply magazines, fortified frontiers, and centrally controlled contributions systems which gradually reduced the need for looting as a survival strategy for the individual soldier. Of course, excesses still occurred and the penalties imposed for failing to provide the stores required could be draconian; but the new methods nevertheless reduced the occasions for friction between soldiers and civilians that had so often produced atrocities in the past.[59]

A second reason favouring greater restraint in the conduct of war in the West was a steady process of deconfessionalization. By 1650 the religious frontiers of Europe had largely stabilized, for the religious rebels had either succeeded in gaining recognition as a state (as with the Dutch Republic) or had been forced either to conform or to leave (as in the Spanish Netherlands). Furthermore, the calamitous changes of fortune experienced by each creed during the period seem to have dented the absolute certainty of many participants that they served as agents of God's purpose: a sense of resignation often replaced the dynamic providentialism that had led men to fight to the death with a clear conscience.[60] In most areas of Christendom, after the peace of

Westphalia in 1648 religion ceased to be an issue for which most states were prepared to go to war. Thus at the turn of the eighteenth century Louis XIV's bid for European mastery met defeat at the hands of a coalition led by the staunchly Calvinist William of Orange, whose most important ally was the Catholic Prince Eugene of Savoy, a minister of the no less Catholic Austrian Habsburgs; while in the Great Northern War, Lutheran Sweden was eventually laid low by an alliance of Lutheran Denmark, Calvinist Brandenburg, Catholic Poland and Orthodox Russia. Of course atrocities still occurred, such as the devastation of the Palatinate by the forces of Louis XIV in 1688–9; but religion played no part in the process and the chorus of condemnation was all but universal. As time passed, deconfessionalization became reinforced by Enlightenment values which enjoined ever greater restraint upon soldiers.[61]

Alongside this gradual intellectual process lay another: a general feeling that in the wars of the mid-seventeenth century Europe had come perilously close to self-destruction. 'Oh, come on!' ran one of the German pastor Paul Gerhardt's hymns, 'Wake up, wake up, you hard world, open your eyes before terror comes upon you in swift, sudden surprise.' A desperate entry in a Swabian peasant family's Bible from 1647 reads: 'We live like animals, eating bark and grass. No one could imagine that anything like this could happen to us. Many people say that there is no God.' A little later in England, writing a few months after the end of the Civil War, John Locke regretted 'all those flames that have made such havoc and desolation in Europe and have not been quenched but with the blood of so many millions'.[62] Political leaders, as well as writers, artists and ordinary people, felt a revulsion towards the excesses of the preceding period and harboured a fervent hope that it should never happen again. As in the aftermath of the First World War, the slaughter had been so great, the spectre of chaos so terrifying, that 'no more war' attitudes became common. Some have detected in these sentiments a climate favourable to the development of absolute states; certainly they created a climate favourable to greater restraint in the conduct of war.[63]

A fourth and final explanation for the growth of restraint in early modern European warfare lay in the steady spread of reciprocity. During the Middle Ages honour and reputation had to some extent ensured observance of the conventions, but they were always reinforced by the threat of vengeance: the kin of a knight slain by treachery would normally seek revenge, creating a blood feud. Where this sanction was lacking, restraint diminished. Thus encounters between knights and members of the lower social orders normally turned into bloodbaths, whoever won: witness the carnage after the various victories of the Swiss or after the defeat of peasant armies. Restraint appeared in such unequal conflicts only when they became protracted: barbarous behaviour by one side, confident of the right-eousness of its own cause and its own invulnerability, changed dra-matically when the other side acquired the capacity to retaliate. Thus in the early stages of the Dutch Revolt, the duke of Alba hanged all prisoners.[64] But this changed abruptly in the autumn of 1573 when the Dutch captured one of Alba's most capable subordinates, the count of Bossu. The Dutch leaders made it clear that, unless the systematic execution of Dutch prisoners ceased, Bossu would be hanged. The Spaniards reluctantly agreed, and negotiations began for the release of Bossu and other Spaniards in exchange for certain rebels in Spanish hands.[65] Enemy troops came to be accepted as soldiers first and rebels second. Likewise, during the Civil War in England, although the king's provost-marshal initially treated captured parliamentarians as rebels and traitors, Parliament's threats to hang all their royalist prisoners in retaliation caused a notable reduction in severity.[66]

Parallel developments occurred at the local level. Where garrisons from opposing sides existed in close proximity, conventions emerged that anticipated the live-and-let-live system on relatively quiet sectors of the trenches on the western front during the First World War: tacit and sometimes even formal treaties of neutrality were concluded between belligerents. In order to remove the intolerable tension of living on permanent alert, rival garrison commanders or neighbouring (but opposed) communities would agree not to attack each other. There was even a ratchet effect, as cooperation on such basic matters led to deals in other areas, such as where each side might safely forage.[67] It took a little longer for the same principle to be accepted in the war at sea. As late as 1622–5 the crews of Flemish privateers were either hanged or thrown overboard ('foot-watering', as it was known) when captured by their Dutch adversaries; but when the Dunkirkers captured no fewer than fifteen hundred Dutch prisoners the foot-watering abruptly ceased.[68]

The spread of reciprocity was not universal, however, and appalling atrocities continued to occur, often with the full support of the state – witness the policy of the German army on hostages throughout the Second World War, the conduct of the Red Army in 1944–5 as it invaded Germany, and the ethnic cleansing and systematic rape that accompanied the Yugoslav Civil Wars in 1991–2000. Perhaps we should not be surprised, for an important aim of state-sponsored propaganda before and during war is specifically to destroy any sense of identification with the enemy by dehumanizing all adversaries so that they can be killed, mutilated and otherwise mistreated with a clear conscience. Evidence of subhuman traits and racial inferiority, as well as alleged atrocities and supposedly implacable malice, all play their part in this process. Thus Nazi Germany prepared its troops for the invasion of the Soviet Union in 1941 by portraying the soldiers of the Red Army as *keine Kameraden* to whom one could do anything, anywhere, at any time, without scruple. 'We must remove any feeling of military comradeship [from our troops],' Hitler instructed his generals before Barbarossa. 'The Communist has never been, and will never be, a comrade. We are engaged in a war of extermination.' Soviet Russia replied in kind. An order distributed to the troops besieging Danzig in March 1945 ended: 'Soldiers of the Red Army, kill the Germans! Kill all Germans! Kill! Kill! Kill!'[69]

In the early modern period the category of *keine Kameraden* applied in Europe to the native Irish, who were killed and enslaved and whose property was destroyed or confiscated with little or no pause for thought. According to his approving biographer, whenever in the 1570s Sir Humphrey Gilbert invaded 'the enemies countrie, he killed manne, woman and child; and spoiled, wasted and burned, by the grounde, all that he might, leavyng nothing of the enemies in saffetie, which he could possiblie waste or consume'; and the way to his head-quarters whenever he campaigned in Gaelic Ireland was flanked by a line of severed heads.[70]

Overseas, such conduct was already the norm. Most Europeans saw their African and Native American adversaries as *keine Kameraden* to whom the Laws of War did not apply. Several justifications were adduced. To begin with, they were pagans. Admittedly, from 1512 onwards a special text (known as the *Requerimiento* and based on Deuteronomy 20:10–16) was read out before each Spanish advance in the Americas, requiring the native peoples of the New World to accept immediately both the authority of the Spanish crown and the tenets of Christianity or face the consequences. Failure to submit instantly legitimized for most Spaniards a war of fire and blood, culminating in the expropriation of all possessions and the enslavement of all persons. Many Westerners further justified this appalling behaviour on the grounds that their overseas opponents corresponded to the peoples described by Aristotle as born to be slaves, to whom few rights under the law remained. It is true that the legitimacy of such conduct was sometimes queried, and that a number of full-dress debates took place in Spain around the year 1550 concerning the Europeans' right to enslave Native Americans, but little changed. Alleged cases of cannibalism, the mass slaughter of sacrificial victims by the Aztec priests, or the mass production of pottery depicting fellatio, sodomy and group sex by some Pre-Columbian peoples all served to justify the Spaniards' view that the Native American peoples were incapable of reading the book of nature implanted in all true human beings by God and therefore stood in need of education – both for their own good and for the good of the whole human community whose integrity could be endangered by cannibalism or 'unnatural' sex even in remote areas like America. Any opposition to the process of education was accordingly viewed as unjust war and the perpetrators therefore received no mercy.[71]

Another reason for the continuing harshness of colonial wars lay in the fact that, to some extent, a measure of brutality was probably essential if the (initially) extremely small numbers of invaders were to retain control several thousand miles from their home base. The point was well put by one of the last of the conquistadores, Richard Meinertzhagen, whose account of the subjugation of Kenya between 1902 and 1906 is strewn with dead bodies. When he prepared his diaries for publication in the 1950s, Meinertzhagen himself was slightly shaken:

On reading through . . . this record I am shocked by the account of taking human life. I do not pretend to excuse it, but perhaps I may explain it. I have no belief in the sanctity of human life or in the dignity of the human race. Human life has never been sacred; nor has man, except in a few exceptional cases, been dignified. Moreover in Kenya fifty years ago, when stationed with 100 soldiers amid an African population of 300,000, in cases of emergency where local government was threatened we had to act, and act quickly.

No doubt Hernán Cortés, commanding only five hundred Europeans in his campaign against the Aztecs in 1519–21, or Francisco Pizarro with less than two hundred Europeans when he destroyed the Inca empire in 1532–3, would have heartily endorsed this rude philosophy.[72]

Yet despite their numerical superiority, the conquerors' victims failed to establish reciprocity. Cooperation between enemies requires neither rationality (for if it works, it will continue), nor trust (thanks to the penalties of defection), nor mutual communication (because deeds speak louder than words). Only durability is essential: some recognition of adversaries from earlier encounters and some certainty that the two sides will meet again. The absence of this vital precondition helps to explain not only the brutality of colonial wars but also the hard war policies followed by Sherman's army on its march through Georgia during the American Civil War, by the army of Morocco on its advance from Seville during the Spanish Civil War, by the German army against Soviet soldiers and civilians during the Second World War, and by the Red Army during its conquest of Germany in 1944–5, just as it had played its part in the destruction of native America. There was no time for reciprocity to develop.[73]

The rules of war followed by most European societies both at home and abroad have thus displayed a remarkable continuity since the sixteenth century. This stems in part from the relative stability of human nature – the advantages of cooperation and the dangers of total collapse were as apparent to Renaissance soldiers as they are today – in part from the lasting influence of the Bible, the Church Fathers and Roman law on Western civilization. But both of these considerations received reinforcement from the weight of practice and precedent – by the frequent appeals to custom in assessing military conduct. It is true that the theoretical restrictions of the *jus in bello* have multiplied; it is also true that those restrictions have been breached at regular intervals. But almost every excess, from the sixteenth century onwards, has been subjected by contemporaries to detailed scrutiny: had the troops been provoked beforehand (for instance, by the previous mutilation of their captured comrades); had they been starved of pay; had the enemy reneged on a previous oath not to fight again? And if no excuses were available, moral condemnation and then legal sanctions ensued. Most of the actions today outlawed by the Geneva Conventions have been condemned in the West for at least four centuries; only the degree and the extent of enforcement have changed over time. Thus every generation of playgoers has understood (despite the bogus Welsh accent) Fluellen's outrage in Shakespeare's *Henry V* upon hearing of the massacre of the unarmed camp followers after the battle of Agincourt:

Kill the poys and the luggage! 'Tis expressly against the law of arms; 'tis as arrant a piece of knavery, mark you now, as can be offert; in your conscience, now, is it not?[74]

Yes, it was against the law of arms in the 1590s, when the play was first performed, as it still is today, constituting just one of the numerous 'self-evident and unalterable' features of the Laws of War that crystallized in early modern Europe and survived virtually intact down to our own day, counterbalancing the contrasts detected by Martin van Creveld.

7

Although Oliver Cromwell used atrocity as a weapon in seventeenth-century Ireland, as the last chapter demonstrated, other commanders displayed some restraint. Admittedly the civil war there began with an attempt by Catholic conspirators to massacre all Protestants in October 1641 – up to 12,000 may have died in the province of Ulster alone – and, during the hostilities that followed, each side initially executed its prisoners out of hand. The return of many 'Wild Geese' (Irish Catholics who had gone abroad to make their living in Europe as professional soldiers) gradually began to change this. Thus in March 1643, after eighteen months of fighting, Colonel Thomas Preston, who had served for many years in the Spanish Army of Flanders, apologized to the opposing commander after hanging a captured enemy soldier. In a personal letter he explained:

The said Lilly, having served in our army and went away to yours, and we having taken him afterwards, we caused the military laws to be put in execution, according to the custom of the country wherein I serve [the Spanish Netherlands], who gives no quarter to such men, as being incapable [i.e., undeserving] thereof; as I hope your lordship . . . would use all such as come away from your army, that you find again in the same nature.[1]

The Irish contingent of the Army of Flanders, in which Preston served, has left copious records in the Spanish archives. So when in 1992 Rolf Loeber, a prominent clinical psychiatrist and (in his spare time) an expert on early modern Irish military affairs, sent me a paper he had written on the 'reception' of continental military practice in seventeenth-century Ireland, I offered to add some material from Spanish sources. Professor Loeber generously suggested that we should *become co-authors of the piece, commissioned by Jane Ohlmeyer for a volume of essays on Ireland in the 1640s and 1650s, and we pooled our expertise.*

When the chapter first appeared, in 1995, few modern historians besides Rolf Loeber had written about the military history of seventeenth-century Ireland. How things have changed! The following year, Thomas Bartlett and Keith Jeffrey edited an excellent volume of essays entitled A Military History of Ireland *(Cambridge, 1996), with a chapter by Jane Ohlmeyer on 'The wars of religion, 1603–60'. In 1999, four important works illuminated the subject further. Kevin Forkan, 'Strafford's Irish Army, 1640–41' (National University of Ireland, Galway, MA thesis), brought together all the printed and many of the manuscript sources concerning the Dublin government's crash programme to adopt continental military practices. Meanwhile Deana Ranken, 'The art of war: military writing in Ireland in the mid-seventeenth century' (Oxford University D.Phil. thesis, 1999), considered Irish writers who dealt with the art of war (such as Garret Barry and the earl of Orrery) as well as those who chronicled the civil wars (although she discussed only those who wrote in English, not those who used Latin or Gaelic). J. Scott Wheeler published* Cromwell in Ireland *(New York), which dealt with the logistics as well as the campaigns of the English conquest. Finally, Rolf Loeber published an article that chronicled the war in County Laois during the 1640s: although the area lacked substantial walled cities, Loeber found over thirty sieges in the decade.[2] The following year, Pádraig Lenihan's* The Confederate Catholics at War, 1641–1648 *(Cork, 2000) provided much important information on how the Catholic armies fought and why, despite their superior numbers, they ultimately lost; while Peter Edwards's* Dealing in Death. The Arms Trade and the British Civil Wars, 1638–1652 *(Stroud, 2000) brilliantly combined continental as well as Irish and British sources.*

This sudden interest is entirely appropriate, because the 'war of the three kingdoms' in the 1640s, far more than the 'war of the three kings' in 1688–91, decided the fate of Ireland for over two centuries. Between 1641 and 1649, an independent Catholic Irish government in Kilkenny conducted its own foreign policy, played host to several foreign ambassadors, and maintained its own armies and navy, for the first time – and the last until 1922. The success of the confederacy in importing the 'Military Revolution' enabled it to hold the Irish Protestants at bay, but not to defeat the English veterans led by Oliver Cromwell. Nevertheless, the failings were not all – and perhaps not primarily – military: Cromwell did not face a united Irish opposition, a crucial advantage that exasperated the confederates' foreign supporters. According to the French ambassador in London,

What really surprises the majority of those who contemplate the affairs of Ireland is to see that people of the same nation and of the same religion – who are well aware that the resolution to exterminate them totally has already been taken – should differ so strongly in their private hostilities; that their zeal for religion, the preservation of their country, and their own self-interest are not sufficient to make them lay down – at least for a short time – the passions which divide them one from the other.[3]

I stand by the conclusion in the chapter that follows: Catholic Ireland's defeat and subjugation by England stemmed essentially from political, not military, factors.

The 'Military Revolution' in Seventeenth-century Ireland

Everyone in Ireland understood the military significance of the rebellion of October 1641. Almost immediately the Lords Justices warned that without immediate intervention from Britain

[This] kingdom will be utterly lost and all the English and Protestants in Ireland destroyed, and so England instead of subjects will have enemies here, who will continually disturb the peace of that Kingdom, as well from hence as from foreign powers . . . and then of necessity England must be forced to undertake a new conquest of this Kingdom, for a politic reformation will then become impossible; and to make a new conquest will be now more difficult and chargeable than in former times, in regard the ports and inland towns and the principal strengths will be immediately lost, as some of them already are ... and the people better disciplined in the rules of war, besides many other advantages they have as well by the return hither of commanders of the Irish who served in foreign nations ... Besides all the mere Irish now in the service of the King of Spain will undoubtedly return hither to join with the rebels.[4]

The Dublin administration perceived with remarkable prescience that the conflict would be qualitatively different from any of the earlier revolts in Ireland because it would dislodge thousands of British settlers and their families, undo English control over large areas of the country, and provoke an unprecedented arms race.

Until recently, however, historians seem to have missed this point. Although the major military innovations in early modern continental warfare have received detailed study, their transfer to Ireland during the first half of the seventeenth century has not. Four key developments, sometimes termed the 'Military Revolution', are at issue: the artillery fortress, the naval broadside, the reliance on firepower in combat, and the application of strategies that deployed several armies in concert. All four appeared in Ireland during the 1640s, and transformed the nature of the conflict.[5]

Warfare in Ireland before 1641 followed two basic patterns. Traditionally the Irish excelled in skirmishes, ambushes, capturing settlers' strongholds and, occasionally, building earthworks. The English, by contrast, concentrated on the control of towns from which they tried to dominate the surrounding countryside. Although many English settlements without walls were burnt by the Irish, formal sieges were rare and even small fortified towns remained relatively impregnable. The capture of Athenry (County Galway, 1576) and Kilmallock (County Limerick, 1583) proved the exception, and even they were soon recovered.

Admittedly artillery was used both to attack and to defend towns before 1500, and it became increasingly common thereafter; but, thanks to the rarity of roads and the ubiquity of bogs, heavy guns tended to be used only against coastal or riverside fortresses – at

Carrigafoyle in 1579, at Smerwick in 1580, at Dunluce in 1584, and most notably at Kinsale in 1601–2. Most of these strongholds boasted 'Italian-style' defensive systems with low, thick walls and quadrilateral bastions protected by artillery. The earl of Kildare built the first artillery fortress recorded in Ireland at Maynooth (County Kildare) in about 1533, defended by numerous heavy guns and a garrison of a hundred, of whom sixty were gunners. The first Gaelic Irish known to have used siege artillery were the O'Donnells, who took Sligo castle with a French gun in 1515.[6]

Some settlers in the Munster plantation in the later sixteenth century, at Mallow in County Cork, and at Castle Island and Castlemaine in County Kerry, also brought artillery and constructed gun platforms; while newcomers in Ulster after 1610 did the same – Sir Thomas Ridgeway at Augher (County Tyrone); Sir Oliver St John at Ballymore (County Armagh) and Sir Thomas Phillips at Limavady (County Londonderry) – but they formed a minority. Elsewhere, only a few plantation centres seem to have received artillery. Thus Richard Boyle, earl of Cork, provided his new town of Bandon (County Cork) with six pieces of ordnance for its defence in 1642,[7] and an early plan of the settlement showed bulwarks designed to carry artillery and, in an unusual design, the long curtain walls built on a shallow V-plan, rather than straight, so that the guns could be fired parallel to the walls without hitting the next bastion.[8] Derry, the largest new town in Ulster, must have been supplied with cannon in the early part of the century by the London Companies, although Lord Deputy Strafford caused their 'best and most useful ordnance be carryed away' before the rebellion (presumably for the campaign in Scotland in 1640).[9]

New-style defences were exceptional, however. By and large, artillery in Ireland before 1641 remained confined to the older cities, even though most lacked walls capable of carrying it. Shortly after the outbreak of the rebellion, for example, the Lords Justices complained that Dublin was in a 'very weak condition to make any defence' with 'the suburbs having no walls and the city walls . . . being made four hundred years ago are very much decayed and have no flankers on them, nor places for men to fight on'. If the city fell, moreover, they feared that Dublin castle would soon follow, 'having been built four hundred years ago, and having on it no modern fortification and the towers being very crazy and in danger of falling, especially when they come to be shaken with the shooting of the ordnance now mounted thereon'.[10] The best improvements to existing fortifications in Ireland were those added at Limerick in about 1590 (most of them still in place during the siege of 1651. See Figure 13). A late sixteenth-century plan indicates a star-shaped redoubt outside the city walls, at least seven new bastions, and a fortified bridgehead.[11] Elsewhere, improvements in fortifications mostly remained limited to gun platforms attached to older walls. However, a number of towns on the south and west coasts with a predominantly Catholic population (including Galway, Limerick, Cork and Waterford) received a citadel, which had the dual purpose of denying access to an invading force and dominating the town. Thus a drawing of the new stronghold at Waterford, dating from 1624–6, shows a gun platform with four cannon facing the settlement.[12] Likewise, Limerick castle was given a polygonal bastion facing the town with a platform for artillery.[13] A citadel could be a mixed blessing, though, because if an enemy occupied it, the adjoining town and port could more easily be bombarded and thus forced to surrender.[14] Finally, another military innovation occurred in late sixteenth-century Ireland: building artillery fortresses on estuaries leading to ports. Duncannon fort, a splendid structure commanding the east shore of the approach to Waterford harbour, built in 1587–9, by 1642 housed several 'great pieces of battery and other ordnance'.[15] The star-shaped fortification at Castle Park, dominating the entrance to Kinsale, completed in 1604, also possessed strong defences.

The proliferation of artillery fortresses placed a new premium on the ability to manufacture heavy guns locally, rather than depend on imports from abroad. However, cannon-founding, whether in iron or bronze, required large capital investment and highly skilled craftsmen, and cannon are known to have been cast in privately owned furnaces at only two sites in pre-war Ireland. Richard Boyle, earl of Cork, established the first at Cappoquin (County Waterford) in 1626.[16] His weapons were probably of medium calibre, since he placed them in the forts of Cork and Waterford to defend the Munster plantation against foreign invaders.[17] The second site lay at Ballinakill (County Laois) where ten (probably iron) three-pounder 'minions' were cast in 1633. The foundry belonged to Sir Thomas Ridgeway, but Lord

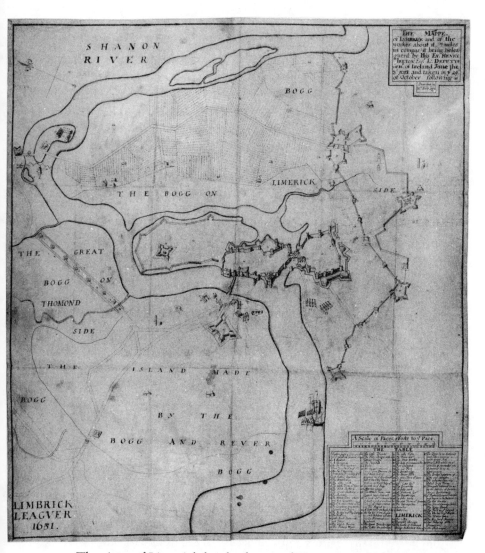

13 The siege of Limerick by the forces of Henry Ireton, 1651
Italian-style additions to the walls of Limerick built in the 1590s forced the
English army commanded by Lord Deputy Henry Ireton to undertake a full
blockade in 1651, constructing a circumvallation that ran for over four
miles (eleven kilometres), reinforced by numerous redoubts. Even so, the
powerful Irish garrison held out from 3 June to 29 October.

Deputy Wentworth (and probably others) owned shares.[18] The iron may have been mined locally, but until 1641 specialists from Liège in the Low Countries operated the foundry. Wentworth, after witnessing a successful trial of the minions at Kilmainham outside Dublin in 1633, praised them as 'the smoothest, and with the closest Grain I ever saw'.[19]

Foreign influence on the military affairs of pre-war Ireland was not confined to architecture and artisans: several foreign military treatises also entered the kingdom. Thus a copy of Gutiérrez de la Vega's *De re militari* was pillaged from a Spanish soldier killed at Smerwick in 1580, and formed the basis for Nicholas Lichefild's translation, published in London two years later; while the defeated commander of Kinsale, Don Juan del Aguila, presented Sir George Carew, lord president of Munster, with a book on fortifications.[20] A few catalogues of private libraries shed some light on the military books available in seventeenth-century Ireland. For instance the marquis of Ormond, who played a crucial military role in the Civil Wars, in 1684–5 owned several relevant early works, including the *Artillery Master* (no known place or date) and J. Perret, *Des fortifications et artifices d'architecture et perspective* (Paris, earliest edition, 1594).[21] The Irish 'master gunner', Samuel Molyneux, who served in Ormond's army and later in the parliamentary army, may have owned several other volumes, which survived in the library of his descendants, such as Nicholas Goldman's *La nouvelle fortification* (Leiden, Elsevier, 1645), and Mattias Dögen's *Architectura militaris moderna* (Amsterdam, Ludovic Elzevir, 1647).[22] Roger Boyle, Lord Broghill (and later earl of Orrery), author of an excellent military treatise that drew partially on his experiences during the wars in Ireland, probably owned Adam Freitag's *Architectura militaris nova et aucta* (first published at Leiden in 1630).[23] In addition, interested Irish readers enjoyed access to the military books, over 150 in number, published in England before 1641.[24] Nevertheless, only one Irishman is known to have brought out a military handbook during the period: Garret Barry, a kinsman of the earl of Barrymore, who served in the Spanish Army of Flanders and at the outbreak of the rebellion returned to Ireland, in 1634 published in Brussels *A Discourse of Military Discipline*, with fourteen tables and diagrams, whose third part bore the mysterious title 'Of Fire-wourckes of rare executiones by sea and lande, as alsoe of firtifasions [sic]'.[25]

Nevertheless, although the Military Revolution thus scarcely touched Ireland directly, many Irishmen came into contact with it in other ways. To begin with, countless Irish soldiers received training in the English army, sometimes abroad – in the Netherlands, France and Brittany – but above all with the English forces stationed in Ireland. According to Barnaby Riche in 1615, Irish had outnumbered English soldiers by a ratio of 3:1 during the Nine Years' War (1594–1603). With a sense of foreboding he wrote, 'I have never reade of any such polycy wher a rebellyous people, that wer every day redy to revolt from ther dutyes to ther soveraygnes, shuld be admytted to the exercse of chevallry: or shuld be Ineured in the practyse of armes . . .'[26] After the war, many of these soldiers left Ireland to join the continental armies, above all the Spanish Army of Flanders.

Some also doubted the wisdom of thus providing former rebels with expert military training, but the victorious English commander, Lord Mountjoy, offered the reassurance that 'it hath ever been seen that more than three parts of the four of these countrymen do never return, being once engaged in any such voyage'.[27] He was wrong: by 1640 the Army of Flanders included some 1300 Irish troops and senior officers, such as Owen Roe O'Neill and Thomas Preston, and both of these commanders, together with several hundred of their veteran compatriots, returned in 1641–2.[28] There they joined not only the thousand or so Irish veterans who simultaneously returned from service in France and Spain,[29] but also the Catholic troops mobilized and trained by Strafford in 1640 as the 'New Army' destined to serve the king in England. According to their commanding officer, these men were not 'poor stinking rascally sneaks[;] thes are brave gallant fellows . . . there cloaths are better, theire persons [are] better and there mettell is better'. He later added: 'I doe not care whoe sees them . . . noe prince in the Christian world hath . . . better men, nor more orderly.'[30] Many of them joined the rebellion and formed the backbone of the confederate armies. To make matters worse, the Dublin government, still trusting the Old English and trying to contain the rebellion, sent out thousands of arms to these Catholic landowners in Leinster. Since many of them later joined the rebellion, most of the weapons fell into enemy hands.[31] Equally serious, from the government's point of view, Irish society on the eve of the rebellion was considerably less militarized than ever before. In the nine counties of Ulster, for example, whereas in 1619 one settler in eight owned a musket, only one in thirty-three did so in 1630 – a mere 700 among over 13,000 adult males; whilst in 1631 Carrickfergus and Derry boasted only twenty muskets apiece for their defence. Throughout the country, landowners abandoned fortified castles in favour of stately manor houses. As a Kerry gentleman, forced by the events of October 1641 to seek refuge in the earl of Cork's stronghold, lamented: 'My house I built for peace, having more windows than walls.'[32]

Yet within a few months several relatively well equipped armies, trained and commanded by professionals with continental experience, clearly outclassed the English forces ranged against them. Thus in November 1641, the English defenders of Drogheda and Dublin sallied forth to defeat the Ulster Catholics but they suffered, according to a later account, from a 'fatal conjuncture of rawe men, young officers and the first occasion'. Their commander attempted to execute the infantry manoeuvre known as the countermarch, standard in continental warfare, whereby the first rank of musketeers fired and withdrew to the back to reload while subsequent ranks fired in turn. The soldiers, however, 'upon the unseasonable word of *countermarch* given out by the officer' became confused, and the Catholics rushed 'in with violence upon those who were put in doubt which way they were to turne their faces, [and] forced the foote to cast away their armes' and flee. Eventually the Irish also surpassed the Scots: at the battle of Benburb in 1646 the confederate Army of Ulster, under Spanish-trained commanders, used the defensive techniques perfected by Habsburg troops to defeat a Scottish force, under Swedish-trained leaders, using the offensive tactics pioneered by Gustavus Adolphus.[33]

At first, to be sure, the rebels lacked artillery; but this defect was partially remedied when they captured several English strongholds. For example, at Newry (County Down) they acquired powder and three heavy guns, which they immediately used to attack Lisburn (County Antrim) in late November 1641. They 'apeared drawn up in Batalia . . . and sent out two devisions, of about six or seaven hundr[ed men] apeece, to compass the Towne, and placed their field-peeces on the high-way to it'.[34] In the event the Irish failed, and the newly acquired weapons lay abandoned in a bog hole; but they still had in

Newry 'a great Iron Battering peece . . . which was left in an old Turret in the towne, throwne off the carriages'.[35] This suggests that the Irish may not yet have possessed the expertise to handle such a gun (or at least to fix it to a gun carriage), but the returning veterans soon provided the missing knowledge. For instance, at the siege of Limerick in June 1642, the Irish under Colonel Garret Barry (see above) captured 'three pieces of ordnance, whereof one of them weighted neer 8000 weight [8 cwt, 4000 kg] mounted', a 'battering piece of such large dimensions, that it took twenty-five oxen to remove it' and fired a 15kg shot.[36] It must have been either a whole or a demi-cannon. Some foresaw that 'with the advantage of his Majesty's ordnance' the rebels 'would fall upon such holds and castles as were then possessed by the English, both in Munster and this county of Clare . . .', and indeed the rebels soon brought a demi-cannon by water and took Askeaton castle 'and all the castles and houlds that were invested by the English' in the county of Limerick. Most places were, not besieged at all but instead surrendered in advance because they could not have withstood battery.[37]

An early, though unconfirmed, reference to confederate cannon-founding occurred in 1642, when news reached Irish supporters on the continent that 'Colonel Richard Plunquet [Plunkett] is at the Earl of Fingall's house making powder and casting artillery'.[38] This could have been either at Fingall's house at Virginia (County Cavan) or, more likely, at Killeen (County Meath). Scattered references also exist to the manufacture of cannon in the midlands. For instance, a smith at Athboy (County Meath), not far from Killeen, is said to have manufactured for the Irish 'a great piece of ordnance' from 140 pots and pans collected in the locality. Scarcely surprisingly, the gun burst when discharged against the walls of Geashill (County Offaly) in 1641. However, another piece of Irish manufacture (called a 'Master-Piece') was effectively employed at the siege of Castle Coote (County Roscommon).[39] Moreover, the Irish were able to operate ironworks at Artully (near Kenmare, County Kerry) around 1645, and at Lissan (County Tyrone), where existing works seized by Niall O'Quinn in 1641 subsequently produced pike heads for the Irish Army of Ulster.[40]

The Irish also augmented their stock of artillery with cannon recovered from ships. For example, at the end of 1642, a French vessel unable to enter the Shannon and blockaded by a parliamentary flotilla landed three pieces of ordnance, sank two ships and recovered eight cannon from them. Shipwrecks provided other opportunities to retrieve artillery: in 1642 a Dutch East Indiaman foundered in foul weather at Dungarvan (County Waterford) and yielded five pieces of ordnance; the *Hopewell*, cast away off Wexford while sailing from London to Dublin, produced five more.[41]

Finally, munitions also arrived intermittently from abroad. One ship, probably sent over from Spanish Flanders and almost captured in October 1642, arrived safely in Wexford with 'two hundred barrels of powder, some muskets, and three pieces of bronze [artillery]' with 'balls of iron'. A continental supporter wrote that these pieces 'will serve to batter the castles in which the heretics make their quarters and defence, and are field pieces as neat as have been seen . . .'[42] At Easter 1643, more ships arrived with ammunition, hand weapons and artillery, paid for by Spain.[43] This, or another shipment, included two iron twenty-four-pounders and a Spanish iron mortar.[44] A further consignment of four demi-cannon from Spain is mentioned in 1648.[45] By then, some towns had assembled considerable arsenals: Wexford, a major confederate port, together with its fort, contained at the time of its surrender to Cromwell in 1649 'near a hundred cannon'.[46]

Most of this information, however, comes from Leinster. The position of the confederate Army of Ulster was very different. A report in October 1642 lamented Owen Roe O'Neill's shortage of artillery in Ulster, noting that if he were to have 'but two pieces of battery and four or five field pieces with store of arms, he would clear all Connaught and Ulster in three months, leaving never a Puritan, English or Scotch, in either Province'.[47] Lacking a major port to which supplies could be directed, Owen Roe probably possessed little or no artillery until, four years later, he captured six to nine pieces, perhaps two of them siege cannon, from the Scots at the battle of Benburb (County Tyrone) in 1646.[48]

Elsewhere armies campaigned, almost certainly for the first time in Ireland, with their own artillery trains. A confederate train in Leinster was first noted in 1643, and by 1646 it consisted of a brass cannon, a brass culverin, two quarter-cannon, carriages and a sleigh.[49] When Thomas Preston's army was defeated at Dungan's Hill in 1647, Colonel

Michael Jones captured 'four demiculverins, each carrying a twelve-pound (5kg) bullet, and 64 fair oxen attending the train', which were added to Jones's seven cannon.[50] On the Protestant side, the outbreak of the first English Civil War prevented the dispatch in August 1642 of artillery intended for the English army in Ireland.[51] However, shortly afterwards a train for the Scottish forces landed in the north with ninety-six officers and artificers (up to that point, the Scots had to make do with a small cannon taken from Carrickfergus castle).[52] By February 1643 the Scots artillery possessed six 'battering pieces', while Ormond had seven.[53] By contrast, the train brought to Ireland by Cromwell contained eleven siege guns and twelve field pieces, which both in magnitude and firepower exceeded all the others operating in Ireland combined![54]

Cromwell also enjoyed far better logistical support. Although in 1647 Owen Roe O'Neill managed to lead his army over the Curlew mountains from Boyle to Sligo because 'his pioneers were at work five or six weeks through Rockey mountains to make way for his Guns',[55] their achievement paled in comparison with the pontoon bridge built by Cromwell's engineers across the river Barrow near New Ross, which according to a writer of the time was 'a stupendious worke' and 'a wonder to all men, and understood by none'.[56] Nevertheless, even Cromwell strove to transport his artillery as much as possible by water: for the 1649 campaign he shipped his battery from Dublin first to Drogheda and then to Wexford.[57]

Access to a seaport was also essential for landing, storage and transfer of supplies; as a safe haven for privateering and other shipping; as winter and training quarters for a garrison; and as the point of departure and return for campaigns to dominate the hinterland. The Irish therefore stood at a serious disadvantage, for in Ulster they lacked any major port (such as Derry or Carrickfergus); in Leinster they never held Dublin, and lost Dundalk and Carlingford; and in the south they also failed to obtain a permanent foothold at Cork, Kinsale, Youghal or Bandon, although for much of the Civil War they held Waterford, Wexford, Limerick and Galway. However, even these key harbours required constant protection from parliamentarian ships and this could only be accomplished effectively in three ways. First, confederate ships could patrol the mouth of the harbour and keep it open for sorties by privateers and merchantmen loyal to their cause. Second, a bulwark capable of dominating the approaches with its artillery could be built. Thus, at Rosslare Point near Wexford harbour, a fort equipped with about seven 'great' guns was built under the supervision of Captain Antonio Vanderipen from Spanish Flanders.[58] Finally, a chain could be stretched from one bank of the harbour to the other in order to prevent ships from getting through, as at Galway in 1643 (although after a blockade of seven weeks the citadel, St Augustine's fort, depleted of supplies, capitulated).[59] Likewise, during the siege of Drogheda in 1642, Sir Phelim O'Neill used a chain to close off the river, but it was later rammed by an incoming ship and broke. Eventually, the besiegers were forced to withdraw.[60]

Artillery fortresses proliferated in Ireland only after the war began. The largest defensive earthworks were made around Dublin: the Down Survey (Figure 14) shows earthen ramparts encircling most of the suburbs to the south and north of the city, reinforced by at least eighteen bastions positioned at regular intervals. A description of these fortifications, dating from 1646, speaks of half-moons before the gates, palisades to strengthen the earthworks, and the destruction of houses outside of the walls to prevent the enemy from taking shelter.[61] Perhaps fortunately, Dublin never underwent a full siege. Soon after the beginning of the rebellion, the Boyle family and its associates in Munster reinforced several towns, including an entrenchment and four gates, probably wooden, at Tallow (County Waterford) in 1643 and improved the town walls of Youghal (County Cork) in 1644.[62] In Leinster, Duncannon fort (County Wexford) received 'brave rampiers' in 1645 under the direction of General Thomas Preston.[63] Pierce Fitzgerald, commissary-general of the confederate horse, built a full bastioned fort (see Figure 15) with a water-filled moat and various earthworks around nearby villages, at Ballyshannon (County Kildare),[64] while Lieutenant-Colonel Walter Cruise's fort at Ardlonan, four miles from Kells (County Meath), was deemed by the New Model Army 'a verie strong place haveing 3 walls within one another, two of them beinge of earth the 3[r]d of stone, all regularly fortified'.[65]

A few Ulster towns also received new defences. At Antrim, in 1642 men and women made 'a Ditch of about 8 feet broad without any Breastwork only the Flankers and Rounds . . .' The appearance of

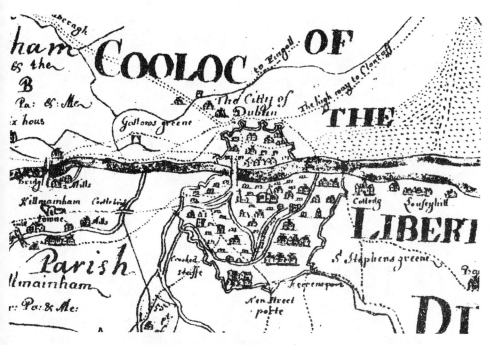

14 The fortifications of Dublin according to the Down Survey, 1650s
After England's military conquest of Ireland in 1649–51, surveyors led by
William Petty (1623–87) measured and mapped the island. According to
John Aubrey's *Brief Lives*, Petty 'employed for the geometrical part . . .
ordinary fellows, some (perhaps) foot-soldiers, that circumambulated with
their box and needles, not knowing what they did, which Sir William knew
right well how to make use of'. Their work, known as the 'Down Survey',
showed roads and walls as well as rivers and settlements. They recorded the
earthen ramparts around Dublin, to the north and south of the river Liffey,
with Trinity College and St Stephen's Green to the east remaining outside.

4000 Irish, however, interrupted the works and the town and its outer
defences were assaulted and burnt in 1649 by the Scots (although they
were unable to destroy 'the Mount and Castle . . . being a place that is
not for a Running party to attack').[66] At Belfast, a bastioned enceinte
was built in 1643, for which Lord Chichester was granted £1000: 'He
planted cannon in the works, and did begin to cut off the highway that
enters Carrickfergus port.' Nevertheless the town was surprised twice,
in 1644 and 1648, indicating the limitations of the improvements.[67]

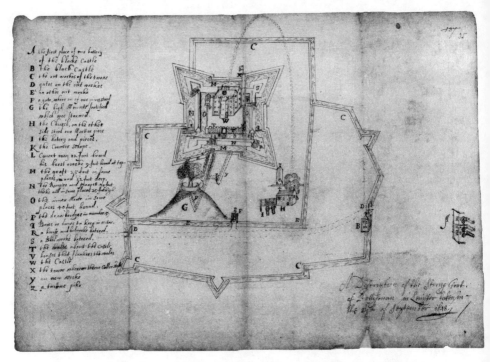

15 The siege of Ballyshannon (County Kildare), 1648

The Fitzgerald family built fortifications of steadily greater sophistication at Ballyshannon, west of Dublin: walls with a few bastions around the town (C); a 'high mounde fortified' (G), a quadrilateral artillery fortress with a moat ('25 foot in some places and 12 feet deep': M), an inner moat ('in some places 40 foot broad': O), and finally the castle (W). Nevertheless, in September 1648, bombardment by siege guns (A, F and I) and a mortar (H, also showing the trajectory of the shells) finally forced its surrender.

The fortifications erected at Limerick in the 1590s received considerable additions during the 1640s, leading the Frenchman La Boullaye-Le-Gouz in 1644 to call it, probably correctly, 'the strongest fortress in Ireland', while Dean Massari wrote a year later that 'it is almost impregnable, being surrounded with a triple wall, the three walls in turn being protected by water'.[68]

Limerick was one of the record number of towns besieged by Cromwell's forces between 1649 and 1652. They rarely used circumvallation, which was time-consuming and labour-intensive, preferring instead a shock approach, by first erecting batteries and bombarding weak segments of town walls or adjacent structures, followed by a general assault. At both Drogheda and Wexford, Cromwell first identified a tall structure near the town wall (a church in Drogheda, a castle at Wexford), and then concentrated on seizing that structure. This gave his soldiers some protection against counterattack and a high vantage point from which to advance upon the town itself. In both cities this strategy proved decisive. Limerick, however, provided a far more serious challenge. In 1651, Cromwell's son-in-law and successor, Henry Ireton, erected an extensive circumvallation (see Figure 13, page 175). Two major forts were constructed (Fort Cromwell and Fort Ireton), forming part of the chain of circumvallation, and a battery of 28 guns and 4 mortar pieces (one of which is said to have thrown a projectile weighing two hundredweight (100 kg)) arrived by sea. Ranged against them, behind the formidable defences, stood experienced troops and at least 34 guns, including two demi-cannons. Eventually a breach was made at a point where the Irish had not reinforced the town wall, yet even Limerick might have held out longer but for treachery within the garrison.[69]

A characteristic feature of Irish warfare during the 1640s was the interdependence of cities and nearby castles. Castles, especially those situated at strategic points such as bridges or fords across rivers, could both safeguard access to the town and give the alarm when enemy forces approached. A location on a river could also prove of economic importance, because one or more mills might be able to operate under the protection of the castle and thus provide much-needed corn, which often could not be ground in the city itself. For example, in 1642, the defenders of Kinsale garrisoned Arcloyne castle and its mill, about one mile outside of the town, 'which lyeth under command of the Castle, and hope we shall keepe it; we had not the use of any Mill these three weeks till now, which caused us (though we have store of Corne) to want [i.e., lack] bread'.[70]

The interdependence of a town and its nearby castles became evident when the town surrendered to the enemy. Surrounding strongholds toppled like packs of cards because, besides the loss of support from the centre, the large forces mobilized to capture a town usually threatened to engulf all the small garrisons in their path.[71] Even before the town fell, nearby fortifications could also prove a liability when seized by an enemy and it was therefore common for the defenders of an endangered town to raze castles in the immediate vicinity. For instance, as the Irish approached Drogheda in 1642, the earl of Ormond (who did not leave Dublin) ordered its garrison to lay waste neighbouring strongholds and villages.[72] Surrounding castles might also be destroyed after a siege was raised, either to improve overall defensive capacity or to take revenge on the gentry who had aided the besiegers.[73] However, to hold down territory it was necessary to occupy all available fortifications. Thus even after the Cromwellians had overrun the country, they felt obliged to maintain a profusion of garrisons: one contemporary source listed 350 of them by early 1652 and estimated that another hundred were still required for total security.[74]

The need to occupy so many strongholds caused many complications. First, with the large number of troops dispersed in garrisons, it became impossible to concentrate an effective field army; second, with some exceptions, since most castles were small, their ability to hold out in the face of an attack remained limited; third, the wide distribution of fortifications often strained the supply network to excess. These drawbacks, however, had to be set against major strategic advantages. Possession of a network of fortified points came in useful when campaigns ended, since most of the armies operating in Ireland lacked large fortified bases for winter quarters. Moreover, they also enabled the occupants to plant corn and keep cattle in the adjoining countryside for their own upkeep, and to raise contributions, thus reducing their dependence on supplies of food from central depots (although they remained heavily dependent on them for ammunition).[75] In this respect, however, Ireland resembled the continent. There too, despite exposure to the Military Revolution for over a century, strategy in most theatres of war continued to revolve around the capture of major fortresses and their penumbra of strongpoints; garrisons normally tied down one-half, if not more, of each state's armed forces (even in wartime); and, almost everywhere, sieges outnumbered battles.

It is true that some areas of Ireland remained totally unaffected by military innovation. Even in 1652, after all major confederate forces had surrendered, English officials lamented the existence of numerous 'crannogs':

vaste great boggs in the middest of which there are firme woody grounds like islands, into which they have passes or casewayes through the boggs where noe more then one horse can goe a breast, which passes they can easily mainteine, or suddainely break up soe as noe horse can approach them, and being inured to live in cabbins and to wade through those boggs they can fetch prey from any part of the countrey to releive themselves and prosecute their designes which are to robb and burne those places that yeild our forces subsistance.

The officials explained that the 'fastnesses being unpassable for horse, and into which foote cannot goe without some experience and hardship to wade in water and tread the bogg . . . Their fastenesses are better to them in point of strength then walled towns.'[76] Yet such 'no go' areas became less numerous than ever before in Irish history, thanks to the ability of pioneers to drive roads and bridges through previously impassable country, opening up new areas to artillery and exposing to destruction strongholds that had formerly been invulnerable. Only the relative scarcity of heavy-calibre weapons before 1649 allowed so many fortifications constructed before the gunpowder revolution to retain a military role.[77]

The 'modern' defences of Ireland required, and received, modern techniques of siegecraft, however: the blockade of Limerick, although the largest, was far from unique. After September 1642 at Castle Forbes (County Longford), the Irish dug many trenches,[78] while at Castle Coote (County Roscommon) in the next year the engineer St Loo, 'an experienced Low-Country soldier', made a 'regular circum-vallation about the castle; yet the garrison so nobly attacked each redoubt, as greatly disappointed the besiegers'.[79] When Thomas Preston besieged Duncannon fort (County Wexford) in 1645, he 'made trenches a farr off, and by degree both daie and night, by triangle and quadrangle worke, came a pistol shott neere the fort . . .' (Figure 16). According to a contemporary writer it was 'the verie best siedge that was yett in Ireland . . . the ordinance and bombs going very thicke',

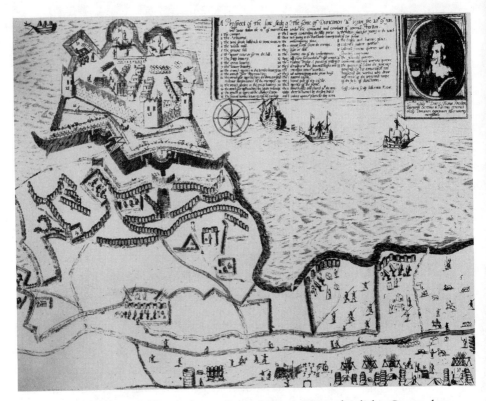

16 The siege of Duncannon fort (County Waterford) by General
Thomas Preston, 1645

Duncannon fort, built by English engineers in the 1580s, commanded access
to the port of Waterford and when it declared for the English Parliament
early in 1645, the Irish confederate council determined on its capture.
Thomas Preston, a veteran of the Low Countries' Wars, began a full siege on
30 January and, by virtue of heavy battery and the careful advance of
trenches, forced its surrender two months later. This print, published at
Kilkenny, was based on the map drawn by Preston's engineer.

and an engraving shows that Preston commanded seventeen guns and
two mortars.[80] At other sieges the Irish dug mines and countermines
(as at Limerick in 1642 and at Birr the following year). They also used
'sows', an apparatus pushed against the walls to shield the miners
attempting to bring down the structure, at the sieges of Ballyally
castle (County Clare), Mallow (County Cork), Rochestown (County

Tipperary), and Tralee castle (where three sows were used).[81] In the case of the great sow used at Ballyally castle in 1641, the structure was:

35 feet long and 9 feet broad; it was made upon four wheels made of whole lumber, bound about with hoops of iron; the axle-trees whereon she ran were great round bars of iron, the beams she was built on being timber. They had cross beams within, to work with their leavers to forcer along as they pleased to guide her. The hinder part of the sow was left open for their men to go in and out at. The forepart of the sow had 4 doors, 2 in the roof, and 2 in the lower part which did hang upon great iron hooks, but were not to open till they came close to the wall of the castle, where they intended to work through the castle with their tools they had provided. The roof of the sow was built like the roof of a house with a very steep ridge; the lower part as the walls of a house. She was double planked with many great oaken planks, and driven very thick with five stroke nails, which nails cost £5, being intended for a house of correction which should have been built at Ennis. This sow was likewise covered over with two rows of hides, and two rows of sheepskins; so that no musket bullet or steel arrow could pierce it, of which trial was often made.[82]

However, we know of no case in which sows proved effective in capturing the castles.[83]

The Irish proved rather more successful in bringing their conduct of the war at sea up to continental standards. Although Randal MacDonnell, marquis of Antrim, still contemplated using galleys to convey his troops to Scotland in 1638, as Gaelic chieftains had always done, in 1645 he invested in a pair of Dunkirk frigates, the finest light warships to be found anywhere in the Western world. They did not sail alone. In July 1642 a 200-ton, eighteen-gun Dunkirk frigate brought over Owen Roe O'Neill and his regiment from Flanders, and by September the Lords Justices reported from Dublin that 'seven or eight ships more, some of them carrying twenty-four pieces of ordnance, are come ... in aid of the rebels'.[84] Between December 1642 and February 1643 confederate agents in the Spanish Netherlands issued at least twenty letters of marque to foreign frigates willing to protect the Irish coast, and keep open the sea lanes to the continent, in return for freedom to capture all enemies of the 'Catholic cause'. By the end of 1642 the Venetian ambassador in London estimated that the confederate fleet consisted of '30 well-armed ships at sea', and for most of the 1640s the confederate navy probably numbered between forty and fifty warships.[85] About half of the crews appear to have been Irish, trained by their Flemish colleagues to the same peak of professional ferocity that in 1649 earned Wexford, one of their principal bases, the epithet of 'the Dunkirk of Ireland, and a place only famous for being infamous'.[86] The *recorded* prizes of the Irish privateers between 1642 and 1650 totalled only 250, but one informed contemporary thought that 'these privateers took over a six year period, from the parliamentary ships of all three kingdoms, 1900 vessels and 1500 captives . . . and this does not include those ships which had been sunk in various encounters'.[87] This record, if true, would have made the Irish privateers more successful than either their English or Flemish counterparts. Small wonder that, in 1649, Prince Rupert led the Royal Navy to southern Ireland in an attempt to join forces with the most successful fleet in his uncle's service: fortunately for Cromwell, Admiral Blake cleared them from Kinsale before they began to jeopardize his lifeline across the Irish Sea to London.

The 'reception' of the Military Revolution in England offers an instructive comparison. As in Ireland, few places possessed modern fortifications in 1642; moreover, most of these lay on the coast, whereas most of the fighting during the Civil War took place inland. Even London only acquired full bastioned defences, initially of earth, after the war began. Few other places of strategic significance constructed a full circuit of Italian-style ramparts during the 1640s: instead, most remained enclosed by outdated medieval walls, occasionally reinforced with a few 'modern' outworks, and wholly susceptible to bombardment. It is therefore strange to find that relatively few places were in fact reduced by artillery until 1645. The explanation, however, is simple: given the highly unsettled state of most of the kingdom during the early war years, with powerful detachments from both sides roaming the roads, it was extremely hazardous to convey a siege train around the country. One risked losing it (as Parliament did at Lostwithiel in 1644, forfeiting forty heavy guns to the king). Just as in Ireland, most towns were therefore taken by storm with no preliminary battery, while the few remaining strongholds suffered bombardment from only a handful of big guns at any one time.[88] Only after their victory at Naseby in June 1645 could the New Model Army move its siege train around at will, and even so its first full-dress siege, involving a full circumvallation and a main field army, did not take place until 1648 (against Colchester). Likewise many battles of the English Civil War, including the decisive engagements at Naseby and Preston (1648), involved no action by field artillery (indeed, at Preston, neither side brought any to the battle); while at other times, field guns were used effectively only to defend entrenched positions against frontal attack.

Again, as in Ireland, the warring parties in England normally controlled territory through mutually dependent systems of large and small garrisons, usually a single major fortress with a network of smaller ones, stretching in a radius of up to thirty miles (50km), both to protect the parent stronghold from blockade and to preserve recruiting and supply grounds. The fall of the main fortification or the defeat of the regionally dominant field army normally caused the surrender of the outlying garrisons, since their military value had ended: between April 1645 and August 1646 the New Model Army forced the surrender of forty-seven strongholds.[89] Finally, although the English navy possessed more and better capital ships than the confederates, it nevertheless proved incapable of keeping the ports of its Irish allies permanently open or of preventing enemy privateers from getting out. In short, Ireland's adjustment during the 1640s to the new ways of warfare pioneered on the European continent proved to be no less rapid and no less impressive than that of England. Even Protestant opponents of the confederation like Sir Arthur Annesley and Sir William Parsons had to admit in December 1646 that '[the Irish now] have their men in a better order of war and better commanded by captains of experience and practice of warr then ever they were since the conquest and these much imboldened by late successes as well in the field as fortresses. They are abundantly stored with armes and munition.'[90] Ireland's eventual defeat and subjugation by England stemmed essentially from political, not military, factors.

8

The importance of the defensive technique normally known as the 'Italian' or 'modern style' first struck me in 1971, when I stood in the ditch surrounding the walls of Berwick-upon-Tweed. Built in the 1560s to defend an English enclave in Scotland, its five huge bastions have survived virtually intact. As I gazed at the flanking embrasures from which artillery would have shot down anyone assaulting the walls, I saw just how the bastion had transformed the balance between defence and offence in warfare. The Army of Flanders and the Spanish Road *began with a discussion of how the 'artillery fortress' (to use the term later popularized by John Lynn) helped to thwart Spain's efforts to suppress the Dutch Revolt, and I included a photograph of the Berwick bastion taken from the spot where I had stood.*

I followed up the theme in The Military Revolution: Military Technology and the Rise of the West, 1500–1800 *(Cambridge, 1988) and made two new claims for the artillery fortress: that the need to blockade it – rather than storm it – directly caused an increase in army size within Europe, and that the new defensive system played a crucial role in European expansion elsewhere. Many disputed the first of my claims, and I responded in the Afterword of the revised edition of the book; but the second claim passed unchallenged. Nevertheless, it seemed to me that a stronger case could be made and, in 1994, James D. Tracy, director of the Center for Early Modern History at the University of Minnesota, offered me a chance to do so when he asked me to speak on the military applications of walls at a conference on 'City walls: form, function and meaning'.*

The Center's conferences bring in scholars from a wide range of disciplines to interact with the excellent University of Minnesota faculty, and discussions after the presentations are always vigorous.

They are also recorded and transcribed, so that shortly after the event each author receives a detailed account of the deadly questions received and the evasive answers offered, with an invitation to improve the paper in readiness for publication. The transcript of the debate following 'my' panel, with four speakers, covered nine pages! I revised my paper in the light of these comments, and of suggestions from others who either heard or read it, but retained the thesis that the artillery fortress played a vital role in the Europeans' ability, first, to hold and, later, to expand their territory around the world.

Several members of the audience pointed out another side to this argument, however: fortified enclaves also attract attack. *Thus the Europeans' strongholds overseas presented a target that any successful challenger had to destroy in order to push the invaders back into the sea. Throughout the early modern period this attraction proved fatal for non-Europeans: the protracted sieges bled armies to death. For example, Sultan Iskandar Muda of Acheh (Sumatra) spent nine years building up his power ready to besiege Portuguese Malacca. In 1629 he led almost 250 ships and perhaps 20,000 men across the straits and, although they raised Western-style siegeworks ('not even the Romans could have made such works stronger or more quickly', according to one of the defenders), the arrival of a relief fleet caused disaster. The Portuguese captured almost all the sultan's fleet and artillery, and only a few of his troops escaped. For the rest of his reign, Iskandar Muda pursued pacific policies.[1]*

Western successes like this depended on two advantages, however: first, keeping the sea-lanes open, so that reinforcements could always get through; and, second, ensuring that improvements in armaments did not imperil a formerly impregnable site. In the mid-twentieth century, both these safeguards failed. At Singapore in 1942, a fortress that had long been unassailable surrendered after the destruction of the warships assigned to keep its sea approaches open. Elsewhere in the Far East, Japanese aerial bombardment created new vulnerability. Although, as with successful surprise attacks elsewhere, an element of complacency on the part of the vanquished played its part (page 67 above), the fatal weakness lay in the West's reliance on enclaves that could, by definition, become isolated and overwhelmed.

The Artillery Fortress as an Engine of European Overseas Expansion, 1480–1750

Historians used to explain the 'rise of the West' in one of two ways: either in terms of some 'moral superiority' or 'manifest destiny' that justified the white man's efforts to seek and retain world domination, or in terms of a presumed advantage of European commercial techniques and organization over all competitors, of joint stock over atomized capital, of companies over 'peddlers', of seamen over landsmen. But subsequent developments have largely discredited the first of these views: the humiliating defeat and temporary collapse of European power in Asia in the mid-twentieth century quickly eroded the idea of white 'moral superiority', while the growth of secular thought rendered Christian triumphalism unfashionable in most quarters. The second 'explanation', however, does retain some value. Although modern research has revealed that 'native' Asian and African economic practices in the sixteenth century were superior to those of contemporary Europe, permanent corporate structures, found only in the West, from the Casa di San Giorgio of twelfth-century Genoa to the various East India companies and public banks of the seventeenth-century Atlantic states, nevertheless did confer a continuity and longevity far greater than that of any non-European merchant consortium.[2]

And yet that advantage reflects social organization as well as business practice. It constitutes but one manifestation of the remarkable ability of relatively small groups of Europeans to function effectively, even when somewhat divided, in the interests of the same general goals. In fact, this 'economy of effort' – from the Crusaders through Cortés and Pizarro, Albuquerque and Coen, to Clive and Cornwallis – appeared most clearly and most decisively in the military and diplomatic spheres, for the West made all its major territorial gains with amazingly small resources.[3] Before 1800, scarcely any triumphs came through superior numbers; rather they arose through a combination, in the terse phrase of Anthony Reid, of 'superior firepower, particularly on shipboard, and fortresses, which they could make virtually impregnable; and [local] allies'.[4] These three related aspects of the efficient use of violence to acquire and maintain supremacy constitute, in effect, a new paradigm for the 'rise of the West': the military explanation.[5]

But what was the precise role of 'fortresses' within this new paradigm? According to Lynn White, doyen of historians of European technology, writing in 1967:

The early sixteenth century in Europe witnessed two revolutions, both of which altered habits of the previous thousand years and each of which, by the later 1500s, had crystallized into patterns that remained nearly intact until the end of the nineteenth century. One was the Protestant Reformation and the defensive response to it in the regions still loyal to Rome. The other was a sudden and profound change in military technology, the chief element of which was the development of light, highly mobile cannon that shot iron balls in fairly flat trajectories. Since the older style of fortifications crumbled before such devices, an entirely new, and enormously costly, apparatus of defense was required. It would be hard to decide which of these simultaneous revolutions had the greater impact on European life, or the most lasting effects.[6]

Appreciation of the value of the new 'apparatus of defense', commonly referred to as the artillery fortress, did not remain confined to Europe. In September 1584, for example, the devout but pragmatic Matteo Ricci in China wrote scathingly of the pusillanimity of his hosts:

Because when two or three Japanese warships come and land on the coast of China, they burn their boats and capture villages and even large cities, putting everything to the torch and sack, without anyone offering resistance . . . It is true that the Chinese have many fortresses, and the towns all have their walls with which to resist the fury of the pirates; but the walls are not of geometric design [i.e., they lacked bastions] nor do they have traverses or moats.[7]

Ricci perceived the absence of artillery fortresses, at least in the coastal areas, as a critical weakness in China's military effectiveness which, he felt, might facilitate Western conquest and (his real objective) the

Christianization of East Asia. Lacking bastions, the Ming empire, he believed, for all its apparent strength might crumble in the face of modest European pressure.[8]

The chronology of the evolution of the artillery fortress in Europe is now relatively clear. Although cannon first appeared in the West in the 1320s, they do not seem to have been used to batter down walls before the 1370s, and the practice remained fairly rare until the 1420s.[9] Nevertheless, from the late fourteenth century onwards, a number of important innovations increased the capacity of fortifications to withstand gunpowder bombardment: first, the addition of guns and gun ports for offensive use as a counterbattery; then, a variety of new structural designs such as 'countersinking' the fort, to minimize the damage done by incoming fire; and later, the introduction of polygonal defensive designs to maximize the opportunities for outgoing fire. But such innovations proved the exception; in most areas the traditional 'vertical system' remained the principal means of defence even though, for a century after 1430, whenever good siege artillery bombarded vertical walls, the outcome was predictable.[10] The verdict of Andreas Bernaldez on the conquest of Granada in the 1480s – 'Great towns, which once would have held out a year against all foes but hunger, now fell within a month' – was echoed by Niccolo Machiavelli concerning the French invasion of Italy of the 1490s: 'No walls exist, however thick, that artillery cannot destroy in a few days.'[11]

In the 1520s, however, this ceased to be true. Thanks to its low, thick walls, broad moats and geometrical bastions, the 'artillery fortress' defied bombardment (see Figure 17). In a report commissioned by the government of Florence in 1526, Machiavelli himself perceived three distinct ways of turning a town into an artillery fortress. Two involved starting from scratch: tearing down the existing walls and either building a new defensive system beyond them, so as to include the suburbs and all points (such as neighbouring high ground) from which an enemy might threaten; or else building a smaller circuit than before, abandoning (and levelling) all exterior areas deemed to be indefensible. However, both of these methods involved substantial expense: not only the money to build the fortress itself, but also high social costs, because the suburbs scheduled for demolition just beyond the medieval walls often contained important buildings such as hos-

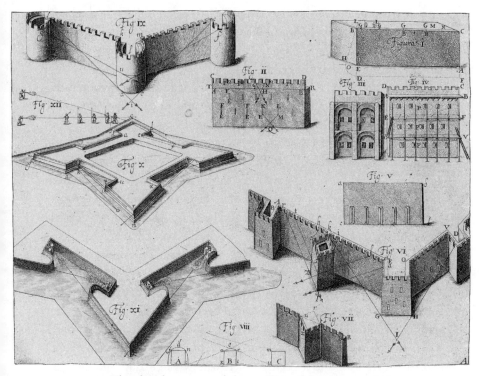

17 The development of the artillery fortress to 1648

Matthias Dögen, a German military theorist, showed in a single picture the evolution of European poliorcetics from the high walls of the Roman and medieval periods, through the round towers of the Renaissance, to the geometric designs pioneered in Italy in the sixteenth century. European engineers soon spread this new design throughout the world.

pitals, religious houses and industrial plants (mills and furnaces). Machiavelli's report of 1526 therefore considered a third technique of installing modern defences which, although less permanent than the others, proved both far quicker and far cheaper: a drastic modification of the existing fortifications, reducing the height and increasing the depth of the existing walls, redesigning the towers and gateways into bastions, and creating an escarpment to give a proper field of fire. Of course earthen ramparts, when unprotected by brick and stone, would not last long (contemporary estimates ranged from four years, with minimal maintenance, up to ten) before the weather eroded them. But they proved relatively fast and cheap to erect; they could absorb incoming fire effectively, and, with enough determined defenders (as at Metz in 1552 or at Haarlem in 1572–3), they could defy even the largest and best-led armies of the day.[12]

By then, however, the new bastioned fortifications had proliferated. Small European states such as Mantua, Monferrat, Lucca and Geneva concentrated on building a single 'impregnable' super-fortress, capable of holding out almost indefinitely, while larger polities invested not in one but in many artillery fortresses in order to create a layered defence-in-depth.[13] Thus, soon after they gained control of the duchy of Milan in the 1530s, the Habsburgs began a comprehensive pro-gramme of fortifications: Cremona and Lodi against Venice in the east; Alessandria and Novara against Savoy in the west; Pavia and, above all, Milan itself as a strategic reserve.[14] Meanwhile, two similar systems evolved in the Low Countries. Already by 1572, when the Dutch Revolt began, 12 Netherlands towns had been turned into artillery fortresses and the walls of 18 more had been partly rebuilt in the Italian style – a total of 27 miles (43km) of new walls. By 1648, however, when the Revolt ended, the Spanish Netherlands alone boasted 28 artillery fortresses and a further 27 towns with partially modernized walls; while the provinces of Holland and Utrecht in the Dutch Repub-lic, which, in 1572 had possessed only one artillery fortress and three more towns with one or two bastions, by 1648 had 13 of the former and 14 of the latter.[15]

Wherever they appeared in Europe, Italian-style fortifications domi-nated the conduct of warfare. As John Cruso, an English military writer, observed in 1632, 'The actions of the modern warres consist chiefly in sieges, assaults, sallies, skirmishes etc., and so affoard but few set battels.' According to Roger Boyle, Lord Orrery, in 1677, 'Battells do not now decide national quarrels, and expose countries to the pillage of conquerors, as formerly. For we make war more like foxes, than like lyons; and you will have twenty sieges for one battel'; while in exactly the same year Johann Behr stated that, in Germany, 'Field battles are in comparison scarcely a topic of conversation . . . Indeed at the present time the whole art of war seems to come down to shrewd attacks and artful fortification.'[16]

The point was expressed most cogently by the principal military

engineer of Louis XIV of France, Sébastien le Prestre de Vauban, in a
tract written c. 1670:

The attack on fortresses has with justice always been considered one of the
most essential elements of the art of war. But since the number of strongholds
has increased to the point where one can no longer enter enemy territory
without encountering many fortified towns, its importance has increased to
the point where one can say that today it alone offers the means of conquest
and conservation. To be sure, winning a battle leaves the victor in control of
the countryside for the time being, but only taking the fortresses will give him
the entire country.[17]

In the Netherlands, for example, where (as noted above) few towns in
his day lacked modern fortifications, in spite of 'over 60 battles and
200 sieges' the country had never been totally subdued. According to
Vauban:

The reason is obvious. A battle lost in the Low Countries normally has few
consequences, for the pursuit of a defeated army continues for only two, three
or four leagues, because the neighbouring fortresses of the enemy halt the
victors and provide a refuge for the vanquished, saving them from being
totally ruined.[18]

As the construction of preclusive frontiers of artillery fortresses continued, in one region of Europe after another sieges eclipsed battles in
importance and wars eternalized themselves.[19]

But what was the chronology and the role of the artillery fortress
outside Europe? The first early modern castle built by the Europeans
in the course of their overseas expansion – indeed, significantly, the
first European building in the tropics – went up at São Jorge da
Mina in West Africa in 1482, following a naval encounter two years
previously between Portuguese and Castilian vessels in the area. Given
the perceived need for speed, the Portuguese crown sent out an
expeditionary force carrying some precut masonry (the foundations,
gates and window frames; the rest was to be supplied locally); and the
completed edifice, although traditional in design (with one fortified
enclosure for defence and another for trade), bore thirty cannon.[20] The

construction of fortified beach-heads had long formed part of the Western military tradition – William the Conqueror built a castle at Pevensey as soon as he landed in England in 1066; the Crusaders, the Venetians and the Genoese all fortified their settlements around the coasts of the Levant, the Aegean and the Black Sea – and it offered a crucial strategic advantage for expansion. Writing between 1505 and 1508 of his experience in Africa and India, the Portuguese conquistador Duarte Pacheco Pereira could already boast that in 'fortresses surrounded by walls . . . Europe excels Asia and Africa'. Islamic sources agreed. The *Tuḥfat-al-Mujâhidîn*, a chronicle of the struggle of the Malabar Muslims against 'the Franks' in southern India, devoted special attention to – and heaped special abuse upon – the large number of forts erected by the Portuguese (starting at Cochin in 1503), which made it almost impossible to drive the newcomers out, for 'their forts could never be taken'.[21] Nevertheless, the traditional vertical designs of the Portuguese described by these writers had become inadequate by the late sixteenth century, when traders from other European states made their presence felt: bastions, ravelins and moats were now added to older constructions like São Jorge, and all new forts were constructed on geometric principles. In the seventeenth and eighteenth centuries, nine European states maintained forty-three fortified stations along the West African coast, from Arguim to Whydah (thirty-one of them crammed into the 300-mile (500km) stretch of the Gold Coast); by 1800, almost all were artillery fortresses.[22]

Portuguese expansion in East Africa, Asia and South America followed much the same course. The coastal fortifications erected in the first phase, often by Portuguese engineers, followed the vertical pattern; from the 1540s, however, new-style complexes, often conceived and directed by Italians, sprang up – starting with the huge bastions of Mazagão (Morocco), Diu (India) and Salvador (Brazil). Everywhere, 'Renaissance' defences gradually gave way to modern ones; from 1558 to 1560, for example, a huge Italian-style fortress encircled and replaced Albuquerque's smaller structure at Ormuz, erected in 1507–15.[23] The process proved slow, however. The splendid drawings by the military engineer Pedro Barreto de Resende, appended to António Bocarro's *Book of Plans of the Fortifications, Cities and Settlements of the State of India*, completed in 1635, depicted 53 seaside strongholds between Sofala and Macao, but scarcely 10 of them could boast Italian-style fortifications: Mascate and Fort Jesus at Mombasa in Africa (the latter specially laid out to a geometrical plan by an Italian architect, Giovanni Battista Cairati, in the 1590s);[24] Baçaim, Chaul, Diu, Damão and São Thomé in India; Jaffna (1618) and Batticaloa (1628) in Sri Lanka; Malacca (1564–8); and the Monte fortress (1620) at Macao.[25] Moreover, even in 1635 some of those still lacked adequate artillery for their defence. Diu, with its massive walls (rebuilt in 1624), possessed only 45 large and 12 small guns (the rest, according to Bocarro, had been taken on the expedition to relieve Malacca in 1629 'where most of them were lost'); Damão had only 27 guns for its 11 bastions, and Chaul only 13 guns for its 9 bastions. Worst of all, 5 of the forts defending Goa, the viceregal capital, boasted only 6 guns between them, and the wall alongside the river had none at all.[26]

Three considerations explain the slow spread of the new defensive technology. First, it cost a great deal of money: the pentagonal citadel at Antwerp, with walls stretching some 1500 yards (1370m), cost 800,000 florins (£80,000) to build between 1567 and 1571; and although using forced labour could reduce the initial cost substantially, the *trace italienne* required a larger garrison. Building 'modern' defences thus represented a major and lasting investment of resources that most taxpayers would gladly avoid for as long as possible.[27] Second, even a state-of-the-art fortress possessed only defensive capacity. It served to protect merchants and their property, and to supply and shelter ships, but that was all. A few outposts and the occasional raid could extend the Europeans' influence perhaps fifty or sixty miles (80 to 100 km) into the hinterland, but no single stronghold could, by itself, control the interior. Construction of isolated fortifications overseas therefore tended to make sense where the Westerners sought to trade, rather than where they sought to settle. As in Europe, to render an entire frontier secure required a defence-in-depth. Third and finally, the military geography of many regions made the costly new fortifications seem irrelevant. In the early sixteenth century, only a few Muslim cities along the shores of the Indian Ocean possessed stone gates and towers, and only one, Aden, possessed a complete circuit of fortifications: 'very well surrounded by walls, towers and turrets, with battlements after our own fashion [*há nossa maneira*]', according to a Portuguese observer in 1513.[28] Most of the other port cities of South Asia sheltered behind wooden stockades, sometimes reinforced with earth, and posed no serious challenge to the Westerners. A few, such as Diu, acquired a citadel, and a former Ottoman engineer fortified Surat in the 1540s, but for most of the sixteenth century the *fidalgos* lacked any indigenous pressure to introduce state-of-the-art fortifications.[29]

The conquest of Malacca by the Portuguese in 1511 epitomized the situation. The city, although a huge trading metropolis (its waterfront was said to measure nine miles (15km) and its population exceeded 100,000), lacked regular fortifications. Moreover, 'most of its artillery – such as it has – resembles muskets', and 'they are very short of gunners and powder'.[30] When the Portuguese arrived, however, the sultan 'greatly fortified their seaboard with stockades of huge thick trees full of numerous cannon large and small and cases crammed with gunpowder'. So the Portuguese commander, Afonso de Albuquerque, burnt a few Muslim ships in order to secure from the sultan a favourable agreement, which included not only restitution for damage done to Portuguese property and advantageous terms of trade but also the demand that the ruler 'should send people to a place that he would tell him of to build a fortress at his own expense'.[31] Since these terms were contemptuously dismissed, Albuquerque at first tried to capture Malacca by naval bombardment (bringing to bear, according to one source, 400 guns).[32] When this failed, the 1500 Portuguese, plus 800 allies (Chinese and Indian), stormed the stockade and the inhabitants fled.

Now, having gained a lodgement, Albuquerque and his men:

with great haste by day, and the use of torches by night, [were] intent on building a castle of timber, with many large trees for the interior and a goodly quantity of cannon, and in a month it had been made strong; and as soon as it had been made secure, we prepared one of stone which we built by dismantling the houses of the Moors, the mosques and others of their buildings. We erected it with great hardship bearing the stones on our backs; and each one of us was day-labourer, mason and stone-cutter.[33]

The work endured and this castle, known as 'A Famosa', still formed part of the defences of the city 130 years later when, despite a complete circuit of walls constructed in the 1560s, which had resisted numerous sieges by its Asian neighbours, it fell to the Dutch.

Throughout the sixteenth century, fortifications built in the cheaper vertical style (like São Jorge da Mina or A Famosa) or with hollow round towers (like the walls of Malacca) proved perfectly adequate against local rulers. Admittedly, improvements became advisable from time to time – as early as 1513, Albuquerque complained that in western India 'the people we are fighting are different now, and [their] artillery, arms and fortresses have now all been transformed to our way of using them';[34] but the Europeans always seemed to retain a decisive advantage. Thus when the sultan of Ahmadnagar laid siege to Portuguese Chaul in 1571, his army of 140,000 men dwarfed the 1100 European defenders, while at the same time other Indian rulers attacked several other Portuguese outposts, thus reducing the chances of relief. The garrison held a perimeter of no more than 600 by 450 yards (550 by 400m), but could shelter behind improvised walls and bastions bearing artillery; moreover, since Chaul was never cut off from the sea, Portuguese ships managed to land reinforcements and supplies, and also used their guns against the besiegers. Nevertheless, the forces of Ahmadnagar gradually took all the outworks until, after six months, they launched a full-scale assault. But it was repulsed and, in the furious counterattack that followed, the Portuguese captured or spiked all the enemy's artillery. The siege was over.[35]

European adversaries were not so easily driven off, however. With the arrival of the Dutch in the Indian Ocean in the 1590s, the Portuguese realized that they faced a new and far more dangerous threat and began to construct geometrical fortifications there. As Philip III observed in 1607: 'Ever since the beginning of the discovery of India, experience has demonstrated the importance of fortresses; and now this seems even greater with the appearance of the [Dutch] rebels in those parts.' The viceroy of Portuguese India was therefore ordered to spend money, first and foremost, on completing Italian-style fortifications already begun, then on founding artillery to defend them, and finally on building more warships.[36] Many other royal letters reiterated the point in increasingly strident tones.[37] At the same time, the Portuguese tried to organize their troops in India to fight in the European manner, for whereas 'street gang' tactics normally worked against native rulers, fire control and superior discipline proved imperative against the Dutch. 'We have tried many times to reorganize our troops in India according to the European manner,' Philip III reported wistfully in 1617, 'since experience has shown that without it we have suffered several important losses. But now that we are at war with the Dutch, who are disciplined soldiers, it is more important than ever.'[38] Yet the losses continued and even multiplied until all the Portuguese fortresses in Sri Lanka and South India, although they had resisted numerous attacks by Asian rulers, fell to the Dutch between 1638 and 1663. The victors, however, took no chances and fortified their gains on a far more impressive scale: thus the walls of Galle in Sri Lanka, with 12 bastions (some of them ninety feet (30m) thick), ran for over a mile, while those of Colombo (with 8 bastions) and those of Negapatam (with 12) stretched further still.[39]

The same defensive pattern prevailed elsewhere in Asia: expensive geometrical fortifications normally only sprang up when and where other Europeans threatened. Thus, as they spread out across Siberia from the 1580s, the Russian explorers and fur-traders built forts at river crossings to protect themselves from local attack and safeguard their links with Muscovy, but these wooden constructions remained modest.[40] In the Philippines, too, the sophisticiation of Spanish fortifications remained limited until other Europeans began to threaten. Even the castle of Santiago at Manila began inauspiciously. In 1588, one Spanish official there informed the king that the fortifications under construction were 'a waste of time and money, because . . . they are made with round towers in the old fashion . . . without a moat or parapet' and thus could not offer interlocking fields of fire. Moreover, 'with what this costs, we could make a fortress in the modern style, with three bastions, instead of a structure so useless that any English or French troops who might besiege it would force it to surrender on the first day of the battery'. The military commandant three years later could only agree, since the defences were 'somewhat out of proportion, being made without architect, advice or plan'.[41] However, the repeated Dutch blockades and attacks after 1600 soon changed the situation, and by 1650 a full enceinte with eleven bastions had been built to surround the heart of the bustling town, while several outlying strategic points (most notably the Cavite peninsula) were also fortified in the 'Italian style'.[42]

In the Americas, fortress-building by the Europeans began early. Between 1509 and 1569, the Spanish crown issued over one hundred orders to erect fortifications in the New World.[43] However, little construction actually took place until the 1550s, when the presence of European enemies threatened the security of the region. The principal ports of the Caribbean began to receive modern fortifications in the reign of Philip II, starting with Havana (briefly captured by the French in 1555) between 1558 and 1577, and accelerating after the devastation caused by Francis Drake's West India raid of 1585–6.[44] By then, however, Drake's circumnavigation in 1577–81 had also provoked a programme of fortification in South America. According to the king himself: 'Many fortresses have been founded and many large garrisons have been established in the Americas in order to discipline and punish the daring of the pirates, who with such defiance and persistence come to those ports in order to rob and cause other damage.'[45] Philip II here referred primarily to the construction of forts in the Straits of Magellan and at Callao, the principal port of Peru; but more soon followed as other English and later Dutch expeditions entered the Pacific, albeit amid controversy: 'Your Majesty well knows,' a minister wearily complained in 1576, 'the disputes that divide engineers: they never agree.'[46] The defences therefore went up slowly; in Chile, the government fortified Valparaíso only in 1594, following a raid on the port by Richard Hawkins, and garrisoned the fort erected by the Dutch at Valdivia during a brief incursion in 1643. Further north, the same Dutch raid stimulated the construction of a complete enceinte around Callao (at a cost of 876,000 pesos: £200,000), and other artillery-bearing fortifications went up around the Spanish Caribbean and along the Pacific coast of Latin America throughout the seventeenth century.[47] Across the Andes, the Portuguese colonists in Brazil also slowly fortified their principal coastal settlements; then, in the eighteenth century, they began to plan impressive polygonal fortifications in the interior to defend the gold mines from possible Spanish attack.[48]

In North America, the various groups of Europeans soon began to build geometrical defences too, first against each other, and later against the indigenous population. At New Amsterdam, the Dutch began a quadrilateral artillery fort with four bastions 'faced outside entirely with stone' in 1635, and along the north side of Wall Street, in 1653, constructed a palisade of sharpened stakes, each twelve feet (3.5m) long, 'to make this city of New Amsterdam defensible', adding two stone bastions in 1660. They also maintained garrisons – at least intermittently – in eight other redoubts patterned on Fort Amsterdam in rural or outlying areas of New Netherland.[49] In the later seventeenth century, the English erected a complete set of bastions around the capital of their new conquest, renamed New York, while the Spaniards built a citadel at St Augustine (Florida) and the French fortified Québec with bastions.[50] Inland, however, where no other Europeans threatened, at first defences generally remained more modest. At Flowerdew Hundred on the James river in Virginia, the colonists erected a small fort in the 1620s with an 'earthen rampart, amounting to half of a bastioned fort, which protected the artillery positioned to guard the stretch of the James River around Windmill Point against cannon fire from sailing vessels; while to the west, a shallower ditch-set stockade, or "quick-set" hedge, defended the settlement from land assault by Native Americans' – a perfect example of the two defensive styles. Not far away, at Harbor View (near the confluence of the Nansemond and the James), a simpler structure went up in the 1640s, with two bastions set into opposite ends of rectangular walls; it formed the precursor of the American frontier 'Indian' forts whose typological descendants can be traced all the way to California.[51]

The Spaniards proved equally pragmatic. Although initially the crown ordered fortresses to be erected in numerous inland locations (even in Mexico City), the conquerors of New Spain – both spiritual and secular – preferred to build their churches to serve as forts in case of need and to construct portable blockhouses along the main roads leading north from the capital (for example, to Zacatecas and Guadalajara) in the 1570s.[52] In the south, officials and settlers constructed numerous forts for defence against their indigenous foes – over 150 of them in Chile alone (96 in the present state of Arauco) – many of them sharing the same rectangular design as those of New England, with two bastions at opposite corners.[53]

The French, however, decided to build full artillery fortresses even in the interior of early modern North America. A popular work on world travel commented laconically on an early French expedition down the Mississippi in the 1680s: 'The Chevalier de la Salle left with a detachment, entered the Illinois area, took possession of the country in the name of Louis XIV, called it Louisiana in honour of this prince, and constructed a fort there; the Spaniards would have built a church, the English a tavern.'[54] In fact, La Salle built two quadrilateral structures in the Mississippi valley, with bastions at each corner (Fort Crèvecœur in 1680 and Fort Louis in 1682), and others followed, but at first all were made of timber and thus possessed limited durability. Fort de Chartres in Illinois, for example, built in 1720 of 'logs the size of a man's leg, square in shape, having two bastions which commanded all the curtains', was soon described as decayed. But in 1753, as part of a chain of forts designed to contain the expansion of the English colonies to the east, the foundations of a large stone fortress with four bastions were laid which, eleven years later, earned praise from a British officer as 'the most commodious and best built fort in North America'. Its precise geometrical shape still stands today – Vauban would have been proud – although the loss of Québec in 1759 rendered the work useless, for the French were forced to cede all their American possessions, and so Fort de Chartres became Fort Cavendish.[55]

In America as in Asia, however, isolated fortresses proved of limited use. They served to create a safe environment for trade and a defence against low-intensity threats, but they could not resist a major assault. The forts erected along the northern frontier of New Spain did not always protect their defenders, let alone the surrounding towns and plantations. Likewise, during 'Bacon's Rebellion' in Virginia, the strongholds built in 1676 to protect the settlements against Native American attack failed to achieve their goal. The French did indeed erect forts that ranged from South Dakota to the Ohio river and south to Louisiana, but only because the local Indian nations welcomed them for purposes of trade and mutual defence; they, too, repeatedly proved incapable of resisting a full-scale attack. Even the more sophisticated forts of New Netherland all fell to the English in 1664 without a shot being fired, and in 1673 the Dutch regained them almost as easily. Only the few fully fledged Italian-style defences, such as Fort San Marcos in Florida (which successfully resisted sieges by the English in 1702 and 1750), proved their worth.[56] But San Marcos, too, could not serve as a base for large-scale offensive operations in the interior. The Westerners in North America – whether French, Dutch, English or

Spanish – could neither transport their artillery inland nor move their own troops fast enough to catch their adversaries in the field. Indeed, they could seldom find their enemies' settlements: 'Every swamp is a castle to them,' lamented Increase Mather during King Philip's War in New England (1675), 'knowing where to find us, but we know not where to find them.' Even in the mid-eighteenth century, the repeated attempts of the French to destroy the Chickasaw failed because they could not locate the Chickasaw towns and, when they did, they found their fortifications (constructed with English assistance) impregnable. Normally, therefore, the Westerners relied on Native American allies and auxiliaries to do their fighting for them.[57]

The indigenous peoples of the Americas, Siberia and the Philippines, although they succeeded in emulating many military techniques of the European invaders, normally failed to build artillery fortresses. Admittedly a number of locations in Mexico and Peru were fortified before the Spanish invasion, but only with vertical defences; others, like Mexico City, possessed vast temples designed like (and, in the event, used like) citadels; while other indigenous strongholds boasted such inaccessible locations that further fortifications seemed unnecessary.[58] The Inca fastness of Ollantaytambo, for example, stood on a rock outcrop so steep that artillery could be used for neither attack nor defence. Apparently, a full process of replication took place only in the north of the continent, where the constant rivalry of the various European invaders led them to teach their Native American allies to construct true Western-style defences. Although in the 'Pequot War' of 1637 the Native Americans still relied on their traditional circular palisade fortifications, forty years later, during 'King Philip's War', their military repertory had expanded dramatically. The Narragansetts of Rhode Island, besides owning moulds and a forge able to make musket and pistol balls and parts for firearms, constructed a fort on a natural island in the 'Great Swamp' which, although it had only palisades for the curtains, 'at one corner . . . they had placed a kind of blockhouse . . . from whence they sorely galled our men that first entered', and a 'flanker' at the other. In December 1675, the fort's capture cost the lives of over seventy colonists.[59] Meanwhile the Susquehannock fort in Maryland defied a siege by English colonists for six weeks in the same year, thanks to its 'high banks of earth, with flankers having many loopholes and a ditch around all'. Other examples of Indian forts with bastions and 'flankers' are reported in New York state, eastern Canada and later, Illinois, where in 1730 the Italian-style defences constructed by the Indians around Fort Fox defied a full-dress French siege for a month.[60] In the end, the Native Americans lost ground, not so much through any technical inferiority but because their numbers dwindled (largely thanks to the inroads of European diseases), while those of the Westerners relentlessly increased (largely thanks to immigration).[61]

Elsewhere, efforts to emulate European techniques of defence and attack proved more successful. Most of the Muslim states of the Middle East possessed an extensive and sophisticated military tradition (both written and practical) of their own and rapidly assimilated Western firearms into their military repertory, albeit often by a process of routine mimesis, copying captured weapons and importing foreign specialists.[62] The Ottoman Turks, for example, at first seemed particularly adept against the West. In 1453 their artillery (mostly cast by Western renegades) demolished the walls of Constantinople; in 1520–1 they captured the strategic strongholds of Rhodes and Belgrade; and in the 1570s they captured both the 'modern' Venetian fortifications of Cyprus (Nicosia, with its eleven bastions, was at the time the most sophisticated fortress-city yet built by Europeans) and the heavily fortified Spanish outposts of Tunis and La Goletta.[63] However, these Turkish successes resulted more from overwhelming force than from the surgical precision with relatively modest forces practised in the West; moreover, after each success the Turks did relatively little to maintain or improve the fortifications they captured. According to Alain Manesson Mallet, a French military writer, in the late seventeenth century: 'Once they [the Turks] have them, they are content to repair the breaches and scarcely take the trouble to preserve the defences, believing that it is useless to spend money to maintain strongholds which the Christians will never attack, thanks to the divisions amongst them . . . As for bastions, these infidels never construct them – unless some renegade shows them how.' Mallet included plates of several fortresses previously taken by the Turks to demonstrate either the lack of subsequent improvements or the imperfect attempts at modernization and, by way of constrast, he also depicted two state-of-the-art artillery fortresses built in Habsburg Hungary.[64] Nevertheless, the Turks almost succeeded with their gamble (if such it was: we rely here only on Western sources). Although they failed to take Vienna in 1683, it should be remembered, first, that the relief army, drawn from several European states, arrived just as the Ottoman siege army neared victory, and second, that it was the Turks at the gates of Vienna and not the Europeans at the gates of Istanbul.[65]

Furthermore, the Turks gladly shared their expertise with others. An interesting early transmission of the Military Revolution of early modern Europe to a Muslim society occurred in Sa'adian Morocco in the sixteenth century. As early as 1541, following the fall of a Portuguese outpost, King John III observed: 'We must recognize that warfare in Morocco has changed. The enemy is now very adept in the arts of war and siegecraft, due in part to the aid of many Turks and renegades, numerous artillery weapons, and the important materials of war.'[66] John III's grandson, Sebastian, experienced the truth of this in spectacular fashion in 1578, when he and his army met defeat and death at the hands of Turkish-trained Sa'adian forces in the battle of Alcazarquivir, while the subsequent conquest of the sub-Saharan Songhay empire in 1590–1 by Moroccan troops – led by a Spanish Muslim renegade and including a detachment of Ottoman musketeers – offered a 'textbook gunpowder conquest', to rank with those of Cortés in Mexico, Pizarro in Peru and Legazpi in the Philippines.[67]

In fact, 'Turks and renegades' made their influence felt all over the Islamic world. The sultanate of Acheh in Sumatra, for example, established direct contact with the 'Raja Rum' (the Ottoman sultan, 'king of the West') in the sixteenth century; letters and gifts were exchanged, and a stream of Turkish military experts came to Indonesia to cast cannon and to fight (according to Malay sources, some three hundred Turks with firearms were fighting for Acheh by 1537). In 1567, the Ottoman sultan even promised to send a fleet to Indonesia to drive out the Portuguese, but in the event it sailed to suppress a revolt in Yemen instead.[68] Sultan Iskandar Muda of Acheh (1607–36) maintained a corps of military slaves, captured when young and trained specially (just like the janissaries), and his soldiers constructed siegeworks of such sophistication that (according to a Portuguese account) 'not even the Romans could have made such works stronger or more quickly' (page 193 above). Elsewhere in South Asia, 'Turks and renegades' frequently rubbed shoulders. At the capture of Goa in 1510, for example, an Italian participant reported that the victors 'killed around two thousand persons of those who resisted us. And these were almost all Turks, and renegade Christians of all sorts; among whom were Venetians and Genoese in largest numbers.'[69] In spite of this salutary example, the total of 'renegade Christians' who earned their living from the local rulers in the region continued to rise – to perhaps five thousand by 1600 – with an even larger number of Turks. Their presence dwindled somewhat in the course of the seventeenth century, at least in Mughal India, and their rewards diminished as native artificers became more experienced; nevertheless, during the civil war between Aurangzeb and his brothers for the Mughal throne in the 1650s, several hundred Europeans and Turks served both as mercenaries and as technical advisers, especially for artillery and siegecraft. Thus, according to François Bernier, Aurangzeb captured the port city of Surat in 1658 only because some Dutch experts 'showed his generals how to use gunpowder mines'.[70]

However, Indian rulers seem to have taken few steps to imitate European fortification styles. According to Niccolo Manucci, an Italian in Mughal service, the Mughal capital at Delhi boasted walls in the 1650s 'one half of brick and the rest of stone. At every hundred paces is a strengthening bastion, but on these there is no artillery.' Slightly earlier, William Methwold of the English East India Company reported that the inland state of Golconda (later Hyderabad) possessed sixty-six fortresses, most of them perched on high rocks or hills and accessible by only one route. Most Indian fortresses were of massive construction: the walls of the Purana Qila at Delhi, built between 1530 and 1545, stood some fifty feet (15 metres) thick and sixty feet (20 metres) high; those of Golconda, four miles (7km) in circumference and later adapted to include artillery platforms, were no less imposing. Against such targets, even the heaviest early modern artillery bombardment (supposing siege guns could be brought up) made little impression, and sieges tended to be decided by blockade rather than cannonade. Thus Aurangzeb brought about a hundred siege guns and 100,000 troops against Golconda in 1687, and also set three mines (each containing sixteen tons of gunpowder) under the walls; but the guns never came close enough to be effective, and when the mines were sprung two had been countermined and blew back on the attackers while the third failed to ignite. In the end, after an eight-month siege, Golconda only fell by treachery when a disaffected nobleman opened one of the gates to the Mughals during a night attack.[71]

Early modern China conformed to much the same pattern. Admittedly China lacked castles, but instead most towns boasted impressive fortifications; indeed, the Chinese character most often translated as 'wall' (*cheng*) is also the character most often translated as 'city'. Thus '*cheng*, a wall, always implies a city; *cheng*, a city, always has walls'.[72] According to a European general in 1860, the walls of Peking stood 'upwards of fifty feet (15 metres) in breadth, very nearly the same in height, in excellent repair, and paved on the top where, I am sure, five coaches-and-four could, with little management, have been driven abreast [along them]'. Those of Nanking, equally formidable, stretched for twenty-two miles (about 35km). In the event, the strength of these defences was never tested by Western guns, but in 1841 during the Opium War, a two-hour bombardment from warships of the Royal Navy on the batteries of Amoy, according to an eyewitness, 'produced no effect whatever; not a gun being found disabled and but few of the enemy killed in them when our troops entered. The principle of their construction was such as to render them almost impervious to the efforts of horizontal fire, even from the 32-pounders.'[73] Small wonder then that (as Matteo Ricci noted) China chose to ignore the 'artillery fortress'.[74]

At the time of the fall of Malacca to the Portuguese in 1511, no town in Southeast Asia seems to have possessed stone walls, and the situation changed only slowly.[75] In Siam, even in the late seventeenth century, only Bangkok had any walled defences: a chain of small forts along the Chao Phrya river, manned by a hundred Christian Luso-Asiatic soldiers under captains 'who drill them every day'. Elsewhere, according to European visitors, the Siamese disdained to fortify strong places 'for fear of losing them, and not being able to retake them'.[76] Likewise, the early modern Vietnamese burnt their wooden settlements when invasion threatened, fleeing to the mountains until security returned. Despite an almost constant state of civil war in the country, the only permanent fortifications remained the walls built across central Vietnam to divide Tongking from Cochin-China; towns and cities were surrounded at most by a bamboo fence (although Hue, at least, boasted a considerable stock of Western artillery by the 1680s).[77] Only Burma proved different; the unification of the country by the Mons of Pegu in the mid-sixteenth century clearly owed a lot to their ability to construct 'impregnable' fortifications in the European manner, although this ability seems to have waned in the seventeenth century.[78]

These mainland states, however, rarely faced a major and sustained European challenge: Felipe de Brito Nicote and his motley crew of mercenaries in Burma (1599–1613) and Louis XIV's naval and military expedition to Siam (1687–8), although surprisingly successful, proved to be isolated episodes.[79] Matters in the Indonesian archipelago were very different, with first the Portuguese and then the Spanish, Dutch, English and French all striving to create permanent fortified bases and to control both the production and trade of certain items. Although the inhabitants of most cities in the archipelago also responded to unstable political conditions by flight, some cities began to acquire walls. To begin with, many urban areas already boasted fortified residential compounds for the great men, and solid stone 'godowns' in which merchants stored their goods against the threat of theft and fire. Furthermore, by 1600 the Javanese cities of Banten, Japara, Tuban, Pati and Surabaya had all acquired perimeter walls – although the largest metropolis in the archipelago, Acheh, rejected them: 'This city [according to a chronicler] is not fortified like other cities because of the very large number of war elephants' able to protect it.[80] The sultan of Makassar displayed rather more ambition. By the 1630s, his capital possessed a large fortress (Sombaopu) around the royal palace which, on the seaward side, boasted walls fourteen feet (over 4 metres) thick, and four bastions equipped with twenty heavy guns donated by Europeans (the Danes, English and Portuguese all maintained factories in the city) and commanded by an Englishman who had converted to Islam.[81]

Other forts of brick also sprang up, until in the 1660s a solid defensive wall studded with forts stretched along the seafront of the city for over seven miles (11km).[82] Both the design of the forts and contemporary documents indicate Portuguese influence, and this should come as no surprise: Makassar had been consistently friendly towards the Portuguese since the arrival of the Dutch in the area, and provided a crucial refuge for them as the Dutch noose tightened elsewhere. After the fall of Malacca in 1641, for example, between 2000 and 3000 Portuguese transferred their activities from Malaysia to Makassar.[83] The Dutch resented this challenge, and in 1667 a fleet of thirty-five ships (including eleven warships) sailed up from Batavia and bombarded the forts along the seafront. Despite a barrage of '12, 18 and 24 pound balls from the enemy', which damaged the masts, sails and rigging of the Dutch ships, the fortresses fell one by one and eventually Makassar made peace (Figure 18). Two years later, however, when it seemed that the sultan had disregarded the agreement, the Dutch returned with Bugis allies and began a formal siege. In June 1669, after six months of bitter fighting, the Dutch managed to explode a mine under the walls of Sombaopu and create a breach twenty yards (18 metres) wide. They then launched an assault that involved fighting so heavy 'That old soldiers have perhaps never heard its like in Europe itself': the Dutch musketeers allegedly fired off 30,000 rounds, yet it still took ten days to complete the capture of the fort.[84]

However, the most remarkable early modern Asian response to Europe's gunpowder revolution occurred in Japan. Writing in the 1590s, the Jesuit missionary Luis Fróis dismissed Japanese fortifications almost as contemptuously as his colleague Matteo Ricci had previously deprecated those of China. Describing Toyotomi Hideyoshi's new fortress at Kyoto, Fróis wrote: 'Although for Japan, where artillery is not used, it is very strong, nevertheless in comparison with Europe it is very weak, because with four pieces of artillery, everything would be destroyed in half a day.' But, even as he wrote, Japan was adapting. In 1578, according to Fróis himself, for the first time the nobles of the island of Kyushu (many of them newly converted to Christianity) began to deploy 'some artillery pieces' in their wars; and, at the same time, the dominant military leader on the main island, Oda Nobunaga, built a new type of defensive fortification at Azuchi, near lake Biwa, by surrounding a promontory with angled stone walls in such a way that they constituted a solid mass of rock and earth, in

18 The reduction of the forts around Makassar, 1667
The Renaissance-style fortifications that defended Makassar (Indonesia)
failed to withstand bombardment by a Dutch fleet in June 1667. The Dutch
first forced the outlying fort of Pannakoke (in the foreground) to surrender
and then attacked Fort Ioupandan (on the skyline) and Sombaopu (labelled
'Hooft Casteel', or citadel). The sultan sued for peace after one day's
bombardment by the Dutch warships.

which each part offered flanking fire to the rest.[85] Although Azuchi
was destroyed in 1582, numerous other cannon-proof castles of similar
design followed between 1580 and 1630, of which some sixty survive,
and Japanese forces built more during the invasion of Korea during
the 1590s (just after Fróis wrote). Several of the new fortresses were
enormous: the star-shaped walls of Kumamoto castle, with forty-nine
towers and two keeps, extended for almost eight miles (13km); so did
those of Osaka castle, composed in part of rocks weighing between
120 and 130 tons each, to a depth in places of almost sixty feet
(20 metres).[86] Although artillery (both Japanese and Western) was

occasionally deployed against these targets – most notably at the siege of Osaka in 1614–15 and during the Shimabara rebellion of 1637–8 – it proved indecisive; the walls were too thick.

The striking resemblance between the geometrical form of these fortifications and the *trace italienne* might suggest that the Japanese imitated the Western design; and, indeed, military conversation with Westerners, among others, formed one of Nobunaga's principal passions. However, no surviving documents demonstrate a connection, and it is noteworthy that Nobunaga also devised the idea of the musketry volley some twenty years *before* it emerged in the West! It seems more likely that the same problem – the vulnerability of vertical defences to artillery bombardment – gave rise to the same solution in both countries. In any case, the impressive network of artillery fortresses developed in early modern Japan helped to preserve its integrity against the West.[87]

But no immunity lasts for ever. In most Islamic societies, the founding and management of artillery became the exclusive preserve of small cadres of foreign specialists, most of them renegades and adventurers with little training and less experience in their craft. In China and Japan, too, technological innovation ceased and by the nineteenth century the military elite had lost the capacity to use their 'new' weapons. Instead of changing their armed forces in order to make the best use of Western military technology, they attempted to adapt Western technology to their existing ideas of warfare; and in this they failed.[88]

The artillery fortress of early modern Europe played a key role in the rise of the West in two distinct respects, one defensive and the other offensive. The sixteenth century saw a strong phase of Islamic expansion, with the Mughals gaining control of some 1.25 million square miles (3.2 million square km) of India, and the Ottomans creating an empire of roughly 1 million square miles (2.5 million square km), which stretched from Morocco, through Egypt and Iraq, to the Balkans and Hungary. So many states and societies succumbed that the resistance of the West to this Islamic tide stands out as unusual. And it was a close-run thing: At Mohacs (1526) and Mezokeresztes (1596) in Hungary, the Turks triumphed; and if they were routed at Lepanto in the Mediterranean in 1571, they nevertheless conquered Cyprus and Tunis in the 1570s and Crete in the 1650s. The artillery fortress proved crucial in limiting the damage. On the one hand, as Vauban rightly observed, 'Winning a battle leaves the victor in control of the countryside for the time being, but only taking the fortresses will give him the entire country' and where artillery fortresses had proliferated to create a defence-in-depth, as in the Maghreb, Hungary and Dalmatia, a rapid Muslim advance proved impossible. On the other hand, the resistance of even a solitary artillery fortress could waste a powerful army, because it could only be starved out and few non-European states could maintain their forces in the field beyond a single campaigning season. The fortress also proved remarkably cost-effective: after the initial outlay (crippling though that could be), the expense of maintaining the masonry, and an adequate garrison amounted to far less than the upkeep of an army capable of defeating adversaries in the field.

Finally, even though they alone did not suffice to create a continental empire, the Europeans' fortified cities overseas nevertheless served to extend their power inland. This occurred in two ways. First, the fortresses offered advantages to indigenous rulers, especially those who lived in fear of a more powerful neighbour: to the king of Malindi in East Africa, faced by the sultan of Mombasa; to the king of Cochin in South India, threatened by the samorin of Calicut; to the Mahicans in northeastern America, beset by the Iroquois. Granting the Europeans permission to erect a fort, and concluding a treaty with them, improved their local importance and their overall security. Without forts capable of offering sustained resistance, alliance with the Europeans, without which Western power would surely have remained confined to the coasts, might not have seemed so attractive to native rulers. Second, and scarcely less important, the capacity of European fortresses to withstand even a prolonged siege offered obvious advantages to local merchants fearful that the wars endemic in most regions might destroy their trading stock. The history of the Europeans in Asia, Africa and North America provides numerous examples of local merchants keeping their goods inside fortified European bases, despite the high tolls and duties exacted, and even lending money to preserve the Western presence in the region. Thus João de Castro, viceroy of India, financed his relief of Diu in 1539 largely from loans provided by Indian merchants living in Goa; and from the 1680s onwards Indian merchants in Southeast India began to make substantial deposits in cash with the agents of the English East India Company in Madras.[89]

The military effectiveness of Western fortifications of course predated the 'Age of Expansion'. Following a wave of invasions during the third century AD, the Romans constructed a network of fortresses along the empire's Rhine frontier – the earliest known example of a defence-in-depth. Then, from the 900s, Fulk Nerra, count of the Angevins, began to construct stone castles to form a similar preclusive frontier around his territory, a technique that quickly spread along all the major land frontiers of medieval Europe: between Capetians and Plantagenets along the Norman border; in the Welsh Marches and around the Pale in Ireland; in Spain during the 'Reconquest'. Castles also served to guard overseas enclaves during the Middle Ages (page 200 above); adding bastions merely allowed the strategy to survive into the gunpowder age.

To return to the 'military paradigm' summarized by Anthony Reid, the artillery fortress constituted the crucial link between the Europeans' naval mastery and their ability to attract and exploit local allies. The invention and diffusion of the 'Italian style' of fortification thus represented an important step in the West's continuing – perhaps unique – ability to make the most of its smaller resources in order, first, to hold its own and, later, to expand to global dominance.[90]

PART III

SIN, SALVATION AND
SUCCESS DENIED

In 1965, the prolific French historian Pierre Chaunu drew attention to the wealth of surviving early modern church records in Europe. He speculated that the quantitative techniques devised by economic historians could also be applied to ecclesiastical history in order to 'measure' religious trends, beliefs and practices. 'What is revolutionary – to be precise: original and fertile – is the serial study of phenomena,' he wrote.[1]

Many church historians heeded this call. Demographers had long realized that the systematic study of the records of baptisms, marriages and burials kept by local clergy held the key to the population history of Europe between the sixteenth century, when parish registers became common, and the national census data of the nineteenth century. Numerous historians also began to exploit the rich archives left by the Inquisition in many Catholic countries – above all Italy, Portugal and the Spanish monarchy (with twenty-two tribunals stretching from Lima to Palermo reporting to a central office in Madrid, whose archives preserve records of over 40,000 trials between 1540 and 1700).[2] Two other ventures in serial religious history proved more controversial, however: the use of visitation records to measure beliefs, and the study of church court records to reconstruct patterns of crime. This final section considers the successes and failures of these two historical initiatives.

9

'Success and failure in the German Reformation', written by Gerald Strauss, ranks as one of the most arresting and influential articles ever printed in the journal Past and Present. It appeared in 1975, and three years later Strauss brought out a book, provocatively entitled Luther's House of Learning: Indoctrination of the Young in the German Reformation. Both publications made extensive use not only of qualitative writings by the reformers themselves, but also of a quantitative source: the 'visitation returns' compiled by senior ecclesiastics who toured the various parishes of each German Protestant state to survey the beliefs and practices of ministers and congregations. Strauss found in these first-hand sources copious evidence of egregious error and ignorance.

Reading 'Success and failure' immediately brought to my mind two parallels. First, very similar material exists in the ecclesiastical records of early modern England: many Puritan divines also lamented the 'incorrigible profanity of the multitude' while Tudor visitation records frequently included examples of error similar to those recorded by Strauss. Having grown up in Nottingham, I recalled with particular relish the vicar of neighbouring Blidworth who in 1583 managed to confuse Judas and Jesus. Second, while reading about the Dutch Revolt I had noted a vigorous debate between historians on when (and, indeed, whether) the United Provinces had been 'Protestantized' during the early modern period.[1] This made me wonder if records from other parts of Protestant Europe would reveal a similar picture to that painted by Strauss; and what would those of Catholic Europe show?

As I pondered these questions, I received an invitation to attend an Anglo-Polish historical conference in Warsaw in April 1978, and decided to work up a paper that applied Strauss's German model to *the rest of Europe, Catholic as well as Protestant. It ran to eighteen typescript pages, with thirty-five notes. Shortly afterwards, I was invited to spend one year as a Visiting Professor at the University of British Columbia in Vancouver. The only condition was that, although I could teach whatever other courses I chose, I must offer the course on 'The Age of Reformation' normally given by Professor Christopher Friedrichs, who had won a fellowship and a sabbatical year. This seemed a small price to pay for a year at such a prestigious institution, and I readily agreed. Chris Friedrichs thereupon offered to let me rent his house, complete with a magnificent library on Reformation history, for the year; and there I began to expand my Warsaw paper. It was hard to keep up. Polish colleagues at the Warsaw conference had already provided a wealth of references on developments in the largest Catholic state in Europe (until 1648). Shortly afterwards, some Scandinavian colleagues introduced me to the incredible records on the successful Protestantization of seventeenth-century Sweden.*

The paper became my 'party piece', a lecture that I gave to many audiences over the next decade. Each provided more material to inte-grate until, by 1990, I had 52 typescript pages of text and 137 notes which I sent to two journals for consideration: the American Historical Review *and* Past and Present. *The former immediately rejected the piece on the grounds that 'The* AHR *seldom accepts articles with more than 30 to 40 pages of text and 20 to 25 pages of notes. It even more rarely publishes review essays of that length.'* Past and Present, *by contrast, agreed to publish provided I could shed about one-quarter of my material and streamline the argument, and the editor forwarded eight papers of advice from members of the editorial board on how to achieve both goals. Their various suggestions, although wildly contradictory, included some wonderful ideas and I submitted a revised text, trimmed to thirty-seven pages, in January 1991: it duly appeared in August 1992 – just over fourteen years after reading the first version in Warsaw.*

Since then, much material has appeared on the religious state of almost every region of early modern Europe. Although generalization is hazardous – all Reformation historians seem invincibly committed to 'exceptionalism': they believe that the country they study followed a unique path – two common denominators stand out. First, the new studies tend to emphasize a distinction between 'conformity' (that is, outward compliance) and 'conversion' (the self-conscious adoption of specific religious beliefs and practices). Gerald Strauss, and those early modern clerics whose testimony he cited, concentrated largely on the second category: they complained that true conversion had not been achieved. Mere conformity did not satisfy them. Although, as a distinguished Reformation historian observed (page 229 below), Strauss had 'graded Luther where Luther himself would have chosen to be tested', both men set inherently unrealistic standards. Changing the practices hallowed by tradition, especially among rural communities (and perhaps 90 per cent of early modern Europeans lived in the countryside), took generations – whether those practices concerned farming or fishing practices, social customs, dress codes or religious beliefs. The imposition of a new creed by pastors could easily turn popular faith into one of 'prevention and protection', with parishioners trying to hide their deep-seated beliefs.[2] Nevertheless, the population for the most part conformed – especially when conformity required actions rather than beliefs or attendance at church. On the one hand, the evolution of a 'Protestant calendar', with holidays to celebrate dates significant for the success of the Reformation, produced mass demonstrations of support for the new faith; on the other, threats from Catholic enemies could turn anti-Catholicism into a glue that helped to bind Protestant states together.[3]

By the seventeenth century, however, changing even outward conformity could prove difficult. In a remarkable tour de force, Karl Bottigheimer and Ute Lotz-Heumann have compared 'Protestantization' in six different areas: Ireland, Wales, Scotland, Norway, Lippe and Brandenburg. Although they detected several important common causes of the 'success' of the Reformation in most (but not all) areas – such as support from the elite, support from the towns and support from the state – they noted significant change over time. Above all, the influence of these three constituencies waned as time passed. This constitutes the second common denominator among the new generation of studies on the question of 'success and failure' in the Age of Reformation: it proved far easier to introduce a new faith before the process of 'confessionalization' got under way, whether the 'old religion' was Catholic, as in Ireland, or Lutheran, as in Lippe and

Brandenburg. After the 1590s, the 'Lords of Dublin', Count Simon or Elector John Sigismund might decide to change their faith, but they could no longer coerce their subjects to follow them.[4]

By then, the confessional approach adopted by the Catholics and the Protestants differed significantly. The Catholics adopted two strategies eschewed by their competitors. First, they sent missionaries into the 'Indies of Europe' to effect the 'spiritual conquest' of the inhabitants of, say, Calabria or Brittany just as earnestly as those of, say, New Mexico or Peru. Second, they explicitly endorsed a 'two-track' faith, keeping what they taught to ordinary people deliberately simple. Whereas Luther and his lieutenants strove to produce a Bible for children (and their illiterate parents), in 1583 Cardinal Borromeo claimed it was 'inappropriate' for Scripture to be read and discussed indiscriminately, because pride and intransigence could lead 'simpler souls' into error. A decade later, the Index of Prohibited Books forbade all vernacular works that conveyed the words of Scripture in any form. In Italy, which had formerly produced more vernacular Bibles than any country except Germany, none appeared between 1567 and 1769; in Spain, no vernacular edition of the Catechism appeared until 1777.[5] Everything depended on direct instruction by the clergy.

Catholics, therefore, gradually came to measure their success in 'conversion' by a different yardstick than most Protestants. Fray Luis de Granada made the point well in his Book of Prayer and Meditation, first written in 1554–5, which went through over a hundred editions by 1700 (twice as many as any other Spanish work) and appeared in almost all European languages, including Greek, and in Japanese. He wrote his book, over five hundred pages long, in the style of a sermon: full of exclamations, questions, parallels and punch-lines. He explicitly set out to reassure the humble. 'Always remember,' he wrote, 'that on the day of judgement, they won't ask us what we read, but what we did.'[6] Few Protestant divines would have written that (nor, for that matter, would they have used 'we' rather than 'you'). Perhaps that is why, as time passed, Catholics increasingly viewed their mission as a success while Protestants despaired: simply put, given the realities of early modern Europe, they were more realistic.

Success and Failure during the First Century of the Reformation

A quarter of a century ago, Gerald Strauss unleashed a fierce debate concerning the pastoral achievements of Protestantism in early modern Germany. Simply stated, he argued that the reformers set out 'to make people – all people – think, feel and act as Christians'; and he claimed that, although in the 1520s many Protestant leaders felt that these goals were being achieved, thereafter triumphalism turned first to disillusion and then to despair. A mass of telling evidence suggested that, at least from the mid-sixteenth to the mid-seventeenth century, the reformers themselves believed that their mission had failed.[7]

Of course, as Strauss himself pointed out, several scholars before him had questioned the extent to which ordinary people were touched by Protestantism, and since 1950 it has been increasingly accepted that (in the celebrated epigram of A. G. Dickens) 'the Reformation was an urban event' – that in the early days it succeeded only in the towns.[8] The true novelty of Strauss's case lay less in the thrust of his argument than in the evidence that underpinned it, for he mobilized not only the published writings of the theologians, but also the pastoral records of the Protestant churches themselves, above all the visitation returns compiled by special commissioners sent out with copious instructions and a detailed questionnaire specifically to assess the behaviour and beliefs of outlying clergy and congregations.[9] The results, starting with the first Protestant visitation in 1527–8, were abysmal. Luther himself wrote movingly of the 'lamentable wretchedness' that he had witnessed as a visitor in Saxony:

Dear God help us, what misery have I seen! The common man, especially in the villages, knows absolutely nothing about Christian doctrine; and indeed many pastors are in effect unfit and incompetent to teach. Yet they are all called Christians, are baptized, and enjoy the holy sacraments – even though they cannot recite either the Lord's Prayer, the Creed or the Commandments. They live just like animals.[10]

According to Strauss's evidence, visitors in most parts of Protestant Germany continued to see similar 'misery' for at least a century after this.[11]

Before entering the debate on how Strauss's evidence should be interpreted, it is important to note that a very similar canvas has been painted for other Protestant areas in the first century after the Reformation. Visitation returns have also been used (together with other sources) to suggest that standards were little better in some Calvinist areas of Germany[12] and in the Dutch Republic,[13] as well as in much of rural England,[14] Scotland[15] and Ireland.[16] There is thus no shortage of complementary material to support Strauss's verdict on Lutheran Germany: that, at least in the eyes of its own leading practitioners, Protestantism had largely failed to arouse a 'widespread, meaningful and lasting response to its message' for one, perhaps two, and in some areas even three generations after the Reformation.[17]

However, despite the apparent consensus concerning so many of the principal Protestant areas of early modern Europe, the evidence presented by Strauss and others has been subjected to heavy criticism. To begin with, it is generally recognized that the criteria adopted for measuring 'success' and 'failure' were, to say the least, narrow. They were certainly not those of (for example) contemporary Catholics, few of whom doubted that the Reformation had been a roaring success. The testimony of leaders like Ignatius Loyola, who believed that only the strongest countermeasures would halt the triumphant advance of Protestantism, is reinforced by the reports of the Catholic clergy charged with extirpating Protestantism in countries won back to Rome concerning the Reformation's evident success at grass-roots level. Thus the foreign priests who arrived in England in 1554 to eradicate all traces of heresy were appalled to find vernacular Bibles chained up in almost every parish church, 'which we removed because of the great damage they were doing in that kingdom'.[18]

So why was this impression of Protestant 'success' not reflected in the visitation records? Three separate explanations may be offered. First, the visitors frequently neglected the cities, where other sources often reveal a learned and diligent clergy serving an enthusiastic and well-informed congregation. Thus many of those whose answers might have given cause for self-congratulation were overlooked. Second, the visitors were neither impartial enumerators patiently compiling a statistical profile of religious awareness, nor yet market researchers testing consumer preferences for competing products. Instead they were collecting data for their local authorities, either to justify their own labours or (more often) to back appeals for better state funding for the performance of God's work: they might thus be tempted to dwell upon any deficiencies encountered in order to persuade their governors of the need for remedial action. In any case they would be well aware of the frequent examples of pride coming before a fall in the Old and New Testaments (as well as in the history of the church) and would be, on balance, more likely to lament than to exult over the state of Christendom at any given time. In short, the visitors were predisposed to discover what was wrong in each parish rather than what was right.[19] Third, and in spite of all this, James Kittelson has pointed out that some of the rural areas covered by visitation returns in fact recorded remarkable successes. His 'report from Strasbourg', covering fourteen country parishes between 1555 and 1580, shows an enviably pious population who knew their catechism satisfactorily, attended church frequently, and partook of the Lord's Supper regularly.[20] Likewise, in England, although there might still be 'dark corners' in the north and west, by the early seventeenth century there were also many areas apparently suffused with light: Archbishop William Laud's annual 'accounts' of the state of both clergy and laity in the province of Canterbury during the 1630s were highly optimistic; while Joseph Hall (bishop of Exeter and Norwich) claimed 'without . . . either arrogance or flattery' that 'the wonder of the world is the clergy of Britain'.[21] To the north, in Scotland, the church leaders of St Andrews in Fife noted in 1600 that 'the peopill convenis sua [i.e., so] frequentlie to preaching that the kirk may nocht convenientlie containe thame' and an overflow chapel had to be opened.[22]

These contradictions have led some scholars to discount the evidence drawn from the visitation records. Some have merely questioned the value of generalizations drawn from sampling. As Kittelson put it, 'Discovering whether pastors . . . achieved their objectives must be accomplished on the basis of parish-by-parish and year-to-year data wherever and whenever possible; sampling techniques merely open the door to false impressions.'[23] Others, however, believe that even evidence drawn from a 'parish-by-parish and year-to-year' analysis of visitation returns would remain suspect because of the nature of the source itself; for, at first sight, both the methods and the questions of the visitors appear unreasonable. We may feel pity for the ministers of Brunswick-Calenberg who were asked, in 1584, 'Can Man exercise his free will in spiritual things?', because even those well enough versed in the language of theology to know that the correct Lutheran answer should be 'No' were then told to justify their response from Scripture.[24] And apparently 'difficult' questions were also put to the laity, such as 'What [does] each man owe to Caesar and the government, and what must he give to God?'. Surely, one might think, by the banks of the Weser, peasants and artisans can have devoted little time to the resolution of such issues? The visitors, at any rate, could find 'not a soul who could give an answer'.[25]

But this objection cannot be sustained. The ignorance revealed by the visitation returns was not due solely to 'difficult questions' and 'unfamiliar language' because, on the one hand, visitations were frequent enough in some areas that the pastors (at least) should have known what to expect while, on the other, both the questions and the correct answers were normally available in advance. Thus before the first general visitation of 1528 in Saxony the Wittenberg reformers compiled and published a pamphlet entitled *The Visitors' Instructions to the Pastors in Electoral Saxony* which offered (in effect) an emergency primer in Lutheran theology. It was intended for pastors to read in advance of their examination, so that they would be tested on material that they had already had an opportunity to prepare.[26] Moreover, questions such as 'What does each man owe to Caesar?', together with the right answers and the appropriate scriptural references, were printed not only in the visitation protocols but also (for the most part) in catechisms. They were therefore widely known, for literally hundreds of catechisms were produced and circulated by diligent pastors and schoolmasters.[27] It is hard to disagree with the verdict of Scott H. Hendrix that the visitors in the sixteenth and seventeenth centuries – and therefore Strauss in the twentieth – 'graded Luther where Luther himself would have chosen to be tested'.[28]

So where should historians stand now? Kittelson is surely right that, if we seek a definitive answer to the question of success and failure, all the available relevant records must be given systematic study. This is particularly true of the visitation returns, since they offer a uniquely detailed range of information on the spiritual life of both ordinary clergy and lay folk. It is true that their proper interpretation presents some methodological difficulties; but so do the other 'serial' sources generated by the Christian churches, such as parish registers, Inquisition records and church court minutes – and yet, in time, members of the historical profession have managed to find ways of exploiting all of them. The records of Protestant visitations must be collected and subjected to the same comprehensive analysis already being applied to those of the Catholic church.[29]

However, even the sample of Protestant visitation returns already available has undermined for ever the triumphalist claims of confessional apologists and some clerical historians that the Reformation enjoyed either uniform success or (a few areas apart) deep popular support in the sixteenth century. On the contrary, the surviving evidence indicates a widespread inability on the part of the reformers – not just in one, but in several different countries – to create an acceptably pious laity within the first century of the Reformation. The evidence of 'failure' is certainly not universal, but it was enough to depress the reformers, and it is also enough to require some tentative explanations from historians.

It is now the space of 160 years since the Protestant faith first appeared publickly there [wrote an Irish Protestant in 1712]; and yet it hath made much smaller progress among the natives than could be wished, there being still (as is it generally believed) six Papists at least to one Protestant in that kingdom, although we have had many advantages which might help to facilitate this work. For we have Scripture and Reason on our side, beyond all contradiction; we have loyal and peaceable principles to ingratiate our Religion with the Higher Powers, and to induce them to promote it; and, some short interruptions excepted, we have had the examples of our monarchs, and the legal establishment, with many other temporal advantages, to recommend it to the people. So that there must be some great impediment in this matter, which ought to be taken away.[30]

The precise 'impediments' which the reformers encountered (in Ireland and elsewhere), as well as the measures by which they sought to 'take them away', might be grouped under two headings: *supply* and *demand*. To begin with the former: a major problem lay in the Protestant message itself, for Christian theology is neither simple nor self-evident. To understand the central doctrines – the Trinity, the Incarnation, the Resurrection and the New Covenant – requires instruction, reflection and (often) correction. In general the pre-Reformation church had not insisted on the need for either priests or laity to master theology, for it regarded as its first task the provision of the 'mysteries' (the sacraments) which enabled Christians to gain salvation. In many areas it was therefore considered enough for the clergy to be able to recite the Lord's Prayer and the Creed; to know what the seven sacraments were; and to be sufficiently familiar with Latin to read the mass. Further learning was neither required nor (usually) provided: there was no Latin instruction specifically for priests, whose schooling before the council of Trent usually seems to have been identical with that of laymen.[31] But the reformers changed the entire thrust of the Christian message. What had passed for piety in the fifteenth century – pilgrimages, processions, veneration of relics – was now normally execrated as superstition; instead, familiarity with the Bible and Christian theology were seen as crucial, because faith alone could save. In Patrick Collinson's terse phrase, 'The successful practice of the Protestant religion required literate skills.'[32]

Now such a transformation clearly could not be achieved overnight, for there are only a limited number of religious virtuosi in the world at any one time, and it takes time to win ordinary people over to new ideas – any new ideas.[33] Nevertheless, the early reformers made a heroic effort to explain their message. Their preferred medium was the printing press, and they began with the Bible and catechism, translated into the vernacular and published in vast numbers. Luther's German New Testament went through 253 editions between 1522 and 1546; 100,000 copies of his *Shorter Catechism* of 1529 were printed before 1563, and 500,000 copies of his German Bible between 1534 and 1574.[34] In England over six hundred separate question-and-answer catechisms were produced between 1540 and 1740.[35] The output of polemics and devotional works was likewise phenomenal: Luther alone published 1351 separate attacks on his Catholic opponents between 1518 and 1546, and his total output (excluding editions of his Bible and assuming a thousand copies for each of his printed works) gives a total of 3,100,000 copies – no small achievement for one man. And many more reformers were at work, apparently prepared to go to any lengths in order to secure the diffusion of their writings: Primus Truber (1508–86) actually invented the first written form of Slovene in order to convert his chosen people.[36]

But the effectiveness of this immense effort hinged upon a critical question: just how many people in early modern Europe could read? Historians have found to their cost that the calculation of literacy rates is a hazardous occupation. Gone are the days when those who studied the subject confidently asserted, largely on the basis of counting signatures on documents, that 40 per cent of townsmen, 5 per cent of country folk and virtually no women could read.[37] Much new evidence has now been adduced to prove that large numbers of people who could not sign their names nevertheless knew and understood the complexities of Christianity. Some people could neither read nor write, yet could memorize and on occasion recite large passages of Scripture or other religious writings, particularly catechisms (indeed the high production rate of catechisms was due precisely to their supposed ability to bridge the gap between oral and literate cultures).[38] Many other people, although they could not even write their names, could certainly read and comprehend.[39]

Even so, the total proportion able to read, understand and evaluate Protestant doctrine by themselves without expert and informed instruction viva voce can hardly have exceeded 50 per cent. To insist under these circumstances that man needed a sound knowledge of Christian doctrine in order to be 'saved' presupposed the existence and maintenance of a numerous, educated and conscientious parish clergy. But that was rarely the case during the first century after the Reformation. Indeed, for some time after Protestantism took root in each country, the local production of clergy of any sort virtually ceased. Thus the ordination register of the archbishop of Merseburg in Saxony reveals a dramatic drop after 1519 (see Table 1) and the pattern was much the same elsewhere. In many English dioceses ordinations entirely ceased for a time – there were none at Durham between 1536 and 1544, none at Exeter between 1544 and 1551 (and only ten between 1553 and 1558), none at York between 1547 and 1551. There may have been, as both the humanists and the early reformers claimed, far too many clerics in Europe on the eve of the Reformation; but for a generation or more afterwards there were far too few.[40]

Table 1 Ordinations at Merseburg (Saxony), 1515–34

1515–19	368
1520–4	113
1525–9	12
1530–4	10

Source: G. Buchwald, ed., *Die Matrikel des Hochstifts Merseburg 1469 bis 1558* (Weimar, 1926), 87–171.

There were three broad reasons for this. In the first place the transition from a Catholic to a Protestant ministry represented a deterioration in clerical status: everywhere the clergy lost their exemption from taxation and other secular obligations; in most countries they also forfeited their right to be tried for offences in a special ecclesiastical court; and, almost everywhere, there was initially little financial support. Thus in Saxony the stipend of most pastors for some years after the Reformation was reduced to the level of a day-labourer's wage; in England only some six hundred of the nine thousand available church livings were considered adequate for the support of an educated minister in 1585; while in Scotland it took a royal commission in the early seventeenth century to secure a sufficient salary for the ministry of the 'kirk by law established'.[41] And yet, in the second place, ordinands were now expected to possess detailed theological knowledge, vocational dedication and verbal dexterity to an unprecedented degree. As Richard Baxter put it in 1655:

O what qualifications are necessary for a man who hath such a charge upon him as we have! . . . How many obscure texts of Scripture to be expounded! How many duties to be performed, wherein ourselves and others may miscarry, if in the matter, and manner, and end, we be not well informed! . . . What men should we be in skill, resolution, and unwearied diligence who have all this to do.[42]

Not surprisingly, amid the uncertainty prevailing immediately after the Reformation, such men became very hard to find. Many of the universities, where the best ordinands were trained, went through a period of acute contraction after the Reformation. According to Erasmus, writing in 1528, 'Wherever Lutheranism has triumphed, education has ceased'; and as late as 1539 the reformer Justus Jonas could still lament that 'Since the Gospel spread throughout the world [i.e., Germany], many universities have been as good as dead.'[43] It was the same story in Scotland: there were no graduands from St Andrews University in the 'Reformation Year' 1559–60, and very few until 1565; while in Holland religious education at the University of Leiden was poor until at least 1600 because there were so few professors that those *in situ* were compelled to teach subjects of which they knew little or nothing. Thus the mathematician Snellius taught Hebrew even though (on his own admission) 'he himself did not understand the rudiments of Hebrew'.[44] Third and finally, once sound theological education got under way most universities seem to have produced a greater supply of cavalry than infantry for the early modern clerical army: that is, in many areas they lavished more attention upon the training of court preachers and professional theologians than on that of humble parsons who would devote their lives to catechism classes and simple sermons. Many of the ablest reformed ministers followed Luther's example and spent a large part of their time writing polemics.[45]

Nevertheless, even had every trained Protestant minister concentrated full time upon pastoral work, there would still have been a clerical shortfall because it was simply not possible to produce a complete team of properly trained reformed ministers immediately after the decision to 'go Protestant'.[46] Sometimes part of the shortfall could be made good via desperate appeals to co-religionists elsewhere for the loan of clergy;[47] but it was seldom enough and so, especially in the early decades, the various Protestant creeds were reluctantly forced to depend heavily upon the services of those clerics already in office, even if their theological commitment to the new orthodoxy was more flexible – or more superficial – than some thought proper. Thus in Saxony at least a third of the clergy in office in 1530 were (like Luther himself) former priests or monks; while in Holland, of the 250 Calvinist ministers known to have been active between 1572 and 1578, at least sixty had previously been ordained into the Catholic church.[48] In Scotland about one-half of the reformed ministry in the 1560s had formerly been Catholic priests or monks (and five ministers had been bishops).[49] England could boast clergy who managed to remain *in situ* throughout all the various changes in religion – Henrician, Edwardian, Marian and Elizabethan – between 1530 and 1570.[50] Clearly the assimilation of such large blocs of conservative (not to say unsympathetic) opinion reduced the level of detailed Christian knowledge dispensed in the parishes affected, and served as a considerable brake on the spread of reformed views.

In time, it is true, a clergy that was both quantitatively and qualitatively acceptable became available in most Protestant countries; the universities were filled with ordinands; and most parishes (at least in prosperous lowland areas) could boast both a graduate minister and a school.[51] But, unfortunately for the progress of the Reformation, the serious disruption caused by a change of creed was seldom something that happened only once. On the contrary, several Protestant areas switched their religion repeatedly. Thus the official creed of the Rhine Palatinate altered at the accession of each new ruler: Lutheran in 1546, Calvinist in 1560, Lutheran again in 1576, Calvinist again in 1583. Each change was marked by the expulsion of all incumbents who would not conform, leaving numerous parishes vacant, so that the pastorate was continually below full strength between 1576 and 1590.[52] Somewhat later, in Scotland, some 200 ministers were 'deprived' between 1639 and 1651, over 300 were turned out after 1662, and around 600 more after 1689 – all for opposing the differing forms of church government (Presbyterian and Episcopalian by turns) decreed by the state;[53] while in England almost 3000 ministers (one-third of the total) were 'ejected' from their livings in the 1640s because they adhered to the episcopal system, and a further 2000 were deprived in the 1660s because they did not. Parishes might remain vacant for years after these brutal changes.[54]

The impact of war on religious practice could be even more

disruptive. Thus in the first phase of the Dutch Revolt, the clergy of each side were prime military targets: the Army of Flanders hanged any Calvinist ministers and elders that they encountered, while the 'Sea Beggars' frequently executed priests, monks and nuns. Slightly later, in the villages around Strasbourg, the hostilities known as the 'Thieves' War' in the 1580s and the 'Bishop's War' in the 1590s, although relatively minor, were enough to interrupt the admirable devotional habits recorded among local people in the preceding decades. Finally, the exemplary piety of the Rhine Palatinate on the eve of the Thirty Years' War was transformed after the failure of Elector Frederick's gamble for the Bohemian crown in 1619–20, for his lands were soon occupied by Spanish and Bavarian forces which immediately expelled all Protestant clergy, sequestered all secularized church property, and imported teams of priests from neighbouring Catholic areas.[55]

Such were the impediments to the early progress of Protestantism on the 'supply side'. And yet, even had all of them been miraculously overcome, and a full complement of dedicated pastors somehow installed permanently in every parish, considerable obstacles remained in the way of effective evangelism on the 'demand side'. For, after the printing-press, the principal means of disseminating the Protestant message was preaching, and here the reformers ran into a further barrier posed by the extraordinary linguistic fragmentation of early modern Europe. In 1789, according to the abbé Grégoire, undertaking a nationwide inquiry into the languages then spoken in France:

In no part of the globe which I know is any national language universally used by the nation. France has within its bosom perhaps eight million subjects, some of whom can hardly mumble a few maimed words or phrases dismembered from our idiom; the others are completely ignorant of it. It is known that in Lower Brittany and in many places beyond the Loire the clergy are still compelled to preach in the local patois under pain of not being understood if they spoke French.[56]

In Holland, despite the desperate shortage of ministers in the early years after the revolt against Spain, when the church at Rotterdam asked their brethren abroad to send a new preacher in 1575 it specified that he should be a local man because 'the ministers from Friesland or the eastern Netherlands will not be understood here by the local people [because of their accent]'.[57] The situation on the Celtic fringe of Britain was even worse because a large part of the population understood no English at all. As John Richardson, rector of Belturbet and chaplain to the duke of Ormond, correctly observed in 1712 of Ireland, 'Until they understand our language, if we would convert them we must apply to them in their own'; and yet the first Protestant New Testament in Irish was printed only in 1602, and the first Bible only in 1685. In Scotland a Protestant catechism in Gaelic was not published until 1653, a Gaelic psalter (and even then only fifty psalms) not until 1659.[58] Oliver Cromwell, lord protector of Scotland, as well as of England and Ireland, may not have been far wrong when he claimed that 'little or no care hath been taken for a very numerous people inhabiting in the Highlands by the establishing of ministry or a maintenance, where the greatest part have scarce heard whether there be an Holy Ghost or not'.[59] In Wales, although a Protestant religious primer – the first book ever printed in Welsh – appeared in 1547, and a New Testament and Prayer Book twenty years later, most ministers in the principality had not been trained in Welsh, and the few graduates among them seem not to have been Welsh-speakers.[60] Although some recognized that Protestantizing Britain's Celtic fringe called for nothing less than the missionary methods employed in the Americas to 'bring the very heathen and savage – whether the poore Indians or the Irish and Welsh – into Christ', those prepared to undertake such work in the local language remained few and far between until the eighteenth century.[61]

However, even where the basic Protestant texts were translated relatively swiftly into the vernacular, and the language of minister and congregation was the same, orally spreading the Protestant gospel to ordinary people still presented problems because, according to the English Puritan William Pemble in the 1630s:

You meet with hundreds that had need be taught their very ABC in matters of religion ... Ask them the meaning of the articles of the faith, of the petitions in the Lords Prayer, or of other common points in Catechisme, and marke their answeres: you shall see them so shuffle and fumble, speake halfe

words and halfe sentences, so hacke and hew at it, that . . . you would think
verily they were born stark naturals and idiots.

Twenty years later another English minister lamented in similar vein
that 'A man may preach long enough to hundreds in the congregation
. . . who will not be able to give any accompt of one sentence they
hear, if they live a hundred years.' The problem was that:

All generally, except they be catechized, or extraordinarily furnished with
parts beyond their neighbors, find it an hard matter to understand the very
common terms in which preachers must expresse themselves . . . For though
a minister thinks he expresseth himself very plain, yet it is almost incredible
what strange conceits most ignorant people have of common notions . . . I am
sure most of our hearers are not arrived (nor even do to their dying day arrive)
unto the understanding of a child of twelve or fourteen years old, bred under
means of Literature.

Many other mid-seventeenth-century Protestant leaders, from almost
all countries, execrated in similar terms the 'incorrigible profanity of
the multitude' who seemed totally, almost congenitally, incapable of
learning and remembering Christian doctrine.[62]

So why, one may ask, did these men not resort to other methods of
disseminating their message? After all, as they no doubt knew, the first
generation of Protestants, perhaps to compensate for their lack of
numbers, had employed several non-literary means of communication
that their successors eschewed, rejected and even condemned.[63] First
came songs. Popular melodies were frequently reissued with Christian
verses, so that (in the words of a Dutch collection of 1540), young
people could 'sing something good, in place of foolish sensual songs'.[64]
The idea soon caught on. *The Gude and Godlie Ballatis*, first printed
in Scotland in 1567, included an item with a chorus that ran gaily
enough:

> Johne, cum kis me now
> Johne, cum kis me now
> Johne, cum kis me by and by
> And mak no mair adow

sandwiched between verses such as:

> God send everie priest ane wyfe
> And everie nunne ane manne
> That they micht live that haly lyfe
> As first the kirk began.

Twenty-five verses of similarly banal anticlerical sentiment followed. It must have been fun to sing in street or tavern, however little one knew of the Protestant gospel. But later, although communal hymn-singing and psalm-singing remained popular, religious and secular music were strictly separated. The *Gude and Godlie Ballatis* were not reprinted after 1621.[65]

The early reformers, although they mostly drew the line at visual imagery in churches, also resorted to woodcuts, engravings and other prints made 'to instruct the common man' (as Luther put it in his introduction to the *Passional* of 1529, a set of Bible stories with facing illustrations), for 'without images we can neither think nor understand anything'. They were essential 'above all for the sake of children and simple folk, who are more easily moved by pictures and images to recall divine history than through mere words or doctrines'.[66] These religious compositions made skilful use of the pre-existing pictorial language that was commonly used by printers and was therefore easily understood by ordinary people: even Luther and Melanchthon wrote texts to accompany woodcut images that depicted deformed animals bearing a curious resemblance to monks. But this, too, did not last. Although religious prints did not totally disappear, once the reformed churches became established they were less prominent, and later Protestant *leaders* rarely made use of them. Collinson has rightly described the reformers as suffering from 'acute visual anorexia'.[67]

In the early days converts were also sometimes made through stage plays that contrasted certain Protestant and Catholic beliefs more clearly than any theological tract. Thus in 1523 the citizens of Bern in Switzerland were entertained by the street performance of a play that satirized the Catholic church's heavy investment in death. *Die Totenfresser* ('The Corpse Eaters') by Nicholas Manuel opened with a sacristan on stage, meditating: 'I like dead people better than fighting or screwing,' he informed his audience. Praying for the dead was 'more fun than baptizing children'. Before long, he was joined by other like-minded clerics of different degrees. They all lamented the onset of the Reformation. 'Of what use can the Gospel be to me?' inquired a bewildered rural dean; 'It's very much against us priests.' He was reassured by, among others, the pope, who reminded everyone that 'Church offerings, weekly or monthly, and annual masses for the dead, bring us in more than enough cash.' But, he warned, there must be no slacking:

> We must use every chance
> To scare hell out of common folk,
> For that is what conceals our deception . . .
> And let's be thankful for the dead
> Who make it possible for us to fleece the living.

Few spectators can have missed the point.[68]

Once their church was established and its enemies outlawed, however, many reformers seem to have forgotten that humour could be as informative as learned exposition. Instead, they excoriated all theatrical performances: 'Wyll not a fylthe playe, with the blaste of a Trumpette, sooner call thyther thousands, than an houres tolling of a Bell, bring to a sermon a hundred?' thundered the Puritan John Stockwood in a sermon of 1578.[69] And yet the continuing educational value of Protestant religious drama was easily demonstrated, as the Puritan divine John Shaw found while ministering to the remote upland parish of Cartmel (Lancashire) in 1644. According to his autobiography, one day he met a man aged about sixty to whom Shaw immediately put the first question in the catechism: 'How many gods are there?' The man replied 'he knew not'. Shaw, 'informing him, asked him again "How he thought to be saved?"'. The man answered 'he could not tell, yet thought that was a harder question than the other. I told him that the way to salvation was by Jesus Christ, God–Man who, as he was man, shed his blood for us on the cross etc.' At this the man, much to Shaw's astonishment, suddenly perked up. '"Oh Sir," said he, "I think I heard of that man you spoke of, once in a play at Kendall, called Corpus Christi play, where there was a man on a tree and blood ran down."' Shaw saw this as clear evidence of the limitations of conventional worship according to the Book of Common Prayer, and several later historians have used the anecdote to prove the continuance of 'dark corners of the land' in mid-seventeenth-century England.[70] Perhaps so; but it also demonstrates the power of drama to explain matters that even regular churchgoers seemed to find difficult. Mystery or passion plays were still performed at Kendal, Chester and elsewhere in the north of England until the 1590s; an elderly man in 1644 can only have seen one as a boy, yet his vivid (and accurate) recollection had outlasted a hundred sermons.[71]

The Protestant leaders seem to have convinced themselves that their religion could – and should – be comprehended only through words. According to J. J. Scarisbrick, it all amounted to a 'streamlining' of the Christian message: 'The Reformation simplified everything. It effected a shift from a religion of symbol and allegory, ceremony and formal gesture, to one that was plain and direct: a shift from the visual to the aural, from ritual to literal exposition, from the numinous and mysterious to the everyday.'[72] But, if the foregoing argument is correct, in early modern Europe the written word and the literal exposition were neither 'plain and direct' nor 'everyday'. And therefore to abolish all media of diffusion except the Word was not a simplification, but rather a complication. Nevertheless, that is precisely what happened. That 'learned minister of God's Holy Word', William Pemble, unconsciously testified to this in his sermon on 'The mischiefe of ignorance', quoted above, when he lamented that 'All meanes of knowledge have been plentifull amongst us – preaching, catechizing, printing – and all these for a long time, sixty yeares and upwards.'[73] Preaching, catechizing and printing, yes; but that scarcely amounted to 'all meanes of knowledge' available.

A clear evolution thus occurred in the use made of the various media by the Protestant evangelists, which helps to explain both the movement's initial 'success' and its later 'failure'. In the early days, when they were desperate for popular support and anxious to demonstrate their distinctness from Catholicism, the reformers made full use of all available channels of communication – print, sermon, music, art, satire and drama. In addition care was taken to identify Protestantism with popular causes. Thus in the 1520s, in Germany, the apostles of the new religion paid special attention to the urban environment (in which, of course, most of them had grown up) and 'tried skilfully to adapt Luther's message to the hegemonic corporate-communal values of their fellow citizens'.[74] But once a loyal, learned congregation grew up, these attitudes and practices changed. Now it was no longer enough just to criticize and ridicule the opposition; there was a whole new theology to explain. Furthermore, once the small learned groups became the elite of an established Church, with the power to coerce all their fellows to attend services, every preacher faced a new dilemma: should he address himself to the familiar, enthusiastic and reassuring faces of the committed, or to the sullen, somnolent or blank stares of the rest? The answer was obvious. Although some ministers struggled to cater for both, offering a number of services for everyone (such as the Sunday sermon) and others just for the godly (Holy Communion, weekday sermons and so on), most pitched their teachings primarily at the true believers.[75] One determined Dutch minister in a rural parish near Dordrecht, for example, managed to devote his weekday sermons for five months in 1584–5 to expounding the Book of Haggai for the edification of his congregation. Yet the Book of Haggai contains but twenty-three verses.[76] Some learned ministers went even further and hand-picked their congregations. In England in the mid-seventeenth century the Puritan John Angier managed to maintain high standards of godliness among his own congregation only by employing 'bouncers' to control those allowed to attend: 'Officers went amongst them to see if there were any intruders [sic],' his biographer proudly related, 'for either they were known by face to them, or they had testimonials from approved ministers or eminent Christians.'[77] Admittedly this practice seems to have been unusual, but throughout the Protestant world many pastors seemed capable of communicating exclusively through tracts and sermons which many of their charges could understand only with difficulty, if at all. A man of refinement, like John Selden, might claim that 'He that takes pleasure to hear sermons enjoys himself as much as he that hears plays', but for the mass of the population it was simply not true.[78]

And, of course, if the Protestant leaders had had their way, Selden would not have been able to hear or enjoy plays at all. Believing that theatres provoked indecency, serious (and sometimes successful) efforts were made in many countries to legislate them out of Christian life. It was the same with festivals (which, it was claimed, led to vice), games (which were said to cause violence), recreation (which produced idleness) and dancing (which allegedly aroused lust). All were proscribed. Instead of trying to identify Protestantism with local values and practices, as Luther and his contemporaries had done, subsequent generations of reformers sought to suppress everything that was not rooted in Scripture. And yet in early modern times such things were too deeply ingrained to be extirpated. As the fun-loving Sir Toby Belch told the Puritan Malvolio when he tried to end the evening carousals in act 1, scene 3, of Shakespeare's *Twelfth Night*:

> Dost thou think, because thou art virtuous,
> There shall be no more cakes and ale?

It needed more than the Reformation to end the appeal of cakes and ale, and more than sermons to fill the gap left by the rituals and religious demonstrations that were now disparaged and discouraged as vain superstition. The campaign of Lent against carnival did nothing to win or retain popular support for the Reformation.[79]

The argument above receives indirect confirmation from the experience of the Roman Catholic church during the age of the Reformation. There is plenty of evidence to suggest that, when they relied primarily on the written and spoken word, the Catholics ran into precisely the same problems as their rivals: lamentable ignorance among the clergy and 'incorrigible profanity' among the masses, particularly in rural areas. Thus in 1578 King Stefan Batory of Poland encouraged the missionary efforts of the Jesuits within his kingdom with the words 'Do not be envious of the foreign lands in Asia and America that your Spanish and Portuguese brethren have won for God. Just near here you have Indians and Japanese [of your own].'[80] The same analogy was drawn by the Jesuits in Italy, who in the 1560s habitually referred to Sicily as 'a real India' and the Abruzzi as 'the Indies of Italy'.[81] Almost a century later things seemed little better: in 1652 a group of missionaries in Corsica, who inquired of villagers 'If there is one God or several, and which of the three divine persons became a man for us', failed to get any answer at all, and concluded 'one might as well be talking Arabic to these people'; while in Apulia a Jesuit missionary who asked a group of shepherds 'How many gods are there?', found some who thought there were a hundred, others who suggested a thousand, and a few who opted for an even higher number.[82]

It might be objected that these examples come from the periphery of Christian Europe. However, the visitation records from the Catholic heartlands in the later sixteenth century often make as dismal reading as those of the Protestant areas. Thus in Luxembourg some priests were found to have committed murder, while others encouraged their concubines to slaughter any illegitimate offspring. Rare was the rural parish in Catholic areas of Germany or Switzerland where mass was celebrated on weekdays.[83] But in most areas the situation soon changed dramatically.

Following the closure of the council of Trent in 1563, the Catholic church modified many of its practices in ways that echoed those of the reformers and sought to defeat the Protestant challenge with similar methods. For example, although the council did not require all clergy to receive special education at a diocesan seminary, many bishops – often supported by the secular authorities – created one. Thus by 1575, 84 of the 200 or so dioceses of Italy already had a seminary, and by 1599 the total had risen to 113; by then, a further 20 existed in Spain.[84] The number of ordained clergy now rose swiftly, after a short but sharp fall during the Reformation crisis, and their quality also improved thanks to the introduction of regular visitations which many Catholic leaders saw (just like their Protestant counterparts) as critical for improving pastoral standards.[85] For Archbishops Carlo and Fed-erigo Borromeo of Milan, visitations became almost an obsession: the former scarcely wrote a letter to a fellow bishop without mentioning them, while the latter organized his visitations like a military operation, with his staff preparing detailed maps and plans of every parish to be inspected. In marked contrast to the contemporary investigations of the Protestants analysed by Strauss, those pursued by the Borromeos found little cause for complaint: a diligent and well informed priest-hood served a laity which, in both social and sacramental terms, was highly satisfactory.[86] Even in areas where the results of the first post-Tridentine visitations were appalling – such as the archdiocese of

Cologne, where, in 1569, 30 per cent of the clergy were found to have concubines, 15 per cent illegitimate offspring and 35 per cent (including almost every member of the chapter) Protestant leanings – subsequent episcopal tours revealed a dramatic improvement. By 1620 concubinage, illegitimate children and religious deviance among the clergy had been more or less eradicated from the area.[87]

Simultaneously, education improved religious awareness among the laity. All over the Catholic world schools were opened and reformed in order to teach sound doctrine to the young. To take a striking example, in 1536 Castellino da Castello opened a 'School of Christian Doctrine' to teach the elements of faith to the children of the city of Milan; but by 1564 there were 28 such schools in the city, instructing some 2000 children, and by 1599 over 120 schools teaching approximately 7000 boys and 6000 girls.[88] Even religious groups founded for other purposes began to devote themselves to education: the Jesuits, founded in 1534 to convert the Muslims of the Holy Land, opened their first school in 1548 at Messina; the Barnabites, a congregation devoted to preaching since 1530, opened a school in 1604 at Milan; and the Oratorians, an association of priests dedicated to raising local religious standards and granted papal recognition in 1575, taught from 1614 at Dieppe. By 1710 the three orders maintained 126 colleges in France alone.[89] Keen attention was also paid, as in Protestant lands, to teaching the catechism to the literate and illiterate alike.[90] In Spain, for example, the records of the Inquisition reveal a steady improvement in religious knowledge even among those brought in for questioning about their orthodoxy: thus the proportion who could recite their catechism perfectly to the Toledo tribunal increased from 40 per cent in 1555 to 80 per cent in 1575, while the proportion who could recite their prayers correctly to the Inquisitors of Cuenca rose from 37 per cent in 1540–63 to 64 per cent in 1564–80, and to 80 per cent in 1581–1600.[91]

This remarkable picture of lay piety, so different from that painted for many Protestant areas, may be ascribed in large part to three factors. First, the Catholics were prepared to compromise with traditional religious customs, and strove to salvage and sanctify many of the traditional practices that many Protestants denounced as either idolatry or vanity – veneration of relics, exorcism, processions and pilgrimage.[92] Moreover, where the Catholic church did suppress, it tried to fill the gap with some new interstitial religious rituals – 'Calvaries', new saints' days, miracles and confraternities.[93] Second, they made full use of all the media available to them: pictures, prints, plays and songs as well as catechisms, schools, sermons and visitations.[94] Thus a vast output of Catholic devotional literature, often printed in large letters on small pages and accompanied by explanatory illustrations, was produced 'for the sake of simple folk';[95] while in the 'dark corners' of the Catholic world specially trained preachers (often drawn from the new religious orders) went on carefully coordinated 'missions' armed with a set of religious pictures, showing the Christian as a pilgrim in the world with the different paths to salvation and perdition, to be used when words alone seemed to puzzle a congregation.[96]

Third, and perhaps most important, the Counter-Reformation church went out of its way to simplify the Christian faith for the benefit of its congregations. In 1578 the *Instructions* issued to the clergy of the archdiocese of Lyon advised parish priests to make only elementary sermons – 'probably nothing more than recitations of prayers and the Ten Commandments together with a brief lecture on the catechism'. Carlo Bascapé, the reforming bishop of Novara from 1593 to 1615, went further and actually warned his clergy to avoid all mention of complex doctrinal problems which the laity would find confusing. This attitude soon spread. In the South Netherlands, ravaged by decades of bitter religious war, the Catholic clergy in the seventeenth century likewise concentrated on providing 'an uncomplicated faith' for their charges.[97] Somewhat later, in France, the Abbé Fleury's *Religious Duties of Masters and Servants* (first published in 1688 and reprinted many times in the eighteenth century) likewise insisted that religion for the masses should be kept straightforward: 'Public instruction . . . must be simple. One must deal only with the catechism: that is to say, with the knowledge of the "mysteries" that is essential for all Christians, and the maxims for regulating behaviour.' And, even then, each exposition should be kept short: 'not too long or too frequent – once a week and only half an hour each time'.[98]

In Poland, meanwhile, some of the Catholic clergy went to even greater lengths to smooth the path of faith for the nobles and gentry who controlled the state. Not only were the articles of belief simplified, but the *szlachta* were bombarded with devotional works (almost all composed by priests) which reassured them not only that salvation certainly awaited all good Catholics, but also that Polish was spoken in Paradise; that even in Hell the superior status of the gentry would be respected, so that they would receive their punishments (if any) away from the sight of lesser mortals; and that God was a constitutional monarch who asked the advice of his celestial diet before taking all major decisions. Defections from the Protestant to the Catholic faith soon became a flood.[99]

And yet, amid all this apparent 'success', some devout Catholics perceived a measure of failure. Thus in the South Netherlands, whereas spectacular results were recorded in the *ad limina* returns of the bishops to Rome during the first half of the seventeenth century, the reports of the rural deans to their bishops were far more pessimistic. It was not a question of insufficient numbers of clergy, for by the 1640s almost every parish had its priest, many chosen after a concursus; nor was the problem infrequent preaching, for the deans usually found that church services and catechism classes were held with due regularity. It was the unwillingness of the laity to attend either that undermined the clerical effort. Government legislation was required before traditional religious practices were abandoned and the people forced reluctantly into the churches. Pastoral theology was thus reduced, according to one modern commentator, 'to commands and prohibitions like barbed wire round a sheep pen'.[100] It seemed a high price to pay for 'success'.

By 1700, only one large Protestant state had achieved all the aims of both reformers and counter-reformers, a state where a pessimistic sense of 'failure' was apparently absent: Lutheran Sweden, a rambling rural kingdom of about 2500 parishes. Although a Swedish Bible and a Protestant church order were introduced under Lutheran guidance during the 1520s, several schisms and deprivations occurred between 1531 and 1611; and not until the 1620s (and the foundation of gymnasia) was a proper education offered for ordinands. Thus far, the Swedish experience differed little from that of other Protestant lands. Thereafter both the quantity and the quality of the clergy improved dramatically, until by 1700 most parishes had two highly trained ministers – one for religious instruction and the other for teaching in the school. But Christian education in Sweden was not confined to church and classroom. All heads of household were required by law to teach young children to memorize their catechism at home, then, either at the growing number of parish schools or at the houses of pastors or church elders, the children learned to read and comprehend what they already knew by heart (Figure 19), and both abilities were examined annually by the minister. After the 1620s the results of these yearly tests were recorded parish by parish, and six grades from 'cannot read' to 'reads acceptably' were awarded; later the examination registers were scrutinized and verified by the rural dean.[101] By the mid-seventeenth century the high standards found elsewhere (if at all) only in great cities like Amsterdam were being achieved on a national scale in the Swedish countryside, and before long they were surpassed. For by the end of the seventeenth century the registers revealed reading literacy rates of 90 per cent for both males and females in the central dioceses (Uppsala and Västerås), with only slightly lower rates in the southern parts. Comprehension of the scriptural set texts was almost equally high. Even the provinces annexed from Denmark in 1658 (Scåne, Hålland and Blekinge) registered high reading and comprehension scores by the end of the century: the ablest clergy in Sweden were drafted into the new parishes with orders to carry out a thorough 'Swedification', and A and B grades rose from below 50 to above 80 per cent, even when a random passage of Scripture was set for reading and explanation.[102] Eventually it was possible to insist that those who could not read a passage of Scripture satisfactorily could not receive a licence to marry.[103]

But why did this remarkable Protestant success remain unique? It was not that the Swedish church had different aims from its fellows, for it did not; rather it enjoyed three practical advantages. First,

19 A Swedish father teaches his children religion, 1840s

Sweden's low population density and harsh climate made it unrealistic to expect religious instruction to take place in a single place for each community, so the task devolved on heads of household. In this panel painting from Leksand, a small Swedish town northwest of Stockholm, done in the 1840s, a patriarch teaches his family – girls as well as boys – to memorize Scripture.

there was total continuity of effort: no foreign invasion or civil war interrupted the patient labours of the ministers, elders and rural deans after the early seventeenth century. Second, and no less important, a total identification of aims existed between church and state, of which their cooperation in the task of 'indoctrinating the young' was but one example.[104] And finally, and perhaps most important of all, no schism occurred within the Swedish Protestant establishment. Not only did the kingdom escape those damaging changes of creed that left parishes deprived for years of any minister: the clergy also remained largely free of the need to engage in polemical exchanges with its rivals and enemies.

Elsewhere things were very different. In Germany the Lutherans were divided for at least a generation after the master's death into Philippists and Gnesio-Lutherans; in the Netherlands Calvinist Gomarists attacked their fellow Calvinist Remonstrants; in Scotland Episcopalians fought Presbyterians; in England Puritans vied with Arminians. And everywhere much time was spent in trying to discredit the Catholics: in France, as perhaps elsewhere, the production of devotional literature was surpassed by the publication of polemics until the 1640s.[105] As Sir Henry Wotton accurately observed, 'The itch of disputing will prove the scab of the churches.'[106]

For many people the schism caused by the Reformation discredited Christianity in general and Protestantism in particular. As early as 1524 the Catholic apologist Josse de Clichthove predicted that the religious split would undermine people's faith; and in 1536 the papal nuncio in Germany, Cardinal Morone, noted sadly that 'since everyone is allowed to believe what he wishes, not only in areas where the princes are contaminated [with heresy] but also in those where they are Catholic, the people are so confused that they do not know which opinion they should adhere to'.[107] Soon even Protestants were forced to admit the same thing. In 1555 a Saxon jurist commented that incessant disputes on the fine points of theology had caused 'lay people and common folk to doubt the very articles of the faith and to hold the preachers, indeed the whole of religion, in contempt'. A generation later, a Calvinist minister in Brussels complained to his colleagues that:

One finds atheists and libertines everywhere, of whom some openly ridicule all religion, calling it a fable and an ornament . . . Others, in order to disguise their contempt for God, say that so many warring creeds have grown up in our Fatherland that they do not know which is the true one, nor which they should believe. Some others hang their coats in the wind and, in their outward behaviour, accommodate themselves to all religions.[108]

Similar claims arose in the British Isles. John Napier's *Plaine Discovery of the Whole Revelation of St John*, published in 1593, asserted that in Scotland the number of 'atheists or newtralls' was set to increase rapidly; while at the Hampton Court conference in 1604 one senior English cleric suggested that his countrymen might be divided into three parts: the godly, who waxed in the Lord's wisdom; the cryptopapists, who wanted the Roman ways back; and those who were 'either indifferent or plain neuter' and 'regard not of what religion they be'. He considered the third to be particularly numerous.[109]

Such, then, were the roots of the despondency among the leaders of the Reformation. They seem to have become obsessed with a particular set of religious values that left no place for any alternatives, and little space for any sense of satisfaction. By the mid-seventeenth century, it is true, Protestantism had become firmly established in large parts of Europe. It had created not one, but several, distinct Christian creeds; it had produced a clergy whose morals, education, religious knowledge and preaching skills were, in general, far higher than ever before; and it had become the functional religion of almost all the inhabitants of England, Scotland, North Germany and Scandinavia, as well as of many people in Switzerland, Hungary, Transylvania, the Dutch Republic and France (and in some of Europe's overseas colonies). A casual traveller to any Protestant church from Saxony to Scotland or from Stockholm to Zurich would have recognized instantly that it was not Catholic: the structure might date from pre-Reformation times, but the liturgy, the music, the layout and the interior decoration had all been transformed. And if the same traveller had surveyed the actual behaviour of Protestant congregations – that is to say, noting what they did, as well as what they did not do – then once again the Reformation would have been seen to have clearly made its mark. It was not just that parishioners everywhere wished to be married in church, wanted their children to be baptized, and desired to be buried in consecrated ground according to the rites of the prevailing local religion; they also, after a while, showed some enthusiasm for the new liturgy – the Book of Common Prayer in England, the Book of Common Order in Scotland, and so on – and vigorously opposed attempts to tamper with it.[110]

But it had been a long, slow process, and by 1650 it was still far from over. At the end of the first century of the Reformation, Protestantism remained in many areas largely what it had been at the start: 'an urban event'. Further research among the visitation returns and other serial sources should pinpoint the precise contours and chronology of the new creed's progress; but it seems unlikely to restore the triumphalist vision of nineteenth-century Protestant historians who saw the 'Reformation process' as a continuous, inexorable and all-engulfing tide and (in Germany) traced Bismarck's creation of a 'new Germany' at Versailles in 1871 back to Luther's defiance of papal authority at Wittenberg in 1517.[111] For historians, as for many reformers, the considerable successes of the first hundred years of Protestantism will no doubt continue to be viewed within a broader framework of failure.

10

The last chapter in this book was the first one undertaken. It is also almost the sole survivor of an abandoned project. Shortly after I started teaching at St Andrews University in 1972, I decided to take advantage of the four-year degree structure to encourage History students to pursue a project in the 'long vacation' between their third and fourth years. I had just read a series of articles in the Annales de Normandie *written by pupils of Pierre Chaunu: each had sampled a local series of early modern court records and tried to chart the changing patterns of crimes revealed. All the studies reported the same marked shift from crimes of violence, which predominated in seventeenth-century trials, to theft, which predominated a hundred years later.[1] I suggested to my colleague Bruce Lenman, an eminent historian of early modern Scotland, that we might ask our students to go through the records of their own locality to see whether the Norman pattern also prevailed there. We arranged palaeography classes and described the different types of record they might encounter; and then we waited. The results were stunning. Students living in England found similar developments in their local records to Chaunu's pupils in Normandy; but the real surprise came from the students living in Scotland, some of whom discovered unexpectedly detailed records about the control of sin. It seemed that every parish had a court that met regularly to discipline people who had blasphemed, got 'beastlie drunk', done anything except attend church on Sunday, or had sexual relations with anyone except their lawful spouse. Cases of fornication – sexual intercourse between unmarried people – formed by far the largest single category of cases judged by most church courts as well as by a few secular tribunals (such as the justice court of Aberdeen, studied by one of the students).*

After a second similar experiment the following year, Lenman and I took three steps. First, we accepted some of the students as doctoral candidates, and coordinated their work on crime in different parts of Scotland. Second, we started teaching a 'special subject' course for undergraduates on the subject, in the hope of attracting more graduate students. Finally we asked the Social Science Research Council in London to fund a survey of all the surviving crime records of early modern Scotland, both to establish what was available and to work out the possibilities for record linkage. In 1977, the Council paid for a graduate research assistant to help us to compile the survey, and Lenman and I began to plan a larger project that would chart the 'taming of Scotland'.[2] We also met with other scholars, including a team of Swedish historians already engaged in the study of crime in their country during the sixteenth and seventeenth centuries, and Christina Larner, who had just completed a survey of Scottish witchcraft cases. Finally, we co-edited a book on crime in Europe since 1550.[3]

Gradually, however, a dreadful realization dawned upon both Lenman and me. The more we searched the legal records, the more evidence we found of cases settled out of court. In Scotland, deeds called 'Acts of Assythment' provided long lists of past felonies, usually committed by members of one family against those of another, and solemnly declared that none would be prosecuted. The Assythment was a pardon: the two families decided to end their feud and agreed to keep the peace in future; they therefore needed to list all the past crimes – including murder, abduction, rape and arson – for which they would no longer seek revenge. This constituted the only court record of all the offences in question: none had been previously reported or tried. Lenman and I realized that, if so many serious crimes had escaped the judicial process, any attempt to quantify crime, or even to suggest trends in the surviving data (as Chaunu's students had done), would prove grossly misleading. We also noted that most European countries possessed a similar instrument for settling serious crimes out of court. In France it was known as the accommodement légal *and, according to one authority, about three-quarters of all* accommodements *registered by the Paris courts in the early seventeenth century 'specify that formal charges were to be dropped as a consequence of the settlement'.[4]*

The only Scottish criminal records that seemed relatively complete (and free of out-of-court settlements) were those kept by the church courts. For a workshop on early modern crime organized by our Swedish colleagues, I therefore analysed the published records of the kirk-session (parish court) of St Andrews between 1573 and 1600, and attempted to link them with surviving demographic and other data. Over that period, the kirk-session (composed of the parish minister with the lay elders and deacons) heard over sixty cases a year and, in the 1590s, tried perhaps 4 per cent of the adult inhabitants of the parish each year. Even more remarkable, over half of all cases related to sex: fornication, adultery and incest. The records of other kirk-sessions at the same time revealed almost exactly the same pattern, with one exception: in St Andrews during the 1590s the punishment for sexual offences shot up and the number of cases dropped dramatically. It seemed that, at least in this respect, the local population had been briefly tamed.

In 1988, I published these findings, the first to be derived from a quantitative survey of surviving church court records in Scotland, in a Festschrift for Rosalind Mitchison, whose own work on the control of sex in early modern Scotland has proved so enlightening. I also delivered them as a paper at a panel on 'Sin and the Calvinists' at the Sixteenth Century Studies Conference. The panel organizer, Raymond Mentzer, persuaded his colleagues to submit expanded versions of the paper, and added two more. One of them was by Michael Graham, then engaged on a wide-ranging survey of the work of Scottish kirk-sessions between 1560 and 1610 for his doctoral thesis. I did not see his contribution until the volume came out in 1994, and I did not realize that he disagreed with my interpretation until his excellent book, The Uses of Reform: Godly Discipline and Popular Behavior in Scotland and Beyond, 1560–1620, appeared two years later.[5]

Graham examined the records of seven kirk-sessions and three presbyteries (none of them complete for the entire period) and made two important deductions. First, he emphasized the role of local factors, and particularly the role of the elite, in determining the zeal with which the church court in each community prosecuted certain categories of offence over time. In the case of St Andrews, he demonstrated that disagreements between the ministers, and between them *and the town magistrates, from time to time undermined the 'great work of discipline' and reduced the number of cases prosecuted. Second, he argued that the strange obsession of apparently all kirk-sessions in their early days with sexual offences demonstrated a shrewd recognition of the courts' limitations: they chose to repress sexual deviance because almost all members of the community supported the official stance – either because it accorded with the Scripture (and thus reduced any risk of provoking divine anger), or because it diminished the number of single mothers dependent on public assistance. Graham argued that only when each community had accepted the church's authority in this matter did its courts start to prosecute other, more controversial, misdemeanours such as excessive drinking or the failure to attend church on Sunday.*

These two observations considerably expand the arguments deployed in the chapter that follows; but Graham also disagreed with me on one important point. He argued that the drop in sexual cases before the St Andrews kirk-session in the mid-1590s did not result from a reformation of morals (pages 278–80 below), although he did not offer a viable alternative.[6] In fact, very few alternatives exist. It is highly unlikely that those guilty of fornication in these years found refuge elsewhere in order to avoid an appearance before the St Andrews court with its punitive fines. Almost every case heard by the session arose because a spinster became pregnant and, since early modern Scotland was a poor country, no parish admitted a pregnant single woman (and therefore the prospect of supporting her and her child) if they could avoid it. Those who did arrive were promptly sent back home again. In fact, some other data presented by Professor Graham support my theory. The kirk-session of the Canongate, a parish in Edinburgh, conducted a similar campaign of savage penalties against fornication in the 1560s; and the number of cases coming before the court fell dramatically.[7] I therefore stand by the thesis stated below: that the combination of more elders patrolling the streets in search of sin with draconian penalties for anyone found guilty virtually eliminated fornication and adultery for a time. Remarkable though it may seem, the Calvinist elite of St Andrews had found – albeit briefly – a deterrent powerful enough to suppress one of the most basic human urges.

The 'Kirk by Law Established' and the 'Taming of Scotland': St Andrews, 1559–1600

In August 1590 Mr James Melville, minister of the church of Scotland, delivered a stirring exhortation to the General Assembly which called for major improvements in the condition of the kirk. One of his principal arguments was:

That discipline was maist necessar in the Kirk, seing without the saming, Chrysts Kingdome could nocht stand. For unles the Word and Sacraments war kiepit in sinceritie, and rightlie usit and practesit be direction of the discipline, they wald soone be corrupted. And therfor certean it was, that without sum discipline na kirk; without trew discipline, na rightlie reformed kirk; and without the right and perfyt discipline, na right and perfyt kirk.

At the end of the session, the Assembly endorsed Melville's stand and resolved that 'Euerie minister sould haiff a copie of the Book of Discipline and peruse it; and euerie presbyterie sould cause thair haill members subscryve the sam; and the refusars to be excomunicat.' Melville's autobiography, which includes the text of his speech, makes it clear that at the forefront of his mind lurked the troubles that he had witnessed for more than a decade in planting a disciplined church in the town of St Andrews in Fife.[8]

St Andrews in the age of the Reformation was the seat of both a university and the metropolitan see of Scotland; it was also a lively burgh, with considerable seaborne trade and jurisdiction over a number of outlying villages.[9] Although in the absence of contemporary registers of births and deaths, or a census, it is hazardous to offer an estimate of the parish's population, it is likely that it consisted of some 4000 people in the early seventeenth century, of whom perhaps 2500–3000 lived in the town.[10] But two considerations suggest that the population in the previous half-century was lower than this. On the one hand, the disruption caused by the Reformation caused both some Catholic clergy and many students to pack their bags; on the other, the plague of 1585–6 'raget till almaist utter vastation' and the principal towns of Scotland, including St Andrews, were left 'almost desolat'.[11] But despite these losses, and perhaps others due to a shift in Scotland's overseas trade to larger and better-appointed harbours in the vicinity, Reformation St Andrews remained a large parish by the standards of sixteenth-century Scotland. It therefore offered a considerable challenge to the architects of the New Jerusalem.

Ministers of the church such as James Melville had at hand three distinct weapons for enforcing their moral standards and their doctrines upon the Scots: certain teachings and traditions of the church; the active support of the secular authorities; and a new and ubiquitous hierarchy of church courts and jurisdictions. All were put to full use. John Calvin, whose example the Scottish reformers chose to emulate, had been impressed by the evidence contained in the Acts of the Apostles and in certain Epistles of St Paul that the first Christian churches had strictly controlled and vigorously censured the social behaviour of their members. In his Ecclesiastical Ordinances of 1541, as well as in later editions of his *Institutes of the Christian Religion*, biblical sanction was claimed for the office of 'elder', whom Calvin made responsible for overseeing the morals and manners of the community.[12]

But who, precisely, comprised the community? Here the example of the early church was less often cited. There were many in the Protestant movement who argued that, as in the time of the Apostles, only true believers should be considered full members of the church; and that therefore only they should be subject to ecclesiastical discipline. This was the stance adopted by Calvinist leaders in both the Dutch Republic and Northwest Germany: only those who had placed themselves 'under the sweet yoke of our chief shepherd Jesus Christ' could be disciplined.[13] But Calvin himself had vehemently opposed this view. For him, the Christian community embraced everyone, sinners and saved alike, and in Geneva he created a special tribunal called the *consistoire*, composed of ministers and elders (some of them also magistrates), to interrogate and judge all who fell from doctrinal and moral purity. Those who erred, whoever they might be, were severely punished –

whether for religious obstinacy (like Miguel Servetus, who was burnt at the stake for heresy) or for moral turpitude (like those convicted of flagrant adultery, who were drowned).[14]

This uncompromising stance was fully endorsed by the leading Scottish reformer, John Knox. Although during his ministry of the English church in Frankfurt (1554–5) and Geneva (1556–8) his elders could deal only with the 'manners and disorders' of the small exile community, in a polemic written at Dieppe in 1559, just before he embarked for Scotland, Knox made a powerful defence of strong discipline, up to and including death for deviants, equally applied to all. And when, the following year, the 'face of a public kirk' was at last established in his homeland, Knox ensured that the Scots Confession recognized 'Ecclesiastical discipline, uprightly ministered as God's word prescribes, whereby vice is repressed and virtue nourished' as one of the three 'notes, signs and assured tokens' whereby the true church might be 'known from that horrible harlot' the church of Rome.[15] The reasoning and the consequences were both spelled out in chapter 7 of another of Knox's literary endeavours of 1560 entitled – perhaps ominously – *A First Book of Discipline*:

As that no Commonwealth can flourish or long indure without good lawes and sharpe execution of the same, so neither can the Kirk of God be brought to purity neither yet be retained in the same without the order of ecclesiastical discipline, which stands in reproving and correcting of the faults which the civil sword either doth neglect or not punish . . . Drunkenness, excesse (be it in aparel or be it in eating and drinking), fornication, oppressing of the poore, . . . wanton words and licentious living tending to slander, doe openly appertaine to the kirk of God to punish them, as God's word commands.

None were to escape scrutiny of their conduct for, the *Book* continued: 'To discipline must all the estates within this Realm be subject, as well the Rulers as they that are ruled; yea and the Preachers themselves, as welle as the poorest within the Kirk.'[16]

It was to enforce Mosaic Law upon all Scots, and to prepare them for the second (and more glorious) coming of the Lord, that powerful new church courts were created. At the parish level a kirk-session, composed of the minister and a number of lay elders and deacons, kept an eye on church fabric and finance and administered poor relief, but spent most of its time on discipline. The records of almost every Scottish kirk-session, from the mid-sixteenth to the mid-eighteenth century, are filled with parishioners who manifestly failed to respect the Lord's Day; with neighbours who, before witnesses, quarrelled and assaulted each other either verbally or physically; and, above all, with couples who admitted, more or less reluctantly, their illicit sexual liaisons. But three eventualities might cause a session to send one of its cases before a higher court – the local 'presbytery' where all the ministers of a given area met together for the examination and ordination of ministers, the supervision and visitation of constituent parishes, the enactment and enforcement of ordinances handed down by higher ecclesiastical tribunals, the correction of manners and morals, and the ultimate sanction of excommunication.[17] The first category of offenders referred to the presbytery were guilty of transgressions deemed to be particularly serious (any offence leading to sentence of excommunication was automatically referred). Others might be 'sent upstairs' because the offender (often a local landowner) either refused to accept the session's authority or repeated his crime frequently. Finally, others still might come before the presbytery because their case offered unusual difficulties.

A case heard by the presbytery of Stirling in 1587 may serve as an example of the first variety. One of the ministers informed his brethren that 'their is ane man dwelland within his said parrochun callit James Wilson . . . quha [i.e., who] hes fallin in the fourt fault of fornicatioun with three soverall wemen, and thairfor inquyrit of the brethir quhat he sould do thairwith'. (Their answer was to summon James Wilson to appear before them under pain of excommunication.[18]) An example of the second category appeared in the minutes of the kirk-session of Auchtermuchty in Fife in 1649. James Sibbald, a miller, was denounced for carting a load of flour on the Sabbath. He appeared before the session, but with an ill grace, and was overheard in the anteroom 'saying "I defy the minister and you and all you session and all that ye can do . . . I cair not for you."' For this evident insubordination he was referred to the presbytery, and 'depairted the session in a werrie disdainful way, muttering wordis quhilkis could not be heard'.[19] A splendid example of the third variety of presbytery disciplinary business – the 'difficult' case – is afforded by the remarkable saga of Janet Dick, whose apparent achievement of a virgin birth troubled the kirk-session of Airth and the presbytery of Stirling on several occasions between 1656 and 1668. Janet, a spinster, 'brought forth a bairn' and yet steadfastly denied ever engaging in sexual intercourse. Examination by midwives beforehand seemed to confirm her story. The kirk was not convinced, but even the most stringent questioning failed to break her story, so she was left 'lying under scandal' (a verdict which virtually deprived her of all civil rights) until the explanation emerged twelve years later. A local man, after being almost killed by a bolt of lightning, admitted that he had 'committed uncleanness' (as he put it) with the girl while she was so soundly asleep that she never woke up. The man was fined for his 'sin', and no cult of the Virgin Janet took root in the central lowlands.[20]

Janet Dick and her clandestine lover, like countless other inhabitants of seventeenth-century Scotland, never seem to have questioned the right of the church courts to judge and to punish them. Open contempt for the system, like that shown by James Sibbald, was rare, and except in the 1650s it was seldom successful. Those who would not bend the knee were relentlessly pursued and, eventually, either imprisoned or forced to flee.[21] It is worth pausing for a moment to examine why.

No doubt there was an element of fear among most ordinary lay folk that resisting or refusing the commands of the church might lead to damnation; but that alone would probably not have been enough to secure obedience – it certainly did not in England.[22] In Scotland, however, fear was heavily reinforced by the comprehensive support for ecclesiastical justice provided by the secular authorities. It is true that the General Assembly of the church failed to persuade the Scots Parliament in 1560 to give the *Book of Discipline* statutory backing; and that Parliament also declined a petition in May 1562 to outlaw those 'horibill vices' described in Leviticus for which 'the eternal God in his Parliament hes pronounced death to be the punishment'.[23] But in 1563 incest and witchcraft were declared capital offences; while in 1567 'notoure and manifest adulterie' joined them, and fornicators were threatened with either a £40 fine or eight days in prison. In the same year, Parliament expressly recognized the kirk's jurisdiction in preaching of the word, administration of the sacraments and correction of manners; and between the 1570s and the 1690s ten separate Acts were passed to make blasphemy into a statutory offence, and fourteen to penalize sabbath breach.[24]

Further down the judicial spectrum, but equally important, magistrates and landlords lent their evident support to the church courts by sitting on the local kirk-session. In most burghs – including St Andrews – the session elders normally included at least one of the town magistrates, and sometimes the minutes note that a sentence was passed on offenders 'the baillies being present', since that made the decision immediately enforceable in the secular as well as in the ecclesiastical courts. Some urban parishes, indeed, openly reserved one or more places specifically for their local law officers.[25] The interlock of church and state was equally apparent in rural areas, not least because the internal divisions of each parish normally reflected the landholding patterns within it: elders were appointed for each barony, since that organism was the basic unit of economic and social life in early modern Scotland.[26] And, as in the towns, those exercising secular jurisdiction were encouraged to participate in the disciplinary work of the church. The acts of the kirk-session of the Gaelic-speaking parish of Cromdale, for example, drawn up in 1702 by the minister and elders 'and with them the laird of Grant, younger, of that ilk, as civil judge, to give his concurrence', ordained that '[i]n regard there are severall scandals committed within the bounds of this pariochen, therefore the civill judge, in the parish's presence, is to be intreated to every session, and his concurrence to suppress immorality is to be required by the minister and elders'. The secular courts returned the compliment: with very few exceptions, town magistrates, sheriffs and holders of heritable jurisdictions went out of their way to support the decisions and laws of the church courts. In the baron court of Stitchill, in 1660, for example:

The said Barroun, takeing to his serious consideratioun how great a necessity Church Discypline of this Paroch has of the assistance and concurrence of the Civil Magistrat and helpe of his authority . . . thairfor the said Barroun heirby judicially decernes and ordaines his ordnar officer of the Barroun [court] to put in execution all Acts and Sentences of the Kirke Sessioun again[st] all persouns whomsoever within this Barrouny and poynd for all penalty and fines to be imposed be them, and take the extract of the Kirke Session their Act for his warrand.[27]

But there was a price to be paid for this apparently perfect union of church and state: the kirk had to accept that it was sometimes inadvisable to follow the *Book of Discipline*'s injunction to proceed against 'all estates within this Realm' with equal energy. Although in 1573 the General Assembly of the church still insisted that 'great men offending in sick crymes as deserve sackcloth should receive the samein as weill as the poor', and although the records of several courts include examples of the successful discipline of local notables, it did not always happen. After all, town magistrates and local landowners often possessed rights of patronage over the parish church and were sometimes impropriators of its tithes: their influence over the minister (and perhaps over some elders) could not be ignored. Their sins might accordingly be either tacitly condoned or else privately settled. Thus in 1585 the provost of Elgin (an elder) confessed himself guilty of the sin of fornication, but was spared public penance in return for the cost of glazing a window in the church; while in Fife, somewhat later, although Lord Lindores was widely 'noted for his whoredom' and the laird of Kemback 'was said by some to be a great whoremaster', their respective sessions chose not to inquire more closely into the matter.[28]

In fact, it has been suggested, these 'tactical concessions' may have 'strengthened rather than weakened the system of Godly Discipline by making it more palatable to the ruling class'.[29] Just how essential secular support really was, whatever concessions it cost, emerged unmistakably in the 1650s when, during the occupation of Scotland by the army of the English Commonwealth, the civil authorities briefly withdrew their backing for ecclesiastical censure. In January 1652 all existing courts and jurisdictions in Scotland were abolished by decree of the conquerors, and the subsequent judicial settlement left no place for either baron courts or church tribunals. In the summer of the following year, a session of the General Assembly was forcibly terminated by English troops and the ministers silenced and sent home. The significance of these events was not lost on contemporaries. In November 1653, for example, the kirk-session of Aberdeen was openly insulted by a servant of the Catholic laird of Pitfodels:

[Alexander Gordon] being demandit whairfoir he did not compeir sooner, he anserit: If it haid not bein to hold in the offiris paines, he had not compeirit now, nor at all. And, being demandit if he did acknowledge us to be ane judicatorie, he anserit: Unles we was authorized be the Comon wealth. And, being demandit again if he wes of our profession [i.e., was a Calvinist], he anserit: He came not to give ane acquittance. And all the whole tyme he carried himselff uncivillie and upbraidlinglie, thanking God that the tymes were not as formerlie.[30]

Such behaviour was only possible as long as the civil authorities in Scotland offered no support for church discipline. Even before the Restoration, this policy was reversed and, from 1660 onwards, church courts everywhere in the kingdom could once more rely on the full support of statute, sheriff, bailie and baron in enforcing their will.[31]

Most of the examples above are taken from the system in its heyday. They illustrate generalities that could be backed up by thousands of other cases in published and manuscript form which are almost identical in nature.[32] But how did it all begin? At what point did the new church courts, created after the Reformation, gain general acceptance; and when, precisely, did they first enter their symbiotic relationship with the established secular jurisdictions? The answer to this problem is not easy to provide, for the survival of the records of the church of Scotland is extremely uneven. In 1905, it was computed that documents from 16 synods, 84 presbyteries and 1324 parishes of Scotland then survived. But many of these sources began only in the eighteenth century, and some of those extant in 1905 – including some of the earliest – have since disappeared.[33] Table 2 shows the survival of pre-1700 church records in 1980.[34]

The parish of St Andrews in the later sixteenth century offers a unique glimpse of the process by which 'godly discipline' was first established in Scotland, for three reasons. First, because its kirk-session register commenced before any other and continued unbroken up to 1600. Second, because many of the events therein recorded are described in detail in the *Diary* kept by James Melville during the 1580s and 1590s.[35] And third, because:

Saint Andrews was in a unique position, and its peculiar advantages allowed it to offer an example to the rest of Scotland. It was small enough to be amenable to tight control, and sufficiently distant from the court and centre of government to be able to manage its own affairs without undue external interference. Its tradition as the ecclesiastical capital made it important enough to attract attention, while its university added the gravity of learning to what was being accomplished.

It offered, as the kirk-session itself claimed, 'the face of ane perfyt reformed kyrk'.[36]

The register of the kirk-session began in October 1559, and the session itself had probably been active for some time before that – perhaps since soon after the town's 'Reformation Day' on Sunday 11 June 1559, when the inhabitants literally awoke 'in a town full of Catholic churches and went to bed that night with a Protestant burgh and a Reformed parish church'.[37] But the early folios of the register contain a strange mixture of administrative, disciplinary and 'consistorial' business (the latter comprising matrimonial, testamentary and other matters previously heard by the archbishop's 'commissary court'). There were two reasons for this, both of them associated with the presence in St Andrews of one of the 'superintendents' created on

Table 2 Survival of Scottish church records, 1560–1700

Period	Kirk-session minutes surviving (in whole or in part)	Presbytery minutes surviving (in whole or in part)
1560–75	3	0
1575–1600	23	11
1601–25	70	23
1626–50	202	45
1651–75	352	62
1676–1700	527	82

the orders of the General Assembly after 1560 to 'visit and plant kirks' in the dioceses of Scotland. John Winram, formerly sub-prior of the Augustinian house at St Andrews and vicar-general of the archdiocese, was elected superintendent for Fife and Perthshire in April 1561, and for the next eleven years he (assisted by the town's kirk-session) handled 124 cases arising from his visits to parishes outside the burgh. All were entered in the session register, normally after the local cases.[38] Furthermore, Winram was at first also charged with 'consistorial' business. Although in 1560 Parliament abolished all papal authority in Scotland, papally appointed bishops were permitted to continue their jurisdiction over matrimonial and other consistorial business, acting in their own names. Since some bishops did not subscribe to the Calvinist Confession of Faith this situation was plainly unsatisfactory, and gradually the 'superintendents' took over the work. This situation changed only with the creation of separate commissary courts, first at Edinburgh in 1564 (for Lothian and for appeals from elsewhere) and shortly afterwards at St Andrews.[39]

The intermingling of consistorial, disciplinary and what later became presbytery matters in the same record renders the analysis of purely kirk-session business before 1573 difficult, though not impossible. To be sure, until the fall of Mary Queen of Scots in June 1567 not all Scots were subject to discipline, for attending Catholic worship that stopped short of the mass was no crime; and Gordon Donaldson has suggested that two alternative churches coexisted in the kingdom between 1560 and 1567.[40] But St Andrews was unusual. On the one hand, the reformed party in the town was unusually strong, for the provost, magistrates and burgh council, along with over three hundred leading citizens, had signed the Protestant 'Band' in July 1559; on the other, the Catholics were disheartened and disoriented, with even Archbishop James Hamilton ambivalent towards the new order. It was therefore possible for the St Andrews kirk-session to deal sternly from the start with sexual offenders (in 1562 adulterers were handed over to the 'bailies present to be civile correctit and punisht according to the order resavit in this citie'), to demand a public recantation from those suspected of favouring Rome (and to imprison or banish those who refused), and to excommunicate those who declined to accept its authority.[41] A campaign to enforce proper observance of the Sabbath began in spring 1568. There were also other efforts to enforce Reformation doctrine that went unrecorded in the register. For example, James Melville recalled seeing, as a student in 1571–2, 'a witche in St. Andros, aginst the quhilk Mr Knox delt from pulpit, sche being set upe at a pillar befor him'. Shortly afterwards he watched her burn to death. At the same time 'Mr Knox' also delivered a series of blistering sermons in the town church, execrating sin and commanding virtue, during which he 'was lyk to ding [i.e., smash] that pulpit in blads, and flie out of it'. But the register is silent about all this.[42]

The situation changed only after 1572. On the national scene, the central government at last provided the reformed church with access to some of the wealth of the former establishment (by the convention of Leith, January 1572), and deprived of office all clerics who refused to accept the Confession of Faith (January 1573). Furthermore, the end of the Civil War in the spring of 1573 ushered in a 'time of repose which God has granted us after our long troubles'.[43] In St Andrews itself, Winram resigned as superintendent in 1572 and left the minister and elders free to pursue local control single-mindedly. Shortly afterwards the session ordained that where a servant was fined for some moral lapse, his or her master should be responsible for payment; and henceforth there was less willingness to commute the normal penalties, imposed specifically to shame the transgressor, for money.[44]

So the 'great work of discipline' in St Andrews really began only in 1573. That year the register commenced – significantly – with an injunction that all members of the session who missed a meeting should be fined 'wythout exceptioun of personis and forgeving to ony man', followed by a supplication to the magistrates that they would 'execut the actis and ordinances' of the session concerning fornicators, adulterers, Sabbath-breakers and 'thame that ar warnit to compeir . . . and comperis not'.[45] It must have proved effective because by 1600 some 1720 parishioners had 'compeired' before the session, an average of over sixty per year.[46] The pattern of their offences, however, is not what one might expect of an ecclesiastical court. Nor does it resemble the duties set out in the instructions issued to the elders of the urban parish of Stirling in 1600, which have been hailed as 'typical': 'To tak attendence to the maneris of the pepill . . .; to attend quhat straingearis

resortis to the toun, and to quhat effect; . . . [and to search for] any
Jesuitis or seminarie Priestis . . . within this toun.'[47]

For it is clear that in St Andrews 'the maneris of the pepill' occupied
the lion's share of all attention, while the movement of 'straingearis'
and papists scarcely received any. And St Andrews was by no means
unique: the few other Scottish parishes with surviving records from
this period show almost exactly the same pattern. So do later ones,
such as the disciplinary records of the Stirlingshire parish of St Ninians
displayed in Table 3, for example.[48] The same applies to several
Calvinist communities outside Scotland. Thus the consistory of
Amsterdam between 1578 and 1600 heard 403 cases, an average of
30 per year, of which 335 (83 per cent) involved moral offences. At
Emden, in Northwest Germany, 80 per cent of the 114 disciplinary
cases tried by the consistory between 1596 and 1600 concerned morals;
while at Nîmes in the south of France, where a kirk-session (*consistoire*) began work in 1561 and handled over 180 cases annually, 80
per cent of all recorded business also concerned morals. It was the same
in other Calvinist communities in France and Switzerland, probably
including Geneva, where between 1559 and 1569 the *consistoire* disciplined some five hundred persons a year – representing perhaps one
adult in fifteen.[49]

Table 3 Kirk-session cases in St Ninians parish, 1653–1719

Offence	Number of cases	per cent
Sexual cases	307	57
Disorderly conduct	162	30
Resistance to authority	46	9
Other	20	4
Total	535	100

Discipline did not take up all the session's time at St Andrews,
however. Between 1573 and 1600 the minister and elders also transacted 361 items of administrative business, such as arranging for

church repairs and the purchase of equipment, for the parish communion service (including an advance examination of the fitness of all
church members to participate) and for catechism classes. And the
1720 whose 'disciplinary' offences are analysed in Table 4 include
those who applied for poor relief (35 cases, almost all after 1597); for
the baptism of illegitimate children or orphans (21 cases); and for the
enforcement of marriage vows about which one partner had had
second thoughts (16 cases recorded – including one ingenious citizen
in 1584 who successfully argued that 'he nevir maid promis of mareage
. . . bot onlie promittit to hir ane kow').[50] Finally, 6 cases of infanticide
and 8 of manslaughter also made a brief appearance before going on
to the civil courts. All these items appear under 'Other' in Table 4.
Few testimonials given to (or required from) God-fearing 'straingearis'
are recorded (34 cases); and fewer cases still of suspected religious
deviance, whether involving witches (8) or Catholics (7). As in seventeenth-century St Ninians – and most other parishes of the kingdom
that have been studied – everything else paled before the apparent
obsession of Scots Calvinists with sex.[51]

Most of the 986 sexual offenders hauled before the session were
charged with fornication (sexual intercourse between two single
persons) – 813 persons – or 'fornication antenuptial' (intercourse
between two persons whose marriage banns had been called but who
had not yet been wed) – 63 persons. Adultery (105 offenders) and
incest (5 offenders) were relatively rare, and bestiality and sodomy do
not appear at all. Given that the entire adult population of the parish
was probably under two thousand, and that around 32 offenders were
prosecuted for sexual misconduct annually, the chances that a young
person would appear before the session at some point were relatively
high.[52]

Almost all the fornicators arrived before the session in much the
same way: a single woman was denounced by a neighbour or by an
elder, either for having given birth or for being about to do so.

[10 August 1580] comperit Beteraige Bredfute and confessit and granted sche
was deliverit off ane maiden bairne to James Wemis

[31 August 1580] comperit Agnes Angous and confessit and granted hir to be

Table 4 Offenders disciplined by the St Andrews kirk-session,
1573–1600

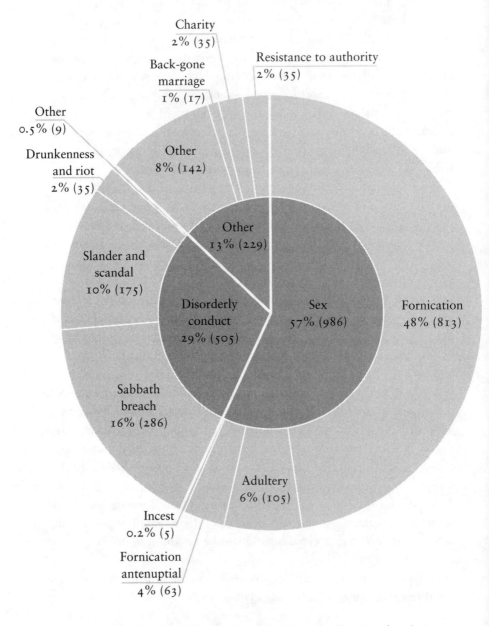

Charity
2% (35)

Back-gone
marriage
1% (17)

Resistance to authority
2% (35)

Other
0.5% (9)

Drunkenness
and riot
2% (35)

Other
8% (142)

Slander and
scandal
10% (175)

Other
13% (229)

Disorderly
conduct
29% (505)

Sex
57% (986)

Fornication
48% (813)

Sabbath
breach
16% (286)

Incest
0.2% (5)

Fornication
antenuptial
4% (63)

Adultery
6% (105)

Total number of offenders: 1720 (1030 males, 690 females)

wyth chylde to Jhone Buge younger, and submitted hir to the discipline off the kirk; and siclyk confessit this to be the thrid tyme she committed fornication.[53]

The session almost always picked on the woman first, because the accusation was so easy to prove: either a girl was pregnant and single or she was not. As the elders of Killearn in Stirlingshire somewhat smugly observed of a pregnant spinster in 1733: 'It is obvious that she has sinned, be the father who it will.'[54]

It was far less easy to establish the father's identity. Some girls refused to tell, although usually everyone knew with whom they had been seen at the relevant time. Others named a man who denied the charge, and in such cases the man was allowed to take an oath of innocence before the whole congregation during time of service. Normally he was allowed a week or so to peruse the oath, with its fearsome penalties for perjury:

Whereas I have been delated for fornication with X, I hereupon swear by the terrible and dreadful name of God the searcher of the secrets of all hearts, that I did never know the said X by having carnal dealings with her. And if this day I swear falsely, I do here before God's people in this congregation renounce my interest in Christ and my right to everlasting happiness in the life to come.

This was usually enough to break the resistance of all but the totally innocent or the invincibly corrupt – and the kirk had no intention of allowing the latter to escape blameless. If a blatantly guilty man still seemed prepared to acquit himself on oath, the session could and did refuse him permission to do so, leaving him neither convicted nor acquitted but, as the phrase went, 'lying under scandal'. This, in effect, meant that he could not go to church, could not leave his parish and could not find work or receive poor relief. He also risked a summons to the local secular court for disturbing the peace.[55]

One of the few alternatives to pregnancy as proof that sexual misconduct had taken place was the discovery of a couple *in flagrante delicto*. In 1589, for example, James Meldrum delated his own wife for adultery with Nicholl Broun. The two parties named appeared before the session 'quha denyit the bill *simpliciter*' despite the fact that witnesses had found Mr Broun hidden 'eftir ten houris at evin, hid secretele in James Meldrumis hous in this citee, behind ane bed heid'. The pair were therefore convicted, and condemned to appear in sackcloth before the congregation on Sunday in respect of their adultery, and before the magistrates 'for the great sklander gevin by thame' in denying the charge.[56] Less spectacular behaviour could also draw unexpected attention to forbidden liaisons: a couple marching purposefully into the countryside at dusk might be followed and spied on; the moans of a couple who had left their bed too near an open window could attract the attention of bystanders; a careless boast of sexual prowess might be reported to the elders for further investigation.[57] But even these cases lacked that element of incontrovertible proof that pregnancy provided, and in the seventeenth century, the charge might have to be reduced from fornication to 'scandalous carriage'. But the St Andrews records scarcely mention this offence: under rigorous questioning, almost all of those accused eventually broke down and confessed.

The kirk disposed of a formidable arsenal of penalties against sexual offenders. Those guilty of lesser misdemeanours might receive a 'rebuke' in private from the session; those whose lapse was greater, but fell short of sexual intercourse, might be rebuked from the pulpit during church service. Parties to grosser offences, however, were each sentenced to pay a fine into the 'poor box' and to appear in public on successive Sundays seated on the church's 'stool of repentance'. In most parishes this was a high, four-legged, backless chair, rather like a modern bar stool, sometimes cleverly constructed so that it would topple over if the sinner failed to sit bolt upright; but elsewhere it was attached to a scaffold with several settings – the higher the setting, the worse the offence. 'The stool,' wrote an English visitor in 1635 'is a public and eminent seat erected about two yards from the ground . . . where the whole congregation may take notice' of the offenders. In some churches, he added incredulously, the stool was capable of holding 'six or eight persons'. At Tyninghame, near Edinburgh, erecting a 'stool' cost £8 for the woodwork and £1 for the stone base: it was clearly a structure of substance.[58]

The usual penalty for fornication included three appearances on the stool on successive Sundays. If the sinner relapsed and fornicated again, six appearances were called for, and those who carried on in this way – charmingly referred to as 'trilapses', 'quadrilapses', and so on – were required to sit on the stool, clothed in sackcloth, on an indefinite number of occasions. While in public view, in this ungainly posture, the offenders endured a lengthy rebuke by the minister, after which they begged forgiveness of those they had wronged (often by shaking hands) and of the congregation at large. In addition they were fined. In St Andrews, until 1593, £2 Scots was normally the price of a case of fornication, double for a relapse, and so on, each party paying the same penalty. Adultery, which led to appearances on the stool for up to nine months, and often a civil punishment, involved a fine of up to £100. These sums were large: average wages in Scotland at this time were less than £1 a week, and the normal weekly collection in rural parishes might be counted in shillings rather than pounds. A few fornications and the occasional adultery were therefore good news for the church treasurer, and indeed for those of the poor who depended on alms from the session. Conversely, the financial hardship caused by the fines, especially to servants (who constituted the largest single category of sexual offender), was considerable, especially on top of the cost of raising the child.

But other penalties also existed. The illegitimate children of sus-pected sinners were often refused baptism until both parents submitted to discipline. Those who showed no contrition, or lacked the money for their fine – a total of at least 114 persons in the period studied – were imprisoned in the church steeple and received only bread and water for up to three weeks before being allowed to crave the church's forgiveness. Twelve more sinners were judged by the ministers and elders to be beyond redemption and suffered summary banishment. For example, Jonet Tod, 'ane common harlot ... nocht worthie of Christian society', was expelled from the burgh in 1598. The session also ordered a further eight persons whose offence was 'aggravated' to stand in the 'jougs' at the market cross, pinioned for an hour or more while passers-by scorned or pelted them. Thus in December 1593, of three women condemned to be 'jokit' for two hours, one had fornicated with the same person a second time; one had fornicated while on poor relief ('being ane that ressavit the puir folkis almous'); and the third had fornicated with several persons ('with Adam Duche

... and certane utheris filthelie, as wes delatit to the session').[59] Adulterers might be put through the full range of available penalties. Thus in December 1594 James Keingzo was 'jokit, cartit, and that throw the haill streitis of the town', before being taken outside the burgh walls where 'the haill scolaris [i.e., all the university students] and utheris, ane great multitude of pepill' cast 'rottin eggis, filth and glar [mud] at him'. Then he was 'at last dowkit [ducked] ower the heid diveris tymes' in the wintry sea, and subsequently condemned to sit in sackcloth 'on the hichest degre of the penitent stuill' until 'the kirk be satisfeit'. After that, the magistrates took over and banished him.[60]

The only other categories of offender who regularly appeared on the stool of repentance were those found guilty of slander or insulting behaviour. In a society where people lived at close quarters, their every action surveyed by countless others, public reputation mattered far more than it does today. To allow an insult to pass unchallenged was, in effect, to admit that it was true. Accusations of misconduct were therefore always taken seriously, not least by the church, which encouraged parishioners to take their slanders to court for fear that otherwise they might settle the matter with fists or worse.[61]

The course of slander cases was as predictable as the sexual hearings. They normally began when a parishioner handed in a complaint that he or she had been maligned by another at a specified time and place. The party named was then called, and both persons involved were required to put down a deposit of £2 – a precaution intended to discourage idle or malicious actions, for the party who lost the case also lost the deposit. At this point either the slander was withdrawn and an apology publicly made or else evidence was produced to justify it. Witnesses were called to speak of the character and reputation of someone accused of theft, witchcraft or some other crime, so that in effect a slander case became a committal hearing on the crime mentioned in the slander. Many of the witchcraft cases heard by the secular courts of early modern Scotland began with an insult that was unsuccessfully challenged in a church court and ended with a public burning for which church and state shared responsibility and costs.[62]

Other forms of slander or insulting behaviour, if proved, were like-wise punished severely – although they stopped short of the death sentence. In 1579, the session ordered John Scot 'in presens off the congregatioun off this citee, to sitt down upone his kneis, confes his offence maed againis the said Jonett [his wife, whom he had falsely accused of adultery] and pronunce this wordis, haldand his awin tung in his hand: "fals tung, thow leid"'. In 1594, a young man found to have threatened his father was condemned to 'compeir in sek claith, beir heddit, and beir futtit, upon the hichest degre of the penitent stuill, with ane hammer in the ane hand and ane stane in the uther hand, as tua instrumentis quhairwith he menassit his father, within ane papir writin in great letteris about his heid thir wordis: "BEHALD THE ONNATURALL SONE PUNISIT FOR PUTTING HAND IN HIS FATHER AND DISHONORING OF GOD IN HIM"''. After that he was, on successive days, to ask forgiveness of his father and of the church congregation; to stand in the jougs two hours; to be carted through the streets while his offence was proclaimed; and to receive solemn warning that 'If he evir offend aganis his father or mother heireftir, in word or deid, that member of his body quhairby he offendis sable cutitt of from him, be it tung, hand or futt.'[63]

This was – and was meant to be – an exemplary sentence, to be carried out 'without mercy, in exampill to utheris to abstein fra the lyke'. The penalty for many non-sexual offenders was merely a fine and a rebuke. Most frequent in this category was 'sabbath breach', a sin committed by doing almost anything on a Sunday except going to church. People were fined for 'sleeping in the meadows in time of sermon', for selling or drinking ale on Sundays 'except it be for the satisfying of nature', as well as for travelling, arguing or beating their wives (or servants) on the Lord's Day. But the commonest offence was working on Sundays: farmers struggling to harvest their crops while good weather lasted, like lax-fishers throwing their nets into the Tay whenever the salmon were running, found themselves summoned to the session and fined if they had done it on the Sabbath.[64] In 1574 it was ordained that every Sunday a magistrate, an elder and two deacons should patrol St Andrews at time of service, seeking out sinners and sluggards; and by 1600 they had brought 286 persons (249 of them men) before the session for sabbath breach.[65]

The offences dealt with by the kirk-session were thus mostly cut-and-dried: a pregnant spinster, a scandal uttered before witnesses, a man found sleeping outside during a church service, or staggering round the streets 'beastlie drunk'. There was no problem of proof, no point in denying guilt. And with the local laird or the bailies sitting on the session, there was little chance of escaping justice and no advantage in challenging the authority of the court. Almost all of those summoned came, confessed, made whatever amends were required of them, and were reconciled to the party they had injured and to the congregation at large. And yet reluctance to 'submit to discipline' was understandably great. To avoid humiliation, some sat on the stool of repentance with their face covered; others carried swords and pistols.[66] Others tried to avoid coming at all: there were thirty-eight cases of 'resistance to authority', ranging from arguments (usually by local landowners) over whether the session's writ extended to a given area, to violent words exchanged between session and accused.[67] A hard core of parishioners seems to have refused to accept the standards set by the session, and appeared several times. Thus eighty-one persons appeared twice or more between 1573 and 1600 for fornication (one person managed six appearances and another five), and seven persons appeared twice for adultery. One person even came three times. But in the 1590s 'repeaters' such as these became rare and, in the whole period under study, resort was made to the ultimate sanction of excommunication only five times.[68] It seemed as if, in St Andrews at least, 'all estates' had indeed become subject to discipline.

This changed situation of the 1590s deserves some further attention. It would be wrong to suppose that the fluctuations in annual totals shown in the appendix (pages 283–7 below) resulted solely from variations in the number of offences committed – that the relative absence of sexual offences in the last decade of the century necessarily indicates a reduction of illicit liaisons. It may, for example, have reflected a new fear among the congregation, following the great plague of 1585–6, that God was not to be scorned. But equally it may have stemmed from the undoubted changes in the priorities and activities of the ministers and the members of the session.[69]

In the first place, the clergy became less complaisant. The record of Robert Hamilton, an early reformer in the town and minister until his death in 1581, had not impressed James Melville, who served in an adjacent parish. 'Efter the first zeall of the Reformation, in Mr Knox and Mr Guildmans dayes,' he wrote in his *Diary*, 'the cauldnes of Mr Robert Hamiltones ministerie, and [the] ignorance and negligence of tham that sould haiff teatched theologie' caused great backsliding and disorder. 'Yea it was evin a pitie to sie that ignorance and profannes that was amangs tham.' But worse was to come: after Hamilton's death there was a hiatus, so that for more than three years there was no resident incumbent at all. James Melville and his uncle Andrew, a Geneva-trained minister and the principal of the 'New College' (St Mary's), therefore decided to help out by preaching at the town church and by stiffening the backbone of the session. The upsurge of business recorded in the register in 1582–4 (see pages 284–7 below) is clearly a reflection of their efforts. But before long there was another reflection: some of their parishioners decided to drive the Melvilles out. For a 'grait space', wrote James, 'ther was na thing bot affixing of plackarts upon the Collage yett [i.e., gate], bosting with batoning, burning and chaffing out of the town'. James Melville confessed that he was afraid, but his uncle Andrew was made of sterner stuff. He immediately assumed the offensive and accused the town magistrates of deliberately keeping the town church vacant, so that they could spend its revenues themselves on 'the goff, archerie, guid cheir etc.'; and in his sermons he excoriated all who opposed him. From the pulpit one day he told James Lermonth of Balcomie, a somewhat dissolute member of a prominent local family who was identified as the author of one of the placards that threatened 'batoning', that he would be punished for his lechery by having no legitimate offspring, and for his threats by being one day beaten to death himself. (Both prophecies, we are assured, eventually came true.) On another occasion, one of Melville's tirades from the pulpit caused the town provost to 'ryse out of his seatt in the middes of the sermont, and with sum muttering of words to go to the dure out throw the middes of the peiple'.[70]

Yet in the end Andrew Melville emerged victorious. The provost, 'convicted in his conscience' by a visit to the local presbytery, 'maid publict satisfaction be acknawlaging of his offence, and craving God and the congregation forgiffnes'; and the town council then agreed to the appointment of a new minister. Although plague struck the town with unusual severity in 1585–6, during which time (according to the register) 'all gude ordour cessit in this citee', it merely served as a prelude to a new moral crusade in the town. The campaign began with the decision, in October 1586, 'that ane generall delatioun be takin throch the haill town of the offendaris of Goddis Law' and was pressed home with rigour and determination by both ministers and elders for over a decade.[71]

Robert Wilkie, a member of the university theology faculty, served as burgh minister from 1586 to 1590, to be followed by David Black, a supporter of Andrew Melville; but almost at once he went 'on strike' and refused to serve until the town agreed to support a second minister. After a year, the local presbytery (which began to operate in 1586) ordered him back to work and in May 1593 Robert Wallace, another Melvillian, joined him as parish minister. Later that year, a new session took office: six elders from the university, twenty-two from the burgh and eleven from rural areas, together with twenty deacons.[72] The quarters of the parishes increased from four to twelve. Although there were, in all, 766 meetings of the various sessions of St Andrews between 1573 and 1600, almost half of them took place in the 1590s (see Table 5).[73] In addition, the presbytery now reinforced the work of the session – and once it split in two, with one part responsible for St Andrews, in 1591, its supervision became ever closer. Although half of the business it transacted between 1586 and 1605 concerned sexual offences, it also dealt with violent and verbal assaults, and with witchcraft and religious dissent.[74]

The explosion of disciplinary business during the 1590s (see below) was naturally related both to the institution of new ministers and to the increased strength of the session; but perhaps of more importance was the presence among the elders of Andrew Melville, now rector of the university and (in the words of R. G. Cant) 'the figure around whom the whole life of the city and university and most of that of Scotland revolved'. He appeared on the session for the first time in January 1591, and was re-elected four times until October 1597.[75]

During the Melville years, 'profanation of the Lord's day' was rigorously punished: of the 286 sabbath-breakers hauled before the session between 1573 and 1600, no less than 181 (63 per cent) appeared after 1594. Likewise, of the 175 cases of slander and scandal,

Table 5 Activity of the St Andrews kirk-session, 1573–1600

Session	Meetings	Session	Meetings	Session	Meetings
1573–4	27	1582–3	36	1591–3*	83
1574–5	20	1583–4	45	1593–4	35
1575–6	14	1584–5	31	1594–5	17
1576–7	18	1585–6	11	1595–7*	42
1577–8	12	1586–7	41	1597–8	52
1578–9	23	1587–8	24	1598–9	62
1579–81*	28	1588–9	37	1599–1600	23
1581–2	36	1589–91*	49		

* = session serving for two years

131 (75 per cent) came before the court during the last decade, and all but 4 of the 35 cases of drunkenness and riot came after 1594. 'Swearing, blasphemy and cursing', which diminished according to the register, were in fact dealt with after October 1596 in a different way. The session empowered each elder and deacon to impose a summary fine on all who 'sueriis, banis or takis Godis name in vane' in their hearing. Those who refused to pay on the spot could have their goods impounded, and those who offered opposition could be imprisoned. The new vigilantes were issued with a special purse in which to collect the fines, and from time to time the proceeds were paid over to the church treasurer.[76]

Sexual offenders were also dealt with differently under the new regime. Savage and exemplary penalties in 1593–4 for adultery and fornication have already been noted (pages 273–4 above). They did not stand alone. After 1593, all fornicators received punitive fines: the full rigour of the 1567 statute was now to be enforced – £40 Scots for the first offence, or eight days in prison, and double for a relapse.[77] The records show that high fines were exacted; but then something remarkable happened. Fornication in St Andrews seems to have ceased! Although 28 cases were investigated in 1594 (which was itself a drop from the 50–60 annual cases of the pre-Melvillian era), there was only one each in 1595 and 1596. Adultery, too, almost disappeared from the register between 1594 and 1597.

There are four possible explanations for this striking development. The first is that, with the penalties increased to such draconian levels, neighbours were reluctant to delate, or elders to prosecute, persons who were manifestly unable to pay such heavy fines.[78] But this ignores the fact that most fornication cases began with the birth of an illegitimate child, which was exceedingly difficult to conceal. Furthermore, 'concealing sin' was itself also liable to a heavy fine.[79] The second possibility is that spinsters who suspected they were pregnant might leave the parish in good time, in order to avoid fine and humiliation. But this, too, is rendered improbable by the common practice of kirk-sessions in sending back unmarried mothers to the parish where their 'sin' had been committed.[80] Third, it is conceivable that Melville and his fellow elders suddenly relented in response to popular hostility to their policies. Certainly in the summer of 1592 there was a 'maist dangerus uproar and tumult of the peiple of St Andros' against Melville following the accidental shooting of a local man in Butts Wynd by a college student practising archery. The 'wicked, malitius misrewlars of the town' (i.e., the magistrates) seized the opportunity to attack one of Melville's power bases – the university – ringing the town alarm bell and inciting the assembled multitude to break down the outer door of the college. A mob got as far as the main rooms, calling for fire, before the tumult was stilled. But the opposition endured. In 1597, one of Melville's most devoted followers was deliberately slain by a group of opponents as he walked in the country.[81] But had these unpleasant events led the session to reduce its vigour, the effect would have been visible in all areas of its disciplinary work; instead of which, although sexual cases dramatically diminished, other categories (as we have seen) soared.

So the only remaining explanation for the relative absence of sexual offences in these years, improbable though it may seem, is that fornication, adultery and the rest had become too dangerous a risk in St Andrews, and that a genuine 'reformation of manners' took place in the burgh.[82] There was certainly a change in the case of sabbath observance because, in the summer of 1600, the session proudly noted that 'the peopill convenis sua frequentlie to preaching that the kirk may nocht convenientlie containe thame', and the university chapel had to be opened as an overflow church for the town.[83]

By then, however, the Melvillian period in St Andrews was over. In 1596 and 1597 the extreme Presbyterian party was defeated in the General Assembly; while David Black, having called the king's mother a whore and Elizabeth Tudor an atheist, was deprived of his ministry, Andrew Melville was dismissed as rector of the university and removed from the kirk-session. Their work, however, was not undone. The same General Assembly in 1596 ordered a session to be created in every parish of the kingdom, with order to 'strik nocht onlie upon gros sinnes, as hurdome, blodshed etc., bot upon all sinnes repugnant to the Word of God, as blasphemie of Gods nam, swearing in vean, banning, profaning the sabathe, disobedience to parents, idle unrewlie annes [i.e., ones] without calling, drunkards, and siclyk . . .'. It seems a perfect description of the recent work of the St Andrews kirk-session, and now it was 'to be an universall rewll throuchout the realme'. James Melville noted it all in his journal with deep satisfaction.[84]

And, except during the Cromwellian occupation of the 1650s, the ecclesiastical tribunals of Scotland remained supreme until the mid-eighteenth century when first a serious schism in the church (the 'Great Secession'), then spectacular improvements in transport, and finally industrial growth began to erode traditional society and its values.[85] Meanwhile, the work of the church courts was seconded by the provision of sound Christian dogma and doctrine over almost all the kingdom via schools, universities, sermons and catechisms. So, through a combination of education and discipline, most Scots came to accept that intercourse would take place only between married partners (and the practice of handfasting, whereby parties cohabited as soon as they were betrothed, entirely died out); that insults should be swallowed rather than expressed; that one should be sober in food, drink and apparel; and that everyone should go to church on Sunday.

Needless to say, Scotland was not alone in its attempts to inculcate godly discipline and inward piety. Almost every state in Europe possessed some sort of Inquisition to enforce Christian standards of behaviour as well as Christian articles of belief: the 'bawdy courts' of England, the *consistoire* in Geneva, the church courts of Lutheran Germany, Denmark and Sweden, the Holy Office in Italy and Spain.[86]

But where Scotland excelled them all was in the intensity of control exercised by her church courts. The Calvinist congregation of Amsterdam in the later seventeenth century probably approached fifty thousand, but the city's consistory handled less than fifty cases annually; even the tribunals of the Spanish Inquisition, each monitoring the actions of up to half a million people, resolved only twenty or thirty cases a year.[87] Yet most Scottish kirk-sessions, although they seldom held authority over more than three thousand parishioners, dealt with far more.

Thanks to this intensity, godly discipline had a further unexpected but highly significant influence on the long-term development of Scotland. In St Andrews, the session in the 1590s helped to turn a sort of 'Montaillou-sur-mer' into a strict, restrained and eminent university town. But this achievement was not unique. By the end of the seventeenth century over five hundred kirk-sessions were active in Scotland, from the Borders to the Northern Isles, all administering the same swift justice, all run by local professionals, and all applying more or less the same standards. The importance of this achievement, in a country of such strong regional and local identities, can hardly be overstated: church building in early modern Scotland far outstripped state building. It played a crucial part in grooming the kingdom for its future role as a major industrial power. By accustoming the workforce to social discipline, and by stressing the value of order, restraint and hard work, the reformed kirk unwittingly became the handmaiden of nascent capitalism. It may have tamed Scotland for another, higher, purpose; but Scotland was tamed all the same.[88]

Appendix: The Disciplinary Work of St Andrews Kirk-session, 1573–1600

The church court (kirk-session) of St Andrews in Fife, as in most other Scottish parishes at the time, spent most of its time dealing with men and women (in almost equal proportions) who had engaged in illicit sex. Fornication (sex between unmarried people), 'fornication antenuptial' (sex between people who had contracted but not yet concluded marriage), adultery (sex between people of whom at least one was married) and incest (sex between persons related in ways proscribed by the Book of Leviticus) accounted for 57 per cent of all business – a total of almost 1000 cases, from an adult population of less than 2000!

[Source: D. Hay Fleming, *Register of the Minister, Elders and Deacons of the Christian Congregation of St Andrews* (2 vols., Edinburgh, 1889–90)]

1. Sexual offenders

	Fornication		Fornication antenuptial		Adultery		Incest	
	M	F	M	F	M	F	M	F
1573	10	10	2	2	2	2	1	1
1574	2	3	1	2	5	4	0	0
1575	6	5	2	2	1	0	0	0
1576	3	4	0	0	0	0	0	0
1577	6	5	1	2	2	2	0	0
1578	2	7	0	0	0	0	0	0
1579	5	10	1	1	1	2	0	0
1580	15	18	0	1	0	2	0	0

1. Sexual offenders – *contd.*

	Fornication		Fornication antenuptial		Adultery		Incest	
	M	F	M	F	M	F	M	F
1581	6	5	0	0	3	2	0	0
1582	12	12	4	4	1	0	0	0
1583	20	23	0	0	1	0	1	0
1584	40	41	2	3	5	4	0	0
1585	10	13	2	3	1	1	0	0
1586	18	23	1	1	0	1	1	1
1587	29	33	2	2	6	4	0	0
1588	20	20	2	2	1	1	0	0
1589	31	30	1	1	2	1	0	0
1590	33	38	1	2	4	4	0	0
1591	23	26	0	0	2	3	0	0
1592	11	14	1	0	3	2	0	0
1593	26	28	1	1	2	2	0	0
1594	12	16	0	0	1	1	0	0
1595	1	0	0	0	1	1	0	0
1596	1	0	1	1	0	1	0	0
1597	4	1	0	1	1	1	0	0
1598	14	16	0	0	2	2	0	0
1599	16	11	2	2	6	6	0	0
1600	13	12	2	1	1	2	0	0
Total	389	424	29	34	54	51	3	2
Total	813		63		105		5	

2. Disorderly conduct

	Sabbath breach		Slander and scandal		Drunkenness and riot		Other	
	M	F	M	F	M	F	M	F
1573	5	0	1	1	0	0	0	0
1574	27	0	0	1	1	0	0	0
1575	2	0	3	1	1	0	0	0
1576	20	2	1	2	0	0	0	0
1577	0	1	1	1	0	0	1	0
1578	0	0	0	0	2	0	0	0
1579	0	0	1	2	0	0	2	0
1580	0	0	1	1	0	0	0	0
1581	0	0	2	1	0	0	0	0
1582	23	0	2	0	0	0	0	0
1583	5	0	0	3	0	0	0	0
1584	0	0	2	1	0	0	0	0
1585	0	0	0	0	0	0	0	0
1586	0	0	1	1	0	0	0	0
1587	0	0	1	2	0	0	0	0
1588	0	0	2	0	0	0	0	0
1589	0	0	0	0	0	0	0	0
1590	5	0	3	6	0	0	0	0
1591	8	0	1	5	0	0	1	0
1592	1	0	1	1	0	0	0	0
1593	6	0	2	0	0	0	0	0
1594	38	5	8	0	10	0	0	0
1595	11	3	11	2	0	0	0	0
1596	13	1	6	2	6	0	0	0
1597	12	8	5	7	0	1	1	0
1598	18	3	18	7	10	0	0	0
1599	34	12	28	9	1	0	2	0
1600	21	2	17	1	3	0	1	0
Total	249	37	118	57	34	1	8	0
Total	286		175		35		8	

3. Other business

	Other		Poor relief/ charity		Back-gone marriage		Resistance to authority	
	M	F	M	F	M	F	M	F
1573	3	3	0	1	1	0	3	2
1574	10	1	0	0	0	0	1	0
1575	5	0	0	0	0	0	4	0
1576	2	2	0	0	0	0	0	1
1577	6	4	0	0	1	0	0	0
1578	0	2	0	0	1	0	0	0
1579	1	0	0	0	0	0	0	0
1580	1	0	0	0	0	0	0	0
1581	1	1	0	0	1	0	0	2
1582	3	4	0	0	0	0	2	0
1583	8	1	0	0	0	1	0	0
1584	0	4	0	0	1	0	0	0
1585	0	2	1	0	2	0	0	0
1586	1	4	0	0	0	0	1	0
1587	9	5	0	0	1	0	1	0
1588	2	3	1	0	0	0	0	0
1589	2	2	0	0	2	0	0	0
1590	3	1	0	0	0	2	0	0
1591	1	2	0	0	0	0	2	0
1592	3	3	0	0	0	1	0	0
1593	5	4	0	0	0	0	0	0
1594	2	0	0	0	0	0	2	0
1595	3	3	0	0	0	2	4	2
1596	0	1	0	0	0	0	4	1
1597	2	0	3	1	0	0	0	0
1598	4	2	1	0	0	0	2	0
1599	6	1	11	5	0	1	0	0
1600	3	1	6	5	0	0	1	0
Total	86	56	23	12	10	7	27	8
Total	142		35		17		35	

4. Annual total of all items of business transacted

	Administrative	Persons disciplined
1573	11	55
1574	12	60
1575	5	32
1576	5	37
1577	5	42
1578	2	14
1579	4	26
1580	1	39
1581	8	24
1582	13	68
1583	15	65
1584	20	103
1585	4	35
1586	12	51
1587	14	85
1588	10	54
1589	17	72
1590	11	102
1591	9	73
1592	2	41
1593	11	78
1594	10	93
1595	6	44
1596	14	38
1597	45	49
1598	50	103
1599	19	145
1600	26	92
Total	361	1720

Notes

Abbreviations

AA Archivo de la Casa de los Duques de Alba, Madrid, Manuscript Collection (with *caja* and folio)

AD Archives départementales

AGI Archivo General de Indias, Seville

AGNM Archivo General de la Nación, Mexico
   CRD Cédulas reales duplicadas

AGPM Archivo General del Palacio Real, Madrid

AGRB Archives Générales du Royaume/Algemeen Rijksarchief, Brussels
   Audience Papiers d'État et d'Audience
   CPE Conseil Privé: époque espagnol
   SEG Secrétairerie d'État et de Guerre

AGS Archivo General de Simancas
   CJH Consejos y Juntas de Hacienda
   CMC Contaduría Mayor de Cuentas (with *época* and *legajo*)
   Estado Negociación de Estado
   MPyD Mapas, planos y dibujos

   SP Secretarías Provinciales

AHN Archivo Histórico Nacional, Madrid

AHR American Historical Review

APO J. H. de Cunha Rivara, ed., *Archivo Portuguez-Oriental* (6 vols., Nova Goa, 1857–76)

ARA Algemene Rijksarchief, The Hague

ASG *AS* Archivio di Stato, Genoa, *Archivio Segreto*

ASP *CF* Archivio di Stato, Parma, *Carteggio Farnesiano*

BCR Biblioteca Casanatense, Rome

BL British Library, London, Department of Western Manuscripts
   Addl Additional Manuscripts
   Cott Cotton Manuscripts
   Eg Egerton Manuscripts
   Harl Harleian Manuscripts

BMO J. Calvar Gross, J. I. González-Aller Hierro, M. de Dueñas Fontán and M. del C. Mérida Valverde, *La batalla del Mar Océano* (3 vols., Madrid, 1988–93)

BNM Biblioteca Nacional, Madrid, Manuscript Section

BNP   Bibliothèque Nationale, Paris, Manuscript Department

Bod   Bodleian Library, Oxford, Department of Western Manuscripts

BPM   Biblioteca del Palacio Real, Madrid, Manuscript Collection

BPU   *Favre* Bibliothèque Publique et Universitaire, Geneva, *Collection Manuscrite Édouard Favre*

BRB   Bibliothèque Royale, Brussels, Manuscript Section

BSLE   Biblioteca del Real Monasterio de San Lorenzo de El Escorial, Manuscripts

BZ   Biblioteca de Zabálburu, Madrid, Manuscripts (with *caja* and folio number)

CCG   E. Poullet and C. Piot, *Correspondance du Cardinal de Granvelle 1565–1586* (12 vols., Brussels, 1877–96)

Chaunu   H. and P. Chaunu, *Séville et l'Atlantique, 1500–1650* (8 vols., Paris, 1955–9)

Co. Do. In.   *Colección de documentos inéditos para la historia de España* (112 vols., Madrid, 1842–95)

CSPD   Calendar of State Papers, Domestic Series

CSPF   Calendar of State Papers of the reign of Elizabeth, Foreign Series

CSPI   Calendar of State Papers relating to Ireland

CSPScot   Calendar of State Papers relating to Scotland and Mary Queen of Scots

CSPSp   M. A. S. Hume, *Calendar of Letters and State Papers relating to English affairs preserved in, or originally belonging to, the archives of Simancas: Elizabeth* (4 vols., London, 1892–9)

CSPV   H. F. Brown, *Calendar of State Papers . . . Venice*, VIII (London, 1894)

Duro   C. Fernández Duro, *La Armada Invencible* (2 vols., Madrid, 1888)

EHR   English Historical Review

Epistolario   Duke of Berwick y Alba, *Epistolario del III duque de Alba* (3 vols., Madrid, 1952)

Groen van Prinsterer, *Archives*   G. Groen van Prinsterer, *Archives ou correspondance inédite de la maison d'Orange-Nassau* (1st series, 8 vols. and supplement, Leiden, 1835–47; 2nd series, I, Utrecht, 1857)

HAG   Historical Archive, Goa

Herrera Oria   E. Herrera Oria, *La Armada Invencible. Documentos procedentes del Archivo General de Simancas* (Valladolid, 1929: Archivo Histórico Español, II)

HMC   Historical Manuscript Commission

HMC Salisbury   Historical Manuscript Commission: Calendar of the Manuscripts of the Most Honourable the Marquis of Salisbury . . . preserved at Hatfield House, III (London, 1889)

IMC   Irish Manuscript Commission

IVdeDJ   Instituto de Valencia de

Don Juan, Madrid,
Manuscript Collection (with
envío and folio number)
KB Koninklijke Bibliotheek, The
Hague, Manuscript Section
KML Karpeles Manuscript
Library, Santa Barbara
CR *Cartas de reyes*
MSP *Medina Sidonia Papers*
Laughton J. K. Laughton, *State
Papers concerning the Defeat
of the Spanish Armada* (2
vols., London, 1895–1900)
Le Glay and Finot A. Le Glay and
J. Finot, eds., *Inventaire
sommaire des archives
départementales antérieures à
1790. Nord, série B* (6 vols.,
Lille, 1863–88)
Maura G. Maura Gamazo, duke of
Maura, *El designio de Felipe II
y el episodio de la Armada
Invencible* (Madrid, 1957)
PEG C. Weiss, *Papiers d'État du
Cardinal de Granvelle* (9 vols.,
Paris, 1841–52)

PMC J. Cortesão and A. Teixeira
de Mota, *Portugaliae
Monumenta Cartographiae* (5
vols., Lisbon, 1960)
PRO Public Record Office, London
AO *Audit Office*
SP *State Papers*
RAH Real Academia de la
Historia, Madrid, Manuscript
Collection
Register D. Hay Fleming, ed.,
*Register of the Minister, Elders
and Deacons of the Christian
Congregation of St Andrews,
comprising the Proceedings of
the Kirk-session and of the
Superintendent of Fife, Fothrik
and Strathearn, 1559–1600,*
Scottish History Society, vols.
I–II (Edinburgh, 1889–90).
Serrano L. Serrano,
*Correspondencia diplomática
entre España y la Santa Sede
durante el pontificado de San
Pio V* (4 vols., Madrid, 1914).
SRO Scottish Record Office

Introduction

1. Trevor-Roper put it thus: he found especially interesting 'the interplay between heavy social forces or intractable geographical facts and the creative or disruptive forces which wrestle with them: the nimble mind, the burning conscience, the blind passion of man' (H. R. Trevor-Roper, *Historical Essays* (2nd edn., New York, 1966), viii). For more examples of Trevor-Roper's fascination with heroic failures, see G. Parker, 'History's Fermi', *The American Scholar* (winter, 1987), 123–7.

2. I refer to the following works: J. H. Elliott, *The Count-Duke of Olivares. The Statesman in an Age of Decline* (New Haven and London, 1986); N. Z. Davis, *The Return of Martin Guerre* (Cambridge, Mass., 1983), and N. Z. Davis, J.-C. Carrière and D. Vigne, *Le retour de Martin Guerre* (Paris, 1982); C. Ginzburg, *The Cheese and the Worms. The Cosmos of a Sixteenth-century*

Miller (Baltimore, 1980); J. Brown, *Immodest Acts. The Life of a Lesbian Nun in Renaissance Italy* (Oxford, 1986); I. Morris, *The Nobility of Failure. Tragic Heroes in the History of Japan* (New York, 1975); and C. Brady, ed., *Worsted in the Game. Losers in Irish History* (Dublin, 1989).

3. Von Neumann's elegant paraphrase of 'Murphy's Law' quoted by J. Campbell, *Grammatical Man. Information, Entropy, Language and Life* (New York, 1982), 73; C. von Clausewitz, *On War* (written in the 1820s; ed. and tr. M. Howard and P. Paret, Princeton, 1984), 119. See also L. Thomas, 'To err is human', in J. Gross, *The Oxford Book of Essays* (Oxford, 1992), 561 – 'Mistakes are at the very base of human thought, embedded there, feeding the structure . . . We are built to make mistakes, coded for error' – and the interesting essays on this subject in R. Beaumont, *War, Chaos and History* (Westport, Conn., 1994).

4. Exactly the same story lies behind the essays in *Spain and the Netherlands 1559–1659. Ten Studies* (London, 1979; 2nd edn., 1990) – see p. 12.

5. See the warnings contained in B. Lenman and G. Parker, 'The state, the community and the criminal law in early modern Europe', in V. Gatrell, B. Lenman and G. Parker, eds., *Crime and the Law. The Social History of Crime in Western Europe since 1550* (London, 1980), 11–48.

6. See also the important data in J. Israel, 'The Dutch role in the Glorious Revolution', in idem, ed., *The Anglo-Dutch Moment. Essays on the Glorious Revolution and Its World Impact* (Cambridge, 1991), 105–63.

7. See N. Eldredge and S. J. Gould, 'Punctuated equilibria: an alternative to phyletic gradualism', in T. J. Schopf, ed., *Models in Paleobiology* (San Francisco, 1972), and A. Somit and S. A. Peterson, *The Dynamics of Evolution: The Punctuated Equilibrium Debate in the Natural and Social Sciences* (Ithaca, 1992). I thank Cliff Rogers for drawing these works to my attention, and for demonstrating their applicability to military history. For a similar model applied to intellectual history, see T. S. Kuhn, *The Structure of Scientific Revolutions* (3rd edn., Chicago, 1996).

8. G. Canestrini, ed., *Opere inedite di Francesco Guicciardini. III: Storia Fiorentina* (Florence, 1859), 105, written in 1508–9. This passage forms virtually the only analytical break in Guicciardini's detailed narrative, which serves to heighten his sense of shock at these events.

9. H. A. Oberman, 'Hus and Luther, prophets of a radical reformation', in R. L. Petersen and C. A. Pater, eds., *The Contentious Triangle: Church, State and University. A Festschrift in Honor of George H. Williams* (Sixteenth Century Essays and Studies, LI, Kirksville, Mo., 1999), 135–64.

10. See C. Haigh, *English Reformations: Religion, Politics and Society under the Tudors* (Oxford, 1993), part 2.

11. The late Michael Roberts made a very similar point in an 'Alternative Inaugural', which he wrote in 1955 and delivered in 1995: 'All historical

enquiry starts with the question "what happened?"; goes on to the question "how?"; and ends up with the far from simple question "why?"; but if we were to suspend our activities until the philosophers reached agreement on the meaning of "why", the chances are that we should never embark upon them at all.' (M. Roberts, 'The naïve historian: an undelivered inaugural', *Comment*, XVIII (Winter, 1995), 6–7.)

12. H. Trevor-Roper, 'History and imagination', in H. Lloyd-Jones, V. Pearl and B. Worden, eds., *History and Imagination. Essays in Honour of H. R. Trevor-Roper* (London, 1981), 358–9.

PART I: PHILIP II: THE WORLD IS NOT ENOUGH

1. IVdeDJ 38/70, apostil from Philip II on a letter from Cardinal Diego de Espinosa, undated but from late in 1569.

2. On the fate of the collection, see G. de Andrés, 'La dispersión de la valiosa colección bibliográfica y documental de la Casa de Altamira', *Hispania*, XLVI (1986), 587–635. For the one manuscript volume published almost in its entirety (BL *Addl* 28,263), see C. Riba García, *Correspondencia privada de Felipe II con su secretario Mateo Vázquez 1567–91* (Madrid, 1959). For more on the sources available for studying the king, see G. Parker, *The Grand Strategy of Philip II* (New Haven and London, 1998), 397–406.

3. The same four repositories also contain, from an entirely different provenance, the extensive archive of two of Philip II's leading ministers: Don Luis de Requesens, ambassador in Rome, lieutenant-general of the Mediterranean fleet, governor of Milan and governor-general of the Netherlands (d. 1576); and of his brother Don Juan de Zúñiga, ambassador in Rome, viceroy of Naples and eventually the king's chief foreign policy adviser (d. 1586). Each exchanged hundreds of letters with the king and thousands with other ministers about royal policy. For an idea of the scale of the collection see F. J. Bouza Álvarez, 'Guardar papeles – y quemarlos – en tiempos de Felipe II. La documentación de Juan de Zúñiga', *Reales Sitios*, CXXIX (1996), 2–15, and CXXXI (1997), 18–33.

4. For a review article on the recent crop of material, see G. Parker, 'Still "Philippizing" after all these years. A review of publications that commemorated the quatercentenary of Philip II's death, 1598–1998', *Tijdschrift voor Geschiedenis*, CXIV (2001), 214–26.

1. David or Goliath? Philip II and His World in the 1580s

Many thanks for assistance with references to David Coleman, Benedict Kiernan and Sanjay Subrahmanyam, and to Fernando Bouza, Richard Kagan and Nancy van Deusen for helpful suggestions and comments. I also acknowledge the inspiration of John Elliott's study, 'The Spanish monarchy and the kingdom of Portugal, 1580–1640', in M. Greengrass, ed., *Conquest and Coalescence. The Shaping of the State in Early Modern Europe* (London, 1991), 48–67.

1. See the Introduction to R. L. Kagan and G. Parker, eds., *Spain, Europe and the Atlantic World. Essays in Honour of John H. Elliott* (Cambridge, 1995), 14–24. The tension between centre and periphery enjoyed great vogue in the third quarter of the twentieth century. In 1961, Edward Shils drew attention to the limited influence of the values and policies promoted at the centre of each pre-modern society in his influential essay 'Centre and periphery', in *The Logic of Personal Knowledge. Essays Presented to Michael Polanyi on his Seventieth Birthday* (London, 1961), 117–30. (My thanks to Richard Groening for bringing this item to my attention.) A decade later, Immanuel Wallerstein chose the centre/periphery dynamic as the organizing theme of *The Modern World System* (3 vols. to date, London and New York, 1974, 1980, 1989).

2. Alas, the presentation did not come as a total surprise. Elliott might have believed that so many of his former students had converged on Oxford simply to celebrate his birthday had not a colleague in America mistaken the date and sent a telegram on 23 June saying 'Congratulations on the birthday; congratulations on the Festschrift'!

3. Elliott, 'The Spanish monarchy and the kingdom of Portugal'.

4. The surviving Florentine canvases (13 of the original 24) are described and illustrated in *Glorias efímeras. Las exequias florentinas por Felipe II y Margarita de Austria* (Valladolid, 1999), 143–209. For more on Philip II and Portugal, see the collected essays of F. J. Bouza Álvarez, *Portugal no tempo dos Filipes. Política, cultura, representações* (Lisbon, 2000); and, on Sebastianism, J. Hermann, *No reino do desejado. A construção do sebastianismo em Portugal, séculos XVI e XVII* (São Paolo, 1998).

5. The same was true for the House of Avis: of the eleven marriages concluded by the last three generations of the Portuguese royal family, eight were with the Habsburgs: R. Valladares, 'Sobre reyes de invierno. El diciembre portugués y los 40 fidalgos (o algunos menos con otros más)', *Pedralbes*, XV (1995), 107.

6. J. I. Tellechea Idígoras, *Felipe II y el Papado. Colección de breves pontificios*, I (Madrid, 1999), 199–202 and 208–9, Pius V to Philip II, 20 Dec. 1568 and 10 Aug. 1569, both holograph.

7. F. J. Bouza Álvarez, ed., *Cartas de Felipe II a sus hijas* (2nd edn., Madrid, 1998), 35, Philip II to his daughters, 3 Apr. 1581; IVdeDJ 56 *carpeta* 21, unfol., Mateo Vázquez to [Hernando de Vega], 17 Apr. 1581. L. Cabrera de Córdoba, *Historia de Felipe II rey de España*, II (1619, Madrid, 1877), 633–4, also claimed that 'crowned, with the sceptre in his hand, he looked like King David'.

8. *APO* fasc. I livro 1, 90–1, Philip II to the city of Goa, 7 Nov. 1580; D. do Couto, *Da Asia: decada X* (Lisbon, 1788), book I, 17–19. A ship from Portugal brought the news to Malacca in November 1581, but Macao only heard in March 1582 via Mexico and Manila – an interesting indication of the relative speed and routes by which news travelled from Europe to the Far East.

9. BL *Eg* 592/38–48v, 'Discurso astronómico' of 1577, at fo. 44. In fact, only 91 degrees (one-quarter of the globe) and six 'hours' separate Sicily and Cuzco.

10. See A. Losada, *Juan Ginés de Sepúlveda a través de su 'Epistolario' y nuevos documentos* (2nd edn., Madrid, 1973), 64–74 and 94–100; O. Niccoli, *Prophecy and People in Renaissance Italy* (Princeton, 1990), 113–20 and 168–88; J. M. Headley, 'The Habsburg world empire and the revival of Ghibellinism', in S. Wenzel, ed., *Medieval and Renaissance Studies*, VII (Chapel Hill, 1978), 93–127; and Headley, 'Rhetoric and reality: messianic humanism and civilian themes in the imperial ethos of Gattinara', in M. Reeves, ed., *Prophetic Rome in the High Renaissance Period. Essays* (Oxford, 1992), 241–69.

11. These publications are surveyed by F. Bosbach, 'Papsttum und Universalmonarchie im Zeitalter der Reformation', *Historisches Jahrbuch*, CVII (1987), 44–76; idem, *Monarchia Universalis. Ein politischer Leitbegriff der frühen Neuzeit* (Göttingen, 1988: Schriftenreihe der historischen Kommission bei der bayerischen Akademie der Wissenschaften, XXXII), chap. 4, and 166–7 (a list of works on the subject published during Philip II's lifetime).

12. L. Díaz-Trechuela, 'Consecuencias y problemas derivados del Tratado en la expansión oriental', in L. A. Ribot García, ed., *El Tratado de Tordesillas y su época*, III (Madrid, 1995), 1519–39; E. H. Blair and J. A. Robertson, eds., *The Philippine Islands, 1493–1898* (55 vols., Cleveland Ohio, 1903–9), XXXIV, 222–8, Rada to the viceroy of Mexico, Cebu, 8 July 1569; and IV, 21–93, Sande's 'Relación' of 7 June 1576 (see ibid., pp. 58–9 and 62–3). For more of the same, see L. Bourdon, 'Un projet d'invasion de la Chine par Canton à la fin du 16e siècle', in *Actas do III Colóquio internacional de estudos Luso-Brasileiros*, II (Lisbon, 1960), 97–121, at p. 101.

13. Quotations from IVdeDJ 25B *carpeta* 22, unfol., Gesio to Philip II, 23 and 24 Feb. 1576 (for more of the same, see ibid., Gesio to Philip II, 23 Apr. 1577); and Blair and Robertson, *The Philippine Islands*, IV, 94–5.

14. BL *Addl* 28, 704/270v–1, Espinosa to the duke of Alba and Don Juan de

Zúñiga, 4 Dec. 1571, on the victory 'la mayor después de la del Vermejo'. On *The Allegory of Lepanto*, see E. Panofsky, *Problems in Titian, Mostly Iconographic* (New York, 1969), 72–3, and M. Tanner, *The Last Descendant of Aeneas. The Hapsburgs and the Mythic Image of the Emperor* (New Haven, 1993), 216–17.

15. Quotations from R. Cueto, '1580 and all that . . .: Philip II and the politics of the Portuguese succession', *Portuguese Studies*, VIII (1992), 150–69, at p. 156: Cristobal de Moura to Philip II, 25 Nov. 1578; F. J. Bouza Álvarez, *Portugal en la Monarquia hispánica (1580–1640). Felipe II, las Cortes de Tomar y la génesis del Portugal Católico* (2 vols., Madrid, 1987), 82 (Castillo); BSLE *Ms* P.I. 20, fos. 44–5, Gesio to Philip II, 16 Nov. 1578. See also the equally forceful views of Pedro Salazar de Mendoza and of Philip II himself quoted in L. Pereña Vicente, *La teoría de la guerra en Francisco Suárez*, I (Madrid, 1954), 76–7.

16. Quotations from W. Scott, ed., *The Somers Collection of Tracts*, I (London, 1809), 164–70; W. T. MacCaffrey, *Queen Elizabeth and the Making of Policy 1572–1588* (Princeton, 1981), 339; and Groen van Prinsterer, *Archives*, 2nd series I, 11, Henry of Navarre to the earl of Leicester, 8 May 1585.

17. *Monumenta historica societatis Iesu*, LX, *Ribadeneira* (Madrid, 1923), 22–9, Ribadeneira to Cardinal Quiroga, 16 Feb. 1580. See also other critics of the king cited by F. J. Bouza Álvarez, 'Servidumbres de la soberana grandeza: criticar al rey en la corte de Felipe II', in A. Alvar Ezquerra, *Imágenes históricas de Felipe II* (Madrid, 2000), 141–79.

18. Bouza Álvarez, *Portugal en la Monarquia hispánica*, 652–6; H. Lapèyre, *El comercio exterior de Castilla a través de las aduanas de Felipe II* (Valladolid, 1981), part 1.

19. For example, see *BMO*, II (Madrid, 1989), 135–6, for the *cédula* of 5 May 1586 for Castile; and AGS *SP* libro 1550 fo. 255, 'O Cardeal' to Philip II, 31 May 1586, for Portugal (see also the protest of the Lisbon merchants in ibid., fos. 395–7, partly published in *BMO*, II, 282–3).

20. F. Checa, *Felipe II. Mecenas de las Artes* (Madrid, 1992), 270; IVdeDJ 99/208, 'Lo que Rodrigo Alvarez portugués pretende'; ibid., fo. 137, Juan de Ibarra to Mateo Vázquez, 3 Feb. 1582, announcing the arrival at Aranjuez of Juan Bautista Antonelli in a boat from Lisbon 'de que se an maravillado'. On the atlas, see pages 103–7 above.

21. BL *Addl* 28,357/498, *cédula* of August 1581.

22. AGS *SP* libro 1550, fos. 46 (Goa: 1 Feb.); 89 (card games: 15 Feb.); 351 and 472 (legal codes: 12 July and 10 Sept.); 416 and 675 (expulsion of Jews: 9 Aug. and 15 Nov.); 534 (Congo: 18 Oct.); 72, 569 and 596 (Japan: 7 Feb., 1 and 8 Nov. 1586).

23. Ibid., fos. 2 (escort: 4 Jan.); 128 (defence of Cape Verde Islands and

Arguim: 8 Mar.); 320 (Brazil: 12 July); 572 (Minha: 25 Oct. 1586); and many more.

24. For attempted English piracy against the Portuguese in 1557, see J. F. Guilmartin Jr., *Gunpowder and Galleys. Changing Technology and Mediterranean Warfare at Sea in the Sixteenth Century* (Cambridge, 1974), 85–94; for the trade war, see *CSPF 1569–71*, 3, 25, 149–50 and 578–9; and *CSPF 1572–4*, 12 (draft treaty between England and Portugal, 1 Jan. 1572).

25. Compare N. J. W. Thrower, ed., *Sir Francis Drake and the Famous Voyage, 1577–1580* (Berkeley, 1984), 60–77 (one brush with a Portuguese galleon off the Celebes: p. 70), with M. F. Keeler, ed., *Sir Francis Drake's West Indian Voyage, 1585–86* (London, 1981), 27–8 (the sack of Santiago in the Cape Verde islands).

26. P. Rois Soares, *Memorial*, ed. M. Lopes de Almeida (Coimbra, 1953), 230. On the outbreak of war in 1585–6, see G. Parker, *The Grand Strategy of Philip II* (New Haven and London, 1998), chaps. 5 and 6.

27. Details from Checa, *Felipe II*, 271–2 and 486, where yet more imperialist examples appear.

28. See the brilliant analysis of the 'messianic imperialism' of these three writers by A. Terry, 'War and literature in sixteenth-century Spain', in J. R. Mulryne and M. Shewring, eds., *War, Literature and the Arts in Sixteenth-century Europe* (London, 1989), chap. 4. See also the other imperialists discussed in F. Fernández Armesto, 'Armada myths: the formative phase', in P. Gallagher and D. W. Cruickshank, eds., *God's Obvious Design. Papers of the Spanish Armada Symposium, Sligo, 1588* (London, 1990), 19–39; P. Fernández Albaladejo, 'Imperio de por sí: la formulación del poder universal en la temprana edad moderna', in G. Signorotto, ed., *L'Italia degli Austrias. Monarchia cattolica e domini italiani nei secoli XVI e XVII* (Mantua, 1993), 11–28; and Pereña Vicente, *Teoría*, 68.

29. IVdeDJ 62/916, Duarte Nunes de Leão to Gabriel de Zayas, 8 Aug. 1585. Checa, *Felipe II*, 281–2, cites the document but with a different reading of the text.

30. Quotations from P. Torres y Lanzas and F. Navas del Valle, eds., *Catálogo de los documentos relativos a las Islas Filipinas existentes en el Archivo General de Indias de Sevilla*, II (Barcelona, 1926), clxxxiii–iv; and F. Colin and P. Pastells, *Labor evangélica de los obreros de la Compañía de Jesús en las Islas Filipinas*, III (Barcelona, 1902), 448–52, Matteo Ricci to Juan Bautista Román, 13 Sept. 1584; J. Guillen Tato, ed., *Museo Naval. Colección de documentos y manuscritos inéditos compilados por Fernández de Navarrete*, XVIII (Nendeln, 1971), fos. 146–60, 'Relación dirigida por Juan Bautista Román', Macao, 28 Sept. 1584, after receiving Ricci's letter (at fo. 159v). On Ricci's acute military sense (and contempt for Chinese military skills), see J. D. Spence, *The Memory Palace of Matteo Ricci* (London, 1983); on the

terror that paralysed maritime China, see K. W. So, *Japanese Piracy in Ming China during the Sixteenth Century* (East Lansing, Mich., 1975).

31. From Bishop João Ribeiro Gaio's 'Derrotero y Relación' of 1584, in the Codex Boxer now at the Lilly Library of Indiana University, quoted, along with other 'universalist' projects of the day, in C. R. Boxer, 'Portuguese and Spanish projects for the conquest of Southeast Asia, 1580–1600', in idem, *Portuguese Conquest and Commerce in Southern Asia, 1500–1750* (London, 1985), chap. 3, 118–36. See also J. M. Headley, 'Spain's Asian presence 1565–1590: structures and aspirations', *Hispanic-American Historical Review*, LXXV (1995), 623–46.

32. Colin and Pastells, *Labor evangélica*, III, 32–3: Melchor Dávalos to Philip II, Manila, 20 June 1585; Blair and Robertson, *The Philippine Islands*, VI, 197–229. On Sánchez's ill-fated mission, see Headley, 'Spain's Asian presence', 638–45.

33. BNP *Fonds français Ms.* 16108/365, M. de St Gouard (French Resident at the court of Philip II) to Catherine de Medici, 20 Aug. 1582.

34. See the reproduction of the bowl, dated 1583, in C. Martin and G. Parker, *The Spanish Armada* (London, 1988), colour plate 25. For a discussion of new ways of portraying St James at this time, see IVdeDJ 62/917, Duarte Nunes de Leão to Zayas, 17 Aug. 1585.

35. *BMO*, I, 395–6, Santa Cruz to Philip II, 9 Aug. 1583 (see also the king's reply of 23 Sept.: ibid., 406.) Pope Gregory XIII also attempted at this moment to rekindle the king's interest in invading England: see ibid., 406–9, Philip II to the count of Olivares, his ambassador in Rome, 24 Sept. 1583 (with supporting documents), in reply to the pope's letter of 16 Aug. proposing the 'Enterprise of England'.

36. R. Villari and G. Parker, *La politica de Felipe II. Dos estudios* (Valladolid, 1996), 110–15, Zúñiga to Philip II, undated but late 1585.

37. Library of Congress, Manuscript Division, *Sir Francis Drake Collection* #3, Medina Sidonia to Philip II, 25 Oct. 1586, minute, point 13. See the similar views of the merchants of Seville in H. Lapèyre, *Une famille de marchands: les Ruiz* (Paris, 1955), 422–3.

38. Maura, 167, Don Juan de Idiáquez to the duke of Medina Sidonia, 28 Feb. 1587; and Herrera Oria, 148–9, same to same, 20 Feb. 1588.

39. *APO*, III, 130–1, Philip III to Viceroy Dom Duarte de Meneses, 23 Feb. 1588.

40. Thomas Beard, *The Theatre of God's Judgements* (1597), quoted with telling examples of the acceptance of this philosophy by Oliver Cromwell (Beard's pupil) and others, in J. Sproxton, *Violence and Religion. Attitudes towards Militancy in the French Civil Wars and the English Revolution* (London, 1995), 52 and 59–61. 'Flavit deus et dissipati sunt' and other 'providentialist' medals of 1588 are reproduced in M. J. Rodríguez-Salgado,

ed., *Armada 1588–1988* (London, 1988), 276–7; Groen van Prinsterer, *Archives*, 2nd series I, 84, François de la Noue to an English correspondent, 17 Aug. 1588. For other examples of English and Dutch providentialism see: M. McGiffert, 'God's controversy with Jacobean England', *AHR*, LXXXVIII (1983), 1151–74; C. Z. Wiener, 'The Beleaguered Isle. A study of Elizabethan and early Jacobean anti-Catholicism', *Past and Present*, LI (1971), 27–62; D. R. Cressy, *Bonfires and Bells. National Memory and the Protestant Calendar in Elizabethan and Stuart England* (Berkeley, 1989), chaps. 7, 9 and 10; D. R. Woolf, *The Idea of History in Early Stuart England. Erudition, Ideology and 'the Light of Truth' from the Accession of James I to the Civil War* (Toronto, 1991), 4–8; and G. Groenhuis, *De Predikanten: de sociale positie van de Gereformeerde Predikanten in de Republiek der Verenigde Nederlanden voor 1700* (Groningen, 1977), 77–107.

41. See numerous examples quoted in J. M. Nieto Soria, *Fundamentos ideológicos del poder real en Castilla (siglos XIII–XVI)* (Madrid, 1988).

42. *Actas de las Cortes de Castilla*, VII (Madrid, 1866), 16–20, royal proposition on 13 July 1583 (the opening address to other sessions of the Cortes normally contained similar rhetoric); *PEG*, V, 643, Philip II to Cardinal Granvelle, 24 Aug. 1559; and BPU *Favre* 30/73v, Philip II to Requesens, 20 Oct. 1573, copy of holograph original.

43. BZ 141/84, Philip II to Mateo Vázquez, 19 Feb. 1586; and IVdeDJ 55/IX/111, same to same, 26 July 1586. See also *CCG*, XII, 534–5 [Sept. 1579], where the king received a letter going to mass, but did not read it until after it ended; and ibid., XI, 277–8, 22 Sept. 1584, where the king claimed he could not read a letter until he had been to vespers to commemorate the anniversary of his father's death.

44. For the king's total seclusion during his 'retreats', see C. Douais, *Dépêches de M. de Fourquevaux, ambassadeur du roi Charles IX en Espagne*, II (Paris, 1900), 3–7, Memoir of Oct. 1568, and José de Sigüenza, *La Fundación del Monasterio de El Escorial* (1605; ed. Antonio Fernández Alba, Madrid, 1988), 92. On sleeping in time of sermon, see Bouza Álvarez, *Cartas de Felipe II a sus hijas*, 113, Philip II to his daughters, [30 Mar.] 1584.

45. AGS *Estado* 527/5, Philip II to Gonzalo Pérez, undated [Mar. 1565].

46. See AGS *Estado* 112/245–50, 226–9 and 216–18, Juana, regent of Castile, to Philip II, 25 Sept., 21 Nov. and 14 Dec. 1556, and 114/257, 'Memorial de las personas con quien se ha de tratar'; M. Ferrandis Torres, *El concilio de Trento*, II (Valladolid, 1934: Archivo Histórico Español, VI), 158–9 and 202–5, report of the 'junta en lo que toca al concilio' to Philip II, 2 Jan. and 26 Feb. 1561; G. Parker, *The Dutch Revolt* (2nd edn., Harmondsworth, 1985), 64–5; José A. García Vilar, 'El Maquiavelismo en las relaciones internacionales: la anexión de Portugal a España en 1580', *Revista de estudios internacionales*, II (1981), 599–643, at pp. 620–42. On the role of Philip's

confessor, see G. Parker, *The World Is Not Enough. The Imperial Vision of Philip II of Spain* (Waco, Texas, 2001), 32–3.

47. Miguel Hernández, *Vida, martirio y translación de la gloriosa virgen y mártir santa Leocadia* (Toledo, 1591), fos. 244v and 247v–8. On the king's attention to relics during his final illness, see Sigüenza, *Fundación*, 175.

48. Some 600 *plegarías* between 1560 and 1568 are registered in AGS *Cámara de Castilla: libros de cédulas*, 321/248–9, 272–5, 184–6v, 299–301, 303 and so on; see also M. Andrés Martín, 'Felipe II y los movimientos reformadores', in F. J. Campos y Fernández de Sevilla, ed., *Felipe II y su época. Actas del Simposium* (2 vols., El Escorial, 1998), II, 411–55, at pp. 425–7; F. J. Bouza Álvarez, *Imagen y propaganda. Capítulos de historia cultural del reinado de Felipe II* (Madrid, 1998), 144–6, on the establishment of prayer stations (1574); BL *Eg* 1506/16–17, Philip II's rescript to Inquisitor-General Quiroga, 8 Mar. 1574, on prayers by special persons.

49. For two examples of 'God has done this,' see BZ 166/92 and 100, Hernando de Vega to Philip II and reply, 9 and 11 Nov. 1586 (upon learning that the annual Indies fleet had arrived safely at Seville). Complaints from IVdeDJ 53/3/56 and BZ 144/36, Vázquez to Philip II and replies, 13 May and 11 Dec. 1574.

50. Serrano, I, 316–17, Philip II to Requesens, 12 Aug. 1566; letter to the duke of Parma quoted (with other similar letters) by J. Zarco Cuevas, 'Ideales y normas de gobierno de Felipe II', in F. Pérez Minguez, ed., *Reivindicación histórica del siglo XVI* (Madrid, 1928), 151–2.

51. Zarco Cuevas, 'Ideales', 151–2, Instruction to Don Diego de Ibarra, 18 Nov. 1590; and KML *MSP: CR* 6/174, Philip II to Medina Sidonia, 15 Dec. 1590.

52. On the first of these escapades, see Bourdon, 'Un projet d'invasion de la Chine'; on the second, B. Bierman, 'Los portugueses y españoles en Camboja al fin del siglo XVI', *Archivo Ibero-Americano*, XXXVIII [año XXII] (1935), 261–70; B. P. Groslier and C. R. Boxer, *Angkor et le Cambodge au XVIe siècle d'après les sources portugaises et espagnoles* (Paris, 1958), 34–62; and M. Phoeun, ed., *Chroniques royales du Cambodge (de 1594 à 1677)* (Paris, 1981), 72–5. Boxer, 'Portuguese and Spanish projects', noted both ventures.

53. On Sri Lanka, see T. Abeyasinghe, *Portuguese Rule in Ceylon, 1594–1612* (Colombo, 1966); and G. D. Winius, *The Fatal History of Portuguese Ceylon. Transition to Dutch Rule* (Cambridge, Mass., 1971). On Taiwan, see Torres y Lanzas and Navas del Valle, *Católogo de los documentos relativos a las Islas Filipinas*, IV, lxxviii–lxxx; and Boxer, 'Portuguese and Spanish projects', 132. In the end Spaniards from the Philippines did maintain settlements on the north coast of Taiwan between 1624 and 1642: see T. A. Andrade, 'Commerce, culture and conflict. Taiwan under European rule, 1624–1662' (Yale Ph.D. thesis, 2000).

54. See E. S. Tenace, 'The Spanish intervention in Brittany and the failure of Philip II's bid for European hegemony, 1589–98' (University of Illinois Ph.D. thesis, 1996); H. Morgan, *Tyrone's Rebellion. The Outbreak of the Nine Years' War in Tudor Ireland* (London, 1993), 206–13; and J. J. Silke, *Kinsale. The Spanish Intervention in Ireland at the End of the Elizabethan Wars* (Liverpool, 1970).

55. For the *Madre* see K. R. Andrews, *Elizabethan Privateering. English Privateering during the Spanish War 1585–1603* (Cambridge, 1964), 73; for the *Valentim*, see PRO AO1/1691/39 and 1/1692/42 (accounts of Fulk Greville and William Ryder for the sale of the cargo – which brought in £44,000, more than the entire cost of the navy for a year!).

56. See Andrews, *Elizabethan Privateering*, 124–34.

57. J. C. Boyajian, *Portuguese Trade in Asia under the Habsburgs, 1580–1640* (Baltimore, 1993), 24–5; and L. de Figueiredo Falcão, *Livro em qve se contem toda a fazenda e real patrimonio dos reynos de Portugal* (Lisboa, 1607; reprinted, 1859), 194–6. (Note that the carrack listed as lost in 1586 was the *São Phelipe* captured by Drake in 1587.)

58. See the tables and commentary in Chaunu, III, 398ff., and VIII part 2, 753ff.

59. See details in A. Teodoro de Matos, 'The financial situation of the State of India during the Philippine period (1581–1635)', in T. R. de Souza, ed., *Indo-Portuguese History. Old Issues, New Questions* (New Delhi, 1985), 90–101. For some doubts concerning the solvency of the Portuguese in Asia, see M. N. Pearson, *Merchants and Rulers in Gujarat. The Response of the Portuguese in the Sixteenth Century* (Berkeley, 1976), 56. The constant state of war in which the Estado da India existed appears clearly in the reports of the viceroys to Lisbon between 1605 and 1622 printed in R. A. Bulhão Pato and A. da Silva Rego, eds., *Documentos remettidos da India ou Livros das Monções*, 10 vols. (Lisbon, 1880–1975).

60. The magnificent survey carried out in 1633–5 by A. Bocarro, *O livro das plantas de todas as fortalezas, cidades e povoações do Estado da Índia Oriental* (3 vols., new edn., Lisbon, 1992), records and depicts the costly new fortifications begun at Mascate (1588), Mombasa (1593), Damão (1615), Diu (1634), and so on. See also chapter 8 above.

61. On the apparent surplus of 1635, see Teodoro de Matos, 'The financial situation', 93; however, the budget omitted the cost of equipping the return fleet that year (a point made to me by L. F. F. R. Thomaz). Moreover, in 1634 Viceroy Linhares expressly stated that the revenues of the Estado did not suffice to cover ordinary expenditure and defence: see HAG *Ms.* 1162/128–9, *Asento* of the council of finance, 16 Aug. 1634. HAG *Ms.* 26/69v–70, Linhares to Philip IV, 7 Dec. 1634, copy, put the debt at 'mais de cuatro milhões [cruzados]'.

62. See P. Bakewell, *Silver Mining and Society in Colonial Mexico: Zacatecas 1546–1700* (Cambridge, 1971), 232; G. Guarda, *Flandes Indiano. Las fortificaciones del reino de Chile, 1541–1826* (Santiago de Chile, 1990); P. E. Hoffman, *The Spanish Crown and the Defense of the Caribbean, 1535–85: Precedent, Patrimonialism and Royal Parsimony* (Baton Rouge, 1980); J. A. Calderón Quijano, *Fortificaciones en Nueva España* (Seville, 1984); and G. Lohmann Villena, *Las defensas militares de Lima y Callao* (Seville, 1964).

63. F. Braudel, *The Mediterranean and the Mediterranean World in the Age of Philip II*, II (London, 1973), 1176; S. A. Skilliter, 'The Hispano-Ottoman armistice of 1581', in C. E. Bosworth, ed., *Iran and Islam* (Edinburgh, 1971), 491–515.

64. See Boyajian, *Portuguese Trade*, 128; G. Parker, *Spain and the Netherlands, 1559–1659* (London, 1979), 193–5; and M. A. P. Meilink-Roelofsz, *Asian Trade and European Influence in the Indonesian Archipelago between 1500 and about 1630* (The Hague, 1962), 386.

65. Parker, *Spain and the Netherlands*, 195–6.

66. Keeler, *Sir Francis Drake's West Indian Voyage*, 56; B. Bailyn, *The New England Merchants in the Seventeenth Century* (Cambridge, 1955), 2–5; K. N. Chaudhuri, *The English East India Company. The Study of an Early Joint Stock Company, 1600–1640* (London, 1965).

67. On Louis XIV's reluctant decision to accept the will of Carlos II, see the brilliant elucidation in A. Lossky, *Louis XIV* (New Brunswick, 1994), 260–2.

68. IVdeDJ 82/444, duke of Sessa (Spanish ambassador in Rome) to Don Balthasar de Zúñiga (Spanish ambassador in Brussels), 28 Sept. 1600, minute. The occasion for this outburst was the rumour that an envoy of the Sharif of Morocco had gone to London to forge an alliance with Elizabeth of England. See the similar views of Don Martín de Padilla the previous year cited in Parker, *Grand Strategy*, 281.

69. *CSPSp*, IV, 690, Padilla to Philip III, 10 Dec. 1601; IVdeDJ 82/419, Sessa to Don Balthasar de Zúñiga, 9 Nov. 1602, minute.

2. Of Providence and Protestant Winds: The Spanish Armada of 1588 and the Dutch Armada of 1688

We thank Dr Peter Le Fevre for bringing some helpful references to our attention. So far as we are aware, the only modern attempt to compare the two invasions is J. L. Anderson, 'Climatic change, sea-power and historical discontinuity: the Spanish Armada and the Glorious Revolution of 1688', *The Great Circle*, V (1983), 13–23. This article concentrates largely on climate.

1. J. Israel, ed., *The Anglo-Dutch Moment. Essays on the Glorious Revolution*

and Its World Impact (Cambridge, 1991), 1 (quoting the *Diary* of Edmund Bohun, an eyewitness) and 128.

2. On William's unpopularity, see Israel, *The Anglo-Dutch Moment*, 42–3 and 142–3; on the consequences of 1688 for British foreign policy, see J. Black, 'The treaty of Rijswijk and the long-term development of Anglo-Continental relations', in H. Duchhardt, ed., *Der Friede von Rijswijk, 1697* (Mainz, 1998), 115–27. On the counterfactual aspects, see J. A. Goldstone, 'Europe's peculiar path: would the world be "modern" if William III's invasion of England in 1688 had failed?', together with C. Pestana's rejoinder, in P. Tetlock, R. N. Lebow and G. Parker, eds., *Unmaking the West. Alternate Histories of Counterfactual Worlds* (New York, forthcoming).

3. 'Flavit deus et dissipati sunt.' In fact this was a Dutch medal: see details on this and other commemorations in M. J. Rodríguez-Salgado, ed., *Armada 1588–1988* (London, 1988), 276–7.

4. See details in J. L. Anderson, 'Combined operations and the Protestant wind: maritime aspects of the Glorious Revolution of 1688', *The Great Circle*, IX (1987), 96–107.

5. BL *Addl* 38,495/28v, Moreau, Polish resident in the United Provinces, to the king of Poland, The Hague, 12 Oct. 1688; a contemporary French writer, Sainte-Marthe, also compared the Spanish Armada of 1588 with the Dutch armada of 1688: see Denis de Sainte-Marthe, *Entretiens touchant l'entreprise du prince d'Orange sur l'Angleterre* (Paris, 1689), 89–93.

6. G. Canestrini and A. Desjardins, *Négociations diplomatiques de la France avec la Toscane* (6 vols., Paris, 1859–86), IV, 737, Filippo Cavriana to B. Vinta, Paris, 22 Nov. 1587; and Laughton, I, 358–62, Sir John Hawkins to Sir Francis Walsingham, 10 Aug. 1588.

7. G. Leti, *Teatro Belgico o vero ritratti chronologici, politici e geografici delle Sette Provincie Unite* (2 vols., Amsterdam, 1690), I, 353–6; BL *Addl* 41,816/ 239, marquis d'Albeville to Secretary of State Lord Middleton, The Hague, 15 Oct. 1688.

8. On the Armada's size see C. Martin and G. Parker, *The Spanish Armada* (2nd edn., Manchester, 1999), 261–5; on the size of Parma's fleet see G. Parker, *The Grand Strategy of Philip II* (New Haven and London, 1998), chap. 8.

9. The 'capital ships' consisted of 13 with between 60 and 68 guns, 7 with between 50 and 56, and 12 with between 40 and 48. The Dutch deliberately held back their first- and second-rate ships, believing that they would prove unstable in the heavy seas to be expected so late in the season. See J. C. de Jonge, *Geschiedenis van het Nederlandsche zeewesen* (2nd edn., 5 vols., Haarlem, 1858–62), III, 41 and 722.

10. See ARA *Staten Generaal* 5625/ii, Memorandum of delegates of the Dutch Admiralty Colleges, The Hague, 16 Oct. 1688; *Hollandse Mercurius*

verhalende de voornaemste saken van staet en andere voorvallen die in en omtrent de Vereenigde Nederlanden en elders in Europa in het jaer 1688 zijn geschiet (Haarlem, 1689), 277; Abraham van Poot, *Engelands Gods-dienst en vryheid hersteldt door syn Hoogheyt den Heere Prince van Oranje* (2 vols., Amsterdam, 1689), 108; A. Montanus, *Het Leven, bedryf en oorlogs-daaden van Wilhem de Derden, koning van Engeland, Schotland, Frankryk en Ierland* (4 vols., Amsterdam, 1703), III, 108–10; de Jonge, *Geschiedenis*, III, 41 and 722; A. N. J. Fabius, *Het leven van Willem III (1650–1702)* (Alkmaar, 1912), 29 and 299; J. C. Mollema, *Geschiedenis van Nederland ter zee* (4 vols., Amsterdam, 1939–42), III, 107; and E. B. Powley, *The English Navy in the Revolution of 1688* (Cambridge, 1928), 35–6 and 71.

11. BL *Addl* 41,816/267, d'Albeville to Middleton, The Hague, 30 Oct. 1688. In the aftermath of the Glorious Revolution, it suited Williamite writers to play down the size of the Dutch army since they maintained that there had *not* been an 'invasion'. Most secondary authorities unconsciously follow this tendency, asserting that William's invasion force was of only around 14,000 men, not realizing that the quoted figure of 14,352 refers only to the regular Dutch infantry and cavalry, omitting the Dutch gunners and the English, Scots, Huguenot and Dutch volunteers, many of whom were professional soldiers. The most authoritative contemporary Dutch sources give the size of the invasion army as 21,000 men while Van den Bos gives 23,000: *Hollandse Mercurius 1688*, 275. Van Poot, *Engelands Gods-dienst en vryheid hersteldt*, I, 107–8, states that 'de hele militie is sterk meer als 21 duisent man soo volontaires als mede de vluchtelingen'. See also Montanus, *Leven, bedryf en oorlogs-daaden*, III, 108–10; *Engeland Beroerd onder de regering van Iacobus de II en hersteldt door Willem en Maria, Prins en Princesse van Oranje* (Amsterdam, 1689), 170; Lambert van den Bos, *Leven en Bedryf van Willem de Derden, koning van Groot Brittanien* (2 vols., Amsterdam, 1694), I, 255 (gives 18,000 foot and 5000 horse); and *The Expedition of his Highness the Prince of Orange for England* [1688], in *Harleian Miscellany* (London, 1744), 438, which also gives over 23,000. Thus the assumption that had there been a battle on Salisbury Plain the Dutch would have been outnumbered by two to one is incorrect; the Dutch would perhaps have been slightly outnumbered but were much superior to James's army in artillery, experience and training, the States-General having sent over their best troops. Several modern historians have been misled into thinking that William III had only 'a fairly modest force for his expedition', of around 12,000 men: see J. R. Western, *Monarchy and Revolution: The English State in the 1680s* (London, 1972), 259–60. Baxter calls it a 'little army': S. B. Baxter, *William III* (London, 1966), 238. The one department in which the Armada of 1588 definitely surpassed that of 1688 was in clergy: the 1588 Armada carried some 198 clerics while in 1688, apart from Gilbert Burnet and a few regimental chaplains, the States-General

commissioned only six Calvinist preachers to accompany the fleet: see Rodríguez-Salgado, *Armada*, 36; ARA *Raad van State* 109, fo. 477.

12. BL *Addl* 41,816/167, Consul Petit to Middleton, Amsterdam, 7 Sept.
1688; ibid. 41,831/167, Peter Wyche to Middleton, Hamburg, 4 Sept. 1688.

13. Ibid. 41,816/231, d'Albeville to Middleton, The Hague, 11 Oct. 1688. As
late as November 1688, however, Sir Robert Holmes still thought the Dutch
fleet was designed to attack France: see J. Black, 'The Revolution and the
development of English foreign policy', in E. Cruickshanks, ed., *By Force or
by Default: The Revolution of 1688-89* (Edinburgh, 1989), 135-58, at
p. 150.

14. BL *Addl* 41,816/209, d'Albeville to Middleton, The Hague, 1 Oct. 1688;
ibid. 41,828/91, Wyche to Middleton, Hamburg, 21 Sept. 1688; ibid. 41,841/
88, Ambassador Carlingford to Middleton, Vienna, 19 Sept. 1688; and
ibid. 41,841/234v, Ambassador Scarborough to Middleton, Lisbon, 3 Nov.
1688.

15. James's Instructions to Dartmouth dated 11 October are quoted by
Powley, *The English Navy*, 28-9.

16. BL *Addl* 41,816/75, Middleton to d'Albeville, London, 23 Sept. 1688.
Middleton was a Scot, which may explain his gross miscalculation.

17. Ibid. 41,816/244, d'Albeville to Middleton, The Hague, 16 Oct. 1688.

18. From a letter sent by Samuel Pepys, secretary of the navy, to Lord
Dartmouth on 8 Nov., quoted in J. R. Tanner, 'Naval preparations of James
II in 1688', *EHR*, VIII (1893), 272-83, at p. 279 n. 57.

19. James's preparations are well discussed in J. Childs, *The Army, James II
and the Glorious Revolution* (Manchester, 1980), 171-81; and C. Jones, 'The
Protestant wind of 1688: myth and reality', *European Studies Review*, III
(1973), 201-22. For Dutch intelligence about them see, for example, the
report sent to Holland in September by a Dutch agent in England, Jacob van
Leeuwen, stating that James was concentrating his forces around London: N.
Japikse, ed., *Correspondentie van Willem III en Hans Willem Bentinck,
eersten Graf van Portland* (5 vols., The Hague, 1927-37), I, part 2, 609.

20. Japikse, *Correspondentie*, I, part 2, 619, Bentinck to an unnamed agent
in England, undated but from Oct. 1688.

21. See, for example, Anderson, 'Combined operations'. However, the author
has since modified his opinion: see idem, 'Prince William's descent upon
Devon, 1688: the environmental constraints', in S. Fisher, ed., *Lisbon as a
Port Town, the British Seaman, and Other Maritime Themes* (Exeter, 1988),
37-55 – which argues that the key consideration was the need to land cavalry
horses.

22. The decision of 11 November is recorded in Japikse, *Correspondentie*, I,
part 2, 623-4. The points for invasion were to be Southampton, failing which
Poole, failing which Exmouth.

23. Herbert's memorandum, warning that the northeastern coast was 'soe dangerex that I hardly think it practicable', is printed in Japikse, *Correspondentie*, I, part 2, 612. The low opinion of Herbert held by William and his entourage is discussed at page 60 above; the letter to Bentinck of 12 Nov. ('Vous voiés que je tiens la course en West, et passerons j'espère demain le pas de Calais') is in Japikse, *Correspondentie*, II, part 3, 53. William's own view of the two alternative landing sites is given in ARA *Collectie Fagel* 507, William III to Grand Pensionary Fagel, Exeter, 26 Nov. 1688.

24. See J. de Lamar Jensen, 'The Spanish Armada: the worst kept secret in Europe', *Sixteenth Century Journal*, XIX (1988), 621–41; and Parker, *Grand Strategy*, chap. 7.

25. AGS *Estado* 165/104–14, Instructions to Medina Sidonia, 1 Apr. 1588; Japikse, *Correspondentie*, I, part 2, 613–17, Instructions for Arthur Herbert, 6 Oct. 1688.

26. In 1588 the Armada passed Torbay on 1 August and reached Calais six days later; a century later the Dutch passed through the Straits of Calais on 13 November and began disembarkation at Torbay on the 15th.

27. Many discussions of this question exist, but in our view the best analysis of the available evidence – which concludes that the 'Naval conspiracy', although it existed, was not decisive in the outcome of the campaign – is that of D. Davies, 'James II, William of Orange, and the admirals', in Cruickshanks, *By Force or by Default*, 82–108.

28. Based upon N. A. M. Rodger, *The Safeguard of the Sea. A Naval History of Great Britain*. I, *660–1649* (London, 1997), 429.

29. See details in Martin and Parker, *The Spanish Armada*, 89–90.

30. The original memorial (drawn up in the joint names of Santa Cruz and Provisioner-General Bernabe de Pedroso) was thought to be lost, but in 1983 it appeared at an auction and was purchased for the Archives of Simancas. Although undated, Santa Cruz sent covering letters to court on 22 Mar. 1586: see *BMO*, II, 44–74. The marquis also sent a preliminary version – which has still not surfaced – more than a month earlier (see BZ 81/88, Santa Cruz to Don Juan de Zúñiga, 13 Feb. 1586, announcing its dispatch). The council of war discussed a précis on 23 Feb. (see AGS *Guerra Antigua* 190/314). This must have been the document seen by the Venetian ambassador in Madrid, and described in his letter to the Doge and Senate on 22 Mar. 1586 (a major security breach!), since no ambassador in Madrid could not have seen a dossier mailed in Lisbon that same day: *CSPV*, 147–8. Copies of the 22 Mar. document were also secured by several ambassadors: for Venice see ibid., 193–5; for London see PRO *SP* 94/2 fos. 124–5; for Paris see BNP, *Fonds français* 16,110/130–6; and so on.

31. Santa Cruz is known to have consulted detailed maps and descriptions of Ireland while preparing his plan: Duro, I, 23.

32. See AGS *Estado* 2218/43, Don Juan de Idiáquez to Archduke Albert, 2 Apr. 1586, on the preparations at Lisbon; Maura, 145ff., on Medina Sidonia's part; and AGS *CMC* 2a/1208 on the embargo of ships to form the squadron of Vizcaya, 10 Apr.–7 May 1586, and *BMO*, II, 179–80, Recalde's patent of 8 June 1586.

33. *BMO*, II, 108–11, Parma to Philip II, 20 Apr. 1586; the letter's arrival is noted in ibid., 195–6, 'Lo que dixó Juan Bautista Piata de palabra a 24 de junio 1586' (a document which itself contains additional information about the plan).

34. Parma devoted only two paragraphs of his letter to the possibility of naval support from Spain, and even then he considered it only in the context of 'the worst case scenario': that somehow details of his plan became known in England. In that case, he suggested, since the king was being forced by Drake's exploits to mobilize a fleet to protect the Atlantic, perhaps this new navy could be used 'either to sail suddenly up here in order to assist and reinforce the troops who have already landed [in Kent] and keep open the seaway between the coasts of Flanders and England; or else – if your fleet is large, well-provided, well-armed and well-manned – it could create a diversion which will draw the English fleet away [from the straits of Dover]': *BMO*, II, 108–11, Parma to Philip II, 20 Apr. 1586.

35. Zúñiga suggested Mary Queen of Scots – preferably married to some more dependable Catholic prince, such as the duke of Parma. But after her execution in Feb. 1587 there was an extended and somewhat acrimonious correspondence between pope and king over the 'investiture': the king wished England to be ruled by his daughter Isabella and her future husband (probably an Austrian Habsburg), but the pope was reluctant to sanction this massive extension of Spanish political power in advance of the conquest.

36. *BMO*, II, 212, *Parescer* of Don Juan de Zúñiga, holograph and undated (but June/July 1586). Before submitting his proposal to the king, Zúñiga certainly consulted others – including Bernardino de Escalante, whose plan closely corresponded to the final proposal: see J. L. Casado Soto, *Discursos de Bernardino de Escalante al rey y sus ministros, 1585–1605* (Laredo, 1995), 110–27, and pages 110 and 112 above.

37. This argument is developed in more detail in G. Parker, *Spain and the Netherlands 1550–1650. Ten Studies* (London, 1979), chap. 7.

38. Although no copy of the masterplan has yet come to light, its existence is clearly indicated in *BMO*, II, 333, Philip II to Parma, 1 Sept. 1586: 'On 26 July I replied at length and in detail to the letter brought by Giovanni Battista Piatti, as I believe you will have seen before receiving this'; and ibid., 387, Parma to Philip II, 30 Oct. 1586, replying to 'your royal letter of 26 July which he [Piatti] brought me'. In its absence, the 'plan' has been reconstructed from the following: *BMO*, II, 387–8, Parma to Philip II, 30 Oct. 1586; 471–

2, royal reply of 17 Dec. 1586; 535–6, Parma to Philip II, 17 Jan. 1587; and 624, Idiáquez to Medina Sidonia, 28 Feb. 1587. In his subsequent letters, the king and Parma never referred to details of the invasion strategy, only to 'la traza acordada' (the plan agreed).

39. AGS *Estado* 1261/87, Philip II to the governor of Lombardy, 7 Aug. 1586; and *BMO*, II, 414, to the viceroys of Naples and Sicily, 12 Nov. 1586. The towns of Spain were ordered to prepare to levy troops on 7 Oct. 1586 (AGS *Guerra Antigua* 189/119–68).

40. On the raid, see Martin and Parker, *The Spanish Armada*, 109–11, the sources listed at p. 113 no. 9, and pages 87–9 above.

41. Instructions in *BMO*, III, 1006–7 and 1067–8, Philip II to Parma, 4 Sept. 1587; and to Santa Cruz, 14 Sept. 1587. It was an oversight to which Parma frequently alluded, but without ever receiving an answer! Cf. AGS *Estado* 592/147–9, Parma to Philip II, 21 Dec. 1587; and *Estado* 594/6–7, 79 and 197, same to same, 31 Jan., 22 June and 21 July 1588.

42. See B. T. Whitehead, *Brags and Boasts. Propaganda in the Year of the Armada* (Stroud, 1994), 76–81. In 1688, despite all the effort expended on propaganda in England and all the promises of support issued by English political, ecclesiastical, military and naval leaders, few declared for William III until it was clear that he had won.

43. The role assigned to Allen in the interim government of England emerges clearly from Philip II's supplementary instructions to Parma on 5 Apr. 1588: AGS *Estado* 165/176–7. For the king's lack of confidence in a rising by English Catholics, see ibid., fos. 174–5, Instructions to Parma, 1 Apr. 1588. In general, see the excellent article of A. J. Loomie, 'The Armadas and the Catholics of England', *Catholic Historical Review*, LIX (1973), 385–403.

44. Admittedly, in March 1588, Philip claimed that 'If I were not needed so much here, to provide what is necessary for that [enterprise] and for many other things, I would be very pleased to join [the Armada] – and I would do so with great confidence that it would go very well for me.' But he doubtless made this strange boast merely to encourage his reluctant commander, Medina Sidonia. The duke's reaction to this royal insight has not survived. KML *MSP: CR* 5/82, Philip II to Medina Sidonia, 11 Mar. 1588.

45. The tense international situation intensified the adverse consequences. In both cases, the invasion could only succeed while all other interested powers (especially France) were temporarily distracted. The invaders had to exploit a favourable conjuncture immediately: they had to deliver the blow swiftly. On the international conjuncture in 1588, see Parker, *Grand Strategy*, chap. 6; for 1688, see the excellent survey of J. P. Carswell, *The Descent upon England. A Study of the English Revolution of 1688 and Its European Background* (London, 1969).

46. On the disruptive effects of this exercise, which involved several large

merchantmen from the returning Indies fleet of 1587 as well as their escorts, see Chaunu, III, 404–10. It is worth noting that Elizabeth raised her fleet of almost 200 ships and almost 16,000 men in just over three months.

47. See the excellent biography of P. Pierson, *Commander of the Armada. The Seventh Duke of Medina Sidonia* (New Haven, 1989).

48. Details from Martin and Parker, *The Spanish Armada*, chap. 11.

49. Contrast Japikse, *Correspondentie*, I, part 1, 57, William III to Bentinck, 14 Sept. 1688, with Gilbert Burnet, *History of His Own Time*, III (Oxford, 1833), 310. The Dutch public was also amazed by the dispatch with which the expedition was made ready, according to G. Leti, *La Monarchie universelle de Louys XIV* (2 vols., Amsterdam, 1689), II, 522.

50. ARA *Staten Generaal* 5625/ii, Delegates of the Admiralty Colleges to the States-General, The Hague, 4 Nov. 1688; ibid., Zeeland Admiralty College to same, Middelburg, 3 Nov. 1688; and de Jonge, *Geschiedenis*, III, 44, 723–4.

51. BL *Addl* 41,816/104, d'Albeville to Middleton, The Hague, 15 July 1688; ibid., fo. 157v, Petit to Middleton, Amsterdam, 24 Aug. 1689. For further details on the recruiting of the 9000 seamen, see ARA *Staten Generaal* 5625/i, Zeeland Admiralty College to the States-General, Middelburg, 14 July 1688; *Resolutien Holland*, 19 Aug. 1688; and *Resolutieën van de Hoogh Mog. Heeren Staten Generael der Vereenighde Nederlantsche Provincien genomen in den jare 1688* (The Hague, n.d.), 481, resolution of 11 Aug. 1688.

52. BL *Addl* 48,186/159v, Petit to Middleton, Amsterdam, 27 Aug. 1688. Some 3000 seamen had already been raised by 26 July when d'Albeville reported to London that 'there are at present but six thousand seamen to be raised, and this has been compassed with a great deal of patience and artifice and the Prince hopes by means of the late rear admiral Herbert [who had just arrived in The Hague from England] to gett over many of His Majesty's seamen: hitherto though they gott but very few or none at all' (ibid. 41,816/124v, d'Albeville to Middleton, The Hague, 26 July 1688). Impressment was extremely rare in the Dutch Republic at this time.

53. Ibid. 41, 816/157v–8 and 165, Petit to Middleton, Amsterdam, 24 Aug. and 3 Sept. 1688.

54. Ibid. 41,828/91, Wyche to Middleton, Hamburg, 21 Sept. 1688. Needless to say, such an enormous mass of shipping was not hired so quickly by normal processes of commercial bargaining but by systematic intervention by the Admiralty Colleges and the States of Holland: see Job de Wildt to Bentinck, undated but from Oct. 1688, in Japikse, *Correspondentie*, I, part 2, 618.

55. There were perhaps 200 mules and horses on the Armada, mainly to help manoeuvre the big siege-guns ashore: AGS *Guerra Antigua* 221/64, 'Relación of 16 Feb. 1588. The duke of Parma planned to embark some 1000 cavalry troopers on his fleet of small ships, but they had to secure their mounts from English stables after the landing: see H. O'Donnell, 'El secreto, requisite para

la Empresa de Inglaterra de 1588', *Revista de Historia Naval*, II, no. 7 (1984), 63–74.

56. According to the supply contracts drawn up by the States-General with the Amsterdam Sephardi 'provisioners-general' Antonio Alvares Machado and Jacob Pereira the following year, a Dutch field army of 20,000 men required for its provisions 200 wagons each drawn by four horses (see BL *Addl* 38,695/73 and 75v, a supply contract dated The Hague, 22 Jan. 1689).

57. Burnet, *History*, III, 299. There has been some dispute over the number of horses. The Polish resident reported that 90 transport vessels in the fleet carried 60 horses each – a total of 5400: see BL *Addl* 38,495/30v, Moreau to the king of Poland, The Hague, 12 Oct. 1688. According to a Dutch planning document, 120 vessels would be required to carry 36 horses each (i.e. 4320 horses in all); and the fleet was to carry 640,000 lbs (290,000kg) of hay as rations for 4000 horses at 16 lbs (7kg) per day each for 10 days: see the 'Memorie' of 19 Sept. 1688 in Japikse, *Correspondentie*, I, part 2, 606. In the end it would seem that some 4000 horses were embarked in October for the cavalry, together with 2–3000 draught animals, of which about 1100 died during the first abortive invasion attempt and were only partially replaced before the fleet set forth again.

58. BL *Addl* 41,816/185 and 251, d'Albeville to Middleton, The Hague, 21 Sept. and 21 Oct. 1688.

59. The Spanish Armada also had its own press but left it behind in Lisbon. The advance propaganda for the English was printed in the Low Countries and was to be carried over by the duke of Parma's forces.

60. BL *Addl* 41,816/186, d'Albeville to Middleton, The Hague, 21 Sept. 1688; and F. J. G. ten Raa and F. de Bas, *Het Staatsche Leger, 1568–1795* (11 vols., The Hague, 1911–18), VII, 6.

61. De Jonge, *Geschiedenis*, II, part 3, 51. The promotion of Herbert was very unpopular with the States-General, as well as with Evertsen and the Dutch navy: see J. Wagenaar, *Vaderlandsche Historie vervattende de geschiedenissen der nu Vereenigde Nederlanden* (21 vols., Amsterdam, 1749–59), XV, 466. But William insisted, even though he too had his doubts – see his letter to Bentinck of 26 Sept. 1688: 'Ce n'est pas le temps de faire voir bravoure, n'y de se battre si l'on le peut éviter; je luy [i.e., to Herbert] l'ay déjà dit, mais il sera nécessaire que vous le répétiez et vous le luy fassiez bien comprendre' (Japikse, *Correspondentie*, I, part 1, 58). It was hardly an expression of confidence! Indeed, no one really seems to have trusted Herbert: see Davies, 'James II, William of Orange, and the admirals', 87–90.

62. BL *Addl* 41,816/239, d'Albeville to Middleton, The Hague, 15 Oct. 1688. Apparently, a few Scotsmen did refuse.

63. Ibid. 41,816/202, d'Albeville to Middleton, The Hague, 28 Sept. 1688. According to Burnet (*History*, III, 308–9), Lords Macclesfield and Mordaunt

were among the English leaders aboard the fleet who resented the tone of *The Prince of Orange his Declaration: shewing the Reasons why he Invades England* (London, 1688), and began to ask why they should fight for such muted aims.

64. BL *Addl* 41,816/209, d'Albeville to Middleton, The Hague, 1 Oct. 1688; ibid., 38,495/45, Moreau to the king of Poland, The Hague, 2 Nov. 1688; and Burnet, *History*, III, 305.

65. See the 'Relaciones de sabado' for 1588–9 in AGS *CJH* 249, *carpetas* 16–17 (Parker, *Grand Strategy*, 199, reproduces one).

66. The sardonic captain was probably Martin de Bertendona: see Martin and Parker, *The Spanish Armada*, 128 and 135 n. 35; AGS *Estado* 165/2–3, Philip II to the Archduke Albert, 14 Sept. 1588.

67. Quotations from Maura, 258–61, Medina Sidonia to Philip II, 21 and 24 June 1588; and Herrera Oria, 210–14, Philip to Medina Sidonia, 1 July 1588.

68. BL *Addl* 41,816/209v, d'Albeville to Middleton, The Hague, 1 Oct. 1688.

69. [J. Whittle], *An Exact Diary of the Late Expedition of His Illustrious Highness The Prince of Orange* (London, 1689), 11–12.

70. BL *Addl* 41,823/77v, Middleton to d'Albeville, London, 15 Oct. 1688.

71. Ibid., 41,816/231, d'Albeville to Middleton, The Hague, 10 Oct. 1688.

72. Ibid., fo. 247, d'Albeville to Middleton, The Hague, 19 Oct. 1688.

73. Ibid., 38,495/40v–1, Moreau to the king of Poland, The Hague, 26 Oct. 1688.

74. [Whittle], *An Exact Diary*, 13–14; according to Whittle 'the total number of the fleet, as they sailed from the Brill, was about four hundred and odd ships' not counting some small craft and boats.

75. BL *Addl* 41,823/76v, Middleton to d'Albeville, London, 8 Oct. 1688.

76. Ibid., fo. 78v, Middleton to d'Albeville, London, 26 Oct. 1688.

77. Ibid., 38,495/54v, Moreau to the king of Poland, The Hague, 9 Nov. 1688.

78. *Journaal van Constantijn Huygens, den zoon, van 21 Oktober 1688 tot 2 September 1696* (2 vols., Utrecht, 1876–7), I, 5–8; N. Japikse, *Prins Willem III, de Stadhouder-koning* (2 vols., Amsterdam, 1930–3), II, 256.

79. Quoted in Carswell, *Descent*, 178.

80. Alan Pearsall, 'The invasion voyage: some nautical thoughts', in C. Wilson and D. Proctor, eds., *1688. The Seaborne Alliance and Diplomatic Revolution* (Proceedings of the International Symposium held at the National Maritime Museum, Greenwich, 5–6 Oct. 1988), 170–1.

81. BL *Addl* 25,377/104, 100, Terriesi to Bassetti, London, 15 and 19 Nov. 1688; according to Terriesi there was a total of 637 vessels in the Dutch armada; see also the *Correspondence of Henry Hyde, Earl of Clarendon, and of His Brother Laurence Hyde, Earl of Rochester, with the Diary of Lord Clarendon from 1687 to 1690* (2 vols., London, 1828), II, 504.

82. A. Boyer, *The History of King William the Third* (3 vols., London, 1702),

I, 237; [Whittle], *An Exact Diary*, 30–1; *The Expedition of His Highness, the Prince of Orange for England*', in Lord Somers, ed., *A Fourth Collection of Scarce and Valuable Tracts* (4 vols., London, 1752), II, 437; G. G. A. Lamberti, *Mémoires de la dernière révolution d'Angleterre* (2 vols., The Hague, 1702), I, 561–3 and 565; F. A. Kazner, *Leben Friedrichs von Schomberg* (2 vols., Mannheim, 1789), I, 287, and II, 269.

83. '*The Expedition*', in Somers, *A Fourth Collection*, II, 258.

84. E. M. Thompson, ed., 'Correspondence of Admiral Herbert during the Revolution', *EHR*, I (1886), 526–7.

3. Treason and Plot in Elizabethan Diplomacy: The 'Fame of Sir Edward Stafford' Reconsidered

Sir Geoffrey Elton made the co-authors aware of their mutual interest in Sir Edward Stafford and encouraged them to collaborate in writing this article: they would like to dedicate it to his memory. They are also grateful to Robert Evans and A. D. Walker-Wraight for valuable suggestions.

1. C. Andrew, Introduction to K. Neilson and B. J. C. McKercher, eds., *Go Spy the Land: Military Intelligence in History* (Westport, 1992), 1 and 13. What the participants *really* wanted to hear in March 1990 was the identity of the 'Fifth Man' in the Kim Philby affair, but Professor Andrew (one of the few who already knew) refused to tell.

2. Published in Neilson and McKercher, *Go Spy the Land*, 49–72. Some of the material appeared in revised form, together with other data, in G. Parker, *The Grand Strategy of Philip II* (New Haven and London, 1998), chap. 7.

3. For full references, see n. 5 below. For the thesis, see R. J. McCue, 'The ambassadorial career of Sir Edward Stafford, Elizabethan ambassador to France, 1583–1590' (Brigham Young University Ph.D. thesis, 1970). I subsequently lectured at the University of Victoria, British Columbia, and found that Dr R. J. McCue had become a senior administrator there. I asked to meet him. 'Of course you won't have heard of me,' he began modestly: nothing prepared him for the grilling he received on Stafford.

4. See pages 86–7 above. Since publication of the article, only one scholar has challenged our verdict. In a review of Harry Kelsey, *Sir Francis Drake: The Queen's Pirate* (New Haven and London, 1998), Simon Adams asserted: 'One very valuable point Kelsey makes is that the attack on Cadiz in 1587 was not planned in advance; Drake took the decision to raid Cadiz *en route*. This is of importance, given the recent claim by Geoffrey Parker and Mitchell Leimon that the plan to attack Cadiz was betrayed to the Spaniards by Sir Edward Stafford. There was no plan to betray' (*Times Literary Supplement*, 23 Oct. 1998). A glance at the sources used by Kelsey (who did not in fact address

Stafford's role) reveals that he relied *inter alia* on the same précis in Hume's *Calendar* that misled Read and Neale (see page 317n. 67 below)! Our claim, based on the original letters in Simancas, still stands.

5. A. F. Pollard, *EHR*, XVI (1901), 572–7, reviewing *CSPS*, IV; C. Read, 'The fame of Sir Edward Stafford', *AHR*, XX (1915), 292–313, and XXXV (1930), 560–6; J. E. Neale, 'The fame of Sir Edward Stafford', *EHR*, XLIV (1929), 202–20 (reprinted in idem, *Essays in Elizabethan History* (London, 1959), 146–69); C. Read, *Mr Secretary Walsingham and the Policy of Queen Elizabeth* (3 vols., Oxford, 1925), III, chaps. 14 and 15; and idem, *Lord Burghley and Queen Elizabeth* (London, 1960), 386–90 and 576 n. 59.

6. One example, a description of Henry III's religious enthusiasm from December 1583, must suffice:

The King is in a mervelous humor of a new confreyrey of Jeronomites, . . . [and] will have his favorites to be of ytt with him; they be clad in a kind of smoaky graye . . . [The King] made in his owne cabinet mesure [to] be taken of every bodye by his own taylor . . . The Duke Espernon was fayne to go owte, not being able to keepe himself from laffinge, and laft at ytt a good while when he came to his chamber, wheratt, as I was informed, the King was extreeme angrie with him. Theire Order is to goe apparelled in the coulor as before, to go barefoote, stones in their hands to knock their breasts when theie be at theire prayers, and to lyve of almes . . . [Last Sunday the King] went thither and for three howers together wore the habit, and took such kowlde that when he came home he fell into [such] a fever and a flux, that men weere in dowbte he would have ended his lyfe with his new order.

W. Murdin, *Collection of State Papers Relating to Affairs in the Reign of Queen Elizabeth from the Year 1571 to 1596* (London, 1759), 383.

7. Details from R. J. McCue, 'The ambassadorial career of Sir Edward Stafford, Elizabethan ambassador to France, 1583–1590' (Brigham Young University Ph.D. thesis, 1970), chap. 1.

8. Guildford Muniments Room, Loseley *Mss*, VIII, fo. 63; IX, fo. 65.

9. PRO *SP* 12/162, no. 31; *SP* 12/152, no. 71; *SP* 46/33 fos. 22–5; *SP* 46/33 fos. 18, 20.

10. BL *Harl* 6993/44.

11. E. K. Chambers, *The Elizabethan Stage* (London, 1923), IV, 100. Stafford's factiousness had perhaps been presaged by a curious incident in Paris in 1580 when he railed against William Wade to his master, Henry Cobham, the English ambassador, as having been placed by 'someone' else: it is not clear by whom, since Wade was a more skilful courtier than Stafford and had retained good relations with both Walsingham and Burghley. But it was probably Walsingham whom Stafford aimed at; and he probably did damage Wade's standing with Cobham. *CSPF, 1579–80*, 428.

12. *CSPScot, 1574–1581,* 606; PRO, *SP* 63/84, no. 3.

13. Read, *Walsingham,* III, 246 n. 2; *CSPF, 1582,* 370.

14. G. D. Ramsay, *The City of London and International Politics at the Accession of Queen Elizabeth* (Manchester, 1975), chap. 3; idem, *The Queen's Merchants and the Revolt of the Netherlands* (London, 1986), 200–1. Ramsay argued that Cecil, as secretary of state, consistently mishandled the 1568–72 diplomatic crisis with the Spanish monarchy because, in the absence of any proper representative in Brussels, he allowed the assumption to pass unchallenged that the duke of Alba, governor-general of the Netherlands, slavishly followed the policies decreed by Philip II in Spain. In fact, the Netherlanders' economic anxiety exerted on Alba a pressure that made him considerably more inclined to peace than the diplomatic exchange with Spain led Cecil to believe.

15. Read, *Walsingham,* III, 243; BL *Sloane MS* 1523, fo. 41; W. Camden, *Annals* (1635 edn.), obituary *sub anno* 1590; C. Wilson, *Queen Elizabeth and the Revolt of the Netherlands* (London, 1970), 130–1.

16. Quoted in D. B. Quinn and N. M. Cheshire, *The New Found Land of Stephen Parmenius* (Toronto, 1972), 10 (translated from the Latin original by Cheshire).

17. See, for examples, *CSPF, 1581–2,* 508; *CSPF, 1583–4,* 242–5; and *CSPF, 1584–5,* 385. See also S. Skilliter, *William Harborne and the Trade with Turkey: A Documentary Study of the First Anglo-Ottoman Relations* (London, 1977); P. E. J. Hammer, 'An Elizabethan spy who came in from the cold: the return of Sir Anthony Standen to England in 1593', *Historical Research,* LXV (1992), 277–95; and G. Parker, 'The worst-kept secret in Europe? The European intelligence community and the Spanish Armada of 1588', in Neilson and McKercher, *Go Spy the Land* 49–72.

18. *CSPF, 1581–2,* 34–5; *CSPF, 1582,* 316; and *CSPF, 1586–8,* 15 and 108. See also L. Stone, *An Elizabethan: Sir Horatio Palavicino* (Oxford, 1956), 323–4.

19. Even Ambassador Cobham, a staunch ally of Leicester, had been irked at his own exclusion from some business and had on occasion treated Walsingham's men less than well: see *CSPF, 1579–80,* 316.

20. *CSPF, 1583–4,* 158 and 183–4.

21. Murdin, *Collection,* 380.

22. *CSPF, 1583–4,* 259 and 272. In the same month, Walsingham urged Stafford that 'hereafter, when you write of some secret matter, let it be in a by-paper and not in your general letter – which I must needs show to divers of the Lords and so either make them privy to the contents of the cipher or vex them if I send it undeciphered' (*CSPF, 1583–4,* 253).

23. *CSPF, 1583–4,* 435.

24. Ibid., 457 and 459.

25. Ibid., 476 and 612; *CSPF, 1584–5*, 11–12 and 120.

26. BL *Cott* Galba E. VI, fo. 171v. See also another 'code' proposed by Stafford in *CSPF, 1583–4*, 183–4. The use of special marks formed a regular part of early modern diplomatic correspondence: see V. Ilardi, 'Crosses and carets: Renaissance patronage and coded letters of recommendation', *AHR*, XCII (1987), 1127–49.

27. Murdin, *Collection*, 396.

28. *CSPF, 1583–4*, 175, 183–4 and 272; *CSPF, 1584–5*, 266.

29. *CSPF, 1583–4*, 474.

30. *CSPF, 1584–5*, 653–4; *CSPF, 1586–8*, 86 and 627.

31. *CSPF, 1585–6*, 221.

32. Murdin, *Collection*, 369. Arundel arrived in Paris just after Stafford, in November 1583; and had entered Spanish employ by February 1585 (if not earlier). He died in December 1587, possibly assassinated by an English exile: McCue, 'The ambassadorial career', 137–41.

33. Leo Hicks, 'The growth of a myth: Father Robert Parsons, SJ, and Leicester's commonwealth', *Studies*, XLVI (spring 1957); D. C. Peck, *Leicester's Commonwealth: The Copy of a Letter Written by a Master of Arts of Cambridge (1584) and Related Documents* (Athens, Ohio, 1985); F. Eguiluz, *Robert Persons, 'el architraidor': su vida y su obra (1546–1610)* (Madrid, 1990), 115–23; and S. Adams, 'Favourites and factions at the Elizabethan court', in R. G. Asch and A. M. Birke, eds., *Princes, Patronage and the Nobility. The Court at the Beginning of the Modern Age, c. 1450–1650* (Oxford, 1991), 265–88.

34. Mendoza mentioned the relationship between Arundel and Lady Stafford: *CSPSp*, IV, 189 and 218. It was doubtless significant that in 1579 Simier had effected Leicester's exile from court by revealing to the queen the secret, kept only from her, of her favourite's marriage to Lettice Knollys. Arundel was distantly related to Stafford's wife.

35. *CSPF, 1584–5*, 266–7 and 312; *CSPF, 1585–6*, 222 and 306–7. Walsingham's suspicion of Lilly proved well founded: he pocketed a pension from Mary. See McCue, 'The ambassadorial career', 62.

36. See the discussion of these fascinating documents in P. Collinson, *Elizabethan Essays* (London, 1994), 48–55, and idem, 'The Elizabethan exclusion crisis and the Elizabethan polity', *Proceedings of the British Academy*, LXXXIV (1993), 51–92.

37. Murdin, *Collection*, 569; W. Camden, *The History of the Most Renowned and Victorious Princess Elizabeth*, ed. W. T. MacCaffrey (Chicago, 1970), 182–3.

38. *HMC Salisbury*, III, 39; *CSPF, 1583–4*, 222 and 269; and Read, 'The fame', 298 (citing PRO *SP* Mary Stuart XV/1).

39. PRO *SP* 12/176, no. 19; *CSPF, 1583–4*, 158; *HMC Salisbury*, II, 67.

40. A. Labanoff, *Letters, instructions et mémoires de Marie Stuart*, VII (London, 1854), 176–91, the bishop of Glasgow to Mary, 21 Mar. 1586, deciphered by Thomas Phelippes; Murdin, *Collection*, 569. Walsingham appears to have regarded the death of Mary as far more important than embarrassing Burghley, and suppressed the information after a private conference with him, but probably did not forgo the advantage to be derived from a wider knowledge of Mary's regard for Stafford.

41. *CSPF, 1585–6*, 672. On the mysterious Delbene, see J. A. Bossy, *Giordano Bruno and the Embassy Affair* (New Haven, 1991), 63, 69–70 and 88–9. Interestingly, the letters of both Delbene and Buzenval had been intercepted by Stafford, who himself copied down extracts and sent them to Burghley: *CSPF, 1586–8*, 125–6.

42. Read, *Walsingham*, III, chap. 15 and p. 406 n. 3. The queen's gift to Croft of £100 per annum in land in September probably indicated royal approval of his conciliatory stance. Raleigh too may have defected to the peace camp by August, which would explain his untypically pro-Spanish activities reported in that month.

43. The secretary still had friends, however: Cobham remained a close associate, and Mildmay asked to share Walsingham's chamber at Fotheringhay: BL *Harl* 287, fo. 71.

44. See, for example, BL *Cott* Galba E. VI, fo. 229, Horatio Palavicino to Burghley, 9 June 1584 (in Italian), complaining that Stafford 'for the past two months is so much given to gambling that it passes all reason, in terms both of the large quantities of money he has ventured and lost, and of the type of people with whom he is mixing'. Palavicino's entire letter concerned Stafford's gambling, predicted the ambassador's 'shipwreck' unless he stopped, and urged Burghley to write an 'affectionate but most severe' letter of discouragement.

45. *CSPF, 1586–8*, 34–5. The Spanish ambassador in Paris, who maintained close contact with Guise, confirmed the first allegation: on 11 May 1586 he informed Philip II that Stafford, desperate for money, had sold secrets to the duke of Guise via Charles Arundel, receiving 3000 crowns in return: AGS *Estado* K 1564/54 (précis in *CSPSp*, III, 575).

46. Murdin, *Collection*, 569. At some point in the autumn of 1586 Burghley also confided to the ambassador that Henry of Navarre had sent a warning 'that the duke of Guise knew some things about the Queen's affairs that it was impossible to know unless her ambassador had revealed them, and complained that Leicester and Walsingham had told the Queen – in the hope of discrediting both Stafford and his patron'. See *BMO* II, 549–50.

47. *Dictionary of National Biography*, s.v. Sir Edward Stafford (written by A. F. Pollard); *CSPF, 1586–8*, 137 and 150–1.

48. *CSPF, 1586–8*, 128–9. In fact Stafford squandered not only his salary

but also a substantial sum sent to him by the queen for distribution to her French supporters: see *CSPSp*, IV, 310–11.

49. Two years previously Elizabeth had written to Marchaumont that she wished that the Dutch 'were no more poisoned with Spanish treasure than M. de Marchmont and Secretary Walsingham is'. (*CSPF, 1583–4, 346*.) Certainly Simier sought to retain her favour; in September 1586 Stafford wrote to Burghley that Simier wanted him to tell the queen, but not Walsingham, whose 'old grudge would make him careless to keep it [secret], that he is in love with the French ambassador's wife's sister's daughter and the ambassador's wife sendeth all her letters for Guise's mother to her sister to deliver, and Simier knoweth all of her daughter who is as far in love with Simier as he with her'. Simier could thus acquire information useful to Elizabeth's service (*CSPF, 1586–8, 86*).

50. *CSPF, 1586–8*, 150 and 267. For evidence that Stafford still believed Walsingham sought to undermine him as late as November 1586, see Bossy, *Giordano Bruno*, 246.

51. PRO *SP* 12/195, no. 54.

52. PRO *SP* 12/195, no. 64.

53. *CSPF, 1586–8*, 215, 266–7, 271 and 336–7.

54. Perhaps, however, Walsingham continued to keep Stafford under surveillance. McCue, 'The ambassadorial career', 67, suggests that Walsingham released both Lilly and Grimstone only against a promise that they would spy on Stafford. And then in December 1587 came the affair of Gilbert Gifford: page 91 above.

55. *CSPSp*, IV, 6–8. On Arundel's relationship to Lady Stafford, see page 314 n. 34 above; for evidence that Mendoza knew that Stafford had sold secrets to Guise, see page 315 n. 45 above. Mendoza's predecessor, Juan Bautista de Tassis, suggested that Stafford might serve as a spy as early as October 1584: *CSPSp*, III, 528.

56. *BMO* II, 618–19 (précis in *CSPSp*, IV, 25–6).

57. See the debate between Conyers Read and Sir John Neale in the articles cited on page 312 n. 5. above. Neither author, be it noted, examined the original correspondence of Mendoza, only the translated précis printed in *CSPSp*. One alternative candidate, Charles Arundel, can be ruled out because he died in December 1587, and yet 'Julio', 'the new friend' (and so on) continued to supply information for another year.

58. *BMO* III, 995.

59. *BMO* III, 1688–9 (précis in *CSPSp*, IV, 189–90 and 192, but missing the vital difference in nomenclature).

60. A glance at Mendoza's dispatches calendared in *CSPSp* indicates that almost all the information derived from 'Julio' and 'the new correspondent' was said to come from a specified minister at the Tudor court – see examples

on page 88 above – and on at least one occasion Mendoza reported that he had asked 'Julio' to send information back to the queen directly (*BMO* III, 388–9).

61. See *CSPSp*, IV, passim: e.g. 189, 198 and 213–14.

62. *BMO* III, 388–9 and 576–7. 'The new friend' asked Mendoza to ascertain which one of these offices he should accept. The king replied that he should stay where he was but, if he could not, to take his seat on the Council and only if that fell through to accept Ireland: *BMO* III, 670. The same letter noted the mistreatment of the 'new friend's' brother in England, which again points to Stafford, whose brother's imprisonment earlier in 1587 had been reported to the king. (See *CSPSp*, IV, 13, 14, 39, 82, and page 91 above.)

63. AGS, *Estado K* 1567/79. In June 1588 he repeated that 'Julio' was not getting his *gajes* (ibid., fo. 85). See also *BMO* III, 1160–1, reporting that, according to 'Julio', 'the ambassador has spent 12,000 crowns of the money sent him by the queen to be distributed to her Huguenot allies'.

64. AGS *Estado K* 1567/53, enclosing two lists (fos. 62a and b).

65. *BMO* II, 556–7.

66. *BMO* III, 150–1. Walsingham's letter (to William Wade, sent to explain the reasons for Mary Stuart's execution to her French relatives) was dated '3 March' (O.S.?).

67. *BMO* III, 201–2 (the king drew a long line in the margin to call attention to this paragraph: see AGS *Estado K* 1566/103). Even Mendoza's own spies in England, who were normally extremely well informed, only provided confirmation on 20 April (which did not arrive in Paris until mid-May – far too late to be of use): *BMO* III, 205–6. H. Kelsey, *Sir Francis Drake. The Queen's Pirate* (New Haven and London, 1998), 289, supported by Simon Adams (page 311 above), claimed that the decision to attack Cadiz was 'one of Drake's typical last-minute decisions' taken only three days beforehand, while his fleet regrouped off Lisbon. On p. 496, he cites three documents in support: (1) Mendoza's letter of 19 April; (2) a letter from Drake to Walsingham on 27 April O.S. (J. S. Corbett, *Papers relating to the Navy in the Spanish War 1585–1587* (London, 1898: Navy Records Society, XI), 107); (3) William Borough's later claim that while off Lisbon he had 'gathered advertisements and notes by a flyboat . . . which came from Cadiz' on 15 April. 'Those notes I delivered as soon as I might to mine Admiral [Drake]; whereupon he resolved, at the first sight of them, to go presently for that place' (Corbett, *Papers relating to the Navy*, 154). In fact, the first two documents do not support Kelsey's argument. Mendoza's letter, based on information sent to Stafford from London on 7 April, warned that Drake would attack Cadiz (a warning confirmed by Mendoza's own spies on 20 April: see above). Drake's own letter, written a week after his successful attack, provided so short an account of his voyage to Cadiz that it implied the

recipient already knew his destination. Borough's testimony, although more convincing, is compromised not only because it was recorded later (probably in August) but also because it was presented as evidence in Borough's trial for cowardice, desertion and fomenting mutiny (see Kelsey, *Sir Francis Drake*, 300–1). Probably, Borough's 'advertisements and notes' merely led Drake to inform his captains (or at least Borough), perhaps for the first time, of the fleet's destination.

68. Dates from Corbett, *Papers relating to the Navy*, 107; and *BMO*, III, 201–2, endorsed with the date of arrival (30 April).

69. AGS *Estado K* 1567/142. Interestingly enough, news of Drake's expedition arrived at Lisbon on 26 April aboard a ship from Emden that had left Bristol on the 12th, and was confirmed by three Norman ships arriving on the 28th. The authorities sent a letter of warning on the 29th – once again, just too late: Chaunu, III, 400 n.

70. *CSPF, 1586–8*, 278–9. Was it significant that Walsingham kept a corrected draft of this letter – one of his few dispatches to Stafford to survive? As soon as Stafford received this and other letters from London he once again hastened to communicate their contents to Mendoza who, on 20 May, was able to send full details to Madrid: *BMO* III, 388–9. According to Mendoza, Stafford claimed that his information derived from letters dated '29 April' (8 May N.S.) from Walsingham, Howard and the queen (the latter written in her own hand to Henry III and thus the one for which, according to Walsingham, the rest had been held up).

71. The 'double-cross' technique of deception is well described in Michael I. Handel, *Strategic and Operational Intelligence in the Second World War* (London, 1987), 23.

72. *BMO* III, 1721–3, 1810; KML, Instructions from Elizabeth to Howard, 20 Dec. 1587 (O.S.), original. For another 'leak' see AGS *Estado K* 1567/97, Mendoza to Philip II, 8 Aug. 1588, containing extremely accurate information from 'Julio' on the strategy devised by the English to combat the Armada, communicated to him by letters from London dated 29 July. The Armada did not encounter the English fleet until 1 Aug.

73. See, for example, the well-informed dispatches of the Florentine ambassadors in Paris for this period: G. Canestrini and A. Desjardins, *Négociations diplomatiques de la France avec la Toscane*, IV (Paris, 1872), 679–817. In July 1587 the king warned about reports circulating that 'the new friend' visited Mendoza's residence on many evenings: see *BMO* III, 670. The king's source was Longlée, the French resident in Madrid, another foreign diplomat who secretly favoured Philip: see Parke, *Grand Strategy*, 221, and n. 79 below.

74. This was precisely what Spain wanted: see AGS *Estado K* 1567/52, Mendoza to Philip II, 5 Apr. 1588: 'I informed Julio, as Your Majesty commanded me ... that he should dissuade his queen from alliance with the French.' See also McCue, 'The ambassadorial career', 55–6.

75. Corbett, *Papers relating to the Navy*, 101–2; K. R. Andrews, *Drake's Voyages. A Reassessment of Their Place in Elizabethan Maritime Expansion* (London, 1967), chap. 7. In fact Drake made such good speed that he never received the new orders.

76. *CSPF, 1586–8*, 181–2.

77. See the jubilation of the same Idiáquez in 1584 when news of Orange's assassination arrived: *CCG*, X, 58–9 and 70–1. In January 1587, the Spanish court noted that Dom Antonio might be assassinated 'without scruple since he is a rebel' condemned 'by virtue of a brief from the pope': *BMO* II, 558–9 (*CSPSp*, IV, 12–13). Elizabeth had been condemned by a papal brief in 1570.

78. Laughton, I, 46: Stafford's original letter has apparently not survived.

79. *CSPF, 1586–8*, 597, 641 and 652; *CSPF, 1588 June–Dec.*, 5. Stafford was not alone in these claims. In November 1587, in a letter filled with details about Parma's preparations, the earl of Leicester (governor-general of the Dutch Republic) still had no idea about their objective: H. Brugmans, ed., *Correspondentie van Robert Dudley, Graaf van Leycester* (3 vols., Utrecht, 1931), III, 284–6. And as the Armada prepared to weigh anchor, the French ambassador in Madrid claimed that it was bound for Zeeland: BNP, *Fonds français* 16, 110/257, M. de Longlée to Henry III, 6 May 1588. But Stafford surely knew better.

80. See, for example, the anonymous report dated 20 Oct. 1587 sent from Paris to Walsingham, printed in *HMC Salisbury*, III, 288–90, bulging with accurate news of Spanish preparations in Flanders, Burgundy and Lisbon.

81. BL *Harl* 6994/98.

82. See *CSPD, 1581–90*, 379–80; *CSPD (Addenda), 1580–1625*, 199–202; and *CSPSp*, IV, 13, 14 and 82. William Stafford still languished in the Tower in August 1588 (*CSPD, 1581–90*, 531).

83. *CSPD (Addenda), 1580–1625*, 223–30 (also printed in *CSPF, 1586–8*, 661–9). The letters, which do not all survive, almost certainly pre-date January 1587, and so did not necessarily invalidate Walsingham's assurances to Stafford (see page 84 above). See also *CSPF, 1588 July–Dec.*, 359.

84. *CSPF, 1586–8*, 548 and 568.

85. *CSPSp*, IV, 190, 196, 213 and 416 for payments; and 416, 430 and 468 for 'Julio's' taciturnity. Stafford even published a pamphlet ridiculing Mendoza's overoptimistic predictions concerning the Armada: see B. T. Whitehead, *Brags and Boasts. Propaganda in the Year of the Armada* (Stroud, 1994), 107–8.

86. *CSPSp*, IV, 470, 477, 501 and 528–9.

87. F. J. Weaver, 'Anglo-French diplomatic relations 1558–1603', *Bulletin of the Institute of Historical Research*, VII (1929), 13–15, gives Stafford's

movements; McCue, 'The ambassadorial career', 99 n. 74, suggests that the queen made Stafford solvent again in 1589.

88. *BMO* III, 216-17 and 388-9.

89. *BMO* III, 1504-5.

90. See the interesting discussion of M. J. Rodríguez-Salgado, 'The Anglo-Spanish War: the final episode in "The Wars of the Roses"?', in idem and S. Adams, *England, Spain and the Gran Armada, 1585-1604* (Edinburgh, 1991), 1-44.

91. P. Collinson, *The English Captivity of Mary Queen of Scots* (Sheffield, 1987), 20.

92. M. Philippson, *Ein Ministerium unter Philipp II: Kardinal Granvella am spanischen Hofe, 1579-1586* (Berlin, 1895), 56; *CSPSp*, IV, 233-4 and 307-8; and *CSPF, 1588 Jan.-June*, 305, 316-17, 350-1, 372-3 and 385.

93. AGS *Estado* 2512/16, 'Copia de la Memoria', and AGS CMC 29/42, unfol., *gastos secretos* of the count of Villamediana, who between 1604 and 1607 disbursed over 700,000 crowns in bribes to English courtiers. (Our thanks to Paul C. Allen for these details.)

94. See the figures in McCue, 'The ambassadorial career', 93-9, and notes.

95. *BMO* III, 1160-1.

96. Adams, 'Favourites and factions', 288.

4. Philip II, Maps and Power

I am indebted for invaluable references and orientation to several scholars in the field, particularly to Peter Barber, David Buisseret, Ulla Ehrenvärd, John Elliott, Richard Kagan and above all the late Richard Boulind. I am also obliged to the curators and staff of the Map Rooms at the National Library of Scotland in Edinburgh, the Kungliga Bibliotek in Stockholm, the Newberry Library in Chicago and the British Library in London for their assistance. Thanks, too, to José Visser and Santiago Martínez for research assistance. This chapter discusses only maps of Europe and America. Space precluded a consideration of the systematic charting of the seas and islands carried out by the pilots of the Casa de la Contratacción (House of Trade) in Seville.

1. AGI *Indiferente General* 738/82, royal apostil on a *consulta* of 5 July 1568. The unfortunate Legazpi had been dispatched from New Spain entirely without maps, being instructed to get hold of Portuguese charts whenever he could, 'even by buying them', in order to find out where he was going (see C. Quirino, *Philippine Cartography* (2nd edn., ed. R. A. Skelton, Amsterdam, 1964), x).

2. Details from C. Fernández Duro, 'Noticia breve de las cartas y planos existentes en la biblioteca particular de S. M. el Rey', *Boletín de la Sociedad*

geográfica de Madrid, XXVI (1889), 361–96, and XXVII (1889), 102–65 (reprinted in *Acta cartographica*, V (1969), 100–99); and F. J. Sánchez Cantón, *Inventarios reales: bienes muebles que pertenecieron a Felipe II* (2 vols., Madrid, 1956–9: Archivo Documental Español, X–XI), nos. 1356–8 (Ortelius) and 4137–50 (maps and globes). Some further details may be found in the originals: AGPM *Sección Administrativa* 235–7: Inventarios 1–3. However, officials compiled these inventories for the public auction of goods specified in Philip II's will: they would have omitted 'classified' items like manuscript maps. Curiously, the final inventory of Charles V's goods listed far more maps – but then he died, officially at least, a private person. See the emperor's maps, charts and globes noted in F. Checa, *Felipe II. Mecenas de las Artes* (2nd edn., Madrid, 1993), 22, 25 and 469.

3. Le Glay and Finot, V, 254. On the general point see J. B. Harley, 'Silences and secrecy: the hidden agenda of cartography in early modern Europe', *Imago Mundi*, XL (1988), 57–76.

4. Geminus may have used the detailed (but now lost) map made a few years before by the royal cosmographer, Alonso de Santa Cruz. According to a letter written by Santa Cruz to Charles V in 1551: 'I have completed a [map of] Spain, of more or less the size of a large tablecloth [*repostero*], showing all the cities, towns and villages, the rivers and the mountains, together with the frontiers of the kingdoms and many other details.' Santa Cruz apparently still possessed the map – four parchment 'skins' wide – when he died in 1572, because the inventory of his maps included 'Una descripción grande de toda España, de punto grande, en un pergamino de cuatro pieles de ancho, arrollada sobre una vara larga'. See 'Minuta del inventario de los papeles que quedaron por muerte de Alonso de Santa Cruz', in M. Jiménez de la Espada, *Relaciones geográficas de Indias: Perú* (Madrid, 1965), I, 289. That appears to be the last mention: see F. Picatoste y Rodríguez, *Apuntes para una biblioteca científica española* (Madrid, 1891), 291.

5. J. H. Hessels, ed., *Ecclesiae Londino-Batavae Archivum*, I (Cambridge, 1887), 81–2, Jerónimo de Roda to Ortelius, Brussels, 30 Sept. 1571, communicating Espinosa's command. See the illustration of 'Martimuñoz' in D. Buisseret, *Monarchs, Ministers and Maps. The Emergence of Cartography as a Tool of Government in Early Modern Europe* (Chicago, 1992), 127.

6. See full details in J. Keuning, 'The history of an atlas: Mercator-Hondius', *Imago Mundi*, IV (1947), 37–62. In 1600 Don Balthasar de Zúñiga, Spanish ambassador in Brussels, reacted with excitement to reports that some maps of his native land had been included in Mercator's *Atlas* and made a special trip to Antwerp to buy a copy. He was disappointed: although 'better than Ortelius', he found that it again contained nothing on Spain (IVdeDJ 82/385, Zúñiga to duke of Sessa, 30 Mar. 1600: my thanks to Paul Allen for drawing this reference to my attention).

7. J. M. Sanz Hermida, 'Las representaciones geográficas y corográficas como elementos de prestigio y representación de la Monarquía: el mapa de España y las descripciones de ciudades de Enrique Cock', in E. Martínez Ruiz, ed., *Madrid, Felipe II y las ciudades de la Monarquía*. II. *Las ciudades: capitalidad y economía* (Madrid, 2000), 289–305. Only two copies of Cock's map survive: Sanz Hermida reproduced one recently acquired by the Biblioteca Nacional in Madrid (p. 290). On the evolution of the 'map of Spain', see A. Hernando, *El mapa de España, siglos XV–XVIII* (Madrid, 1995).

8. See the penetrating remarks on cartographic methods at this time by M. A. de Lavis-Trafford, *L'évolution de la cartographie de la région du Mont-Cenis et de ses abords aux 15e et 16e siècles* (Chambéry, 1949), 121–5.

9. P. de Medina, *Primera y segunda parte de las grandezas y cosas notables de España* (Alcalá de Henares, 1548; 2nd edn., ed. Diego Pérez de Mesa, Alcalá, 1595). On the Ptolomaic maps, see R. Almagià, 'The first "modern" map of Spain', *Imago Mundi*, V (1948), 27–31; and Hernando, *El mapa*, 91–115. It is possible that the handful of more accurate cityscapes in the second edition of Medina derived from the views made of all major Spanish cities by the Dutch artist, Anton van den Wyngaerde, who travelled around Spain in the 1560s at Philip II's express 'command and instruction to paint the pictures of several of my principal cities': see page 102 above.

10. Royal order printed by B. van 't Hoff, *Jacob van Deventer: Keizerlijk-koninklijk geograaf* (The Hague, 1953), 36. This amplified an earlier command issued in April 1558. For van Deventer's earlier cartographic series, see C. Koeman, *Gewestkaarten van de Nederlanden door Jacob van Deventer, 1536–1545* (Alphen-aan-den-Rijn, 1994), with facsimiles and an introduction.

11. A magnificent facsimile edition of this project for the North Netherlands exists: C. Koeman, J. Visser and P. C. J. van der Krogt, *De stadsplattegronden van Jacob van Deventer* (8 vols., Alphen-aan-den-Rijn, 1992–8). For the southern provinces see the less accurate facsimiles in C. Ruelens, *Atlas des villes de Belgique au XVIe siècle* (Brussels, 1884). Of the originals, BNM *Ms Res.* 200 contains 105 finished plans from the provinces of Holland, Zeeland and Gelderland; and *Ms Res.* 207 contains 74 plans from Hainaut, Cambrai, Artois and Flanders. The third volume (no doubt containing town plans from the remaining provinces) has been lost. A collection of 152 draft copies, which resurfaced at an auction in 1859, are now distributed between various regional archives in the kingdom of the Netherlands and the Royal Library, Brussels.

12. On Wyngaerde's surviving corpus, see the definitive edition of R. L. Kagan, ed., *Spanish Cities of the Golden Age: The Views of Anton van den Wyngaerde* (Berkeley, 1989); on Cock's later attempt, see the brilliant reconstruction of Sanz Hermida, 'Las representaciones geográficas', 296–305. The decision not to print Wyngaerde's views in 1572 may also reflect

the publication of a rival (but inferior) series of 'views' done of Spanish cities by Joris Hoefnagel in G. Braun and F. Hogenburg, *Civitates orbis terrarum* (Cologne, 1572).

13. P. Miquelez, *Catálogo de los códices españoles de la Biblioteca del Escorial*. I. *Relaciones históricas* (Madrid, 1917), 252-4, printed Páez's *Interrogatorio*; N. Salomon, *La Campagne de la Nouvelle Castille à la fin du 16e siècle d'après les* Relaciones Topográficas (Paris, 1964), offered a full account of the surveys. BNM *Ms* 5589/64, 'Ynterrogatorio', mentions '13 or 14 volumes' of 'relaciones'; AGS *Estado* 157/102-5 contains the orders sent to magistrates in October 1575 commanding their cooperation in making the surveys, and a copy of the printed questionnaire.

14. F. J. Bouza Álvarez, 'Monarchie en lettres d'imprimerie. Typographie et propagande au temps de Philippe II', *Revue d'histoire moderne et contemporaine*, XLI (1994), 206-20, at p. 213. However, the second edition of Pedro de Medina's *Grandezas de España* (1595) certainly did make use of them: see the evidence in Miquelez, *Catálogo*, 257.

15. A. de Morales, *Las antigüedades de las ciudades de España* (Alcalá de Henares, 1575), fos. 4v-5; F. de Guevara, *Comentarios de la pintura* (c. 1564; Madrid, 1788), 219-21. See also Kagan, *Spanish Cities*, 44-5. Picatoste y Rodríguez, *Apuntes*, 86-89, provides a useful biography of Esquivel, mostly drawn from Guevara and Morales. See also the interesting remarks on Esquivel and his methods in F. Vázquez Maure, 'Cartografía de la peninsula: siglos 16 a 18', in *Historia de la cartografía española* (Madrid, 1982), 61; and in M. I. Vicente Moroto and M. Esteban Piñero, *Aspectos de la ciencia aplicada en España del Siglo de Oro* (Valladolid, 1991), 473-82.

16. Quotation in Picatoste y Rodríguez, *Apuntes*, 88; 'Atlas' in BSLE *Ms* K.I.1. Each map measures approximately 12 by 18 inches (30 by 43cm). The relationship between Esquivel's survey and the Escorial Atlas is inferred from four circumstances. (1) The calligraphy and cartography of the Escorial Atlas clearly date from the reign of Philip II. (2) The detailed maps of Spain in the Atlas appear to have no precursors and must therefore be the result of some special ground survey carried out by triangulation. (3) Such a survey would have taken several years and could only have been undertaken with a licence from the Crown. (4) Only Esquivel is known to have undertaken such a survey during the reign of Philip II.

17. See three important articles of G. de Reparaz-Ruiz, 'La cartographie terrestre dans la péninsule ibérique aux 16e et 17e siècles, et l'œuvre des cartographes portugais en Espagne', *Revue géographique des Pyrénées et du Sud-Ouest*, IX (1940), 167-202; 'Le plus ancien levé d'une nation européenne. Une carte topographique du Portugal au 16e siècle', in L. de Matos and R. Ricard, eds., *Mélanges d'études portugaises offerts à M. Georges le Gentil* (Lisbon, 1949), 271-313; and 'The topographical maps of Portugal and Spain

in the sixteenth century', *Imago Mundi*, VII (1950), 75–82. The calculation of 1:430,000 comes from Vázquez Maure, 'Cartografía', 62.

18. Kungliga Bibliothek, Stockholm, *Ms* M.163 (formerly *Ms Sparwenfeldt* 17). According to the entry on its flyleaf, the volume was acquired in Madrid in the 1690s by Johan Gabriel Sparwenfeldt, along with 24 maps by Lavanha. No trace of these maps has been found, so conceivably they formed another (perhaps finished?) copy of the 21 maps now in the Escorial, plus 3 more now lost. Certainly the Stockholm codex, which has apparently never been studied in detail, is connected with the Escorial maps because (1) much of the writing in both manuscripts is the same; (2) both deal with the same places; and (3) some such set of coordinates would have been essential for the compilation of the Escorial Atlas. It is worth noting that Lavanha kept very similar records for his survey of Aragon in 1610–11: *PMC*, III, 51. On Sparwenfeldt's purchases in Spain, see C. U. F. Jacobowsky, *J. G. Sparwenfeldt. Bidrag till en biografi* (Stockholm, 1932), 123–52

19. It seems probable that the Escorial cartographers, like Seco, had access to the official map which was compiled from these data because the similarities between their map and Seco's are overwhelming (even the errors – mistaken configuration of rivers and so on – are the same). But they are not identical. The Escorial maps of Portugal contain several details that Seco's lacks, so the prototype must have been on a larger scale than Seco's, and it must have been completed before he began: certainly before 1560, when the pirate edition was made, and probably before 1550. If so, the Portuguese were the first to produce a national map based on modern surveying techniques. Unfortunately, this presumed official map has not survived, but the observations on which it was based, probably dating from the 1530s, are to be found in a codex (now preserved in Hamburg) which lists the geographical coordinates of about 1000 places in Portugal (the Seco map has 1154): see A. Ferreira, C. de Morais, J. da Silveira and A. Girão, 'O mais antiga mapa de Portugal (1561)', *Boletim do centro de estudos geograficos*, II, nos. 12–13 (Coimbra, 1956) and 14–15 (Coimbra, 1957). See also the cautionary comments in *PMC*, II, 79–86. Reparaz-Ruiz, 'Une carte topographique', 309–14, suggested that the Portuguese map was compiled principally by Pedro Nunes, an accomplished cartographer, assisted by Seco and others, and noted the parallels between the Seco map and the Escorial 'Portugal' maps.

20. AGPM *Cédulas reales* 6/210–12, warrants in favour of Lavanha (400 crowns a year), Georgio (250) and Onderiz (200), all 25 Dec. 1582. The king also named the first two professors at his new Academy of Mathematics in Madrid: see Vicente Moroto and Esteban Piñero, *Aspectos*, 81.

21. It is of course possible that the Escorial Atlas was only a rough working copy of which the finished version (now lost) was purchased by Sparwenfeldt in the 1690s and never seen again: see n. 18 above.

22. BCR *Ms* 2174/43 and 132–3, Philip II to the viceroy of Naples, 1 Feb. 1566 and 11 Mar. 1575, register copies. On the spate of government-sponsored maps of Italy from the later sixteenth century, see J. Marino, 'Administrative mapping in the Italian states', in Buisseret, *Monarchs, Ministers and Maps*, 5–25. Spanocchi's 'Descripción de las marinas de todo el reino de Sicilia' (c. 1578) remains in manuscript: BNM Ms 788; Turriano's work may be admired in F. G. Martin Rodríguez, *La primera imagen de Canarias. Los dibujos de Leonardo Torriani* (sic) (Santa Cruz de Tenerife, 1986).

23. See G. Parker, *The Grand Strategy of Philip II* (New Haven and London, 1998), 62–5, for details and reproductions. On Velasco, see Vicente Moroto and Esteban Piñero, *Aspectos*, 399–406.

24. See C. Fernández Duro, *Disquisiciones naúticas. IV: los ojos en el cielo* (Madrid, 1879), 309–10, G. B. Gesio to Philip II, 18 Jan. 1579, on the attempt to establish the longitude of Mexico during the lunar eclipse of 1577.

25. See the documents on Jaume Juan's mission printed by Vicente Moroto and Esteban Piñero, *Aspectos*, 437–43, and in M. L. Rodríguez Sala, ed., *El eclipse de luna. Misión científica de Felipe II en Nueva España* (Huelva, 1998). See also U. Lamb, 'The Spanish cosmographic juntas of the sixteenth century', *Terrae incognitae*, VI (1974), 51–62 (although she dates the eclipse 'October 1584'). D. Goodman, *Power and Penury. Government, Technology and Science in Philip II's Spain* (Cambridge, 1988), 67, records that observations were also coordinated with colleagues in China. By an uncanny coincidence, an English expedition to North America tried to 'time' the eclipse of the sun predicted for June 1582 in order to calculate longitude: see D. B. Quinn, *English Plans for North America* (New York, 1979: *New American World. A Documentary History of North America to 1612*, III), 242, Sir Humphrey Gilbert's Instructions.

26. See AGNM *CRD* II/27, *expediente* 62, Philip II to the viceroy of New Spain, 12 Mar. 1583 (asking about Domínguez's maps); and Goodman, *Power and Penury*, 82 n. 12. The 1584 eclipse ended at 7.31 p.m. according to Jaime Juan's 'clock with wheels', but at 7.22 according to the observed position of a fixed star, and at 7.20 according to the observed elevation of the moon – significant differences when trying to establish the exact longitude of a place! For the difficulties in interpreting the indigenous maps, see B. E. Mundy, *The Mapping of New Spain. Indigenous Cartography and the Maps of the Relaciones Geográficas* (Chicago, 1996), and D. Sacchi, *Mappe dal nuovo mondo: cartografie locali e definizione della Nuova Spagna (secoli XVI–XVII)* (Turin, 1997). See also the efforts to produce cityscapes of Spanish American towns recorded by R. L. Kagan with F. Marías, *Urban Images of the Hispanic World, 1493–1793* (New Haven and London, 2000).

27. For examples of the king's routine acquisition of maps (both 'printed and painted on canvas') from the Netherlands in the 1560, see Kagan, *Spanish*

Cities of the Golden Age, 48–9; and L. Voet, 'Les relations commerciales entre Gérard Mercator et la maison Plantinienne à Anvers', *Duisburger Forschungen*, VI (1962), 169–229. For espionage, see G. de Andrés, 'Juan Bautista Gesio, cosmógrafo de Felipe II y portador de documentos geográficos desde Lisboa para la Biblioteca de El Escorial en 1573', *Bolétin de la real sociedad geográfica*, CIII (1967), 365–74; and W. A. R. Richardson, 'An Elizabethan pilot's charts (1594): Spanish intelligence regarding the coasts of England and Wales at the end of the 16th century', *Journal of Navigation*, LIII (2000), 313–27.

28. The Galician map of areas affected by plague in April 1598 may be found in AGS *MPyD* LI–11.

29. For the Mercator purchases (made from Plantin) see Voet, 'Les relations commerciales', 204–5. The Latin edition of Saxton in Philip II's library (see Fernández Duro, 'Noticia breve', 164) may have been purchased in 1585 because in that year the English ambassador in Paris complained of efforts made by Catholic exiles in Spanish pay to get hold of copies of the work: see BL *Harl* 288/163–4v 'Secret advertisement', 1 Dec. 1585. For the 1574 incident, see IVdeDJ 88/378, *Presupuestos* of the count of Olivares; for details on the invasion plans of the 1570s, see Parker, *Grand Strategy*, chap. 5.

30. *BMO*, I, 420–1, and III, 1113–16, Parma to Philip II, 30 Nov. 1583 and [25 Sept.] 1587. For its author, see ibid., III, 1461 and 1463, Heighington and Mendoza to Philip II, 27–28 Nov. 1587. J. P. R. Lyell, 'A commentary on certain aspects of the Spanish Armada drawn from contemporary sources' (Oxford University B. Litt. thesis, 1932; and Houghton Library, Harvard University, *fMs* Eng 714), 14–25, described three more surveys of the English coast, formerly in the Cabra archive, and dated them to 1586–7; but this cannot be correct because they speak of William of Orange (d. July 1584) as still alive. Perhaps they too date from 1583 and were sent to Lisbon four years later?

31. BNM *Ms Res.* 237, 'Recueil et pourtraicte d'aulcunes villes maritimes et ... portz et leurs advenues', 1586; M. L. Martín-Meras, *Atlas de Oliva* (Madrid, 1987), reproducing BPM *Ms* II/1271, an atlas of Europe's coasts done between 1580 and 1588 (see chart VI for Ireland, England and Scotland – shown as separated by sea!); and BNM *Ms* 5785/168, Escalante's map.

32. Only one printed copy of the *Derrotero* (the one Medina Sidonia sent to the king on 2 April 1588) has survived: AGS *Estado* 431/17, reproduced in Herrera Oria, 156–80. A manuscript copy of this printed version exists in BL *Addl* 17,638/1–19. The *Derrotero* seems to have been the duke's own idea. See KML *MSP: CR* 5/129–30, Don Juan de Idiáquez to Medina Sidonia, 28 Mar. 1588: 'Lo de la carta y derrotero que Vuestra Señoría ha mandado hazer para su viaje, se ha tenido por cosa acertadíssima'.

33. Herrera Oria, 180 and 155, undated notes exchanged between Philip II and Don Juan de Idiáquez.

34. Quotations from the *Derrotero* in ibid., 168–9. See the perceptive remarks of M. J. Rodríguez-Salgado, 'Pilots, navigation and strategy in the *Gran Armada*', idem and S. Adams, eds., *England, Spain and the Gran Armada, 1585–1604* (Edinburgh, 1991), 134–72, at pp. 148–9 and the map at p. 150; and Richardson, 'An Elizabethan pilot's charts', 314–16.

35. Duro, I, 499, Medina Sidonia to Philip II, 2 Apr. 1588; AGS *Contaduría del Sueldo* 2nd series, 283, unfol., 'Asiento con Ceprián Sánchez maestre de hazer cartas de marear'. Sánchez was paid 40 escudos on 4 April 'por 80 quarterones de cartas de marear con sus braxeajes de las costas de España, Ynglatierra y Flandes, que por horden del duque de Medina Sidonia estava aziendo para repartir en los navios de la dicha armada'. In the event 85 charts were delivered on 12 May, and Sánchez was paid a further 297 escudos. The document does not indicate whether the charts were all the same. The Armada included 130 ships.

36. The maps are discussed in *PMC*, III, 81, where it is noted that 'both are folded down the middle, which suggests that they belonged to an atlas'; however, it seems more likely that the centrefold indicates that they were mounted on a hinged board (*cuarterón*) for use on ships, as Medina Sidonia had intended. On stylistic grounds, *PMC* attributes the unsigned charts to Luis Teixeira rather than to Ciprián Sánchez. The link between the Spanish Armada and the two charts (both of them sold at an auction in London in 1937) may be inferred from the following: (1) given the offices they held (both Sánchez and Teixeira were 'royal cosmographers'), these manuscript charts were likely to have been official, not private, commissions; (2) these are the only known Portuguese charts of the period that include 'soundings' – something specified in Medina Sidonia's contract with Sánchez; (3) the only occasion on which the king's fleet sailed up the Channel, and would therefore have needed such special charts, was in 1588. It is possible that both items came from the Andalusian flagship *Nuestra Señora del Rosario*, which Sir Francis Drake captured intact in August 1588. M. J. Rodríguez-Salgado, ed., *Armada 1588–1988* (London, 1988), 217, reproduces one of them.

37. Don Fernando de Lannoy's map – reproduced in Buisseret, *Monarchs, Ministers and Maps*, 139 – is discussed in L. Febvre, *Philippe II et Franche Comté* (Paris, 1911), 114 n. 1; and G. Parker, *The Army of Flanders and the Spanish Road 1567–1659. The Logistics of Spanish Victory and Defeat in the Low Countries' Wars* (2nd edn., Cambridge, 1990), 83. It is clear that Lannoy had completed the map *before* he knew the Spaniards were coming. On the 'Spanish Road', see chapter 5 above.

38. Both maps are also discussed and reproduced in Parker, *Army of Flanders*, 102–5. The originals are in AD Doubs *États* C264, unfol., endorsed: 'Pour le passage de la gendarmerie et pour les estappes'.

39. ASP *CF* 109 (*Paesi Bassi* 4), unfol., Don Sancho de Londoño to the duke

of Parma, 21 Nov. 1568; AA 166/2, unfol., 'Relación de Juan Despuche y Don Alonso de Vargas sobre el país y río' (the title was written in Alba's own hand). The duke purchased other maps locally during his Maas campaign: see Le Glay and Finot, V, 235-6.

40. Details from S. Groenveld and J. Vermaere, 'Zeeland en Holland in 1569. Een rapport voor de hertog van Alva', *Nederlandse Historische Bronnen*, II (1980), 103-74 (including the text of the report by Gabriel Serbelloni, Chiappino Vitelli and Bartolomeo Campi); and A. de Smet, 'A note on the cartographic work of Pierre Pourbus, painter of Bruges', *Imago Mundi*, IV (1947), 33-6.

41. 'Sgrooten's maps, presently in BRB *Ms* 21,596, are described by L. Bagrow, *A. Ortelii catalogus cartographorum* (Gotha, 1928: Petermann's Mitteilungen, Erganzungsheft CXCIX), I, 58-69; and A. Bayot, 'Les deux atlas manuscrits de Chrétien Sgrooten', *Revue des bibliothèques et archives de Belgique*, V (1907), 183-304. AA 70/12 contains 51 manuscript military maps and plans commissioned by the duke for his campaigns in Italy, Portugal, and, above all, the Netherlands. L. J. Spaenjaerdt Speckman, *Francesco de Marchi (1504-77). Italiaans vestingbouwkundige in Spaanse dienst en de Nederlandse vestingen* (Leiden, 1972), described and reproduced maps from Florentine archives that, he claimed, were commissioned by the duke of Alba from Francesco de Marchi; but M. Schroor and C. van den Heuvel, *De Robles atlassen. Vestingbouwkundige plattegronden uit de Nederlanden en een verslag van een veldtocht in Friesland in 1572* (Leeuwaarden, 1998), 29, prove that the collection dates from the early seventeenth century. It has nothing to do with the duke of Alba. Marchi *did* work for Margaret of Parma in the 1560s, however, and prepared - and almost printed - a detailed treatise on fortifications graced by 170 beautifully engraved plates. See the fascinating history of his work by B. de Groof and G. Bertini, 'Francesco de Marchi y la Monarquía Española', in C. J. Hernando Sánchez, ed., *Las fortificaciones de Carlos V* (Madrid, 2001), 389-411.

42. Schroor and van den Heuvel, *De Robles atlassen*, describe the 63 maps, currently held in repositories in Austin, Texas, and Dresden, Germany, and the Rijksarchief in Friesland in 1998 published a facsimile edition.

43. For details of these last two collections see C. van den Heuvel, 'Een atlas voor Gilles de Berlaymont, baron van Hierges', *Caert-Thresoor*, XV (1996), 57-69; and E. H. Waterbolk, 'Viglius of Aytta: sixteenth-century map collector', *Imago Mundi*, XXIX (1977), 45-8. On the campaigns, see G. Parker, *The Dutch Revolt* (revised edn., Harmondsworth, 1985), 140-2 and 156-68.

44. Details from A. Paz y Melía, *Séries de los mas importantes documentos del archivo y biblioteca del Exmo. Señor Duque de Medina Celi* (Madrid, 1915), 162-5 ('Inventario de los bienes que quedaron por muerte del duque

Don Juan de la Cerda', 1575); and J. M. March, *Don Luis de Requesens en el gobierno de Milán 1571–3* (2nd edn., Madrid, 1946), 27–8: inventory at Requesens's death in 1576.

45. For some perceptive remarks see Schroor and van den Heuvel, *De Robles atlassen*, 31 (and accompanying notes). For specific items, see Le Glay and Finot, V, 349–50 and 381; 'Sgrooten's 2-volume *Orbis terrestris descriptio* of 1588–92 (BNM *Ms Res.* 266); and two volumes prepared later by Pierre le Poivre from earlier originals (BRB *Ms* 19,611 and BPM *Ms* II/523). All these items deserve publication and detailed study.

46. M. Gracia Rivas, *La 'invasión' de Aragón en 1591. Una solución militar a las alteraciones del reino* (Zaragoza, 1992), 191–212, reproduced Spanocchi's splendid maps. On Lavanha's survey and map, see *PMC*, IV, 69–70 and pl. 423.

47. BPM *Ms* II/2459, 'Poesías varias', fo. 118, advertisement (undated but probably 1598). The disappearance of the map collection of the count-duke of Olivares, chief minister of Philip IV, may give a false impression of seventeenth-century Spanish cartography. Clearly, Olivares commanded extensive and impressive cartographic resources: to give a single example, in 1627, when Spain again planned the invasion of England and Ireland, Olivares explained his Grand Strategy to the Genoese ambassador in Madrid with the aid of 'six very clear and distinct maps' of the proposed invasion area (J. H. Elliott, *The Count-Duke of Olivares. The Statesman in an Age of Decline* (New Haven, 1986), 282). It would be interesting to know the provenance of these maps. Elliott, *Richelieu and Olivares* (Cambridge, 1984), 28, offers another example of the riches of Olivares's map-room, this time concerning the Netherlands.

48. R. L. Kagan, '*Arcana Imperii*–: Maps, knowledge and power at the court of Philip IV' (to appear in the facsimile edition of a rediscovered atlas completed for Philip IV in the 1620s by Pedro Teixeira Albernaz). I am very grateful to Professor Kagan for sharing with me his important paper in advance of publication. Della Faille quoted in O. van der Vijver, 'Lettres de Charles della Faille, SJ, cosmographe du roi à M. F. van Langren, cosmographe du roi à Bruxelles, 1643–5', *Archivum historicum societatis Iesu*, XLVI (1977), 73–183, at p. 172. Interestingly, della Faille seemed not to know of Pedro Teixeira's map of Portugal, included in the atlas he presented to the king in 1630. Philip IV's filing system was no better than that of his grandfather.

49. AGRB *CPE* 1573/164–6, 'Aviso de Miguel Florencio van Langren'. The Habsburgs took a long time to recover cartographical competence. In 1764, the Imperial Council of War in Vienna ascribed Austria's defeat in the Seven Years' War in part to the lack of maps: see R. J. W. Evnas, 'Essay and reflection: frontiers and national identities in Central Europe', *International History Review*, XIV (1992), 480–502, at pp. 489–90.

PART II: THE CENTURY OF THE SOLDIER

1. M. L. Doglio, ed., *Lettere di Fulvio Testi*, III (Bari, 1967), 204, Testi to Francesco Montecuccoli, Jan. 1641; T. Hobbes, *On the Citizen (De cive*, 1641; English edn. by R. Tuck and M. Silverthorne, Cambridge, 1998), 29; J. S. Levy, *War in the Modern Great Power System, 1495–1975* (Lexington, 1983), 139–4.

5. The Treaty of Lyon (1601) and the Spanish Road

1. V. Saletta, 'Il viaggio di Carlo V in Italia', *Studi Meridionali*, IX (1976), 322–3 (my thanks to Bonner Mitchell for this reference).
2. CCG, I, 284–7, Granvelle to Philip II, 30 May 1566. The cardinal had already suggested this itinerary to the king three years before, but Philip found the letter too long and seems to have looked only at a summary that missed out this part! (See AGS *Estado* 524/4 and 8, same to same, 10 Mar. 1563, with Philip's note asking his secretary to *sacar puntos* (make a précis).) Interestingly, almost 70 years later a councillor of state in Madrid, anxious to find the safest route from Lombardy to the Low Countries, reviewed exactly the same five itineraries, demonstrating the comprehensive nature of Granvelle's grasp: AGS *Estado* 3338/31, marquis of Los Balbases to the count-duke of Olivares, 26 Jan. 1633.
3. CCG, I, 469–74, Granvelle to Philip II, 15 Sept. 1566. The Genoese ambassador in Madrid also saw the advantages to Philip II of a route between Lombardy and Luxembourg that ran 'quasi sempre su'l suo [almost always on his own territory]', and described what would become the Spanish Road accurately: ASG *AS* 2412a (*Spagna* 3a), Tommaso Sauli to the Doge and council of Genoa, 6 Nov. 1565.
4. See AGS *Estado* 1219/18 and 192, itineraries prepared in 1566; fo. 177, duke of Savoy to Philip II, undated but late 1566, announcing that he was sending a messenger who would report with pictures as well as in writing' on the routes to the Netherlands; and fo. 261, Philip II to the governor of Lombardy, 30 Oct. 1566, instructing the dispatch of a 'man who can make a good painting to show the nature of the area through which the troops will pass'. For eyewitness accounts of this journey, see AA 165/23, 'Relación del viaje que su excelencia hizo de Italia a Bruselas, 1567', probably written by Francisco de Ibarra; and BPM *Ms* II/1791, 'Jornada del ejército español en Flandes, año 1567', by Camillo Gravarona, in Italian. For a brief modern account, see G. Parker, *The Dutch Revolt* (2nd edn., Harmondsworth, 1985), 102–3.

5. AGS *Estado* 609/88, Instruction of Archduke Ernest of Austria to Don Diego Pimentel, his envoy to Philip II, 30 Jan. 1595; BRB *Ms* 16,149/41v–45, marquis of Aytona to Philip IV, 19 Dec. 1631, copy.

6. *Epistolario*, I, 647–9 and 654, Alba to Margaret of Parma, 16 June and 10 July 1567, for the 'Spanish Road' courier chain; and III, 121–3, Alba to Philip II, 24 May 1572, for the decision to send duplicates.

7. Le Glay and Finot, V, 332, payment of 7543 livres (£75) to cover expenditure by the postmaster in 1588–90, including arranging postal stations through Lorraine and Burgundy to Savoy; *BMO*, II, 108–11, Parma to Philip II, 20 Apr. 1586, and II, 195–6, 'Lo que dixo Juan Bautista Piata'; see also pages 51–2 above. On 'average' journey times for couriers, see G. Parker, *The Grand Strategy of Philip II* (2nd edn., New Haven and London, 2000), 52–4.

8. For some idea of the scale, see J. Gentil da Silva, *Banque et crédit en Italie au XVIIe siècle* (2 vols., Paris, 1969), and C. M. Cipolla, *The Fontana Economic History of Europe*, II (London, 1974), chap. 2. For a particular example see AGS *CMC* 2a/23, unfol., *Cuenta* of Gabriel de Alegría 1587–90, who paid 1.5 million crowns (£334,000) in cash to the leaders of the French Catholic League, much of it received from money convoys travelling up the Spanish Road.

9. S. Goulart, *Mémoires de la Ligue*, I (3rd edn., Amsterdam, 1758), 600: Philippe Duplessis-Mornay's 'Discourse to King Henry III on ways of reducing Spanish power'. The same month, news reached Italy that 'The French intend to prohibit the passage of the Spanish infantry at a certain bridge in Lorraine': AGS *Estado* 1259/235, Baron Sfondrato to Philip II, Turin, 21 Apr. 1584.

10. AGRB *Manuscrits Divers* 5459/374–5v, Granvelle to Philip II, 28 Oct. 1584 (imperfectly printed in *CCG*, XI, 376). These remarks apparently arose from the rejection by the Grisons (overlords of the Valtelline) in June 1584 of a treaty concluded the previous year that allowed Philip II's troops to pass through the valley one company at a time: see AGS *Estado* 1258/55–6 and 1259/45. A decade before, an earlier governor of Milan had tried to persuade Philip to intervene in the Valtelline in order to secure a corridor through which troops could pass. See AGS *Estado* 1239/35–6, marquis of Ayamonte to Philip II, 22 May 1574, enclosing a detailed description and a coloured panorama of the valley (see A. Cámara, *Fortificación y ciudad en los reinos de Felipe II* (Madrid, 1998), 106). On that occasion, the king declined to act for fear of antagonizing the French, whose couriers to Venice also crossed the Valtelline: AGS *Estado* 1239/194, Philip II to Ayamonte, June 1574.

11. See details in J. L. Hanselmann, *L'alliance Hispano-Suisse de 1587* (Bellinzona, 1971), and, for some later developments, R. Bolzern, *Spanien, Mailand und die katholische Eidgenossenschaft. Militärische, wirtschaftliche und politische Beziehungen zur Zeit des Gesandten Alfonso Casati (1594–1621)* (Lucerne, 1982), 22–5.

12. AGRB *Audience* 204/124, Count Peter-Ernest of Mansfelt to Philip II,

22 Dec. 1592. He sent Spanish troops into Lorraine to keep the Road open: ibid., fos. 153-7, same to same, 29 Jan. and 7 Feb. 1593.

13. AGS *Estado* 1272/160, draft articles agreed by the Grisons on 27 July 1592. See also the correspondence on the subject in 1593 between the governor of Milan and the Spanish ambassador in Rome: ibid., fos. 134-5. The pope disapproved of the agreement.

14. AGS *Estado* 1269/8, *consulta* of the council of state, 25 May 1591, on letters from the duke of Terranova. The council also examined all documents on the matter since 1588. See also Bolzern, *Spanien, Mailand und die katholische Eidgenossenschaft*, 75, and note 10 above.

15. Archives de l'État, Geneva, *Registre du Conseil* 96/209-209v, report of Chapeaurouge dated 22 Dec. 1601. A précis appears in F. de Crue, 'Henri IV et les députés de Genève', *Mémoires de la Société d'Histoire et d'Archéologie de Genève*, XXV (1901), 239-683, at pp. 471-2. For the Saluzzo affair told exclusively from Spanish documents, see J. L. Cano de Gardoquí, *La cuestión de Saluzzo en las comunicaciones del imperio español, 1588-1601* (Valladolid, 1962).

16. On 15 Nov. 1601 Sully, Henri IV's finance minister, approved payment 'to the secretaries and archivist of the Audit Office at Chambéry for securing the documents concerning the lands of Bresse, and other territories taken in exchange for the marquisate of Saluzzo': Archives Nationales, Paris, 120 AP 10/42v.

17. AGS *Estado* 1290/42, 'Relación del paso de Flandes' by Juan de Urbino, 12 May 1601: a remarkably detailed account of the new 'Spanish Road' and its problems. Originally, a painted panorama accompanied his description, but this has apparently been lost.

18. Archives Communales de St Claude (Jura) BB 6/83, register of deliberations of the town council, 25 May 1601. Two weeks before, perhaps after the visit of Juan de Urbino (see preceding note), the council discussed in detail the route to be followed by the troops as they travelled from Grésin, via Chézery, to Clairvaux: ibid., fo. 76, meeting of 11 May 1601.

19. J. E. M. Lajeunie, 'Correspondance entre Henri IV de France et Philippe de Béthune, ambassadeur de France à Rome, 1602-1604', *Mémoires de la Société d'Histoire et d'Archéologie de Genève*, XXXVIII (1952), 189-475, at pp. 270-1, Béthune to Henri, 19 Aug. 1602; AGS *Estado* 1291/177 and 181, Don Mendo Rodríguez de Ledesma, Spanish ambassador in Savoy, to Philip III, 5 and 24 Aug. 1602; J. Berger de Xivrey and J. Guadet, *Recueil de lettres missives de Henri IV*, VIII (Paris, 1872), 835, 839-42, 845-55 and 856-8, Henry IV to Jean de Beaumanoir, maréchal de Lavardin, 6, 10, 15, 18 and 28 July, 19 Aug. and 2 Sept. 1602.

20. AGS *Estado* 622/175, Don Balthasar de Zúñiga, Spanish ambassador to the archdukes, to Philip III, 21 Jan. 1603.

21. See AGS *Estado* 1291/72, Count Fuentes, governor of Milan, to Philip III, 31 July 1602, on the decision to send in 22 companies at Savoy's request; and details on the location – and cost – of each garrison in AD Savoie, *SA* 6603–7615. See the map based on these data in N. G. Parker, 'The Spanish Road and the Army of Flanders. A study in the formation and disintegration of a European army, 1567–1647' (Cambridge University Ph.D. thesis, 1968), between pp. 58 and 59. For the size of the armies using the Spanish Road, see idem, *The Army of Flanders and the Spanish Road. The Logistics of Spanish Victory and Defeat in the Low Countries' Wars, 1567–1659* (revised edn., Cambridge, 1990), 278–9.

22. AGS *Estado* 1291/149, 'Memoria que a dado el gobernador de Vicançon [Besançon] sobre el paso de Saboya a Borgoña', forwarded by Don Mendo Rodríguez de Ledesma on 22 Jan. 1602.

23. AGS *Estado* 1293/25 and 77, Fuentes to Philip III, 5 May and 7 Sept. 1604. Bolzern, *Spanien, Mailand und die katholische Eidgenossenschaft*, 88, provides an excellent map of the new 'Spanish Road', which reached the Rhine at Waldshut and from there passed through Habsburg territories – Further Austria and Alsace – to Lorraine, thus avoiding Franche-Comté. See also AGRB *Audience* 1953/1, unfol., Archduke Albert to the governor of Luxembourg and the duke of Lorraine, 31 Aug. 1604, for further details.

24. AGS *Estado* 1294/43, Fuentes to Philip III, 31 Mar. 1605. In an earlier letter, however, the count gave another reason for separating the two groups: 'I shall send the Italians through Savoy, in order not to jeopardize our good standing with the Swiss by causing disorders – something that the Spanish who have to cross will not do' (ibid., fo. 32, same to same, 24 Feb. 1605)! On the size of the expedition, see Bolzern, *Spanien, Mailand und die katholische Eidgenossenschaft*, 93, and AGS *Estado* 1294/30, 'Relación' of the army of Milan, Feb. 1605.

25. Details, and detailed plans, in A. Giussani, *Il forte di Fuentes. Episodi e documenti di una lotta secolare per il dominio della Valtellina* (Como, 1905). The fortress was eventually destroyed in 1796, and the English poet Wordsworth wrote a fine sonnet about its ruins, which his wife also described in her journals (1821–2): see W. Knight, ed., *The Poetical Works of William Wordsworth*, VI (London, 1896), 328–32.

26. AGS *Estado* 1296/68 and 70, Fuentes to Philip III, 9 and 23 June 1607, supply details on this 'expedition that never was'. On the Valtelline's violent history in the early seventeenth century see R. C. Head, *Early Modern Democracy in the Grisons, 1470–1620* (Cambridge, 1995).

27. See AGS *Estado* 1294/64, Fuentes to Philip III, 27 Apr. 1605, and 1295/ 181–6, letters of the count of Oñate to Philip III, May 1605, on Savoy's insistence on prepayment; and 1296/26, Fuentes to Philip III, 26 May 1607, on Savoy's refusal of passage.

28. Bolzern, *Spanien, Mailand und die katholische Eidgenossenschaft*, 93, gives figures. For the Mantuan struggle, see G. Parker, *Europe in Crisis, 1598–1648* (2nd edn., Oxford, 2001), chap. 4.

29. AGS *Estado* 1923/23, duke of Feria to Secretary Arosteguy, 16 Feb. 1619, describing the proposed route for the troops in detail; and ibid., 87 and 112, Feria to Philip III, 30 Sept. and 30 Oct. 1619, concerning their itinerary and the refusal of the Swiss to allow the passage of troops bound for Flanders. See also Bolzern, *Spanien, Mailand und die katholische Eidgenossenschaft*, 93.

30. AGS *Estado* 1924/120, 'Relación' of the musters of the various regiments as they crossed the Rhône between 17 July and 11 Aug. 1620. For Geneva's disquiet, see Archives de l'État, Geneva, *Registre du Conseil* 119/87v, 97v, 99, 122, 123, 126 and 152v, entries between May and Aug. 1620; and *Portefeuille Historique* 2650, letters of Isaac Wake, English ambassador in Savoy, 8 May and 4 July 1620. The expedition left a trail of damage and unpaid bills behind it: see the complaints of 'foulles' and 'despenses soufferts au passaige des trouppes d'Yspaigne passés en Flandres' in 1620 from the towns of Modane and St Jean de Maurienne: AD Savoie *SA* 7431, 7461, 7470, 7471, 7479 (all for St Jean) and 7530, 7551 (for Modane).

31. Details in AGS *Estado* 3335/114–16, Juan de Ayzaga to Philip III, Bormio, 15 Nov. 1620, enclosing plans of the proposed fortress. On the link between the treaty of Lyon and the Valtelline problem see the short but suggestive article of P.-F. Geisendorf, 'Le traité de Lyon et le pont de Grésin, ou d'une cause parfois méconnue des troubles des Grisons au 17e siècle', *Mémoires de la Société d'Histoire et d'Archéologie de Genève*, XL (1960), 279–86.

32. *Nieuwe Tijdinghe*, 26 May 1621, p. 8. I thank Ad Meskens for supplying me with a copy of this advertisement.

33. I also thank Dr Meskens for drawing the existence of this map to my attention. On the map, currently in the University Library at Louvain, see A. Meskens, 'De doos van Pandora. Een kaart van Michiel Coignet', *Gewina*, XX (1997), 32–4. The copy published in *Cahiers d'histoire*, XLVI (2001), 301, comes from the Bibliothèque Municipale, Besançon, *Collection Chifflet* 184/66v, with the title 'Table chorographique de Michel Coignet, d'une nouvelle voye et route pour la conduite des marchands et négotians depuis l'Italie aux Païs Bas, par ce païs et comté de Bourgogne, authorisée par les archiducs Albert et Isabel, en l'an 1621'. My thanks to Denise Turrel for these details. Note that this itinerary closely resembled that recommended by the 'governor of Besançon' in 1602: see page 134 above.

34. L. Pearsall Smith, *The Life and Letters of Sir Henry Wotton*, II (London, 1907), 221, Wotton to Sir T. Aston, 18 Dec. 1621; AGS *Estado* 1926/128, 'Relación' of Philip IV's garrisons, Jan. 1622.

35. AGS *Estado* 2036/52, *consulta* of 9 June 1622 on letters from Archduchess Isabella dated 23 May. Note that Philip IV – no doubt at the prompting of

Don Balthasar de Zúñiga – expressed surprise that the council ruled out the 'Spanish Road' since 'I have not heard that the duke of Savoy raised any objection to the regular passage [of troops].' For the 1623 expedition, see AGS *Estado* 1926/238–9, 'Relación' of the troops dispatched, and fo. 251, Juan Carlos de Guzmán, the army's commander, to Philip IV, Como, 18 Oct. 1623.

36. AGS *CJH* 522, unfol., 'Relación del estado que tienen las cosas del servicio de Su Magestad en Esguizgaros', by Alfonso Casati, 3 Apr. 1623.

37. For explanations, see R. Pithon, 'Les débuts difficiles du ministère de Richelieu et la crise de la Valteline (1621–27)', *Revue d'histoire diplomatique*, LXXIV (1960), 298–322; and idem, 'La Suisse, théâtre de la guerre froide entre la France et l'Espagne pendant la crise de la Valteline (1621–26)', *Revue suisse d'histoire*, XIII (1960), 33–53. Figures from AGS *Estado* 3337/15–18, reports from Nicolás Cid to Philip IV, Aug. 1631, and 3340/115, Feria to Philip IV, 7 Aug. 1633.

38. AGRB *Audience* 2068/2, unfol., duke of Lorraine to Archduchess Isabella, 18 Aug. 1633, copy, with details on the abortive crossing of the Burgundian regiment; AGRB *SEG* 207/293–4v, Isabella to Philip IV, 24 Oct. 1633, minute. For more on the passage of troops along the Spanish Road through Lorraine, see G. Cabourdin, *Terre et hommes en Lorraine (1550–1635). Toulois et comté de Vaudémont*, I (Nancy, 1977), 61–2; on roads in the area see pp. 70–4.

39. J. H. Elliott, *The Count-Duke of Olivares: The Statesman in an Age of Decline* (New Haven and London, 1986), 464: *consulta* of the council of state, 17 Sept. 1633, *voto* of Olivares.

40. AGS *Estado* 3341/254 and 258, 'Relaciones' of the size of the army, July 1631. AGRB *SEG* 34, the Order Book of the cardinal-infante as he led his army from Milan to Brussels, gives his exact itinerary (because each order notes the date and place of issue) as well as furnishing a unique source on the journey of a Spanish army from Lombardy to the Low Countries. See also the account of D. Aedo y Gallart, *Le voyage du prince Don Fernande, Infante d'Espagne* (Antwerp, 1635).

41. See details in Parker, *Army of Flanders*, 77–9 and 279; D. Goodman, *Spanish Naval Power, 1589–1665. Reconstruction and Defeat* (Cambridge, 1997), 24–6; and R. A. Stradling, *The Armada of Flanders. Spanish Maritime Policy and European War, 1568–1668* (Cambridge, 1992), chaps. 6–7.

42. J. J. Poelhekke, *De Vrede van Munster* (The Hague, 1948), 272, the count of Castrillo to Philip IV, 3 June 1646; E. Prestage, ed., *Correspondência diplomática de Francisco de Sousa Coutinho, durante a sua embaixada em Holanda, 1643–50*, II (Coimbra, 1926), 256, Sousa Coutinho to John IV, 17 Nov. 1647, quoting the French ambassador in The Hague.

6. The Etiquette of Atrocity: The Laws of War in Early Modern Europe

My thanks for assistance and references in preparing this chapter go to John Beeler, Mitzy Carlough, Charles Carlton, Steven Collins, Robert Cowley, Barbara Donagan, Fernando González de León, Mark Grimsley, J. F. Guilmartin Jr., Russell Hart, Sir Michael Howard, Jefferson McMahan, Allan Millett, Jane Ohlmeyer, Mark Shulman, Nancy van Deusen, Joanna Waley-Cohen and, most of all, John Lynn.

1. P. Genard, *Les poursuites contre les fauteurs de la Furie Espagnole ou du Sac d'Anvers de 1576* (Antwerp, 1880), 6−21 (from depositions made on oath to a committee of inquiry in the city, 2−5 Dec. 1577); G. Gascoigne, *The Spoyle of Antwerp* (London, 1576; facsimile edn., Amsterdam, 1969); *A Larum for London* (performed at some point between 1594 and 1600, first published 1602; ed. W. W. Greg, Malone Society reprints, 1913). On the place of atrocities in the 'core curriculum' of Dutch schools, see E. P. de Booy, *De weldaet der scholen. Het plattelandsonderwijs in de provincie Utrecht van 1580 tot het begin der 19e eeuw* (Utrecht, 1977), 60−3 and 278−9.

2. M. van Creveld, 'The Gulf crisis and the rules of war', *MHQ. The Quarterly Journal of Military History*, III, no. 4 (summer 1991), 23−7.

3. See the suggestive article of J. A. Lynn, 'How war fed war: the tax of violence and contributions during the *Grand Siècle*', *Journal of Modern History*, LXV (1993), 286−310; and F. Redlich, *De praeda militaris: Looting and Booty, 1500−1815*, Vierteljahrschrift für Sozial-und Wirtschaftsgeschichte, Beiheft XXXIX (Wiesbaden, 1956).

4. For details see, respectively, A. Gentili, *De jure belli, libri III* (1588−9; complete edn., Hanau, 1598), 2.19 (English edn., Oxford, 1933); J. P. Myers, '"Murdering heart . . . murdering hand": Captain Thomas Lee of Ireland, Elizabethan Assassin', *Sixteenth Century Journal*, XXII (1991), 47−60; G. Parker, *The Army of Flanders and the Spanish Road: The Logistics of Spanish Victory and Defeat in the Low Countries' Wars, 1567−1659* (2nd edn., Cambridge, 1990), 66.

5. For example, vol. VIII of the *Tractatus universi juris* (Venice, 1584) contained five major treatises on the Laws of War written in Italy between about 1360 and 1560: see G. Soldi-Rondinini, 'Il diritto di guerra in Italia nel secolo XV', *Nuova rivista storica*, XLVII (1964), 275−306. See also P. Contamine, *War in the Middle Ages*, tr. M. Jones (Oxford, 1984), 260−302; Redlich, *De praeda militaris*, I; and F. H. Russell, *The Just War in the Middle Ages* (Cambridge, 1975).

6. H. E. J. Cowdrey, 'The Peace and the Truce of God in the eleventh century', *Past and Present*, XLVI (1970), 42−67; and J. T. Johnson, *The Just War*

Tradition and the Restraint of War: A Moral and Historical Inquiry (Princeton 1984), 124–8.

7. An early example of modern Articles of War was the *Lex pacis castrensis* (1158) of Emperor Frederick Barbarossa; the first code enacted as permanent legislation by a state was issued by the States-General of the Dutch Republic in 1590. For a detailed discussion of the Articles of one state, see B. Donagan, 'Codes and conduct in the English Civil War', *Past and Present*, CXVIII (1988), 65–95.

8. Fairfax quoted, amid an important discussion of theory and practice of the Laws of War in seventeenth-century England, in Donagan, 'Codes and conduct', 78.

9. See H. J. Cohn, 'Götz von Berlichingen and the art of military autobiography', in J. R. Mulryne and M. Shewring, eds., *War, Literature and the Arts in Sixteenth-Century Europe* (London, 1989), chap. 2; K. M. Brown, *Bloodfeud in Scotland, 1573–1625: Violence, Justice and Politics in an Early Modern Society* (Edinburgh, 1986), 5; and Redlich, *De praeda militaris*, 2–3. Gentili, *De jure belli*, 3.8 (English edn., 2:323–7), provides an interesting discussion of suitable punishments for defeated leaders.

10. I. Gentles, 'The impact of the New Model Army', in J. S. Morrill, ed., *The Impact of the English Civil War* (London, 1991), 99. See also D. Underdown, *Pride's Purge: Politics in the Puritan Revolution* (Oxford, 1971), chaps. 4–5.

11. B. de Ayala, *De iure et officiis bellicis et disciplina militari, libri III* (Douai, 1582), 1.2 (quotations from the 2-vol. edn. of J. Westlake (Washington, DC, 1912), 1:10–11). Ayala was born in Antwerp in 1548, son of a Spanish father and a Netherlands mother. He studied at Leuven University and in 1580 petitioned for the post of auditor-general of the Army of Flanders on the basis of his Netherlands birth (AGRB *Audience* 1818/3, unfol., petition of 9 Feb. 1580). He received the job three months later and held it until his death in 1584. F. de Vitoria, *Relectio de iure belli* (1539; ed. L. Pereña Vicente, Madrid, 1981), 182, had advanced virtually identical arguments.

12. For the theories see J. T. Johnson, *Ideology, Reason and the Limitation of War: Religious and Secular Concepts, 1200–1740* (Princeton, 1975), esp. 134–46; idem, *Just War Tradition*, esp. 94–103; and J. R. Hale, 'Incitement to violence? English divines on the theme of war, 1578–1631', and 'Gunpowder and the Renaissance: an essay in the history of ideas', in idem, *Renaissance War Studies* (London, 1983), 487–517. For a later example of the lack of influence of theory on the practice of war, see A. Starkey, 'War and culture, a case study: the Enlightenment and the conduct of the British army in America, 1755–1781', *War and Society*, VIII (1990), 1–28.

13. *BMO*, I, 535, 'Lo que responde a Su Santidad'; AGS *Estado* 947/110, Philip II to the count of Olivares, his ambassador in Rome, 22 July 1586.

14. See S. L. Adams, 'The Protestant cause: religious alliance with the West

European Calvinist communities as a political issue in England, 1585-1630' (Oxford University D. Phil., 1973); G. Groenhuis, *De Predikanten. De Sociale Positie van de Gereformeerde Predikanten in de Republiek der Verenigde Nederlanden voor* c. 1700 (Groningen, 1977), 77-107; S. A. Arnoldsson, *Krigspropagand i Sverige före Trettioåriga Kriget* (Gothenburg, 1941), and pages 29-33 above.

15. Ayala, *De iure*, 1.2.23 (16-17). The phrase 'heinous offence' is significant since it was used by lawyers to denote capital crimes.

16. Ibid., 1.2.14-15 (11-12).

17. Gentili, *De jure belli*, 3.7 (English edn., 2:320); A. de Freitas de Meneses, *Os, Açores e o Dominio Filipino (1580-1590)* (Angra do Heroísmo: Instituto Histórico da Ilha Terceira, 1987), I, 66, marquis of Santa Cruz to Philip II, Aug. 8 1588; Starkey, 'War and culture', 14-15; and D. Syrett, 'The failure of the British effort in America, 1777', in J. Black and P. Woodfine, eds., *The British Navy and the Use of Naval Power in the Eighteenth Century* (Leicester, 1988), 174-5.

18. F. de Valdés, *Espeio y deceplina militar* (Brussels, 1589), fo. 40v. See also S. de Londoño, *Discurso sobre la forma de reduzir la disciplina militar* (Brussels, 1589), fo. 23v: '[soldiers have] more opportunities to misbehave than any other group of people'.

19. *CSPI, 1586-8*, 161, Thomas Woodhouse to Geoffrey Fenton, 23 Sept. 1586, after the battle of Ardnary. C. H. Carlton, *Going to the Wars: The Experience of the British Civil Wars, 1638-1651* (London, 1992), 174.

20. See the admirable discussion in M. Walzer, *Just and Unjust Wars: A Moral Argument with Historical Illustrations* (2nd edn., New York, 1992).

21. Carlton, *Going to the Wars*, 174. The same response is documented in non-Western cultures; see, for example, the brutal treatment of Canton in 1650, after its recapture by the Manchu, in M. Martini, *Bellum Tartaricum, or the Conquest of the Great and Most Renowned Empire of China* (London, 1654), 189-90.

22. Joshua 6:21, 24.

23. See Soldi-Rondinini, 'Il diritto di guerra', 299; V. Schmidtchen, *Kriegswesen im späten Mittelalter: Technik, Taktik, Theorie* (Weinheim, 1990), 65-71; A. Vanderpol, *La doctrine scolastique du droit de guerre* (Paris, 1919), 146-9; P. Contamine, 'Ransom and booty', in idem, *War and Competition between States* (Oxford, 1991), 163-93; and Redlich, *De praeda militaris*, 17-19. For twentieth-century views, see W. V. O'Brien, *The Conduct of Just and Limited War* (New York, 1981).

24. The flooding of Walcheren - seemingly the first such example of the war - was reported by de Wacken and Beauvoir to the duke of Alba, Middelburg, 27-28 June 1572: AGRB *Audience* 343/84f. The constant danger of inundation in Holland during the 1570s is well described in G. 't Hart, 'Rijnlands

Bestuur en Waterstaat rondom het Beleg en Ontzet van Leiden', *Leids Jaarboekje* LXVI (1974), 13-33.

25. AGS *Estado* 560/91, Valdés to Don Luis de Requesens, 18 Sept. 1574. This document is printed and discussed by M. C. Waxman, 'Strategic terror: Philip II and sixteenth-century warfare', *War in History*, IV (1997), 339-47.

26. See W. Hays Park, 'Rolling Thunder and the law of war', *Air University Review*, XXXIII, no. 2 (Jan.–Feb. 1982), 2-23; and idem, 'Linebacker and the law of war', ibid., XXXIV, no. 2 (Jan.–Feb. 1983), 2-30.

27. AGS *Estado*, 561/122, Philip II to Requesens, 22 Oct. 1574. See the remarkably similar logic used to rule out the strategic bombing of the Red River dikes in a memorandum of John T. McNaughton, assistant US secretary of defense, 18 Jan. 1966, in M. Gravel, ed., *The Pentagon Papers: The Defense Department History of United States Decision-Making on Vietnam* (Boston, 1971), IV, 43-8. For another unusual modern example of restraint, the decision not to drop the first atomic bomb on Kyoto, see O. Cary, *Mr Stimson's Pet City: The Sparing of Kyoto, 1945* (Moonlight Series no. 3, Kyoto, 1975).

28. François de La Noue, *Discours politiques et militaires* (1587; ed. F. E. Sutcliffe, Geneva, 1967), 391-401 and 638-42.

29. J. H. Elliott, 'Revolution and continuity in early modern Europe', in J. H. Elliott, *Spain and Its World, 1500-1700: Selected Essays* (New Haven, 1989), 92-113; P. Clark, ed., *European Crisis of the 1950s: Essays in Comparative History* (London, 1985); G. Parker, *Europe in Crisis, 1598-1648*, (2nd edn., Oxford, 2001).

30. W. Beech, *More Sulphur for Basing: or, God Will Fearfully Annoy and Make Quick Riddance of His Implacable Enemies, Surely, Sorely, Suddenly* (London, 1645). See also the fire-eating tract written in the Netherlands in 1583 by Luis Valle de la Cerda, *Avisos en materia de estado y guerra para oprimir rebeliones* (Madrid, 1599), fos. 31-3v, 37v-9, justifying the execution of all rebels, with references from Deuteronomy, Cicero, the Justinian Code, Cyprian, Augustine and Thomas Aquinas.

31. Donagan, 'Codes and conduct', 86; G. Parker, *Spain and the Netherlands, 1559-1659: Ten Studies* (London, 1979), 110.

32. B. Whitelocke, *Memorials of the English Affairs* (Oxford, 1853), III, 351.

33. *Henry V*, act 3, sc. 3, lines 7-18; [duke of Wellington], *Despatches, Correspondence and Memoranda of Field Marshall Arthur, Duke of Wellington* (Kraus reprint, Millwood, NY, 1973), I, 93, Wellington to George Canning, 3 Feb. 1820. See also the excellent discussion in J. W. Wright, 'Sieges and customs of war at the opening of the eighteenth century', *AHR*, XXIX (1934), 629-44; and M. H. Keen, *The Laws of War in the Late Middle Ages* (London, 1965), 119-33.

34. Carlton, *Going to the Wars*, 173.

35. Quotations from Archief van het Aartsbisdom Mechelen (Belgium), *Fonds Kloosters: Cortenberg*, 2/345 ('Den capiteijn antwoerde nu de furie over was, niet en souden cunnen doet'); and E. Symmons, *A Military Sermon, Wherein by the Word of God, the Nature and Disposition of a Rebel Is Discovered* (Oxford, 1644), 35. My thanks to Craig Harline for the first reference and to Barbara Donagan for the second.

36. F. de Vitoria, '*Relectio de iure belli*', in A. Pagden and J. Lawrance, eds., *Political Writings*, (Cambridge 1991), 293-327.

37. AGS *Estado* 554/14, Requesens to Philip II, 30 Dec. 1573. Explicit discussions of the customs of war by leading military practitioners are exceedingly rare. For a detailed account of the duke of Alba's policy towards rebellious towns, albeit based on secondary sources, see L. van der Essen, 'Kritisch onderzoek betreffende de oorlogvoering van het Spaans leger in de Nederlanden in de XVIe eeuw, namelijk de bestraffing van opstandige steden. I. Tijdens het bewind van Alva', *Mededelingen van de Koninklijke Vlaamse Academie van Wetenschappen, Letteren en Schone Kunsten van België: Klasse der Letteren*, XII, no. 1 (1950).

38. *CCG*, IV, 231-4, Morillon to Granvelle, 3 June 1572, records Mechelen's refusal to accept a garrison. Alba's determination to make the town pay for this may be found in *Epistolario*, III, 187, 193-4 and 197, Alba to Philip II, 21 Aug. and 6 Sept. 1572, and to Cardinal Pacheco, 1 Sept. 1572. His later justifications appear in ibid., III, 219-21, 230-1 and 238-9, Alba to Philip II, 2 and 13 Oct. 1572, and Alba to Don Juan de Zúñiga, [27] Oct. 1572.

39. *Co. Do. In.*, LXXV, 127, Esteban Prats to Philip II, 30 Nov. 1572; Jean Richardot quoted by L. P. Gachard, *Rapport sur les différents séries de documents concernant l'histoire de la Belgique qui sont conservés ... à Lille* (Brussels, 1841), 234. See other contemporary letters concerning the brutality of the sack in *CCG*, IV, 455-68, 490-4, 504 and 547.

40. L. Didier, *Lettres et négociations de Claude de Mondoucet* (Paris, 1891), I, 48, Mondoucet, the French agent who accompanied Alba on campaign, to Charles IX, 25 Sept. 1572; and *Epistolario*, III, 249, Alba to Philip II, 19 Nov. 1572.

41. Van der Essen, 'Kritisch onderzoek', 23-6.

42. 'I recall that the burning of the town of Duren [in 1543] by the emperor Charles V secured the submission of the whole province of Gelderland in a single day': *Epistolario*, III, 248. Alba to Philip II, 19 Nov. 1572.

43. *Epistolario*, III, 239, Alba to Zúñiga, [27] Oct. 1572. Even as the sack of Mechelen continued, Oudenaarde, Dendermonde, Leuven, Diest and Tongeren all sent delegates to surrender and ask for mercy.

44. See B. Donagan, 'The Thirty Years' War: the view from England' (paper given at the Sixteenth-Century Studies Conference, Philadelphia, 1991).

45. See the details in G. Droysen, 'Studien über die Belagerung und Zerstörung

Magdeburgs, 1631', in *Forschungen zur deutsche Geschichte* (Göttingen, 1863), III, 433–606; A. Cunningham and P. Grell, *The Four Horsemen of the Apocalypse: Religion, War and Famine in Reformation Europe* (Cambridge, 2000), 178–82; and K. Wittich, *Dietrich von Falkenberg, Oberst und Hofmarschall Gustav Adolfs: Ein Beitrag zur Geschichte des dreissigjährigen Krieges* (Magdeburg, 1892). On the propaganda surrounding this event, see W. Lahne, *Magdeburgs Zerstörung in der zeitgenössischen Publizistik* (Magdeburg, 1931); and Donagan, 'The Thirty Years' War'.

46. Details in Ian Gentles, *The New Model Army in England, Ireland and Scotland, 1643–1653* (Oxford, 1992), 357–63.

47. J. T. Gilbert, *A Contemporary History of Affairs in Ireland* (Dublin, 1880), II, 270, Ormond to Charles II, Sept. 1649. All other quotations come from J. Burke, 'The New Model Army and the problems of siege-warfare, 1648–51', *Irish Historical Studies*, XXVII (1990), 1–29.

48. Gentili, *De jure belli*, 3.7 (English edn., 2:315). For examples of executions following unconditional surrender, see van der Essen, 'Kritisch onderzoek', 31–5; Haarlem in 1573: J. W. Spaans, *Haarlem na de Reformatie: Stedelijke cultuur en kerkelijk leven, 1577–1620* (Hollandse historische reeks XI, The Hague, 1989), 44–6; and several towns in England and Ireland in 1648–51: Burke, 'The New Model Army'.

49. Two published fragments of seventeenth-century court-martial records give some idea of their work: J. Adair, 'The court martial papers of Sir William Waller's army, 1644', *Journal of the Society for Army Historical Research* XLIV (1966), 205–23; G. Davis, ed., 'Dundee court-martial records, 1651', *Scottish Historical Society Miscellany*, III (Scottish History Society, 2nd series, XIX, Edinburgh, 1919), 3–67. For the Spanish Army of Flanders see also L. van Meerbeeck, *Inventaire des archives des tribunaux militaires* (Gembloux, 1939).

50. See IVdeDJ 36/40, 'Lo que a Su Magestad ha parecido advertir sobre la relación de los excessos que se dize se han hecho en los Estado de Flandes'; ibid., 44/57–8, (Mateo Vázquez to Philip II, 11 and 15 Apr. 1574; and ibid., 45/329, the reports of the 'Juntas grandes y particular'.

51. See P. Génard, 'La furie espagnole: Documents pour servir à l'histoire du sac d'Anvers en 1576', *Annales de l'Académie royale d'archéologie de Belgique*, XXXII (1876); and K. S. Bottigheimer, 'The Restoration land settlement in Ireland: a structural view', *Irish Historical Studies*, XVIII (1972), 9–12.

52. Keen, *Laws of War*, 133, 243–4 and 254–7.

53. In AGRB *SEG* 11/82v, Parma's instruction for Don Alonso de Lerma, 29 Dec. 1588, sent to negotiate the ransom of captured soldiers from the Spanish Armada. See data on earlier exchange and ransom practices in Contamine, 'Ransom and booty', 173–93.

54. The *cuartel general* of 25 October 1599 was reissued on 14 May 1602 and 18 Oct. 1622; see copies in ARA *Staten van Holland* 2604 nr. g; and BRB *Ms* 12,622–31, fos. 273–5v. The English versions of the 1602 and 1622 arrangements were printed as an appendix to H. Hexham, *The Principles of the Art Militarie Practiced in the Warres of the Vnited Netherlands* (London, 1637); see M. J. D. Cockle, *A Bibliography of Military Books up to 1642* (London, 1900), 108–9. An important collection of documents on the ransom and exchange of prisoners by and from the Spanish Army of Flanders may be found in AGRB *SEG*, 175bis/46–72.

55. L. van Meerbeeck, 'Le service sanitaire de l'armée espagnole des Pays-Bas à la fin du XVIe siècle et au XVIIe siècle', *Revue internationale d'histoire militaire*, XX (1959), 493, notes that a French military hospital abandoned in the Spanish Netherlands in 1677 was immediately placed under special protection, guaranteed by the joint insignia of France and Spain.

56. AGS *Estado* 2251, unfol., Philip IV to Don Francisco de Melo, 17 May 1644.

57. AHN *Estado libro* 972, unfol., Marquis Sfondrato to Don Miguel de Salamanca, 4 June 1640. See also a position paper prepared by the Spanish High Command at this time, regretting the restraints imposed on their conduct of war by the ability of the peasants to contract out of hostilities by paying contributions: AGRB *CPE* 1573/259–62v (papers of Pieter Roose); and the examples from the Thirty Years' War cited by Redlich, *De praeda militaris*, 45. On the medieval safeguards, see Keen, *Laws of War*, 251–3.

58. HMC *Twelfth Report, Appendix Part ix: Beaufort Manuscripts* (London, 1891), 60, the marquis of Worcester (formerly Lord Glamorgan) to Charles II, c. 1666. For the military changes mentioned in this paragraph, see G. Parker, *The Military Revolution: Military Innovation and the Rise of the West, 1500–1800* (2nd edn., Cambridge, 2000), chaps. 1–2.

59. See Redlich, *De praeda militaris*, 58–77; and Lynn, 'How war fed war'.

60. See B. Donagan, 'Understanding Providence: the difficulties of Sir William and Lady Waller', *Journal of Ecclesiastical History*, XXXIX (1988), 433–4; and B. Worden, 'Oliver Cromwell and the sin of Achan', in D. Beales and G. Best, eds., *History, Society and Churches: Essays in Honour of Owen Chadwick* (Cambridge, 1985), 125–45.

61. See G. Bacot, *La doctrine de la guerre juste* (Paris, 1987), chap. 3; G. Best, *Humanity in Warfare: The Modern History of the International Law of Armed Conflicts* (London, 1980), chap. 1; M. Howard, ed., *Restraints on War: Studies in the Limitation of Armed Conflict* (Oxford, 1979), 5–6; and Johnson, *Ideology, Reason and the Limitation of War*, chap. 4.

62. Gerhardt and Locke quoted in T. K. Rabb, *The Struggle for Stability in Early Modern Europe* (Oxford, 1975), 119–20; the peasant Bible in G. Parker, *The Thirty Years' War* (2nd edn., London, 1977), 160.

63. Rabb, *Struggle for Stability*, argues the case for the chaos of the mid-century wars giving rise to absolutism anc also produces a dazzling array of 'no more war' writings and pictures.

64. AGS *Estado* 554/146, Requesens to Philip II, 30 Dec. 1573.

65. Details in A. Gerlo and R. de Smet, eds., *Marnixi epistulae. De briefwisseling van Marnix van Sint-Aldegonde. Een kritische uitgave* (Brussels, 1990), I, 206–32.

66. Carlton, *Going to the Wars*, 249–52. But there were exceptions: some royalists continued to hang captured parliamentarians out of hand (see examples in ibid., 255–64); and the parliamentarians in the Second Civil War showed far more rigour towards their defeated enemies (see Burke, 'The New Model Army').

67. For examples of early modern live-and-let-live systems, see H. Drouot, *Mayenne et la Bourgogne, 1587–1596: Contribution à l'histoire des provinces françaises pendant la Ligue* (Paris, 1937), I, 309–15; J. S. Morrill, *The Revolt of the Provinces: Conservatives and Radicals in the English Civil War, 1630–1650* (London, 1976), 36–42; and H. Salm, *Armeefinanzierung im dreissigjährigen Krieg: Der niederrheinisch-westfalische Reichskreise, 1635–59*, Schriftenreihe der Vereinigung zur Erforschung der neueren Geschichte, XVI (Münster, 1990), 164–76. For the First World War, see T. Ashworth, *Trench Warfare, 1914–1918: The Live and Let Live System* (New York, 1980).

68. R. A. Stradling, *The Armada of Flanders: Spanish Maritime Policy and European War, 1568–1668* (Cambridge, 1992), 40–5.

69. Quotations from C. Streit, *Keine Kameraden: Die Wehrmacht und die sowjetischen Kriegsgefangenen, 1941–45* (Stuttgart, 1978), 9; and C. Duffy, *Red Storm on the Reich: The Soviet March on Germany, 1945* (London, 1991), 274. Both works document the meticulous execution of these policies. See also H. Boog et al., *Das deutsche Reich und der zweite Weltkrieg*, IV (Stuttgart, 1983), 413–40; and O. Bartov, *Hitler's Army: Soldiers, Nazis and War in the Third Reich* (Oxford, 1991), 106–78.

70. T. Churchyard, *A Generall Rehearsall of Warres Wherein Is Five Hundred Severall Services of Land and Seas* (London, 1579), sig. Qii, Qiiiv.

71. See P. Seed, 'Taking possession and reading texts: establishing the authority of overseas empires', *William and Mary Quarterly*, XLIX (1992), 183–209; P. W. Powell, *Soldiers, Indians and Silver: The Northwards Advance of New Spain, 1550–1600* (Berkeley, 1969), part 3; A. Pagden, *The Fall of Natural Man: The American Indian and the Origins of Comparative Ethnology* (Cambridge, 1982), 80–90; and, more generally, Johnson, *The Just War Tradition*, 69–84. H. Strachan, 'Essay and reflection: on total war and modern war', *Journal of International History*, XXII (2000), 341–70, noted that technology and geography have traditionally helped Western nations to fight wars that were 'total' for their enemies but 'limited' for them.

72. R. Meinertzhagen, *Kenya Diary (1902–1906)* (London, 1983), 178. By way of example, see the author's personal tally at pp. 143–4, 146, 152 and 158, and the quotations in R. F. Jones, 'The Kipkororor Chronicles', *MHQ. The Quarerly Journal of Military History*, III, no. 3 (spring 1991), 38–47. Church-yard, *A Generall Rehearsall*, sig. Qiv, advanced a remarkably similar justifica-tion for the brutality of the English in Elizabethan Ireland: there were so few troops and so few victuals, he asserted, that a policy of terror was unavoidable.
73. R. Axelrod, *The Evolution of Cooperation* (New York, 1984), 173–89.
74. *Henry V*, act 4, sc. 7, lines 1–4.

7. The 'Military Revolution' in Seventeenth-century Ireland

The authors are much indebted to Paul Kerrigan, Jane Ohlmeyer and Robert Stradling for making available to them published and unpublished material. They are also grateful for comments by Magda Stouthamer-Loeber on an earlier draft of this chapter.
1. HMC *Calendar of the manuscripts of the marquis of Ormonde*, new series (8 vols., London, 1902–20), I, 57, Preston to Ormond, 26 Mar. 1643 (O.S.).
2. See R. Loeber, 'Warfare and architecture in County Laois through seven-teenth-century eyes', in P. G. Lane and W. Nolan, eds., *Laois: History and Society. Interdisciplinary Essays on the History of an Irish County* (Dublin, 1999), 377–413. Further relevant recent titles include M. Bennett, *The Civil Wars Experienced. Britain and Ireland, 1638–1661* (London, 2000); J. P. Kenyon and J. H. Ohlmeyer, eds., *The Civil Wars: A Military History of England, Scotland and Ireland, 1638–1660* (Oxford, 1998); P. Lenihan, ed., *Conquest and Resistance: War in Seventeenth-century Ireland* (Leiden, 2001), especially pp. 345–70, 'Conclusion: Ireland's Military Revolution(s)'; M. Ó Siochrú, ed., *The Kingdoms in Crisis: Ireland in the 1640s* (Dublin, 2001), with an important essay on military affairs by P. Lenihan; and J. R. Young, ed., *Celtic Dimensions of the British Civil Wars* (Edinburgh, 1997).
3. J. H. Ohlmeyer, Introduction, in idem, ed., *Ireland from Independence to Occupation, 1641–1660* (Cambridge, 1995), 20, Ambassador Bellièvre to Secretary of State Brienne, London, 13 Nov. 1648. I thank Professor Ohlmeyer for drawing recent works on Irish military history to my attention, for fostering my interest in early modern Irish history, and for introducing me to Rolf Loeber.
4. HMC *Ormonde Mss*, new series, II, 10.
5. See G. Parker, *The Military Revolution: Military Innovation and the Rise of the West, 1500–1800* (2nd edn., Cambridge, 2000). For Ireland see C. Falls, *Elizabeth's Irish Wars* (New York, 1970) and P. Kerrigan, 'Fortifications in Tudor Ireland', *Fortress* VII (1990), 27–39.
6. G. A. Hayes-McCoy, 'The early history of guns in Ireland', *Galway Archae-*

ological Society Journal, XVIII (1938–9), 54–5; A. M. Freeman, ed., *The Annals of Connacht* (Dublin, 1983), 631.

7. G. Bennett, *The History of Bandon* (Cork, 1862), 67.

8. P. O'Flanaghan, *Bandon* (Dublin, 1988), map 6.

9. J. Hogan, ed., *Letters and Papers relating to the Irish Rebellion between 1642 and 1646* (IMC, Dublin, 1936), 4.

10. HMC *Ormonde Mss*, new series, II, 33.

11. Kerrigan, 'Fortifications', 35.

12. G. A. Hayes-McCoy, ed., *Ulster and Other Irish Maps, c. 1600* (IMC, Dublin, 1964), pl. XVI.

13. BL *Addl* 24, 200, survey by Nicholas Pynnar, 1624.

14. M. D. O'Sullivan, 'The fortification of Galway in the sixteenth and early seventeenth centuries', *Journal of the Galway Archaeological and Historical Society*, XVI (1934), 34.

15. P. M. Kerrigan, 'Irish castles and fortifications in the age of the Tudors, part 2 – 1558 to 1603', *An Cosantoir* (1984), 276. It was built under the supervision of Geoffrey Fenton, who presumably had some knowledge of warfare since he had translated Guicciardini's *Wars of Italy* (London, 1579); Hogan, *Letters*, 151.

16. *CSPI, 1625–32*, 110.

17. J. Bruce, ed., *Letters and Papers of the Verney Family* (London, 1853), 125.

18. W. Knowler, ed., *Letters and Dispatches of the Earl of Strafforde . . .* (2 vols., London, 1739), I, 128, 145 and 163; A. B. Grosart, ed., *The Lismore Papers* (10 vols., London, 1886–8), 1st series, III, 209; H. F. Kearney, 'Richard Boyle, ironmaster', *Journal of the Royal Society of Antiquaries of Ireland*, LXXXII–LXXXIII (1952–3), 161; Sir A. Vicars, *Index to the Prerogative Wills of Ireland* (Dublin, 1897), 37.

19. Knowler, *Letters*, I, 163; W. Nolan, 'The historical geography of the ownership and occupation of land in the barony of Fassadinin, Kilkenny, c. 1600–1850' (University College, Dublin, Ph.D. thesis, 1975).

20. K. Duncan-Jones, *Sir Philip Sidney, Courtier Poet* (New Haven, 1991), 229; R. Loeber, 'Biographical dictionary of engineers in Ireland, 1600–1730', *Irish Sword*, XIII (1977–9), 31.

21. HMC *Ormonde Mss*, new series, VII, 514–15.

22. Trinity College, Dublin (printed books) vvi, 45.

23. He copied many of its illustrations for his own book, entitled *A Treatise of the Art of War* (London, 1677). The link with Freitag initially became evident to Rolf Loeber from the mention of Freitag's work in Orrery's play *Mr Anthony*.

24. M. J. D. Cockle, *A Bibliography of English Military Books up to 1642, and of Contemporary Foreign Works* (2nd edn., London, 1900).

25. Barry also published a translation, in similarly barbarous English, of the

official history of Spinola's victorious siege of Breda: see H. Hugo, *The seige* [*sic*] *of Breda* (Leuven, 1627). Remarkably, the end of the Irish wars did not spawn a spate of publications similar to those celebrating the end of the Eighty and the Thirty Years' Wars on the continent in 1648. Only a few military commanders who had served in Ireland thought it worthwhile to publish military tracts after 1660, most notably Roger Boyle, later earl of Orrery, who published *A Treatise of the Art of War* (London, 1677), and Sir James Turner, who wrote *Pallas armata. Military Essays of the Ancient Grecian, Roman and Modern Art of War* (London, 1683). On Barry, see D. Ranken, 'The art of war: military writing in Ireland in the mid-17th century' (Oxford University D.Phil., 1999), 46–55; on Orrery, ibid., 55–68. Another exception was master gunner Samuel Molyneux, who published an educational treatise on gunnery and ballistics. This work, of which only one copy appears to have survived (at Trinity College, Dublin, lacking its title page and date of publication), relied on trigonometry and exemplified the empirical and statistical basis of the 'New Learning' which emerged in the 1650s. Officers who had served during the Irish Civil War and in the subsequent Down Survey – Miles Symner, Samuel Molyneux, William Petty, Benjamin Worsley – formed the core of the Dublin Philosophical Society. Although civilians eventually also contributed to this Irish equivalent of the Royal Society of London, military officers took the initiative. See T. C. Barnard, 'The Hartlib circle and the origins of the Dublin Philosophical Society', *Irish Historical Studies*, XIX (1974), 56–71.

26. E. M. Hinton, 'Rych's "An Anatomy of Ireland" with an account of the author', *Publications of the Modern Language Association of America*, LV (1940), 96.

27. Mountjoy to Privy Council, 1 May 1601, quoted in R. D. FitzSimon, 'Irish swordsmen in the imperial service in the Thirty Years War', *Irish Sword*, IX (1969–70), 22.

28. In January 1640 the 18 companies of Irish infantry (in a single tercio) serving in the Army of Flanders numbered 199 officers and 1071 men: see the Memorial of Pieter Roose, 28 Jan. 1640 (AGRB CPE 1574/81–99). Interestingly, according to this document the Irish units had changed from arquebus to musket in 1633–4, but the English still carried the lighter arquebus. Although by 1640 only one Irish regiment served in the Spanish Netherlands, there had been four in 1636: B. Jennings, *Wild Geese in Spanish Flanders 1582–1700* ... (IMC, Dublin, 1964), 8–14; and R. A. Stradling, *The Spanish Monarchy and Irish Mercenaries: The Wild Geese in Spain 1618–68* (Dublin, 1994), 164–5. For an account of the Irish military community in Flanders see G. Henry, *The Irish Military Community in Spanish Flanders, 1586–1621* (Dublin, 1992); and idem, 'Ulster exiles in Europe, 1605–41', in B. Mac Cuarta, ed., *Ulster 1641* (Belfast, 1993), 37–60.

29. Precise numbers are elusive, but the Irish units serving in Spain fell to one

regiment in 1643, and in the French army from seven regiments in 1641 to one in 1643. It must be presumed that many of these 'missing' troops returned to their native land: personal communication from Robert Stradling.

30. Bod. *Carte Mss* I/214, 131, St Leger to [Ormond], 21 July and 17 Aug. 1640. See also the data in K. Forkan, 'Strafford's Irish army, 1640–1' (National University of Ireland, Galway, MA thesis, 1999).

31. H. Hazlett, 'A history of the military forces operating in Ireland, 1641–9' (Queen's University, Belfast, Ph.D. thesis, 1938), 117. Strafford made a substantial arms purchase in Holland in 1638 (Sheffield City Library, Wentworth Woodhouse Muniments XI a. 126, Wentworth to Boswell, 26 Oct. 1638) and boasted in Feb. 1639 that 'our standing army of one thousand horse and two thousand foot will be in very good condition; besides we have eight thousand spare arms and twelve field pieces, and eight greater for battery, ready upon their carriages' (Knowler, *Letters*, II, 281, Wentworth to Newcastle, 10 Feb. 1639). (Thanks to Michael Perceval-Maxwell for these references.) For more on Irish arms imports from abroad, see P. Edwards, *Dealing in Death. The Arms Trade and the British Civil Wars, 1638–1652* (Stroud, 2000), 189–96.

32. Examples taken from R. Gillespie, 'Destabilizing Ulster, 1641–2', in Mac Cuarta, *Ulster 1641*, 107–21, at pp. 110–11. Also see BL *Addl* 4770/283, listing the settlers and their weapons in c. 1630: the 13,092 'men' listed in the nine counties possessed 7226 swords, 3085 pikes, 700 muskets, 384 calivers, 836 snaphances (a light flintlock), 69 halberds and 11 lances.

33. J. T. Gilbert, ed., *History of the Irish Confederation and the War in Ireland, by Richard Bellings*, I (Dublin, 1882), 33–4. On Bellings, who wrote in the 1670s, see Ranken, 'The art of war', 98–117; on Benburb, see Stradling, *Spanish Monarchy*, 91; for more on the Irish war effort, see P. Lenihan, *The Confederate Catholics at War, 1641–1648* (Cork, 2000).

34. I. Ryder, *An English Army for Ireland* (London, 1987), 8; Hazlett, 'Military forces', 114 and 119; 'The battle of Lisnegarvey, AD 1641', *Ulster Journal of Archaeology*, I (1853), 242–3.

35. Cited in T. Fitzpatrick, *The Bloody Bridge and Other Papers relating to the Insurrection of 1641* (Dublin, 1903, reissued Port Washington, NY, 1970), 121–2 and 124; Sir J. Turner, *Memoirs of His Own Life and Times* (Edinburgh, 1829), 20.

36. *A More Exact Relation of a Great Victory . . .* (London, 1642), 3–3v; Bennett, *Bandon*, 82. See also the new study of K. Wiggins, *The Anatomy of a Siege: King John's Castle, Limerick, 1642* (Woodbridge, 2001).

37. Hogan, *Letters*, 117–18; T. C. Croker, *Researchers in the South of Ireland* (London, 1824), 40–1.

38. HMC *Reports on the Franciscan manuscripts preserved at the convent, Merchants' Quay, Dublin* (Dublin, 1906), 121–2.

39. W. A. McComlish, 'The survival of the Irish castle in an age of cannon', *Irish Sword*, IX (1969–70), 17.

40. D. Massari, 'My Irish campaign', *The Catholic Bulletin*, IV (1916), 218; E. McCracken, 'Charcoal-burning ironworks in seventeenth- and eighteenth-century Ireland', *Ulster Journal of Archaeology*, XX (1957), 134.

41. HMC *Franciscan Mss*, 229; Hogan, *Letters*, 88; *La courageuse résolution d'une dame irlandoise* (Paris, 1642), 6.

42. HMC *Franciscan Mss*, 199 and 206.

43. J. T. Gilbert, ed., *A Contemporary History of Affairs in Ireland (1641– 1652)* I (Dublin, 1879), 32; idem, *History of the Irish Confederation*, II, 331.

44. Gilbert, *History of the Irish Confederation*, I, 151.

45. Gilbert, *Contemporary History*, I, 184; Edwards, *Dealing in Death*, 189– 96.

46. T. Carlyle, ed., *Oliver Cromwell's Letters and Speeches* (5 vols., London, 1870), II, 197.

47. HMC *Franciscan Mss*, 206.

48. C. Hollick, 'Owen Roe O'Neill's Ulster army of the confederacy, May– August 1646', *Irish Sword*, XVIII (1991), 224 and 226; Gilbert, *Contemporary History*, I, 116; G. A. Hayes-McCoy, *Irish Battles. A Military History of Ireland* (Belfast, 1989), 174–99.

49. HMC *Ormonde Mss*, I, 58; Gilbert, *History of the Irish Confederation*, VI, 84.

50. C. H. Firth, *Cromwell's Army* (London, 1902, reprinted London, 1992), 150.

51. Ryder, *English Army*, 22.

52. D. Stevenson, *Scottish Covenanters and Irish Confederates: Scottish-Irish Relations in the Mid-seventeenth Century* (Belfast, 1981), 72; Gilbert, *Contemporary History*, I, 419.

53. C[ambridge] U[niversity] L[ibrary] *Ms Ee.3.39*, fo. 1; see also Stevenson, *Scottish Covenanters*, 321 and 323–4. A listing of the artillery train in Munster in 1645 can be found in CUL *Ms Ee.3.40*, fos. 4v–5v; C. MacNeill, ed., *The Tanner Letters* . . . (IMC, Dublin, 1943), 315.

54. Firth, *Cromwell's Army*, 169 n.1.

55. [E. Hogan, ed.], *The History of the Warr in Ireland . . . by a British Officer of the Regiment of Sir John Clotworthy* (Dublin, 1873), 58.

56. Gilbert, *Contemporary History*, II, 55 and 102; J. S. Wheeler, *Cromwell in Ireland* (New York, 1999).

57. In contrast, the confederate army rarely made use of shipping to transport cannon, possibly because of the provincial division of its forces, although Preston shipped his guns from Athy (County Kildare) to Carlow on the river Barrow, a distance of about 12 miles (20km): Gilbert, *Contemporary History*, I, 262.

58. [J. Lodge], *Desiderata curiosa Hibernica* (2 vols., Dublin, 1772), II, 159; Carlyle, *Cromwell's Letters*, II, 191.

59. P. Walsh, 'Rinmore Fort: a seventeenth-century fortification at Renmore, Galway', *Journal of the Galway Archaeological and Historical Society*, XLI (1987–8), 120–1.

60. Hogan, *Warr in Ireland*, 16.

61. National Library of Ireland, *Ms* 4617 unfol.

62. Grosart, *Lismore Papers*, 1st series, V, 221; 2nd series, V, 120; R. Loeber, 'Biographical dictionary of engineers in Ireland, 1600–1730', *Irish Sword*, XIII (winter, 1977), 106; R. Caulfield, ed., *The Council Book of the Corporation of Youghal* (Guildford, 1878), 546–7 and 550.

63. Gilbert, *Contemporary History*, I, 102–3.

64. Gilbert, *History of the Irish Confederation*, VI, 84; Lord W. FitzGerald, 'The FitzGeralds of Ballyshannon (County Kildare), and their successors thereat', *County Kildare Archaeological Society Journal*, III (1899–1902), 425–52.

65. R. M. Young, ed., 'Diary of the proceedings of the Leinster army under Governor Jones', *Ulster Journal of Archaeology*, III (1897), 153–61, quoted at p. 157; HMC *Tenth Report, Appendix IV* (London, 1885), 87; D. F. Cregan, 'Some members of the confederation of Kilkenny', in S. O'Brien, ed., *Measgra I gCuimhne Mhichíl Uí Chléirigh* (Dublin, 1944), 43; M. J. Moore, *Archaeological Inventory of County Meath* (Dublin, 1987), 117.

66. Hogan, *Letters*, 20 and 95.

67. *CSPI*, 1633–47, 393 and 561; HMC *Tenth Report, Appendix IV*, 92.

68. J. Hill, *The Building of Limerick* (Cork, 1991), 31; Massari, 'Campaign', 221.

69. J. G. Simms, 'Hugh Dubh O'Neill's defence of Limerick, 1650–1651', *Irish Sword*, III (1957), 115–23; Gilbert, *Contemporary History*, III, 238–9 and 253. For a brief account see I. Gentles, *The New Model Army in England, Ireland and Scotland, 1645–1653* (Oxford, 1992), 377–80.

70. J. F. Fuller, 'Kinsale in 1641 and 1642', *Journal of the Cork Historical and Archaeological Society*, XIII (1907), 2; Loeber, 'Warfare and architecture', 395.

71. For example, when Galway fell in 1651, all surrounding castles also surrendered or were abandoned: R. Dunlop, ed., *Ireland under the Commonwealth* . . . (2 vols., Manchester, 1913), II, 616.

72. Gilbert, *Contemporary History*, II, 247–8.

73. R. Cox, *Hibernia Anglicana, or the History of Ireland from the Conquest thereof by the English to This Present Time* . . . (2 vols., London, 1689–90), II, 92; N. Barnard, *The Whole Proceedings of the Siege of Drogheda* (London, 1642), 71; Grosart, *Lismore Papers*, 1st series, V, 102. For instance, when the town of Bandon became an isolated enclave, men from the town assailed

seven castles in its neighbourhood, some of which they burnt and slighted, while others they subsequently maintained for the outlying defence of the town.

74. C. H. Firth, ed., *The Memoirs of Edmund Ludlow Lieutenant-General of the Horse in the Army of the Commonwealth of England 1625–1672* (2 vols., Oxford, 1894), I, 497.

75. BL *Eg* 81/21ff. Agreements of surrender to the Cromwellians make this abundantly clear and show widespread evidence of soldiers who were active farmers.

76. Firth, *Ludlow*, I, 498.

77. This, too, was true on the continent, where old-style fortifications in remote locations could still defy the full force of the Military Revolution: see Parker, *Military Revolution*, 8.

78. J. Lodge, *The Peerage of Ireland*, ed. M. Archdall (7 vols., Dublin, 1789) II, 141–3n.

79. F. Grose, *The Antiquities of Ireland* (2 vols., London, 1791), I, 83–4; Gilbert, *Contemporary History*, I, 82.

80. Gilbert, *History of the Irish Confederation*, IV, frontispiece; P. Lenihan, 'Aerial photography: a window on the past', *History Ireland*, I, no. 2 (1993), 9–13.

81. T. C. Croker, 'Narratives illustrative of the contests in Ireland in 1641 and 1690', *Camden Society*, XIV (1841), 16–19; Hazlett, 'History', 120; P. C. Power, *History of South Tipperary* (Cork, 1989), 66; M. Hickson, ed., *Ireland in the Seventeenth Century; or, the Irish Massacres of 1641* (2 vols., London, 1884), II, 108 and 117.

82. Croker, 'Narratives', 117–18.

83. Gilbert, *History of the Irish Confederation*, I, xlv; Gilbert, *Contemporary History*, III, 229; Grosart, *Lismore Papers*, 2nd series, V, 79.

84. Henry, 'Ulster exiles', 57–8; HMC *Ormonde Mss*, II, 191.

85. *Calendar of state papers . . . existing in the archives . . . of Venice, 1642–3* (London, 1925), 211. For further details see J. H. Ohlmeyer, 'Irish privateers during the civil war, 1642–50', *Mariner's Mirror*, LXXVI (May 1990), 120–1.

86. *Irish Monthly Mercury*, issue I (London, 1649), 3. Also see J. H. Ohlmeyer, 'The "Dunkirk of Ireland": Wexford privateers during the 1640s', *Journal of the Wexford Historical Society*, XII (1988–9), 23–4.

87. R. O'Ferrall and R. O'Connell, *Commentarius Rinuccinianus . . .* ed. Revd S. Kavanagh (IMC, 6 vols., Dublin 1932–49), I, 519–20, quoting Dr Walter Enos of Wexford (reference kindly communicated by Jane Ohlmeyer).

88. W. G. Ross, 'Military engineering during the Great Civil War, 1642–1649', in F. G. Day, ed., *Professional Papers of the Corps of Royal Engineers* (Royal Engineers Institute occasional papers London, 1887), XIII, 86–205.

89. Details in the excellent study by M. E. Lewis, 'The use of ordnance in early modern warfare, with particular reference to the English Civil War 1642-9' (Manchester University unpublished MA thesis, 1971). See also the useful review article of M. J. Braddick, 'An English military revolution?', *Historical Journal*, XXXVI (1993), 965-75.

90. BL *Eg* 917/25v: 'State of the kingdom of Ireland' by Sir A. Annesley and Sir W. Parsons, 10 Dec. 1646. Reference kindly communicated by Jane Ohlmeyer.

8. The Artillery Fortress as an Engine of European Overseas Expansion, 1480–1750

I am grateful to Tonio Andrade, Thomas Arnold, Bernard Bachrach, Edward Farmer, Alan Gallay, Richard Kagan, George Milner, John Nolan, John Richards, Sanjay Subrahmanyam, James Tracy and Nancy van Deusen for valuable suggestions concerning this essay.

1. D. Lombard, *Le sultanat d'Atjéh au temps d'Iskandar Muda (1607–36)* (Paris, 1967), 83–100; C. R. Boxer, 'The Achinese attack on Malacca in 1629, as described in contemporary Portuguese sources', in J. Bastin and R. Roolvink, eds., *Malayan and Indonesian Studies: Essays Presented to Sir Richard Winstedt on his Eighty-fifth Birthday* (Oxford, 1964), 105–21.

2. Niels Steensgaard discerned two stages in this process: first the arrival of the Portuguese, who enjoyed a crucial advantage over Asian traders because they did not have to sell their stock within a single monsoon season like their 'native' rivals, and the arrival of the Dutch, who deployed a centralized trade system and a single stock of capital (whereas the Portuguese had maintained hundreds of entrepreneurs under their protection). See 'Tourists, tents and traders. An interview with Niels Steensgaard', *Itinerario*, XVIII, no. 1 (1994), 36–7.

3. See R. Hassig, *Aztec Warfare: Imperial Expansion and Political Control* (Norman, 1988), 105–9 and 208–20; S. Subrahmanyam, *The Political Economy of Commerce: Southern India, 1500–1650* (Cambridge, 1990), chap. 5; and S. Chaudhury, 'Trade, bullion and conquest. Bengal in the mid-eighteenth century', *Itinerario*, XV, no. 2 (1990), 21–32.

4. A. R. Reid, *Southeast Asia in the Age of Commerce 1450–1680: II, Expansion and Crisis* (New Haven, 1993), 271.

5. The concept first appeared in F. C. Lane, *Venice and History* (Baltimore, 1966), chaps. 23 and 24, and was developed by N. Steensgaard, 'Violence and the rise of capitalism: F. C. Lane's theory of protection and tribute', *Review*, V (1983), 247–73. See also G. Parker, *The Military Revolution. Military Innovation and the Rise of the West, 1500–1800* (rev. edn.,

Cambridge, 2000), chaps. 3–4; and idem, ed., *The Cambridge Illustrated History of Warfare: The Triumph of the West* (Cambridge, 1995).

6. L. White Jr., *Medieval Religion and Technology. Collected Essays* (Berkeley, 1986), 149 (from 'Jacopo Aconcio as an engineer', first published in *AHR*, LXII (1967)).

7. Matteo Ricci to Juan Bautista Román, 13 Sept. 1584, quoted on page 25 above. However, Ricci was not quite correct: some geometrical defences have been discovered in Chinese sources: see J. Needham and R. D. S. Yates, *Science and Civilisation in China*, V, *Chemistry and Chemical Technology*, part 6, *Military Technology: Missiles and Sieges* (Cambridge, 1994), 260–5. Moreover, some Chinese vertical walls proved thick enough to resist even the most ferocious artillery bombardment: see page 212 above; on the very different response of Japan, see pages 214–16.

8. Ricci by no means stood alone in this: see the optimistic views of other Europeans in the Orient quoted on pages 20, 25–7 above.

9. See H. Koller, 'Die mittelalterliche Stadtmauer als Grundlage staatliche Selbstbewusstseins', in B. Kirchgässner and G. Scholz, eds., *Stadt und Krieg* (Sigmaringen, 1989), 9–25. France soon became the European centre of artillery warfare, but by the 1490s Spain had 180 large and medium pieces and five state-run gun and powder factories: see W. F. Cook, 'The cannon conquest of Nasrid Spain and the end of the Reconquista', *Journal of Military History*, LVII (1993), 52.

10. See the important chronology of the increasing force of artillery in C. J. Rogers, 'The military revolutions of the Hundred Years' War', in idem, ed., *The Military Revolution Debate* (Boulder, 1995), 68–73; and the brilliant studies of the spread of the 'new style' by A. Fara, *Il sistema e la città. Architettura fortificata dell' Europa moderna dai trattai alle realizzazion, 1464–1794* (Genoa, 1989); and idem, *La città da guerra nell' Europa moderna* (Turin, 1993).

11. A. Bernaldez, *Memorias*, quoted in Cook, 'The cannon conquest', 43; Machiavelli, *Art of War*, quoted in Parker, *Military Revolution*, 10. See also the similar views of the late fifteenth-century military engineer di Giorgio discussed in F. P. Fiore, 'L'architettura militare de Francesco di Giorgio: realizzazioni e trattati', in C. Cresti, A. Fara and D. Lamberini, eds., *Architettura militare nell' Europa del XVI secolo* (Siena, 1988), 40.

12. Machiavelli's 'Relazione di una vista fatta per fortificare Firenze', in S. Bertelli, ed., *Niccolo Machiavelli: Arte della guerra e scritti politici minori* (Milan, 1961), 295. See also the perceptive discussion of D. Lamberini, 'La politica del guasto. L'impatto del fronte bastionato sulle preesistenze urbane', in C. Cresti et al., *Architettura militare*, 223–34.

13. See the interesting discussion in J. F. Pernot, 'Guerre de siège et places-fortes', in V. Barrie-Curien, ed., *Guerre et pouvoir au XVIIe siècle* (Paris,

1991), 129–50; and in T. Arnold, 'Fortifications and the Military Revolution: the Gonzaga experience, 1530–1630', in Rogers, *Military Revolution Debate*, 201–26.

14. See A. S. Tosini, 'Cittadelle lombarde di fine '500: il castello di Milano nella prima età spagnola', in C. Cresti et al., *Architettura militare*, 207–17; S. Leydi, *Le cavalcate dell' ingegnero. L'opera di Gianmaria Olgiati, ingegnere militare di Carlo V* (Modena, 1989); and D. Parrott, 'The utility of fortifications in early modern Europe: Italian princes and their citadels, 1540–1640', *War in History*, VII (2000), 127–53. The Venetian Republic did the same: see M. E. Mallett and J. R. Hale, *The Military Organization of a Renaissance State. Venice c. 1400 to 1617* (Cambridge, 1984), 409–28.

15. Data taken from W. Brulez, 'Het gewicht van de oorlog in de nieuwe tijden. Enkele aspecten', *Tijdschrift voor Geschiedenis*, XCI (1978), 386–406, based *inter alia* on a comparison of the town plans made by Jacob van Deventer in the 1560s and by Johan Blaeu in the 1640s. For the spread of the artillery fortress in the Low Countries see C. van den Heuvel, *Papiere Bolwercken. De introductie van de Italiaanse stede- en vestingbouw in de Nederlanden (1540–1609) en het gebruik van tekeningen* (Alphen aan den Rijn, 1991).

16. J. Cruso, *Militarie Instructions for the Cavallrie* (Cambridge, 1632), 105; Roger Boyle, earl of Orrery, *A Treatise of the Art of War* (1677), quoted in Parker, *Military Revolution*, 16; J. Behr, *Der aufs Neuverschantzte Turenne* (1677), quoted in C. Duffy, *The Fortress in the Age of Vauban and Frederick the Great, 1660–1789* (London, 1985), 13–14. See also the useful discussion in F. Tallett, *War and Society in Early Modern Europe 1495–1715* (London, 1992), 50–4.

17. S. le Prestre de Vauban, *Mémoire pour servir d'instruction dans la conduite des sièges et dans la défense des places* (c. 1670, but misdated 1704: Leiden, 1740), 3–5, checked against the manuscript copy in the Anne S. K. Brown Military Collection, Hay Library, Providence, Rhode Island, fols. 1–1v.

18. S. le Prestre de Vauban, *Traité de l'attaque des places* (manuscript in the Anne S. K. Brown Military Collection, Hay Library, Providence, Rhode Island, in the same volume as the *Mémoire*, 2nd pagination, 1–2). This passage does not appear in Vauban, *De l'attaque et de la défense des places*, (2 vols., The Hague, 1737–42. but written c. 1704), although in other respects the two works are almost identical. The Brown manuscript appears to be an interim draft, written at some point between 1670 and 1704.

19. This ceased to be true only when various governments in the later eighteenth century chose to invest in roads rather than in walls. The cost was much the same, but the speed of movement permitted by the new road network finally rendered a defensive system based on heavily fortified strongpoints both ineffective and uneconomical. See Parker, *Military Revolution*, chap. 5;

reinforced by H. Eichberg, 'Zirkel der Vernichtung oder Kreislauf des Kriegs-gewinns? Zur Ökonomie der Festung im 17. Jahrhunder', in Kirchgässner and Scholz, *Stadt und Krieg*, 105–24.

20. See details in J. Vogt, *Portuguese Rule on the Gold Coast, 1469–1682* (Athens, Ga., 1979), 19–31; and A. W. Lawrence, *Trade Castles and Forts of West Africa* (Stanford, 1964), 103–79 and pls. 2–36.

21. D. Pacheco Pereira, in J. Barradas de Carvalho, ed., *Esmeraldo de situ orbis* (Lisbon, 1991), 190–1; Zain al-Din, *Tohfut-ul-Mujahideen*, in D. Lopes, ed., *Historia do Portugueses no Malabar por Zinadim* (Lisbon, 1898), 73 (see further data on the forts of the 'Franks' at pp. 36, 47 and 58–9). Pacheco, who played a prominent role in the exploration of the West African coast in the 1480s and served in Portuguese Asia in 1500–5, wrote his treatise between 1505 and 1508. Zain al-Din composed his account in the 1580s.

22. Full details in Lawrence, *Trade Castles and Forts*. This concentration is easily explained. Elsewhere in West Africa, the inlets and lagoons allowed the Europeans to control trade with the artillery aboard their ships, but the 'Gold Coast' offered no natural harbours, and the ships therefore had to anchor some distance from the coast; hence the need for fortresses ashore. (My thanks to Graham Connah for this point.)

23. See the magnificent illustrations of these locations in R. Moreira, ed., *História das fortificações portuguesas no mundo* (Lisbon, 1989), 114, 150–3, 170–1, 176–9, 256–7 and 259. The same late transition from medieval to modern architecture occurred in Spanish North Africa: see J. B. Vilar, *Mapas, planos y fortificaciones hispánicos de Tunez (siglos XVI–XIX)* (Madrid, 1991), 354–474, and idem, *Mapas, planos y fortificaciones hispánicos de Marruecos (siglos XVI–XX)* (Madrid, 1992), 337–454.

24. Cairati also supervised the construction of artillery fortresses at Basseim and Damão in India. See details in C. R. Boxer and C. de Azevedo, *Fort Jesus and the Portuguese in Mombasa 1593–1729* (London, 1960); J. Kirkman, *Fort Jesus. A Portuguese Fortress on the East African Coast* (Oxford, 1974); and W. A. Nelson, *Fort Jesus of Mombasa* (Edinburgh, 1994).

25. I. Cid, ed., *O livro das plantas de todas as fortalezas, cidades e povoações do Estado da India oriental* (3 vols., Lisbon, 1992) is a modern version of the manuscript in the Evora public library containing colour depictions of 48 forts (a sketch-map of their location may be found in I, 21). The manuscript was also published, with black and white plates and many additional sub-sequent printed sources, in A. B. de Bragança Pereira, *APO*, IV, part 2. Another manuscript copy in BNM (*Ms* 1190 and *Ms Res.* 202) contains 53 plates. For details on these and three other extant manuscript copies of the work, see *PMC*, V, 59ff. On the new circuit of walls at Malacca, see P. Y. Manguin, 'Of fortress and galleys. The 1568 Acehnese siege of Malacca, after a contemporary bird's-eye view', *Modern Asian Studies*, XXII (1988), 607–28.

26. Cid, *O livro*, II, 132-5.

27. H. Soly, 'De bouw van de Antwerpse citadel (1567-71). Sociaal-economische aspecten', *Tijdschrift voor Geschiedenis*, XXI (1976), 549-78. Because every part of the construction process was paid for (by the citizens of Antwerp), the detailed surviving accounts of this enterprise offer an important index of overall cost. Labour represented almost three-quarters of the expenditure. Rijksarchief in Gelderland, Arnhem, *Archief van het huis Bergh*, 539, unfol., Herman van den Berg to Archduke Albert, 24 Jan. 1604, claimed that he had managed to fortify Venlo in the 'new style' for 9000 florins (£900) instead of 60,000, through the use of forced labour. For the higher cost of defending Italian-style defences, see Mallett and Hale, *Military Organization*, 445.

28. 'O livro Duarte Barbosa', in *Colecção de noticias para a historia e geografa das nações ultramarinas*, iI (2nd edn., Lisbon, 1867), 262.

29. The view of W. G. L. Randles, 'The artilleries and land fortifications of the Portuguese and of their adversaries in the early period of the discoveries', in *Limits of the land and sea: proceedings of the VIIIth international reunion for the history of nautical science* (Cascais, 1998), 329-40.

30. A. Bausani, ed., *Lettera di Giovanni da Empoli [1514]* (Rome, 1970), 132; letter from 19 Portuguese captives in Malacca to Albuquerque, 6 Feb. 1510, in R. A. de Bulhão Pato, ed., *Cartas de Affonso de Albuquerque* (Lisbon, 1893), III, 5. The captives claimed that Malacca's 10,000 buildings included only 500 of adobe, the rest being of 'straw like those of India'. However, the mosques at least were made of stone because, as Empoli recorded, Albuquerque recycled them for 'A famosa'. For a brilliant survey of Malacca before the conquest, see L. F. F. R. Thomaz, 'The Malay sultanate of Melaka', in A. R. Reid, ed., *Southeast Asia in the Early Modern Era. Trade, Power and Belief* (Ithaca, 1993), 69-90.

31. Bausani, *Lettera di Giovanni da Empoli*, 135-6. The explicit reference to gunpowder weapons among the defenders of Malacca contradicts the oft-quoted account in the 'Serajah Melayu', which stresses the fear and surprise caused by the Europeans' bombardment: 'What may be this round weapon that yet is sharp enough to kill us?': C. C. Brown, ed., 'Serajah Melayu or "Malay Annals"', *Journal of the Malay Branch of the Royal Asiatic Society*, XXV, nos. 2-3 (1952), 158. However, the 'Serajah' was compiled from oral traditions in 1612, whereas Empoli (an eyewitness) wrote in 1514; moreover, although the Malaccans may have possessed gunpowder weapons, it seems unlikely that they were as effective, or were deployed as effectively, as those of the Europeans.

32. A. De Gubernatis, *Storia dei viaggatori italiani nelle Indie orientali* (Livorno, 1875), 376 (from an anonymous Italian account of the fall of Malacca).

33. Bausani, *Lettera di Giovanni da Empoli*, 138. Empoli reported the same

pattern at the capture of Goa in 1510: as soon as the city fell, Albuquerque began to construct a stone castle (p. 121).

34. Bulhão Pato, *Cartas de . . . Albuquerque*, I, 127, Albuquerque to King Manuel, 30 Nov. 1513; *'artelheria e armas e fortalezas he ja tudo tornado a nosa husamça'* – alas, he did not provide the details.

35. See R. O. W. Goertz, 'Attack and defence techniques in the siege of Chaul, 1570-1', in L. de Albuquerque and I. Guerreiro, eds., *Il Seminário internacional de história indo-portuguesa*, (Lisbon, 1985), 265-92. See also the useful general overview of M. N. Pearson. *The Portuguese in India*, New Cambridge History of India, I, book 1 (Cambridge, 1991), 56-9.

36. R. A. de Bulhão Pato, ed., *Documentos remetidos da India ou livros das Monções* (Lisbon, 1893), I, 90-100, Philip III to the viceroy of India, 18 Jan. 1607. Characteristically, the king concluded his long hortatory letter by regretting that he could send no money to implement any of the new policies enjoined.

37. See, for example, ibid., I, 1-18, Philip III to the viceroy of India, 26 Feb. 1605, inquiring about the progress of fortification in all the major centres of Portuguese India; and ibid., I, 322-36, same to same, 13 and 17 Feb. 1610, ordering improvements to the fortification of numerous bases with artillery bastions (while again regretting that no money could be sent). After a hiatus following the conclusion of a truce with the Dutch, the pressure resumed: see ibid., IV, 273ff., same to same, 20 Jan. 1618, ordering the viceroy to repair and modernize all fortifications in the Estado da India; ibid., VI, 297ff. and 439ff., same to same, 22 and 24 Mar. 1620; and so on.

38. Ibid., IV, 168-9, Philip III: instructions to Viceroy Redondo, 21 Mar. 1617. See also the reminder, Philip III to viceroy, 23 Jan. 1618, and the viceroy's discouraging replies of 8 Feb. 1619 and 8 Feb. 1620 (ibid., IV, 287-8, and V, 326-8).

39. Details from P. E. Peiris, *Some Documents relating to the Rise of the Dutch Power in Ceylon, 1602-1670* (Colombo, 1929), 67-8; and P. Baldaeus, *Naauwkeurige beschrijvinge van Malabar en Choromandel* (Amsterdam, 1672), I, 155 (Negapatam) and II, 106 (Colombo). See also the excellent illustrated descriptions in W. A. Nelson, *The Dutch Forts of Sri Lanka: The Military Monuments of Ceylon* (Edinburgh, 1984).

40. B. Dmytryshyn, E. A. P. Crownhart-Vaughan and T. Vaughan, eds., *Russia's Conquest of Siberia* (Portland, 1985), 22 and 41 (a woodcut illustration of an *ostrog*); and G. V. Lantzeff and R. A. Pierce, *Eastward to Empire: Exploration and Conquest on the Russian Open Frontier to 1750* (London, 1973), 110-14 and 124.

41. M. L. Díaz-Trechuelo Spínola, *Arquitectura española en Filipinas (1565-1800)* (Seville, 1959), 43-4, Juan Bautista Román to Philip II, 6 July 1588, and Governor Desmariñas to Philip II, 20 June 1591.

42. Ibid., passim; and R. Reed, *Colonial Manila: The Context of Hispanic Urbanism and Process of Morphogenesis* (Berkeley, 1978), chap. 5.

43. See the list of *cédulas* in A. de Altolaguirre y Duvale, *Gubernación espiritual y temporal de las Indias* (6 vols.), Colección de documentos inéditos de Ultramar, 2nd series, XXI–XXVI (Madrid, 1927–32), II, 36–52, under the rubric *De las fortificaciones y fuerzas*.

44. See P. E Hoffman, *The Spanish Crown and the Defense of the Spanish Caribbean, 1535–85: Precedent, Patrimonialism and Royal Parsimony* (Baton Rouge, 1980), passim; and K. R. Andrews, *The Spanish Caribbean: Trade and Plunder, 1530–1630* (New Haven, 1978), 81–107. See also the instructions given to Juan de Texeda in 1588 and to Juan Bautista Antonelli in 1593 to fortify the main harbours of the Caribbean, in D. de Encinas, *Cedulario indiano* (Madrid, 1596; 4 vols., facsimile edn., Madrid, 1945–6), IV, 46–52 and 68–70.

45. G. Lohmann Villena, *Las defensas militares de Lima y Callao* (Seville, 1964), 1, Philip II to the viceroy of Peru, 9 Apr. 1582. See also the useful survey of J. A. Calderón Quijano, *Las defensas indianas en la Recopilación de 1680. Precedentes y regulación legal* (Seville, 1994).

46. AGS *Guerra Antigua* 81/346, *consulta* of 20 Nov. 1576, concerning Juan Bautista Antonelli's criticism of planned fortifications at Cartagena de Indias. See also D. Angulo Iñiguez, *Bautista Antonelli. Las fortificaciones americanas del siglo XVI* (Madrid, 1942).

47. Lohmann Villena, *Las defensas*, 93 and 116; J. A. Calderón Quijano, *Fortificaciones en Nueva España* (2nd edn., Madrid, 1984), passim; and G. Guarda, *Flandes Indiano. Las fortificaciones del reino de Chile, 1541–1826* (Santiago de Chile, 1990), 13–14 and 60–74 (Valdivia), 49–55 (the Straits of Magellan) and 150–1 (Valparaíso). See also J. Gorbea Trueba, 'La arquitectura militar en la Nueva España', *Estudios de historia Novohispana*, II, (1967), 213–32; and A. Cámara, *Fortificación y ciudad en los reinos de Felipe II (Madrid, 1998)*.

48. See F. A. Dutra, 'Matías de Albuquerque and the defense of Northeastern Brazil, 1620–1626', *Studia* (1973), 117–66; and R. M. Delson, 'The beginnings of professionalization in the Brazilian military: the eighteenth-century Corps of Engineers', *The Americas*, LI (1995), 562–4.

49. See E. B. O'Callaghan and B. Fernow, eds., *Documents relative to the Colonial History of the State of New York* (15 vols, Albany, 1853–67), I, 365, 422, 440–1 and 499; V. 280; B. Fernow, ed., *The Records of New Amsterdam from 1653 to 1674* (7 vols., Albany, 1897), I, 72–3; and A. C. Aimone, 'New Netherland's military experience', *De halve maen*, LI (Oct. 1976), 15–17, and LI (Jan. 1977), 13–14.

50. On these and other fortresses, see A. Gallay, *Colonial Wars of North America, 1512–1763. An Encyclopedia* (New York, 1966), 600–11 (Québec),

664–7 (St Augustine), and so on; and I. K. Steele, *Warpaths. Invasions of North America* (Oxford, 1994), chaps. 2–6.

51. C. T. Hodges, 'Private fortifications in seventeenth-century Virginia: a study of six representative works', in T. R. Reinhard and D. J. Pogue, eds., *The Archaeology of Seventeenth-Century Virginia*, (Richmond, 1993), 192–3 and 199; and the numerous entries in Gallay, *Colonial Wars*.

52. For details, see P. W. Powell, *Soldiers, Indians and Silver: The Northward Advance of New Spain, 1550–1600* (2nd edn., Berkeley, 1969), 151. For the order to create a fortress in Mexico City, see Altolaguirre y Duvale, *Gobernación espiritual*, II, 45 (*cédula* of May 1536).

53. Guarda, *Flandes Indiano*, 182–98 ('El frente interno'). A plan of Angol in 1637 shows the typical geometrical design used against the Araucanians (see p. 198).

54. Abbé Delaporte, *Le voyageur françois* (Paris, 1769), quoted by S. Wilson, 'Colonial fortifications and military architecture in the Mississippi Valley,' in J. F. McDermott, ed., *The French in the Mississippi Valley* (Urbana, 1965), 103.

55. Wilson, 'Colonial fortifications', 119; Gallay, *Colonial Wars*, 114–16; and D. Buisseret, *Historic Illinois from the Air* (Chicago, 1990), 28–9, 38–9 and 40 (an excellent map of the French fortresses in North America during the Seven Years' War). Fort de Chartres has now been restored to its mid-eighteenth-century condition (information kindly supplied by Benjamin Rota).

56. For useful sketches, see Gallay, *Colonial Wars*, 58 (Bacon's Rebellion), 489–91 (the loss of New Netherland) and 499–500 (its recovery), and 666 (San Marcos). On New Spain, see Powell, *Soldiers, Indians and Silver*, passim.

57. Mather quoted by J. L. Axtell, *The European and the Indian. Essays in the Ethnohistory of Colonial North America* (Oxford, 1981), 145; Gallay, *Colonial Wars*, 124–9, on the Chickasaw. I thank Alan Gallay for enlightenment on this point.

58. See Hassig, *Aztec Warfare*, and idem, *War and Society in Ancient Mesoamerica* (Berkeley, 1992), passim.

59. Details in W. Hubbard, *The History of the Indian Wars in New England* (Boston, 1677; ed. S. G. Drake, Roxbury, 1865), I, 146–7; and P. M. Malone, *The Skulking Way of War: Technology and Tactics among the New England Indians* (Lanham, 1991), 73–4. The fort in the 'Great Swamp' thus resembled an Irish 'crannog': see the description of one from the 1650s on page 187 above. The Narragansetts also constructed a stone fort with two bastions that remained undiscovered by the colonists until after the war; Malone, *Skulking Way*, 74–5.

60. Thomas Mathew's contemporary, account, quoted by A. L. Ferguson, 'The Susquehannock fort on Pitscataway Creek', *Maryland Historical Magazine*, XXXVI (1941), 1–9. For other examples, see Steele, *Warpaths*, 66–7 and

113; and Gallay, *Colonial Wars*, 219–22 (on Fort Fox, with two contemporary maps) and 424–5 (Indian forts in Maryland). See also the judicious remarks of L. H. Keeley, *War Before Civilization* (Oxford, 1996), 71–81; and A. Gallay, *The Indian Slave Trade: The Rise of the Indian Empire in the American South, 1670–1717* (New Haven, 2002), 172–5, 180–91, 269–74.
61. For another surprisingly successful indigenous replication of European techniques of fortification, albeit from outside this period, see J. Belich, *The New Zealand Wars and the Victorian Interpretation of Racial Conflict* (Harmondsworth, 1986), 49–50, 106–7, 251–2 and 294–7.
62. See the perceptive remarks of J. Aubin in *Bulletin critique des annales islamologiques*, VI (1990), 153–5. D. Ralston, *Importing the European Army: The Introduction of European Military Techniques and Institutions into the Extra-European World, 1600–1914* (Chicago, 1990), 43–78, begins his analysis of 'the reform of the Ottoman army' only in 1750 and therefore sheds little light on this; but see the interesting case studies of C. F. Finkel, 'French mercenaries in the Habsburg-Ottoman war of 1593–1606: the desertion of the Papa garrison to the Ottomans in 1600', *Bulletin of the School of Oriental and African Studies*, LV (1992), 451–71; R. Murphey, 'The Ottoman attitude towards the adoption of western technology: the role of the *Efrenci* technicians in civil and military applications', in J. L. Bacqué-Grammont and P. Dumont, eds., *Contributions à l'histoire économique et sociale de l'empire ottoman* (Louvain, 1983), 287–98; and S. Christensen, 'European-Ottoman military acculturation in the late Middle Ages', in B. P. McGuire, ed., *War and Peace in the Middle Ages* (Copenhagen, 1987), 227–51.
63. On the Venetian fortification programme in Croatia/Dalmatia, see Mallett and Hale, *Military Organization*, 429–60; and J. Vrandecic, 'The military revolution comes to Croatia' (forthcoming). On Habsburg efforts in Hungary, see L. Zangheri, 'Gli architetti italiani e la difesa dei territori dell'Impero minacciati dai turchi', in Cresti et al., *Architettura militare*, 243–51; and R. Schäfer, 'Festungsbau an der Türkengrenze. Die Pfandschaft Rann im 16. Jahrhundert', *Zeitschrift des historisches Vereins für Steiermark*, LXXV (1984), 31–59.
64. A. M. Mallet, *Les travaux de Mars, ou l'art de la guerre* (3rd edn., The Hague, 1696), III, 317–33, from 'Livre sixième: De la milice des Turcs', with a discussion of prints of Satu Mare, Budapest, Szolnok and Neuhausel (Nové Zámsky). This section did not appear in Mallet's first edition of 1672, but was added in the second in 1684–5, following the relief of Vienna.
65. A point made by W. J. Hamblin, 'Gunpowder weapons and medieval Islamic military theory' (a paper graciously sent to me by Dr Hamblin in October 1989). On the remarkable logistical achievements of the Ottoman empire, see C. Finkel, *The Administration of Warfare: The Ottoman Military Campaigns in Hungary, 1593–1606*; Beihefte zur Wiener Zeitschrift für die

Kunde des Morgenlandes, XIV (Vienna, 1988); and R. Murphey, *Ottoman Warfare 1500-1700* (London, 1998).

66. See W. F. Cook, *The Hundred Years' War for Morocco. Gunpowder and the Military Revolution in the Early Modern Muslim World* (Boulder, 1994), 193. On the spread of Western military techniques to other Islamic states in North Africa, see A. C. Hess, *The Forgotten Frontier. A History of the Sixteenth-century Ibero-African Frontier* (Chicago, 1978), and idem, 'Fire-arms and the decline of Ibn Khaldun's military elite', *Archivum ottomanicum*, IV (1972), 173-99.

67. See Cook, *The Hundred Years' War*, 258.

68. Details from A. R. Reid, 'Sixteenth-century Turkish influence in western Indonesia', *Journal of Southeast Asian History*, X, no. 3 (1969), 395-414.

69. Piero Strozzi – a Florentine, hence his rejoicing – writing on 10 Dec. 1510, just after the capture of Goa, quoted by Subrahmanyam, *Political Economy*, 255. See numerous other examples of 'renegades' in A. D. da Costa, 'Os Portugueses e os Reis da India', *Boletim do Instituto Vasco da Gama*, XIII (1932), 1-45; XV (1932), 1-38; XVIII (1933), 1-28; and XX (1933), 1-40; and M. A. Lima Cruz, 'Exiles and renegades in early sixteenth-century Portuguese Asia', *Indian Economic and Social History Review*, XXIII (1986), 249-62, esp. 259-62.

70. D. F. Lach and E. J. van Kley, *Asia in the Making of Europe* (3 vols., Chicago, 1993), III, 726, quoting François Bernier and John Fryer. See also S. Subrahmanyam, 'The *Kagemusha* Effect: the Portuguese, firearms and the state in early modern South Asia', *Moyen Orient et Océan Indien*, IV (1987), 97-123; J. F. Richards, *The Mughal Empire*, New Cambridge History of India, I, book 5 (Cambridge, 1993), 220-2; N. Manucci, *Storia do Mogor, or Mogul India 1653-1708* (ed. W. Irvine, 4 vols, London, 1906-8), I, 309 and 313; and F. Bernier, *Travels in the Mogul Empire, AD 1656-68* (ed. A. Constable, London, 1891), 31-2. (Bernier served as Aurangzeb's personal physician.)

71. Manucci, *Storia do Mogor*, I, 183-4; William Methwold (writing in the 1620s), quoted in Lach and Van Kley, *Asia in the Making of Europe*, III, 1023. See also S. Toy, *The Strongholds of India* (London, 1957), 53-60 (Golconda) and 123 (Delhi); and J. F. Richards, *Mughal Administration in Golconda* (Oxford, 1975), 48-51.

72. See N. Schatzman Steinhardt, 'Representations of Chinese walled cities in the pictorial and graphic arts', in J. D. Tracy, ed., *City Walls. The Urban Enceinte in Global Perspective* (Cambridge, 2000), 421. Even the earliest Chinese pictograms denoting 'town', in the Shang oracle bones of the second millennium BC, were written in the shape of a square or rectangular enclosure, above the drawing of a man: see Needham and Yates, *Science and Civilisation in China*, V, part 4, 243.

73. Quotations from H. Knollys, *Incidents in the China War of 1860, Compiled from the Private Journals of General Sir Hope Grant* (Edinburgh, 1875), 198–9; and J. Ouchterlony, *The Chinese War* (London, 1844), 174–5. Note, however, that (according to Ouchterlony) rapid naval broadsides did destroy the granite-built gun batteries on the Pearl river defending Canton.

74. Conversely, Western fortifications might succumb to Chinese attack: in 1661–2 the Ming loyalist leader Coxinga – albeit with the aid of a renegade – conducted a successful siege of Fort Zeelandia, the Dutch headquarters on Taiwan; see the account of C. R. Boxer, 'The siege of Fort Zeelandia and the capture of Formosa from the Dutch, 1661–23', *Transactions and Proceedings of the Japan Society of London*, XXIV (1926–7), 16–47, reprinted in idem, *Dutch Merchants and Mariners in Asia, 1602–1795* (London, 1988), chap. 3; for the role of the renegade, see p. 41. See also H. Franke, 'Siege and defense of towns in medieval China', in F. A. Kierman and J.K. Fairbank, eds., *Chinese Ways in Warfare* (Cambridge, Mass., 1974), 151–201; and Needham and Yates, *Science and Civilisation in China*, V, part 4, 260–5.

75. See Bausani, *Lettera di Giovanni da Empoli*, 132–3, written in 1514, and specifically contrasting the 'walled cities, houses, buildings, castles of great strength, and artillery of every sort like our own' found in China with the lack of fortifications in Indonesia.

76. Lach and Van Kley, *Asia in the Making of Europe*, III, 1202 and 1216 (based on the accounts of Louis XIV's envoy to the court of Siam, Simon de la Loubère, published in 1691, and of the French missionary Nicholas Gervaise, published in 1688).

77. L. Cadière, 'Le quartier des Arènes. I. Jean de la Croix et les premiers Jésuites', *Bulletin des amis du Vieux Hué*, XIV, no. 4 (1924), 312 (citing a report of 1683); Lach and Van Kley, *Asia in the Making of Europe*, III, 1264(from the 1631 'Relation' of Christoforo Borri), 1281 (citing Alexandre de Rhodes in 1641), and 1298. For other examples of 'flight' as a reaction, see also Parker, *Military Revolution*, 122 (Malaya).

78. See V. B. Lieberman, 'Europeans, trade and the unification of Burma c. 1540–1620', *Oriens extremus*, XXVII, no. 2 (1980), 203–26; Reid, *Southeast Asia*, 78–82; and Lach and Van Kley, *Asia in the Making of Europe*, III, 1122–46.

79. See Lach and Van Kley, *Asia in the Making of Europe*, III, 1124–8 and 1193–4 for details.

80. See Reid, *Southeast Asia*, 87–8.

81. Details from Lach and Van Kley, *Asia in the Making of Europe*, III, 1444 (from the eyewitness description of Seyger van Rechteren, who visited Makassar in 1635); G. Vermeulen, *De gedenkwaerdige Voyagie* (Amsterdam, 1677), 67; and Reid, *Southeast Asia*, 88. A map of this date from the 'Secret Atlas of the East India Company' showing Sombaopu, in colour, is in A. R.

Reid, 'Southeast Asian cities before colonialism', *Hemisphere*, XXVIII, no. 3 (1983), 144.

82. Idem, 'The rise of Makassar', *Review of Indonesian and Malaysian Affairs*, XVII (1983), 141-2. However (Professor Reid informs me), one can see today from the substantial ruins that the bricks used were thinner than European ones.

83. Personal communication from Anthony Reid, 24 Mar. 1995; see also Lach and Van Kley, *Asia in the Making of Europe*, III, 1446 (citing Domingo Fernández de Navarrete, who visited Makassar in 1657).

84. Details from the eyewitness accounts in Reid, 'The rise of Makassar', 150; Vermeulen, *Voyagie*, 53-71; and W. Schouten, *Reys-togten naar en door Oost Indien*, (2nd edn., Amsterdam, 1708), 85-93. See also the pictures of the Dutch bombardment of Pannakkukang in Reid, *Southeast Asia*, II, 279, and in Schouten, *Reys-togten* (plate 18 above). L. Andaya, *The Heritage of Arung Palakka: A History of South Sulawesi (Celebes) in the Seventeenth Century* (The Hague, 1981), 130-3, offers a good account of the fall of Makassar to the combined forces of the Dutch and of Arung Palakka's Bugis.

85. Ricci, quoted on page 195 above; L. Fróis, *História do Japão* (ed. J. Wicki, Lisbon, 1984), V, 315 (sub anno 1591-2, part of an interesting chapter comparing various types of building in Europe and Japan); see also III, 141-2 (for 1578), IV, 54-5 (for 1584), and so on. See the discussion in J. P. Oliveira e Costa, 'A introdução das armas de fogo no Japão pelos Portugueses a luz da história do Japão de Luís Fróis', *Estudos orientais*, III (1992), 126-8. Other, more favourable, European descriptions of Japanese castles appear in M. Cooper, ed., *They Came to Japan. An Anthology of European Reports on Japan, 1543-1640* (Berkeley, 1965), 131-41.

86. See Parker, *Military Revolution*, 142-3, and references at p. 232.

87. For Nobunaga's love of military conversation, see A. Valignano, *Sumario de las cosas de Japón* (1583; ed. J. L. Alvarez-Taladriz, Tokyo, 1954), 152. For the spontaneous development of musketry volley, see Parker, *Military Revolution*, 140.

88. Richards, *The Mughal Empire*, 288-9; and N. Perrin, *Giving up the Gun. Japan's Reversion to the Sword* (New York, 1979). In Ch'ing China too, despite the keen interest of many government officials in military technology, most innovations involving firearms remained the work of foreigners of limited practical experience: see J. Waley-Cohen, 'China and Western technology in the later eighteenth century', *AHR*, XCVIII (1993), 1525-44. See also Ralston, *Importing the European Army*.

89. Information kindly provided by Sanjay Subrahmanyam and Blair B. Kling. See also Parker, *Military Revolution*, 134; and H. Furber, *John Company at Work. A Study of European Expansion in India in the Late Eighteenth Century* (Cambridge, Mass., 1948), 204f.

90. For a discussion of the continuing characteristics of Western warfare, see Parker, *Cambridge Illustrated History of Warfare*, 364–73.

PART III: SIN, SALVATION AND SUCCESS DENIED

1. P. Chaunu, 'Une histoire religieuse sérielle', *Revue d'histoire moderne et contemporaine*, XII (1965), 3.
2. For comprehensive studies of two countries, based on impressive mass data-processing, see J. Dupâquier, ed., *Histoire de la population française*, II (Paris, 1988); E. A. Wrigley and R. Schofield, *The Population History of England, 1541–1871. A Reconstruction* (2nd edn., Cambridge, 1989), and E. A. Wrigley et al., *English Population History from Family Reconstruction 1580–1837* (Cambridge, 1997). For the scale of Inquisition records and some preliminary statistics, see G. Henningsen and J. Tedeschi, eds., *The Inquisition in Early Modern Europe. Studies on Sources and Methods* (DeKalb, Ill., 1986).

9. Success and Failure during the First Century of the Reformation

An early version of this paper was prepared for the Anglo-Polish historical Conference held in Warsaw in 1978. My thanks are due to numerous commentators, both then and later: in general to various lecture audiences in Britain, Ireland, Europe and North America; in particular to Simon Adams, Robert Bireley, Thomas A. Brady, James K. Cameron, Patrick Collinson, Nicholas Davidson, Geoffrey Dickens, Alastair Duke, Geoffrey Elton, Carl G. Estabrook, Dermot Fenlon, Christopher R. Friedrichs, Ian Green, Christopher Haigh, John Henderson, James M. Kittelson, Philomena Kilroy, Bruce Lenman, William S. Maltby, Heiko A. Oberman, Jane Ohlmeyer, Wolfgang Reinhard, Bob Scribner, Lesley M. Smith and Gerald A. Strauss. Anyone familiar with the field will immediately realize that all these scholars could scarcely be expected to agree with a single interpretation of Reformation history, whether offered by me or anyone else. It may be that none of them will wish to accept my argument; certainly none of them should be held responsible for my errors. But I am still most grateful for all of their comments, criticisms and references.

1. Recorded, with many other striking examples, by R. B. Manning, 'The spread of the popular reformation in England', *Sixteenth-century Essays and*

Studies (later, *Sixteenth Century Journal*), I (1971), 35–52. Other sources given in notes 7 and 13 below.

2. E. M. Kern, 'The "universal" and the "local" in episcopal visitations', in M. Reinhart, ed., *Infinite Boundaries. Order, Disorder and Reorder in Early Modern German Culture* (Kirksville, Mo., Sixteenth Century Essays and Studies, XL), 35–54, makes much the same point. For three recent case studies, see C. S. Dixon, *The Reformation and Rural Society: The Parishes of Brandenburg-Ansbach-Kulmbach, 1528–1603* (Cambridge, 1996); M. C. Questier, *Conversion, Politics and Religion in England, 1580–1625* (Cambridge, 1996); and A. M. Poska, *Regulating the People: The Catholic Reformation in Seventeenth-century Spain* (Leiden, 1998) – with special reference to the Galician diocese of Ourense. See also note 62 below.

3. See, for two examples, D. Cressy, *Bonfires and Bells. National Memory and the Protestant Calendar in Elizabethan and Stuart England* (Berkeley, 1989); and R. Hutton, *The Rise and Fall of Merry England: The Ritual Year, 1400–1700* (Oxford, 1994).

4. K. S. Bottigheimer and U. Lotz-Heumann, 'The Irish reformation in European perspective', *Archiv für Reformationsgeschichte*, LXXXIX (1998), 268–309.

5. For details, see A. Prosperi, *Tribunali della coscienza: inquisitori, confessori, missionari* (Turin, 1996); R. B. Bottigheimer, *The Bible for Children. From the Age of Gutenberg to the Present* (New Haven and London, 1996); G. Fragnito, *La Bibbia al rogo: la censura ecclesiastica e i volgarizzamenti della Scrittura, 1471–1605* (Bologna, 1997); and P. Rodríguez, *El catechismo romano ante Felipe II y la inquisición española. Los problemas de la introducción en España del Concilio de Trento* (Madrid, 1998).

6. Details from E. Rhodes, 'Spain's misfired canon: the case of Luis de Granada's *Libro de la oración y meditación*', *Journal of Hispanic Philology*, XV (1990), 43–66, quotation at p. 56. Many thanks to Andrew Pettegree, to Karl and Ruth Bottigheimer and to Ute Lotz-Heumann for help in framing this introduction.

7. G. Strauss, 'Success and failure in the German Reformation', *Past and Present*, LXVII (1975), 30–63; idem, *Luther's House of Learning: Indoctrination of the Young in the German Reformation* (Baltimore, 1978), quotation at p. 307. Strauss addressed various objections and criticisms in 'The Reformation and its public in an age of orthodoxy', in R. P. Hsia, ed., *The German People and the Reformation* (Ithaca, NY, 1988), 194–214.

8. A. G. Dickens, *The German Nation and Martin Luther* (London, 1974), 182. The most celebrated formulation of this view appeared in B. Moeller, *Reichsstadt und Reformation* (Gutersloh, 1962), tr. H. C. E. Midelfort and M. U. Edwards as *Imperial Cities and the Reformation* (Philadelphia, 1972). It was not, of course, universally true – there were some towns (such as

Cologne, Mainz, Liège and other cities of episcopal residence) where Protestantism made little or no progress, and some rural areas (especially in South Germany and the Alpine lands) where reformed views appear to have gained widespread support – but Dickens's formulation fits the facts in most areas. For the Low Countries, see J. Decavele, *De dageraad van de reformatie in Vlaanderen (1520–1565)* (2 vols., Brussels, 1975); J. G. C. Venner, *Beeldenstorm in Hasselt, 1567: achtergrond en analyses van een rebellie tegen de prins-bisschop van Luik* (Leeuwaarden, 1989); for France, see H. Heller, *The Conquest of Poverty: The Calvinist Revolt in Sixteenth-Century France* (Studies in Medieval and Reformation Thought, XXXV, Leiden, 1986); for England, see the various articles in C. Haigh, ed., *The English Reformation Revised* (Cambridge, 1987); for Scotland, see M. Lynch, 'From privy kirk to burgh church: an alternative view of the process of Protestantisation', in N. A. T. MacDougall, ed., *Church, Politics and Society: Scotland, 1408–1929* (Edinburgh, 1983), 85–96; for Ireland, see N. Canny, 'Why the Reformation failed in Ireland: *une question mal posée*', *Journal of Ecclesiastical History*, XXX (1979), 423–50; see also the retort of Karl Bottigheimer, 'The failure of the Reformation in Ireland: *une question bien posée*', *Journal of Ecclesiastical History*, XXXVI, (1985), 196–207. For the 'failed Reformation' in some cities, see H. C. Rublack, *Gescheiterte Reformation: Frühreformatorische und protestantische Bewegungen in süd- und westdeutschen geistlichen Residenzen* (Stuttgart, 1978). For evidence of a South German rural reform movement, see P. Blickle, *Die Gemeindereformation: Die Menschen des 16. Jahrhunderts auf dem Weg zum Heil* (Munich, 1985); F. Conrad, *Reformation in der bäuerliche Gesellschaft: Zur Rezeption reformatorischer Theologie im Elsass* (Veröffentlichungen des Instituts für europäische Geschichte Mainz, CXVI, Wiesbaden, 1984). Far more detailed research is required on this topic, however, before we can be sure that the Blickle school has reconstructed the religion of ordinary country people rather than merely that of their local village elites.

9. Although the practice of visitation was ancient – dating back to the Synod of Tarragona in AD 516 – the aims of sixteenth-century visitors were new, for they investigated religious beliefs and practices, whereas medieval visitors had surveyed mainly church fabric and Christian instruction. It is true that, in the Middle Ages, the Inquisition had asked searching questions of lay persons concerning their religious beliefs, but – even in a 'hotbed of heresy' like Montaillou – the interrogations only concerned suspects. The idea of going out into the villages and examining the entire lay congregation was entirely new. See H. Jedin, 'Einführung', in E. W. Zeeden and H. Molitor, eds., *Die Visitation im Dienst der kirchlichen Reform* (Katholisches Leben und Kirchenreform im Zeitalter der Glaubensspaltung, XXV, Münster, 1967), 4f.

10. Luther's preface to his *Kleine Catechismus* (Wittenberg, 1529), in *D. Martin Luthers Werke: Kritische Gesamtausgabe* (Weimar, 1883), XXX.1, 265.

11. See the fascinating examples in Strauss, 'Success and failure', passim; idem, *Luther's House*, chaps. 12–13.

12. See, for example, G. A. Benrath, 'Das kirchliche Leben Heidelbergs in den Jahren 1593 bis 1595', *Heidelberger Jahrbuch*, X (1966), 49–82; idem, 'Les visites pastorales dans le Palatinat électoral au 16e siècle', in *Sensibilité religieuse et discipline ecclésiastique: les visites pastorales en territoires protestants (Pays Rhénanes, Comté de Montbéliard, Pays de Vaud), XVIe–XVIIe siècles* (Recherches et documents, XXI, Strasbourg, 1975), 68–77; B. Vogler, 'Die Entstehung der protestantischen Volksfrömmigkeit in der rheinischen Pfalz zwischen 1555 und 1619', *Archiv für Reformationsgeschichte*, LXXII (1981), 158–95.

13. Dutch historians were among the first to recognize that Protestantism failed to affect the population at large until the early seventeenth century – partly because the state resolutely refused to coerce its citizens to attend any church – but they believed the Dutch experience to be unique: see P. Geyl, 'De protestantisiering in Noord Nederland', in idem, *Kernprobleme van onze geschiedenis* (Utrecht, 1937); L. J. Rogier, *Geschiedenis van het katholicisme in Noord-Nederland in de 16e en 17e eeuwen* (2 vols., Amsterdam, 1945). For more recent surveys, see J. A. de Kok, *Nederland op de breuklijn Rome-Reformatie: numerieke aspekten van protestantisiering en katholieke herleving in de noordelijke Nederlanden, 1580–1880* (Assen, 1964); but see also the important debate in *A. A. G. Bijdragen*, XIII (1965), 149–80; A. T. van Deursen, *Plain Lives in a Golden Age. Popular Culture, Religion and Society in Seventeenth-century Holland* (Cambridge, 1991), part 4; and, above all, A. C. Duke, *Reformation and Revolt in the Low Countries* (London, 1990), chaps. 9–11.

14. For a selection of regional examples, see F. D. Price, 'Gloucester diocese under Bishop Hooper', *Transactions of the Bristol and Gloucester Archaeological Society*, LX (1939), 51–151; W. G. Hoskins, *Essays in Leicestershire History* (Liverpool, 1950), 19–22; C. Hill, 'Puritans and "the dark corners of the land"', *Transactions of the Royal Historical Society*, 5th series, XIII (1963), 77–109.

15. See the useful overview by M. Lynch, 'Calvinism in Scotland, 1559–1638', in M. Prestwich, ed., *International Calvinism, 1541–1715* (Oxford, 1985), 225–55, esp. pp. 247ff. By 1596 there were still only 539 ministers to serve the 1080 parishes in the kingdom, 'and the land is overflowit with atheisme and all kind of vice, ther being above foure hundreth paroch kirks destitute of the ministrie of the word' – not counting the numerous vacant parishes in the highlands and islands: T. Thomson, ed., *Acts and Proceedings*

of the General Assembly of the Kirk of Scotland (3 vols., Maitland Club, XLIX, Edinburgh, 1839–45), III, 876.

16. An inquiry conducted in 1622 revealed that there were only 380 certified preaching ministers distributed among the 2492 parishes of the established church: see A. Clarke, 'Varieties of uniformity: the first century of the Church of Ireland', in W. J. Sheils and D. Wood, eds., *The Churches, Ireland and the Irish* (Studies in Church History, XXV, Oxford, 1989), 118. See also the articles by Canny and Bottigheimer cited in n.above; A. Ford, *The Protestant Reformation in Ireland, 1590–1641* (Frankfurt, 1985).

17. Strauss, *Luther's House*, 303, 307f.

18. Many Catholics in the 1540s and 1550s expressed alarm at the Protestants' 'success'. The examples in the text come from *Monumenta Ignatiana*, i.7, *Sancti Ignatii de Loyola . . . epistolae et instructiones* (Monumenta Historica Societatis Iesu, XXIV, Madrid, 1908), no. 4709, Loyola to Canisius (in Vienna), 13 Aug. 1554; J. I. Tellechea Idigoras, *Fray Bartolomé Carranza: documentos históricos* (5 vols., Archivo documental español, XVIII–XIX, 1–2, XXXII–XXXIII, Madrid, 1962–76), III, 29 (Interrogatorio 62 in the Carranza trial, 1562). The frequency of Bibles in English parish churches has been confirmed from selected churchwardens' accounts by R. Hutton, 'The local impact of the Tudor Reformation', in Haigh, *English Reformation Revised*, 118.

19. Indeed some returns listed only failings. At Strasbourg, for example, the title of the annual summary of returns changed after 1562 from 'A Relation of the Church Visitation' to '[A List of] Several Errors and Failings in the Church Visitation'; see J. M. Kittelson, 'Successes and failures in the German Reformation: the report from Strasbourg', *Archiv für Reformationsgeschichte*, LXXIII (1982), 159. This should not surprise us. The collection of grievances to be turned into *gravamina* for redress was a standard procedure of government in early modern Germany. It is also worth noting that, in England, the Puritans collected their lists of 'scandalous clergy' mainly in order to convince the government of the need for a more stringent Reformation: see P. Collinson, *The Religion of Protestants: The Church in English Society, 1559–1625* (Oxford, 1982), 100–8.

20. Kittelson, 'Successes and failures'; idem, 'Visitations and popular religious culture: further reports from Strasbourg', in K. C. Sessions and P. N. Bebb, eds., *Pietas et Societas: New Trends in Reformation Social History* (Sixteenth Century Essays and Studies, IV, Kirksville, 1988), 89–101. It should be noted, however, that the territory ruled by Strasbourg was very small – fourteen parishes – so that the obstacles to effective evangelism were far less than in (say) rural Saxony. The only extensive rural areas that seem to have been Protestantized in the sixteenth century with any real success were those with important local industries such as Flanders and Holland: see J. Decavele,

Het eind van een rebelse droom: opstellen over het calvinistisch bewind te Gent, 1577–1584 (Ghent, 1984), 32–60; Duke, *Reformation and Revolt*, 231f.

21. W. Scott and J. Bliss, eds., *The Works of William Laud* (7 vols., Oxford, 1847–60), II, 317–70; Collinson, *Religion of Protestants*, 92, quoting Hall's *Concio synodica* of 1624. See also the more optimistic survey of English clerical achievements by P. Collinson, 'Shepherds, sheepdogs and hirelings: the pastoral ministry in post-Reformation England', in W. J. Sheils and D. Wood, eds., *Ministry, Clerical and Lay* (Studies in Church History, XXVI, Oxford, 1989), 185–220.

22. *Register*, II, 925–6. See also chapter 10 above.

23. Kittelson, 'Visitations and popular religious culture', 91. 'Systematic' studies of visitation records have also been called for by P. T. Lang, 'Die Bedeutung der Kirchenvisitation für die Geschichte der frühen Neuzeit', *Rottenberger Jahrbuch für Kirchengeschichte*, III (1984), 207–12; also the contributors to E. W. Zeeden and P. T. Lang, eds., *Kirche und Visitation: Beiträge zur Erforschung des frühneuzeitlichen Visitationswesens in Europa* (Spätmittelalter und frühe Neuzeit: Tübinger Beiträge zur Geschichtsforschung, XIV, Stuttgart, 1984).

24. See details in Strauss, *Luther's House*, 279: no one was able to give a satisfactory answer. See also the 'ridiculous and impossible' questions from ecclesiastical visitors in England, in R. W. Ketton-Cremer, *Norfolk in the Civil War: A Portrait of a Society in Conflict* (2nd edn., Norwich, 1985), 65f. and 240–52.

25. Strauss, *Luther's House*, 278.

26. There is an excellent account of the origins and course of the first Saxon visitation in S. C. Karant-Nunn, *Luther's Pastors: The Reformation in the Ernestine Countryside* (Transactions of the American Philosophical Society, LXIX, no. 8, Philadelphia, 1979), 21–7. Note, however, that there were also 'follow-up' questions that could not be prepared in advance. At p. 26 Karant-Nunn records that one visitor prepared 'typical Catholic retorts to correct answers in order to see how firm the pastors' conviction was'. See also Strauss, *Luther's House*, 263f.

27. I. Green, *The Christian's ABC: Catechisms and Catechizing in England, c. 1530–1740* (Oxford, 1996) (with a list of all catechisms written for use in England and a content analysis based on a detailed study of 60 of them); Strauss, *Luther's House*, 161–5 (suggesting that perhaps one in every three Lutheran pastors 'drew up a substantial catechism of his own'). In the Dutch Republic in the seventeenth century, catechisms were more common in schools than Bibles: see E. P. de Booy, *De weldaet der scholen: het plattelandsonderwijs in de provincie Utrecht van 1580 tot het begin der 19e eeuw* (Amsterdam, 1977), 43.

28. S. H. Hendrix, 'Luther's impact on the sixteenth century', *Sixteenth Century Journal*, XVI (1985), 4.

29. See U. Mazzone and A. Turchini, eds., *Le visite pastorali: analisi di una fonte* (Annali dell' Istituto storico italo-germanico, XVIII, Bologna, 1985); J. Aubin and D. Ramada Curto, eds., *La recherche en histoire de Portugal*, I (Paris, 1989), 49–55; E. W. Zeeden, ed., *Repertorium der Kirchenvisitationsakten aus dem 16. und 17. Jahrhundert in Archiven der Bundesrepublik Deutschland* (Stuttgart, 1982–); C. Nubola and A. Turchini, eds., *Fonti ecclesiastiche per la storia sociale e religiosa d'Europa: XV–XVIII secolo* (Bologna, 1999).

30. J. Richardson, *A Short History of the Attempts that Have Been Made to Convert the Popish Natives of Ireland to the Establish'd Religion* (London, 1712), iv–v.

31. See S. T. Nalle, *God in La Mancha. Religious Reform and the People of Cuenca, 1500–1650* (Baltimore, 1992), chap. 3; P. Heath, *The English Parish Clergy on the Eve of the Reformation* (London, 1969), 77–90; F. Heal and R. O'Day, Introduction, in idem, eds., *Church and Society in England: Henry VIII to James I* (London, 1977), 4; I. Luxton, 'The Reformation and popular culture', in ibid., 65. However, there is also much evidence of rising educational standards among the clergy in (for example) R. R. Post, *Kerkelijke verhoudingen in Nederland voor de Reformatie* (Utrecht, 1954); O. Vasella, *Untersuchungen über die Bildungsverhältnisse im Bistum Chur* (Jahresbericht der historisch-antiquarischen Gesellschaft von Graubünden, LXII, Chur, 1932), 125–70; F. Rapp, *Réformes et Réformation dans le diocèse de Strasbourg, 1450–1525* (Paris, 1974).

32. P. Collinson, *The Birthpangs of Protestant England: Religious and Cultural Change in the Sixteenth and Seventeenth Centuries* (London, 1988), 74. The Protestants' dismissal of 'good works' as 'supererogatory', and their concepts of 'justification' and 'predestination', may have made their message even harder for ordinary people to grasp because it left very little for them to *do* except read (if they could), listen and think. See also the perceptive remarks of Duke, *Reformation and Revolt*, 263–7; C. Eire, *War against the Idols: The Reformation of Worship from Erasmus to Calvin* (Cambridge, 1986), 10–25; P. L. Berger, *The Sacred Canopy: Elements of a Sociological Theory of Religion* (New York, 1969), 123–49.

33. An interesting modern parallel is the attempt to create and educate 'socialist man' in the various countries of Eastern Europe after 1948. By 1990 the result seemed to most observers to be more 'failure' than 'success'.

34. Details quoted by R. Engelsing, *Analphabetentum und Lektüre: Zur Sozialgeschichte des Lesens in Deutschland zwischen feudaler und industrieller Gesellschaft* (Stuttgart, 1973), 28ff.; see also, however, the cautionary comments of R. Gawthrop and G. Strauss, 'Protestantism and literacy in early modern Germany', *Past and Present*, CIV (1984), 31–55.

35. I. Green, ' "Reformed pastors" and *bons curés*: the changing role of the parish clergy in early modern Europe', in Sheils and Wood, *Ministry, Clerical and Lay*, 282.

36. Details from M. U. Edwards, 'Statistics on sixteenth-century printing', in P. N. Bebb and S. Marshall, eds., *The Process of Change in Early Modern Europe: Essays in Honor of Miriam Usher Chrisman* (Athens, Ohio, 1988), 152f. and 161; R. Yaron, 'Ein Truber-Fund in Jerusalem', *Byblos*, XXVII (1978), 204–20. See also the admirable general remarks of E. Eisenstein, *The Printing Press as an Agent of Change* (Cambridge, 1979), 303–450; N. Z. Davis, 'Printing and the people', in idem, *Society and Culture in Early Modern France* (Stanford, 1975), 189–226; the articles in H.-J. Köhler, ed., *Flugschriften als Massenmedium der Reformationszeit* (Stuttgart, 1981).

37. See, for example, the studies of D. Cressy, *Literacy and the Social Order: Reading and Writing in Tudor and Stuart England* (Cambridge, 1980), chap 8; R. A. Houston, *Scottish Literacy and the Scottish Identity: Illiteracy and Society in Scotland and Northern England, 1600–1800* (Cambridge, 1985), chap. 5.

38. See examples in M. Aston, *Lollards and Reformers* (London, 1984), 199ff.; E. Cameron, *The Reformation of the Heretics: The Waldenses of the Alps, 1480–1580* (Oxford, 1984), 66; K. Thomas, 'The meaning of literacy in early modern Europe', in G. Baumann, ed., *The Written Word: Literacy in Transition* (London, 1986), 104f. An interesting example of clever but illiterate children being trained to memorize passages of Scripture and the catechism, and then pass it on, appears in D. C. Mactavish, ed., *Minutes of the Synod of Argyll, 1639–61* (2 vols., Scottish History Society, 3rd series, XXXVII–XXXVIII, Edinburgh, 1943–4), II, 170.

39. The evidence here is of various sorts. It includes the testimony of visitors to Scottish churches who observed that the majority of the congregations – female as well as male – followed the weekly lesson in their own Bibles; the existence all over northern Germany of a network of *Winkelschulen* ('corner schools') which, although transient and casual, offered cheap elementary education to large numbers of girls as well as boys; and the claims of several trustworthy contemporaries that they had taught themselves to read (and sometimes to write). See T. C. Smout, 'Born again at Cambuslang: new evidence on popular religion and literacy in eighteenth-century Scotland', *Past and Present*, XCVII (1982), 114–27; C. R. Friedrichs, 'Whose house of learning? Some thoughts on German schools in post-Reformation Germany', *Historical Education Quarterly*, XXII (1982), 731–7; M. Spufford, 'First steps in literacy: the reading and writing experiences of the humblest seventeenth-century spiritual autobiographers', *Social History*, IV (1979), 405–35.

40. Complaints taken from Karant-Nunn, *Luther's Pastors*, 9ff.; J. A. Hoeppner Moran, 'Clerical recruitment in the diocese of York, 1340–1530: data and commentary', *Journal of Ecclesiastical History*, XXXIV (1983), 54.

Figures from M. Bowker, 'The Henrician Reformation and the parish clergy', in Haigh, *English Reformation Revised*, 75–93; R. Whiting, *The Blind Devotion of the People: Popular Religion and the English Reformation* (Cambridge, 1989), 138. It should be remembered, however, that Protestantism did not require as many ministers as Catholicism because, on the one hand, one man could preach to hundreds while many chantry priests were required to say masses for souls and, on the other, most reformed pastors were aided in their pastoral duties by lay readers, elders and deacons.

41. Details from Karant-Nunn, *Luther's Pastors*, 38–52; K. E. Wrightson, *English Society, 1580–1680* (London, 1982), 207f.; W. R. Foster, *The Church before the Covenants: The Church of Scotland, 1596–1638* (Edinburgh, 1975), 156–72. For an example of the same financial problems facing reformed pastors in the Dutch Republic, see C. C. Hibben, *Gouda in Revolt: Particularism and Pacifism in the Revolt of the Netherlands, 1572–1588* (Utrecht, 1983), 114–18. Of course, many rural priests *before* the Reformation had also been very poorly paid.

42. R. Baxter, *Gildas Salvanius: The Reformed Pastor* (London, 1655); quoted in Green, ' "Reformed pastors" and *bons curés*', 258.

43. *Opus epistolarum D. Erasmi*, eds. P. S. and H. M. Allen (12 vols., Oxford, 1906–58), VII, 366, Erasmus to Pirckheimer, 20 Mar. 1528; F. Paulsen, *Geschichte des gelehrten Unterrichts* (3rd edn., 4 vols., Leipzig, 1919), I, 201. University enrolments throughout Germany did indeed fall dramatically in the 1520s, and did not regain their healthy earlier levels until after 1555: see figures in D. Hay, 'Schools and Universities', in G. R. Elton, ed., *The New Cambridge Modern History*, II, *The Reformation, 1520–59* (Cambridge, 1958), 431–3; W. J. Wright, 'Evaluating the results of sixteenth-century educational policy: some Hessian data', *Sixteenth Century Journal*, XVIII (1987), 411–26.

44. *Early Records of the University of St Andrews* (Scottish History Society, 3rd series, III, Edinburgh, 1926), 154–9 and 262–72; C. A. Tukker, 'The recruitment and training of Protestant ministers in the Netherlands in the sixteenth century', in D. Baker, ed., *Miscellanea historiae ecclesiasticae*, III (Leuven, 1970), 212 n. 4.

45. For some further examples, see J. B. Neveux, *Vie spirituelle et vie sociale entre Rhin et Baltique au XVIIe siècle* (Paris, 1967), part 1, chap. 1.

46. In the province of Holland, for example, only 30 out of 179 parishes had a minister by 1573 (when Catholic worship was prohibited), and only 111 (or 62 per cent) had one by the end of 1578. In all, probably only 250 pastors were active in the province during these six years – a total that can scarcely compare with the 1500 or so secular clergy resident there before the Reformation. Where there had been one priest for every 60 parishioners, there was now only one minister for every 350. Of course the 1500 priests had not been spread evenly throughout the province, but even so they were no doubt more widely spread than the 250 pastors. See Duke, *Reformation and Revolt*, chap. 9.

47. See, for example, the appeals of several newly established churches in Holland to the Dutch church in London between 1572 and 1578, pleading for ministers: J. H. Hessels, ed., *Ecclesiae Londino-Batavae archivum* (4 vols., Cambridge, 1887–97), III.1, docs. 207, 210, 220, 310, 312 and 488.

48. Details in Karant-Nunn, *Luther's Pastors*, 9ff. (R. W. Scribner believed that the total number of former Catholic clergy who became Lutheran pastors in Saxony may have been higher than one-third: personal communication, 11 May 1989); Duke, *Reformation and Revolt*, 221f.; Rogier, *Geschiedenis van het katholicisme in Noord-Nederland*, I, 16f.

49. The classic study of G. Donaldson, 'The parish clergy and the Reformation', in D. MacRoberts, ed., *Essays on the Scottish Reformation, 1513–1625* (Glasgow, 1962), 129–44, has been somewhat modified by the figures in C. H. Hawes, *Scottish Parish Clergy at the Reformation, 1540–1574* (Scottish Record Society, new series, III, Edinburgh, 1972), which argues that fewer than 500 of the 3400 Scottish Catholic clergy in post in 1559 changed their allegiance to the reformed church. Nevertheless, they made up about one-half of the early reformed ministry.

50. C. Cross, 'Priests into ministers: the establishment of Protestant practice in the city of York, 1530–1630', in P. N. Brooks, ed., *Reformation Principle and Practice: Essays in Honour of Arthur Geoffrey Dickens* (London, 1980), 203–25, argued that so many ex-priests and ex-monks stayed on in the city between 1533 and 1553 that York in effect remained Catholic until Mary formally restored the Roman faith. Likewise, under Elizabeth, of the 268 ministers recorded in the diocese of Gloucester in 1563, 70 had been Marian priests and a further 84 had been both Marian priests and Protestant pastors under Edward VI.

51. B. Vogler, 'La politique scolaire entre Rhin et Moselle: l'exemple du Duché de Deux-Ponts, 1555–1619', *Francia*, III (1975), 236–320, estimated that by 1620 there was one school per parish in the Rhine Palatinate, Hessen-Kassel and parts of Saxony, Brunswick and Württemberg (pp. 261–2). The record of lowland Scotland was almost as good by the later seventeenth century: see Houston, *Scottish Literacy*, 113–15.

52. The Palatinate nevertheless enjoyed a number of advantages in clerical terms: its livings were relatively rich and well endowed; it was supplied by two major universities (Heidelberg and Strasbourg); and it was easily accessible to refugee ministers from elsewhere. See B. Vogler, *Le clergé protestant rhénan au siècle de la Réforme, 1555–1619* (Strasbourg, 1976), 84–7 and 361–4.

53. D. Stevenson, 'Deposition of ministers in the church of Scotland under the covenanters, 1638–51', *Church History*, XLIV (1975), 321–35; G.

Donaldson, 'The emergence of schism in seventeen-century Scotland', in D. Baker, ed., *Schism, Heresy and Religious Protest* (Studies in Church History, IX, Cambridge, 1972), 277-94.

54. Details in I. Green, 'The persecution of "scandalous" and "malignant" parish clergy during the English Civil War', *EHR*, XCIV (1979), 507-31; idem, *The Re-establishment of the Church of England, 1660-1663* (Oxford, 1978), chap. 8; J. H. Pruett, *The Parish Clergy under the Later Stuarts: The Leicestershire Experience* (Urbana, 1978), chap. 1.

55. Details from G. Parker, *The Dutch Revolt* (rev. edn., London, 1985), 154; Kittelson, 'Visitations and popular religious culture', 91f.; L. J. Abray, *The People's Reformation: Magistrates, Clergy, and Commons in Strasbourg, 1500-1598* (Ithaca, NY, 1985), 96ff.; A. Egler, *Die Spanier in der linkrhein-ischen Pfalz, 1620-1632: Invasion, Verwaltung und Rekatholisierung* (Mainz, 1971), 134 and 149; F. Maier, *Die bayerische Unterpfalz im dreis-sigjährigen Krieg: Besetzung, Verwaltung und Rekatholisierung* (New York, 1990), 142ff. and 289ff. See also the perceptive general remarks on war and confessionalization in R. P. Hsia, *Social Discipline in the Reformation: Central Europe, 1550-1750* (London, 1989), 130-3.

56. Quoted by H. Mitchell, 'The world between the literate and the oral traditions in eighteenth-century France: ecclesiastical instructions and popular mentalities', in R. Runte, ed., *Studies in Eighteenth-century Culture*, VIII (Madison, 1979), 48. Grégoire followed up his denunciation of patois with a questionnaire, sent to all parishes of France, which revealed scarcely three million Frenchmen able to speak 'pure French'. See A. Gazier, ed., *Lettres à Grégoire sur les patois de France, 1790-4: documents inédits* (Paris, 1880), 293. It is therefore noteworthy that the first religious works published in patois – whether Breton, Provençal or Occitan, and whether written by a Huguenot or Catholic pen – only appeared in the 1640s or later, a full century after the Reformation took root in France. See C. Anatole, 'La Réforme tridentine et l'emploi de l'Occitane dans le pastorale', *Revue des langues romanes*, LXXVII (1967), 1-29. However, some religious items in patois circulated in manuscript: A. Croix, *La Bretagne aux 16e et 17e siècles: la vie, la mort, la foi* (Paris, 1981), 1207, records manuscript Breton catechisms from 1575, 1622 and 1646.

57. Hessels, *Ecclesiae Londino-Batavae archivum*, III.1, 278-9, consistory of Rotterdam to the Dutch church in London, 4 Jan. 1575. It was the same in Germany, where most intellectuals spoke a form of High German that had originated in Saxony (Luther's homeland) in the fourteenth century. Two hundred years later it was still almost as unintelligible as Latin to the ordinary folk of Switzerland or Brunswick. See L. E. Schmidt, *Untersuchungen zur Entstehung und Struktur der neuhochdeutschen Schriftsprachen* (Cologne, 1966), passim.

58. Richardson, *Short History*, 11, 14f. and 26f.; V. E. Durkacz, *The Decline of the Celtic Languages: A Study of Linguistic and Cultural Conflict in Scotland, Wales and Ireland from the Reformation to the Twentieth Century* (Edinburgh, 1983), chap. 1.

59. Cromwell, quoted in Mactavish, *Minutes of the Synod of Argyll*, II, xiv. For further details, see ibid., viii–x, 36f., 170 and 198; W. Ferguson, 'The problems of the established church in the west highlands and islands in the eighteenth century', *Record of the Scottish Church History Society*, XVII (1969), 15–31. A slightly more optimistic view was taken by J. Kirk, 'The kirk and the highlands at the Reformation', *Northern Scotland*, VII (1986), 1–22; idem, 'The Jacobean church in the highlands, 1567–1625', in L. Maclean, ed., *The Seventeenth Century in the Highlands* (Inverness, 1986), 24–51. Even the creation of the Society in Scotland for the Propagation of Christian Knowledge in the 1690s did not help much in the highlands and islands, for its schools were at first not allowed to teach in Gaelic, and places like Glenelg were left to the devices of such pastors as the Revd Daniel Maclachlan, whose ministry did not long survive the publication of his pamphlet *An Essay upon Improving and Adding to the Strength of Great Britain and Ireland by Fornication* in 1755. He died in Jamaica.

60. See G. Williams, *History of Wales, III, Wales c.1415–1642, Recovery, Reorientation and Reformation* (Oxford, 1987), 295 and 314ff.; A. H. Dodd, *Studies in Stuart Wales* (Cardiff, 1952), 39ff.; O. Williams, 'The survival of the Welsh language after the union of England and Wales: the first phase, 1536–1642', *Welsh Historical Review*, II (1964–5), 67–93.

61. J. Brinsley, *A Consolation for our Grammar Schooles* (London, 1622), quoted with other interesting material in V. Salmon, 'Missionary linguistics in seventeenth-century Ireland and a North American analogy', *Historiographia linguistica*, XII (1985), 321–49. See also Clarke, 'Varieties of uniformity'.

62. Quotations from *The Workes of that Learned Minister of God's Holy Word Mr William Pemble* (3rd edn., London, 1635), 558f. (from his sermon 'The Mischiefe of Ignorance'); S. Ford, *A Sermon of Catechizing* (London, 1655), fos. ii–iii. See also the telling examples quoted in Wrightson, *English Society*, 183–221. Recent historians have suggested, however, that the problem was not 'profanity', but 'conformity': that most ordinary people preferred consistency and tradition in their faith, adhering to the old ways simply because they *were* the old ways. See the perceptive remarks (for three separate areas) by Whiting, *Blind Devotion of the People*, chaps. 12–13; Vogler, 'Entstehung der protestantischen Volksfrömmigkeit', 191–5; Duke, *Reformation and Revolt*, chap. 10.

63. The following discussion owes much to the pioneering studies of R. W. Scribner. See, above all, his excellent survey of the German material, 'Oral culture and the diffusion of Reformation ideas', in his *Popular Culture and*

Popular Movements in Reformation Germany (London, 1987), chap. 3. See also the important discussion of the cultural forms used by English Protestants in Collinson, *Birthpangs of Protestant England*, chap. 4.

64. J. van Biezen and M. Veldhuys, eds., *Souterliedekens, 1540: facsimile-edition* (1984), 31. This was the first complete rhymed psalter to be printed in Europe: based on a Dutch version of the Bible that derived from Luther's German translation, it went through 33 editions by 1613.

65. A. F. Mitchell, ed., *The Gude and Godlie Ballatis* (Scottish Text Society, XXXIX, Edinburgh, 1897), passim, quotation at pp. 158–60. See also the prominence of religious musical pamphlets in the items surveyed by K. C. Sessions, 'Song-pamphlets: media changeover in sixteenth-century German publicization', in G. P. Tyson and S. S. Wagonheim, eds., *Print and Culture in the Renaissance: Essays on the Advent of Printing in Europe* (Newark, Del., 1986), 110–19. Collinson, *Religion of Protestants*, 238, notes the growth of a 'godly consensus', once Protestantism had been firmly established in England, that 'psalms and ballads could never coexist'. On the general role of music in post-Reformation Christianity, see J. A. Bossy, *Christianity in the West, 1400–1700* (Oxford, 1985), 161–7.

66. See R. B. Bottigheimer, 'Martin Luther's children's Bible', *Wolfenbütteler Notizen zur Buchgeschichte*, XV, no.2 (1990), 152–61, and idem, 'Bible-reading, "Bibles" and the Bible for children in early modern Germany', *Past and Present*, CXXXIX (1993), 66–89. See also R. W. Scribner, *For the Sake of Simple Folk: Popular Propaganda for the German Reformation* (Cambridge, 1981).

67. Further analysis available in C. Andersson, 'Popular imagery in German Reformation broadsheets', in Tyson and Wagonheim, *Print and Culture*, 120–50; C. C. Christensen, *Art and the Reformation in Germany* (Athens, Ohio, 1979); T. Watt, *Cheap Print and Popular Piety, 1550–1640* (Cambridge, 1991); Collinson, *Birthpangs of Protestant England*, 115–21 (quotation from p. 119).

68. N. Manuel, *Die Totenfresser*, ed. F. Vetter (Leipzig, 1923), I, 19–21, 96–8, 109–10 and 201–14. The play is discussed at length in S. E. Ozment, *The Reformation in the Cities: The Appeal of the Reformation to Sixteenth-century Germany and Switzerland* (New Haven, 1975), 111–16; but see also Andersson, 'Popular imagery', 136–43.

69. Stockwood quoted in J. W. Blench, *Preaching in England during the Late Fifteenth and Sixteenth Centuries: A Study of English Sermons, 1450–c.1600* (Oxford, 1964), 306. See also the prohibition of mirth in the 1580s quoted in ibid., p. 310: 'For the voyce of the preacher ought to be the voyce of the cryer, which should not pipe to make the people daunce, but mourne to make them weepe.'

70. From C. Jackson, ed., 'The Life of Master John Shaw', in *Yorkshire*

Diaries and Autobiographies in the Seventeenth and Eighteenth Centuries (Surtees Society, LXV, Durham, 1877), 138f.; discussed, *inter alia*, in C. Hill, *Society and Puritanism in Pre-Revolutionary England* (London, 1964), 250f. On English mystery plays and other multi-media performances, see Luxton, 'Reformation and popular culture'; Cross, 'Priests into ministers', 219; and M. Spufford, *Small Books and Pleasant Histories. Popular Fiction and Its leadership in Seventeenth-century England* (London, 1981), 154.

71. This point was also made by A. N. Galpern, *The Religion of the People in Sixteenth-century Champagne* (Cambridge, Mass., 1976), 84. I. Cowan, *The Scottish Reformation* (London, 1978), 187–8, notes that the kirk of Scotland also systematically banned religious drama; while Collinson, *Birthpangs of Protestant England*, 101, quotes a particularly revealing statement from the dean of York, who forbade the performance of a religious play in 1567 on the grounds that 'Though it was plausible forty years ago, and would now also of the ignorant sort be well liked, yet now in this happy time of the Gospel I know the learned will mislike it.' In Poland, Germany and the Netherlands, it is true, Protestants (like Catholics) wrote religious plays; however, they were often for performance in schools rather than in public. See J. A. Parente, *Religious Drama and the Humanist Tradition: Christian Theater in Germany and in the Netherlands, 1500–1680* (Leiden, 1987), passim; J. Tazbir, 'Le rôle de la parole dans la propagande religieuse polonaise', *Revue d'histoire moderne et contemporaine*, XXX (1983), 28.

72. J. J. Scarisbrick, *The Reformation and the English People* (Oxford, 1984), 163. See the similar statement of P. Collinson, 'The Elizabethan church and the new religion', in C. Haigh, ed., *The Reign of Elizabeth I* (London, 1984), 171. The opposite approach of the Counter-Reformation church is stressed by P. Parent, *L'architecture des Pays-Bas méridionaux (Belgique et nord de la France) aux XVIe, XVIIe et XVIIIe siècles* (Paris, 1925), who noted that the sermons, sculptures, paintings, organs, sumptuous materials and architectural form of baroque churches in the area were all carefully designed in order to convey exactly the same overall impression.

73. *Workes . . . of Mr William Pemble*, 558. See above, pages 237–8.

74. T. A. Brady, *Turning Swiss: Cities and Empire, 1450–1550* (Cambridge, 1985), 151ff. For example, many of the criticisms voiced by Luther in his tracts of 1520 (against the use of Roman Law and other 'novelties') also appeared in the *gravamina* drawn up by the Diet of Worms in 1521: see G. Strauss, ed., *Manifestations of Discontent in Germany on the Eve of the Reformation* (Bloomington, 1971), x and 52–63.

75. This problem is examined in depth by E. G. Léonard, 'La notion et le fait de l'église dans la Réforme protestante', in *Relazioni del X congresso di scienzi storichi* (5 vols., Florence, 1955), IV, 75–110. See also three excellent case studies: E. Cameron, 'The "godly community" in the theory and practice of

the European Reformation', in W. J. Sheils and D. Wood, eds., *Voluntary Religion* (Studies in Church History, XXIII, Oxford, 1986); P. Collinson, 'The English Conventicle', in ibid.; J. Kirk, 'The "privy kirks" and the antecedents: the hidden face of Scottish Protestantism', in ibid. For a concrete example, take Ralph Josselin, minister of Earls Colne in Essex, who divided his congregation into those who 'seldom hear', 'my sleepy hearers' (the majority) and 'our society' of godly souls. He chose to concentrate his efforts on the last category, although it numbered in the end only 34 communicants. See Wrightson, *English Society*, 220, drawing on A. Macfarlane, ed., *The Diary of Ralph Josselin, 1616–1683* (London, 1976).

76. Duke, *Reformation and Revolt*, 261; further details kindly communicated to me by Duke. It could be argued that, since Haggai was the first prophet to be sent to the people of Israel after the Babylonish captivity, and was charged with restoring the temple and true worship in Jerusalem, his book was of unusual importance; but 20 sermons on 23 verses still seems excessive.

77. E. Axon, ed., *Oliver Heywood's Life of John Angier of Denton* (Chetham Society, new series, XCVII, Manchester, 1937), 79.

78. Selden, quoted in R. P. Lessenich, *Elements of Pulpit Oratory in Eighteenth-century England* (Cologne, 1972), 1. It is true that Samuel Pepys did prefer sermons, but the views of a man who masturbated while at church – even (according to his own testimony) in the queen's chapel during the Christmas service in 1667 – should perhaps not be taken as representative. See R. Latham and W. Matthews, eds., *The Diary of Samuel Pepys* (10 vols., Berkeley, 1979–83), VII, 365; VIII, 588; IX, 184. For the unpopularity of sermons, see Wrightson, *English Society*, 218f.; for the popularity of Sunday games, see M. Ingram, *Church Courts, Sex and Marriage in England, 1570–1640* (Cambridge, 1987), chap. 3.

79. Collinson has suggested that the Elizabethan and early Stuart clergy persecuted popular culture far more than popery: Collinson, *Birthpangs of Protestant England*, passim (for example, p. x: 'It was minstrels more than mass-priests who proved to be the enemy'). It is true that many Catholic leaders also adopted an aggressive attitude towards popular culture, but the war of Lent against carnival generally came later in Catholic lands. See, in general, P. Burke, *Popular Culture in Early Modern Europe* (London, 1978), chap. 8. In some areas, the struggle continues to this day: see, for example, J. de Pina Cabral, *Sons of Adam, Daughters of Eve: The Peasant World View of the Alto Minho* (Oxford, 1986), 137–50.

80. J. Tazbir, 'La conquête de l'Amérique à la lumière de l'opinion polonaise', *Acta Poloniae historica*, XVII (1968), 15.

81. See the suggestive article by A. Prosperi, ' "Otras Indias": missionari della Contrariforma tra contadini e selvaggi', in G. Garfagnini, ed., *Scienze, credenze occulte, livelli di cultura* (Florence, 1982), 205–34.

82. Examples quoted by P. Burke, 'Le domande del vescovo e la religione del popolo', *Quaderni storici*, XLI (1979), 541f. It should be remembered that 'How many gods are there?' was the very first question in most catechisms. However, my colleague Nicholas Davidson has suggested two possible explanations for the bizarre answers: first, the question implied (to those who did not already know the correct response) an answer in the plural. Second, experience might have taught those who did know that the best way to get rid of tiresome intruders was to make the most outrageous answer possible to the first question, for then they were sure to give up in horror and leave one alone.

83. Data drawn from M. S. Dupont-Bouchat, W. Frijhoff and R. Muchembled, *Prophètes et sorciers dans les Pays-Bas, 16e–17e siècles* (Paris, 1978), 61ff.; A. Franzen, ed., *Die Visitationsprotokolle der ersten nachtridentinischen Visitation im Erzstift Koln* (Münster, 1960), 123f.; O. Vasella, *Das Visitationsprotokoll über den schweizerischen Klerus der Bistums Konstanz von 1586* (Quellen zur schweizer Geschichte, new series, section 2, V, Bern, 1963), 132f.; A. Hahn, *Die Rezeption des tridentinischen Pfarrerideals im westtrierische Pfarrklerus des 16. und 17. Jahrhunderts* (Publications de la section historique de l'Institut Grand-Ducal de Luxembourg, XC, Luxembourg, 1974), 174f., 276ff. and 379ff.

84. Details from K. M. Comerford, 'Italian Tridentine diocesan seminaries: a historiographical study', *Sixteenth Century Journal*, XXIX (1998), 999–1002; and F. Martín Hernández, 'Felipe II y la reforma del clero español: los seminarios', *Ciudad de Dios*, CCXI (1998), 1005–26. For similar developments in the Netherlands, see the detailed studies of J. Roegiers, 'De oprichting en de beginjaren van het bischoppelijk seminarie te Gent (1569–1623)', *Handelingen van het maatschappij voor geschiedenis en oudheidkunde te Gent*, new series, XXVII (1973), 2–192; and P. de Clerck, 'De priesteropleiding in het bisdom Ieper (1565–1626)', *Annales de la Société d'émulation de Bruges*, C (1963), 7–67. For Germany, see M. Arneth, *Das Ringen um Geist und Form des Priesterbildung im Säkularklerus des 17. Jahrhunderts* (Würzburg, 1970), part 2. See also the evidence on the parallel evolution of Protestant and Catholic discipline in W. Reinhard, 'Gegenreformation als Modernisierung? Prolegomena zu einer Theorie des konfessionellen Zeitalters', *Archiv für Reformationsgeschichte*, LXVIII (1977), 226–52; idem, 'Zwang zur Konfessionalisierung: Prolegomena zu einer Theorie des konfessionellen Zeitalters', *Zeitschrift für historische Forschung*, X (1983), 257–77; and L. Schorn-Schütte, 'The Christian clergy in the early modern Holy Roman Empire: a comparative social study', *Sixteenth Century Journal*, XXIX (1998), 717–31.

85. A temporary shortage of clergy was even experienced in several areas where Protestantism made little direct impact: see, for example, Croix, *Bretagne aux 16e et 17e siècles*, 1161f.; G. Cabourdin, *Terre et hommes en*

Lorraine (1550–1635): Toulois et Comté de Vaudémont (Nancy, 1977), 562. But the size of the second estate rose in Catholic lands almost continuously from the late sixteenth to the mid-eighteenth century. In Castile, to take a single example, the clerical population rose from 91,000 in 1591 to 200,000 in 1737: see F. Ruiz Martin, 'Demografia eclesiástica hasta el siglo XIX', in Q. Aldea Vaquero and J. Vives Gatell, eds., *Diccionario de historia eclesiástica de España* (4 vols., Madrid, 1972–5), II, 682–733.

86. See A. D. Wright, 'Post-Tridentine reform in the archdiocese of Milan under the successors of St Charles Borromeo, 1584–1631' (University of Oxford D.Phil. thesis, 1973), 299–303. For a good example of Borromeo in action, see A. G. Roncalli, ed., *Gli atti della visita apostolica di S. Carlo Borromeo a Bergamo (1575)* (5 vols., Florence, 1936–57), esp. III–V, on the areas of the diocese outside the city of Bergamo. It has been suggested that, in some cases at least, the responses of parish priests to questions from the visitors about the religious beliefs of their congregations were 'understated' – that is, most priests sought to protect rather than to denounce their flocks; but that would scarcely have been possible in the teeth of the relentless questioning of Borromeo and his lieutenants. See M. Venard, 'Les "notes" de l'hérésie selon les visites pastorales du XVIe siècle', in B. Chevalier and R. Sauzet, eds., *Les réformes: enracinement socioculturel* (Paris, 1985), 375–81; R. Sauzet, *Les visites pastorales dans le diocèse de Chartres pendant la première moitié du XVIIe siècle: essai de sociologie religieuse* (Rome, 1975), 95–113.

87. Details from Franzen, *Visitationsprotokolle*, 123f.; J. Meier, 'Die katholischer Erneuerung des Würzburger Landskapitels Karlstadt im Spiegel der Landskapitelsversammlungen und Pfarreivisitationen, 1579–1624', *Würzburger Diozesängeschichtsblätter*, XXXIII (1971), 51–125. For evidence of similar progress in seventeenth-century France, see the excellent studies of J. Ferté, *La vie religieuse dans les campagnes parisiennes, 1622–1695* (Paris, 1962); L. Pérouas, *Le diocèse de La Rochelle de 1648 à 1724, sociologie et pastorale* (Paris, 1964); J. F. Soulet, *Traditions et réformes religieuses dans les Pyrénées Centrales au XVIIe siècle* (Pau, 1974); R. Sauzet, *Contre-Réforme et réforme catholique en Bas Languedoc: le diocèse de Nîmes au XVIIe siècle* (Louvain, 1979).

88. P. F. Grendler, *Schooling in Renaissance Italy: Literacy and Learning, 1300–1600* (Baltimore, 1989), 335–7. For an example from northern Europe, see O. Henrivaux, 'Les écoles dominicales de Mons et de Valenciennes et les premiers catéchismes du diocèse de Cambrai', in M. Cloet and F. Daelemans, eds., *Godsdienst, mentaliteit en dagelijks leven* (Brussels, 1988), 129–5.

89. Figures calculated from J. de Viguerie, *L'institution des enfants: l'éducation en France, 16e–18e siècle* (Paris, 1978), 61.

90. The most influential Catholic catechism was that drawn up following the council of Trent (in 1566) which adopted the same scholastic 'dialogue' form

as the Protestant ones, but a host of others soon followed. See de Viguerie, *Institution des enfants*, 39ff.; J. R. Armogathe, 'Les catéchismes et l'enseignement populaire en France au 18e siècle', in H. Coulet, ed., *Images du peuple au 18e siècle* (Paris, 1973), 103-21.

91. See J.-P. Dedieu, 'Chrétienisation en Nouvelle Castille: catéchisme, communion, messe et confirmation dans l'archevêché de Tolède, 1540-1650', *Mélanges de la casa de Velázquez*, XV (1979), 261-94; S. T. Nalle, 'Religion and reform in a Spanish diocese: Cuenca, 1545-1650' (Johns Hopkins University Ph.D. thesis, 1983), 229; idem, 'Inquisitors, priests and the people during the Catholic Reformation in Spain', *Sixteenth Century Journal*, XVIII (1987), 557-87.

92. In the remoter areas of Portugal, even in the twentieth century, priests who claimed the ability to mobilize supernatural resources for the benefit of their parishioners were popularly known as *bruxos* (witches). See Pina Cabral, *Sons of Adam, Daughters of Eve*, 201.

93. See the excellent analysis in P. T. Hoffman, *Church and Community in the Diocese of Lyon, 1500-1789* (New Haven, 1985), 168-70. See also W. Frijhoff, 'La fonction du miracle dans un minorité catholique: les Provinces-Unies au XVIIe siècle', *Revue d'histoire de la spiritualité*, XLVIII (1972), 151-78. On saints, it is worth noting that there were no canonizations between 1523 and 1588 – presumably a reflection of the doubts cast on the efficacy of saints by the reformers – but 55 between 1588 and 1767: P. Burke, 'How to be a Counter-Reformation saint', in K. von Greyerz, ed., *Religion and Society in Early Modern Europe, 1500-1800* (London, 1984), 46.

94. Thus medieval 'mystery plays', which in Protestant lands were largely suppressed, were replaced by religious drama in Catholic lands. Over 7500 Jesuit plays were written in the German-speaking lands alone between 1553 and 1773 to help the faithful to understand and believe: see J. M. Valentin, *Le théâtre des Jésuites dans les Pays de Langue Allemande: répertoire chronologique des pièces représentées et des documents conservés (1553-1773)*, (2 vols., Stuttgart, 1983-4). This material is discussed in R. Bireley, 'Early modern Germany', in J. W. O'Malley, ed., *Catholicism in Early Modern History* (Reformation Guides to Research, II, St Louis, 1988), 19. For specimens of Counter-Reformation stained glass, see Croix, *Bretagne aux 16e et 17e siècles*, pl. 176-84. For one well researched regional example of how the various techniques of communication used by the Catholic church reinforced each other, see R. P. Hsia, *Society and Religion in Münster, 1535-1618* (New Haven, 1984), chap. 6.

95. See S. T. Nalle, 'Literature and culture in early modern Castile', *Past and Present*, CXXV (1989), 90-3; G. Bollême, *La bibliothèque bleue: anthologie d'une littérature 'populaire'* (Paris, 1976), 35.

96. For 'missions' in general, see N. S. Davidson, *The Counter-Reformation*

(Oxford, 1987), 41–3. For some detail, see the evocative set of *cartes* painted on sheepskin from seventeenth-century Brittany in Croix, *Bretagne aux 16e et 17e siècles*, 1222–9, pl. 153–61 and 185–92. Some Catholics had recognized from the start that 'The written word of God, as the Lutherans call the Gospel, cannot always be productively presented to the simple folk according to its bare words or literal meaning' (according to Johannes Bachmann, a Catholic polemicist, in 1527), but it took time to concert an alternative strategy of conversion: see M. U. Edwards, 'Catholic controversial literature, 1518–1555', *Archiv für Reformationsgeschichte*, LXXIX (1988), 203. In Ireland, the Counter-reformers used Gaelic poetry and spoken Irish as their principal media, and some even welcomed the general illiteracy of their compatriots because it protected them so effectively against the teaching of the heretics: see the subtle analysis of N. Canny, 'Religion, politics and Gaelic Irish literature, 1580–1750', *Past and Present*, CV (1982), 91–116.

97. On the creation of *een probleemloos geloof* (an uncomplicated faith) in the South Netherlands, see M. Cloet, *Het kerkelijk leven in een landelijke dekenij van Vlaanderen tijdens de XVIIe eeuw: Tielt van 1609 tot 1700* (Leuven, 1968), 496–508, esp. p. 507; K. de Raeymaecker, *Het godsdienstig leven in de landdekenij Antwerpen, 1610–1650* (Leuven, 1977), 136–52; L. Braeken, *De dekenij Herenthals, 1603–69: bijdrage tot de studie van het godsdienstig leven in het bisdom Antwerpen* (Leuven, 1982), 84f., 94ff. and 207ff. Among the few exceptions that came in for detailed discussion were the distinctions between Catholicism and the other Christian faiths. Thus the catechism of the archdiocese of Mechelen included in the third lesson, 'Of faith', the following exchange: 'Q. Is it true that everyone can be saved through their faith? A. So the heretics teach, but they are mistaken, because without the true faith salvation is impossible.' In the fourth lesson, 'Of Scripture and tradition': 'Q. Are the heretics' Bibles also Holy Scripture? A. No way, because they are falsified in many places … Q. Is Scripture entirely clear and can everyone understand it well? A. Not so: rather it is obscure in many places, and therefore it is very dangerous for unlettered folk to read it': *Catechismus oft Christelycke Ghedeylt … voor de catholijcke Jonckheydt van het aertsbischdom … Mechelen* (1689), quoted with other telling material by M. Cloet, 'De gevolgen van de scheiding der Nederlanden op religieus, cultureel en mentaal gebied, van c. 1600 tot 1650', in J. Craeybeckx, F. Daelemans and F. G. Scheelings, eds., *1585: op gescheiden wegen/1585: On Separate Paths* (Leuven, 1988), 68–9.

98. Details from Hoffman, *Church and Community*, 83; Davidson, *Counter-Reformation*, 32–3; C. Fleury, *Les devoirs des maîtres et des domestiques* (Amsterdam, 1688), 85f. 'I am well aware,' the abbé graciously conceded, 'that holding a conversation with a lackey just up from the country or a kitchen scullion is not pleasant', but Christ did it and so must Christ's ministers. See

also the fascinating information on 'simplifying the faith' in a rural French parish, in G. Bouchard, *Le village immobile: Sennely-en-Sologne au XVIIIe siècle* (Paris, 1972), 283–343. Protestant attempts to simplify the faith have been noted in Germany by Bottigheimer, 'Bible-reading', 88; and in England by Green, ' "Reformed pastors" and *bons curés*', 281–2.

99. On the 'primitivization' of religion in Poland, see the brilliant article by J. Tazbir, 'La polonisation du Catholicisme après le Concile de Trente', *Memorie domenicane*, new series, IV (1973), 223ff. For a Protestant parallel, see L. Grane, 'Teaching the people: the education of the people in the Danish Reformation', in L. Grane and K. Hørby, eds., *Die dänische Reformation vor ihren internationalen Hintergrund* (Göttingen, 1990), 179ff.

100. Quotation from T. B. W. Kok, *Dekenaat in de steigers: kerkelijk opbouwwerk in het Gentse dekenaat Hulst, 1598–1648* (Tilburg, 1971), 254. See also other material in ibid., 368, 372 and 403; the works by Braeken, de Raeymaecker and Cloet cited in n. 97 above. It is noteworthy that the more optimistic vision provided by the historians of French Catholicism recorded in n. 87 above depends almost entirely on the reports of bishops to Rome, not of rural deans to bishops: see the strictures of Sauzet, *Visites pastorales*, 101ff. For a helpful survey of the many impediments (by no means all of them religious) to the spread of Catholicism in the later sixteenth and seventeenth centuries, see John A. Bossy, 'The Counter-Reformation and the people of Catholic Europe', *Past and Present*, XLVII (1970), 51–70.

101. An example is reproduced in E. Johansson, 'The history of literacy in Sweden', in H. J. Graff, ed., *Literacy and Social Development in the West: A Reader* (Cambridge, 1981), 169. See also E. Johansson, *The History of Literacy in Sweden in Comparison with Some Other Countries* (Umeå University Educational Reports, XII, Umeå, 1977); idem, 'Literacy studies in Sweden: some examples', in E. Jackson and I. Winchester, eds., *Records of the Past: Exploring New Sources in Social History* (Ontario Institute for Studies in Education, informal series, XIII, Toronto, 1979), 211–39. This paragraph owes much to conversations with Egil Johansson, Jan Sundin, Marja Taussi Sjöberg and other members of the Demographic Database at Umeå University, to all of whom I am most grateful.

102. See further material in H. J. Graff, *The Legacies of Literacy: Contrasts and Contradictions in Western Culture* (Bloomington, Ind., 1987), 223–30. The value of this data has been questioned by G. Strauss, 'Lutheranism and literacy: a reassessment', in von Greyerz, *Religion and Society in Early Modern Europe*, 119: 'But what sort of literacy was this? People couldn't write a line – they were obliged only to learn to read. And whether they understood what they read is a question to which statistics cannot supply an answer. I am inclined to doubt that they did.' Having seen some of the Swedish evidence

myself (at the Demographic Database in Umeå), there seems little doubt that comprehension was high.

103. Churches in other countries were able to insist on a *knowledge* of the basic texts before calling marriage bans: see, for example, the decree of the kirk-session of St Andrews in Scotland from 1594, in *Register*, II, 439, imposing a penalty of £2 – as well as a prohibition of the wedding – for any suitors who could not 'repeat' the Lord's Prayer, Creed and Commandments. This fine was exacted from eight persons between 1597 and 1599: ibid., 839f., 848, 872, 880, 886 and 890. But to have insisted on a *reading* knowledge would have condemned the population either to extinction or to sin on a grand scale.

104. For another example, see the church's propaganda campaign in favour of Sweden's intervention on the continent to save the Protestant cause: S. A. Arnoldsson, *Krigspropagand i Sverige före trettioåriga kriget* (Gothenburg, 1941). See, on the Swedish church in general, M. Roberts, 'The Swedish church', in idem, ed., *Sweden's Age of Greatness, 1632–1718* (London, 1973), 132–73.

105. French printing figures from H. J. Martin, *Livres, pouvoirs et société à Paris au XVIIe siècle (1598–1701)* (2 vols., Geneva, 1969), I, 61–98. On the German disputes, see the penetrating remarks of R. W. Scribner, *The German Reformation* (London, 1986), 51f.; Strauss, 'Reformation and its public', 209; Edwards, 'Catholic controversial literature'; idem, 'Statistics on sixteenth-century printing'.

106. H. Wotton, 'Panegyrick to King Charles' (written c. 1630) in idem, *Reliquiae Wottoniae* (4th edn., London, 1685), 147. The Catholics by and large managed to avoid internal disputes after the initial trauma of the Reformation, until the bitter quarrels of the Jansenists and Jesuits in the second half of the seventeenth century. For a suggestion that this dispute lost support for the Catholic church as a whole, see M. Vovelle, *Piété baroque et déchrétienisation en Provence au XVIIIe siècle* (Paris, 1973), 271, part 2, chap. 3 passim.

107. Clichthove's *Anti-Lutherus* (1524) and other similar works are discussed by K. Werner, *Geschichte der apologetischen und politischen Literatur der christliche Theologie* (5 vols., Schaffhausen, 1867), IV, 92–3; Morone quoted by B. M. Hallman, 'Italian "natural superiority" and the Lutheran question, 1517–46', *Archiv für Reformationsgeschichte*, LXXI (1980), 143. For further evidence, this time from Protestant sources, that the Reformation movement was running wild by 1524–5, see the telling quotations in S. C. Karant-Nunn, 'What was preached in the German cities in the early years of the Reformation?', in Bebb and Marshall, *Process of Change in Early Modern Europe*, 81–96.

108. Melchior von Osse quoted in Strauss, 'Reformation and its public', 209;

Hessels, *Ecclesiae Londino-Batavae archivum*, III.1, 679–81, Daniel de Dieu to the Dutch church at London, 9 Aug. 1582. See similar comments in ibid., II, 625–8, passim; see also Hibben, *Gouda in Revolt*, 102–11.

109. J. Napier, *A Plaine Discovery of the Whole Revelation of St John* (Edinburgh, 1593), sig. A3ᵛ; Collinson, *Religion of Protestants*, 200. See also G. Alexander, 'Bonner and the Marian persecutions', in Haigh, *English Reformation Revised*, 167; N. S. Davidson, 'Unbelief and atheism in Italy, 1500–1700' forthcoming).

110. See the important revisionist essays by J. Morrill, 'The church in England, 1642–9', in idem, ed., *Reactions to the English Civil War* (London, 1982), 89–114; B. Reay, 'Popular rel gion', in idem, ed., *Popular Culture in Seventeenth-century England* (London, 1985), 91–128; E. Lund, 'The impact of Lutheranism on popular religion in sixteenth-century Germany', *Concordia Journal*, XXIII (1987), 331–41; D. Hirst, 'The failure of godly rule in the English republic', *Past and Present*, CXXXII (1991), 33–66; E. Duffy, 'The godly and the multitude in Stuart England', *Seventeenth Century*, I (1988), 31–55; J. Dawson, ' "The face of ane perfyt reformed kyrk": St Andrews and the early Scottish Reformation', in J. Kirk, ed., *Humanism and Reform: The Church in Europe, England and Scotland, 1400–1640* (Studies in Church History, subsidia, VIII, Oxford, 1991), 413–35; J. Maltby, *Prayer Books and People in Elizabethan and Early Stuart England* (Cambridge, 1998).

111. See the admirable analysis of the 'Luther to Bismarck' school of history by T. A. Brady, 'From the sacral community to the common man: reflections on German Reformation studies', *Central European History*, XX (1987), 229–45.

10. The 'Kirk by Law Established' and the 'Taming of Scotland': St Andrews, 1559–1600

This paper grew out of a study of crime in early modern Scotland funded by the British Academy and the (then) Social Science Research Council. It was originally prepared for a workshop on the history of crime organized by Jan Sundin and held at Stockholm in 1983. I should like to thank in the first instance the other members of the workshop – Bruce Lenman, Ken Lockridge, Birgit Petersen, Heinz Schilling, Marja Taussi Sjöberg, Jan Sundin and Martin Vejbrink – for their invaluable comments. I am also most grateful to Nancy Wood for research assistance. In both preparing and revising the paper I acknowledge with gratitude the assistance of James K. Cameron, Jane Dawson, Leah Leneman, Rosalind Mitchison, R. N. Smart and David Underdown. Finally, I learned much from the students of St Andrews University to whom I taught Scottish Reformation history, particularly James Pratt, who graduated in 1986 and was killed in a mountain accident the next year. I dedicate this chapter to his memory.

1. See, for example, B. Boutelet, 'Étude par sondage de la criminalité dans le bailliage du Pont de l'Arche (17e–18e siècles). De la violence au vol, en marche vers l'escroquerie', *Annales de Normandie*, XII (1962), 235–62, based on a sample of 88 cases; and J.-C. Gegot, 'Étude par sondage de la criminalité dans le bailliage de Falaise (17e–18e siècles). Criminalité diffuse ou société criminelle', ibid., XVI (1966), 103–64, based on only a few more.

2. P. Rayner, B. Lenman and G. Parker, *Handlist of Records for the Study of Crime in Early Modern Scotland (to 1747)* (Edinburgh, 1982: List and Index Society, special series, XVI). In the end, Lenman and I supervised only three theses on Scottish crime: Catherine Ferguson, 'The taming of the Anglo-Scottish Border in the seventeenth century' (St Andrews, 1981); Stephen Davies, 'Law and order in Stirlingshire, 1637–1747' (St Andrews, 1983); and Gordon DesBrisay, 'Crime and social control in seventeenth-century Aberdeen' (St Andrews, 1988). Lesley Smith, who rediscovered the records of the Justice Court of Aberdeen, began research on the control of crime during the 1650s at St Andrews but completed it at Oxford (see n. 21 below).

3. V. A. C. Gatrell, B. Lenman and G. Parker, eds., *Crime and the Law. The Social History of Crime in Western Europe since 1550* (London, 1980).

4. See our cautionary article: B. Lenman and G. Parker, 'The state, the community and the criminal law in early modern Europe', in Gatrell, Lenman and Parker, *Crime and the Law*, 11–48 (quotation, from Alfred Soman, at p. 21 n. 17). Other researchers remain convinced of the value of counting court cases, however, and have dismissed our article as too pessimistic. See J. C. V. Johansen and H. Stevnsborg, 'Hasard ou myopie: réflexions autour de deux théories de l'histoire de droit', *Annales: Économies, sociétés, civilisations*, XLI (1986), 601–24; and H. Roodenburg, *Onder censuur. De kerkelijke tucht in de gereformeerde gemeente van Amsterdam, 1578–1700* (Hilversum, 1990), 19–23. Naturally, Lenman and I did not expect our findings to please those who had invested several years in counting and analysing thousands of court cases!

5. M. F. Graham, *The Uses of Reform: Godly Discipline and Popular Behavior in Scotland and Beyond, 1560–1610* (Leiden, 1996): he discusses the St Andrews data at pp. 77–97, 190–201 and 205–220. In all, cases from St Andrews made up 40 per cent of his total database.

6. Graham, *The Uses of Reform*, 75 n. 9, informs readers that 'Parker's approach is sound, but his study is marred by errors of fact and dubious interpretations.' However, Graham's citations throughout come from the 1988 version and not from the 1994 revised text (in the same volume that contained his own essay!), where the 'errors of fact' to which he refers have been corrected. At p. 213 he speculates that 1595 and 1596 (only) saw a

'gradual shift of sexual cases out of the session and into the bailies' court, for which the records have not survived'. Quite apart from the total lack of evidence, this seems implausible for two reasons. First, the punishment of sexual offences yielded huge fines for the church in these years (a point made in the 1994 but not in the 1988 version of my paper: see page 279 above), and it seems unlikely that a court would willingly renounce such a lucrative source of funds for its charitable work. Second, as Graham himself points out, the number of sexual offences tried by the session started to rise again in 1597.

7. Graham, ibid., 100–2. I thank Andrew Pettegree and Jason Nye for help in interpreting the sources concerning St Andrews; the criticisms of Professor Graham's interpretation, however, are mine and not theirs.

8. *The Diary of Mr James Melvill, 1556–1601* (Bannatyne Club, XXXIV, Edinburgh, 1829), 188–9 and 195. There is another edition of Melville's holograph manuscript (in the National Library of Scotland): R. Pitcairn, ed., *The Autobiography and Diary of Mr James Melville* (Wodrow Society, III, Edinburgh, 1842). All citations that follow are, however, from the 1829 edition.

9. H. Scott, *Fasti ecclesiae scotticanae* (Edinburgh, 1925), V, 177ff., gives the exact size of the parishes in and around St Andrews. Cameron was disjoined from St Andrews in 1646; Strathkinness and Boarhills in the nineteenth century. The parish of St Leonards, inside the burgh, was used by all members of the university and was entirely separate from St Andrews parish.

10. The first true census for the parishes of Fife, compiled in 1755, gave St Andrews a population of 5877 persons: see J. G. Kyd, *Scottish Population Statistics including Webster's Analysis of the Population since 1755* (Scottish History Society, 3rd series, XL, Edinburgh, 1952), 38–41, combined total for St Andrews and Cameron parishes. Attempting a back-projection from this figure is hazardous, but might be attempted along the following lines. Webster judged that the parish in 1755 possessed 1177 'fighting men', aged between 18 and 56 years. The record of those who subscribed to the 1643 Solemn League and Covenant in the parish of St Andrews contains 985 names. Of these, 140 were members of the university and therefore belonged to the parish of St Leonards, reducing the total for St Andrews parish to 845. Since only adult males were included among the subscribers, it seems reasonable to suppose that the 845 might be roughly equated with Webster's category of 'fighting men'. Using Webster's carefully calculated ratio of fighting men to the total population (1:5), a parish of some 4250 is indicated for the year 1643. (See the list in St Andrews University Archives, Typ/BE.C43 TSS2: *A solemne League and Covenant* [Edinburgh, 1643], 15–43.) Continuing backwards, the earliest surviving tax record for St Andrews, the burgh stent-roll for 1618, contains the names of 486 householders, but covers only the

burgh, not the parish, and omits those who (like all university personnel) were exempt from taxation. If we assume five persons to have constituted the average household, the population of the burgh proper in 1618 may have approached 2500 (St Andrews University Archives: *Ms* B65/20/3). Happily, these tentative calculations are supported by (1) an order by the kirk-session to prepare 2000 communion tokens in July 1590; and (2) a letter from the ecclesiastical historian David Calderwood, written to the archbishop of St Andrews in 1615, which claimed 'there are in fact more than 3000 regular comunicants' in the parish (*Register*, II, 677).

11. See J. M. Anderson, ed., *Early Records of the University of St Andrews* (Scottish History Society, 3rd series, VIII (Edinburgh, 1926), 154-9 and 262-72, for matriculation and graduation rolls during the period 1556-65. These reveal no graduation ceremony in 1559-60, on account of the troubles, and very few graduates from then until 1565. Matriculations were more or less halved during 1560-3, while in 1559 the record states 'Hoc anno, propter tumultus religionis ergo exortos, paucissimi scholastici ad hanc universitatem venerunt' (p. 266). The plague of 1585-6 is recorded in Melville's *Diary*, 148 and 162.

12. See the excellent discussion of the sources of the notion of 'discipline' in J. K. Cameron, 'Godly nurture and admonition in the Lord: ecclesiastical discipline in the reformed tradition', in L. Grane and K. Horby, eds., *Die dänische Reformation vor ihrem internationalen Hintergrund* (Göttingen, 1990), 264-76.

13. See A. C. Duke, 'The ambivalent face of Calvinism in the Netherlands, 1561-1618', in M. Prestwich, ed., *International Calvinism 1541-1715* (Oxford, 1985), 109-34, esp. 130f.; and H. Schilling, 'Reformierte Kirchenzucht als Sozialdisziplinierung. Die Tätigkeit des Emder Presbyteriums in den Jahren 1557-62', in W. Ehbrecht and H. Schilling, eds., *Niederlande und Nordwestdeutschland* (Cologne/Vienna, 1983), 261-327.

14. See the accounts given by R. M. Kingdon, 'The control of morals in Calvin's Geneva', in L. P. Buck and J. W. Zophy, eds., *The Social History of the Reformation* (Columbus, 1972), 5-16; and E. W. Monter, 'The consistory of Geneva, 1559-1569', *Bibliothèque d'Humanisme et Renaissance*, XXXVIII (1976), 467-84. See also the important discussion of J. K. Cameron, 'Scottish Calvinism and the principle of intolerance', in B. A. Gerrish and R. Benedetto, eds., *Reformatio perennis: Essays on Calvin and the Reformation in Honor of F. L. Battles* (Pittsburgh, 1981), 113-28.

15. 'The forme of prayers and ministration of the sacraments' of 1556 was published in D. Laing, ed., *The Works of John Knox* (Wodrow Society, Edinburgh, 1855), IV, 155-214 – see esp. 203-6: 'The order of ecclesiasticall discipline'; and the 'Answer to a great number of blasphemous cavillations' of 1559, in ibid., V, 17-468 – see 208-32 on the need to punish. See also the

Scots 'Confession of faith', chap. 18, in W. C. Dickinson, ed., *John Knox's History of the Reformation in Scotland* (2 vols., London, 1949), II, 266–7. It is worth noting that both Luther and Calvin had identified only two 'marks' of the true church – right teaching of the gospel and right administration of the sacraments – and that the idea of discipline as a third seems to derive from Bucer: see A. N. Burnett, 'Church discipline and moral reformation in the thought of Martin Bucer', *Sixteenth Century Journal*, XXII (1991), 439–56; and J. C. Spalding, 'Discipline as a mark of the true church in its sixteenth-century Lutheran context', in C. Lindberg, ed., *Piety, Politics and Ethics: Studies in Honor of George W. Forell* (Sixteenth Century Essays and Studies, III, Kirksville, 1984), 119–38.

16. J. K. Cameron, ed., *The First Book of Discipline* (Edinburgh, 1972), 165–6 and 173: 'The seventh head: of ecclesiastical discipline'.

17. See the excellent summary of the duties of the presbyteries at this time in J. Kirk, ed., *Stirling Presbytery Records 1581–1587* (Scottish History Society, 4th series, XLVII, Edinburgh, 1981), xviii; and idem, ed., *The Second Book of Discipline* (Edinburgh, 1980), 102–14.

18. Kirk, *Stirling Presbytery Records*, 258–9. Mr Wilson appeared the very next week and was sentenced 'to mak publict repentence, in his awin parroche kirk four soverall Sondayis in tyme of sermond, bair fuittit in linning clathis' (ibid., 260).

19. Quoted in J. di Folco, 'Discipline and welfare in the mid-seventeenth century Scots parish', *Records of the Scottish Church History Society*, XIX (1977), 169–83, at 176. Throughout the 1640s and 1650s, the burgh of Auchtermuchty was apparently riven by dissent among the elders, between the minister and some of his elders, and between the session and a group of parishioners. See further details in ibid., 176–7.

20. SRO CH2/722/6, entries in the register of the presbytery of Stirling for 1 and 8 Oct. 1656; 26 Jan. 1659, 20 Mar. 1661; and CH2/722/7, entries for 21 Sept. 1664, and 29 Apr., 22 July, 22 Aug., 16 Sept. and 18 Nov. 1668. This case was generously brought to my attention by Dr Stephen J. Davies of Manchester Metropolitan University.

21. See the example of an Edinburgh delinquent pursued in 1653–5 by letter to Aberdeenshire whither she had fled in hope of avoiding censure, in L. M. Smith, 'Scotland and Cromwell: a study in early modern government' (University of Oxford, Ph.D. dissertation, 1980), 236. In the eighteenth century some sessions even placed 'Wanted' advertisements in newspapers requesting information about missing suspects: see R. Mitchison and L. Leneman, *Sexuality and Social Control: Scotland 1660–1780* (Oxford, 1990), 34. See also W. Mackay, ed., *Records of the Presbyteries of Inverness and Dingwall, 1643–1688* (Scottish History Society, XXIV, Edinburgh, 1896), 60 and 84: the case of William McPherson, in 1675, 'adulterer and thereafter fornicator

in Inverness, haveing appeared several yeares *in sacco*, evidenceing his publick remorse for his said gross sins, supplicated the presbytery [of Inverness] to be absolved'. But the assembled ministers seemed to feel that a few further years in sackcloth were called for, and the petition was refused. So in 1677 the unfortunate man went away to Holland to become a soldier: possible death at the hands of the Catholic French must have appeared preferable to endless humiliation before his fellow parishioners.

22. The most influential account of the 'bawdy courts' of Reformation England is that of C. Hill, *Society and Puritanism in Pre-Revolutionary England* (2nd edn., New York, 1967), chap. 8. Subsequent research, however, has not endorsed his negative, unsympathetic account. See, for example, R. B. Manning, *Religion and Society in Elizabethan Sussex* (Leicester, 1969); R. A. Marchant, *The Church under the Law: Justice, Administration and Discipline in the Diocese of York, 1560–1640* (Cambridge, 1972); J. A. Sharpe, 'Crime and delinquency in an Essex parish 1600–1640', in J. S. Cockburn, ed., *Crime in England 1550–1800* (Princeton, 1977), chap. 4; R. Houlbrooke, *Church Courts and the People during the English Reformation, 1520–1570* (Oxford, 1979); P. Collinson, *The Religion of Protestants* (Oxford, 1982), 62–70; S. Lander, 'Church courts and the Reformation in the diocese of Chichester 1500–1558', in C. Haigh, ed., *The English Reformation Revised* (Cambridge, 1987), chap. 2; and, above all, M. J. Ingram, *Church Courts, Sex and Marriage in England, 1570–1640* (Cambridge, 1987).

23. Quoted in Dickinson, *Knox's History of the Reformation* II, 49. The petition continued with a vintage piece of Knoxian moral blackmail: 'and seing that kings are but His lieutenants, having no power to give life where [God] commands death, . . . so will He not fail to punish you for neglecting his judgments'. It is interesting to note that the English Parliament also refused to back a disciplinary package at this time: see J. C. Spalding, *The Reformation of the Ecclesiastical Laws of England, 1552* (Sixteenth Century Essays and Studies, XIX, Kirksville, 1992).

24. Details from T. Thomson, ed., *Acts of the Parliaments of Scotland* (Edinburgh, 1814), II, 539 and III, 24–5 and 38; and Lenman and Parker, 'The state, the community and the criminal law', 37. Interestingly enough, persons convicted of the 'sins' of sodomy and bestiality were also executed – but without the passage of any statute to that effect! It was the opinion of one great eighteenth-century Scots lawyer that they were tried and condemned solely on the basis of the book of Leviticus: see J. Erskine, *An Institute of the Laws of Scotland* (1773; revised edn., Edinburgh, 1838), 1105.

25. From 1599 onwards, for example, the kirk-session of Glasgow resolved that the persons elected as provost and bailies of the burgh should always be enrolled among the elders. See G. Donaldson, *Scotland: James V – James VII* (Edinburgh, 1971), 225. It was significant, however, that although some

magistrates normally sat on each session, they never predominated, thereby threatening the church's independence: see the perceptive remarks in J. Kirk, *Patterns of Reform: Continuity and Change in the Reformation Kirk* (Edinburgh, 1989), 273–5.

26. See Davies, 'Law and order in Stirlingshire', chap. 4. It is worth noting that the baron courts had also supported ecclesiastical jurisdiction before the Reformation. In 1529, for example, all tenants of the barony of Alloway were ordered to accept any censures imposed by the church within forty days, and anyone condemned by the church for adultery was automatically to lose his land: see M. H. B. Sanderson, *Scottish Rural Society in the Sixteenth Century* (Edinburgh, 1982), 12. Statutes against adultery had also been passed by the Scots Parliament – for example in 1551 – but the sanctions stopped at outlawry: see the important discussion in J. Wormald, ' "Princes" and the regions in the Scottish Reformation', in N. A. T. MacDougall, ed., *Church, Politics and Society: Scotland 1408–1929* (Edinburgh, 1983), 65–84, esp. at 82 n. 4.

27. SRO CH2/983/1, p. 1: minutes of the parishes of Cromdale, Inverallen and Advie, 14 Dec. 1702; G. and C. B. Gunn, eds., *Records of the Baron Court of Stitchill, 1655–1807* (Scottish History Society, L, Edinburgh, 1905), 21: declaration of 26 Nov. 1660 – that is, directly after the restoration of Charles II. For further examples, and some excellent general remarks, see B. P. Lenman, 'The limits of godly discipline in the early modern period, with particular reference to England and Scotland', in K. von Greyerz, ed., *Religion and Society in Early Modern Europe 1500–1800* (London, 1984), 124–45.

28. Examples from Mitchison and Leneman, *Sexuality and Social Control*, 74 (with more cases from a later period at 224–8); and di Folco, 'Discipline and welfare', 171. Counter-examples in which the great were made to submit to discipline are noted in Kirk, *Patterns of Reform*, 275–6; and K. M. Brown, 'In search of the godly magistrate in Reformation Scotland', *Journal of Ecclesiastical History*, XL (1989), 553–81, at 566–71.

29. See the perceptive remarks of Lenman, 'The limits of godly discipline', 135f. Graham, *The Uses of Reform*, 267–8, also stressed 'tactical concessions' over sin.

30. J. Stuart, ed., *Selections from the Records of the Kirk-Session, Presbytery and Synod of Aberdeen* (Spalding Club, XV, Aberdeen, 1846), 121. Mr Gordon was sent to the presbytery and was there excommunicated for papism and disobedience.

31. On these policy changes see Smith, 'Scotland and Cromwell', chap. 9; and idem, 'Sackcloth for the sinner or punishment for the crime? Church and secular courts in Cromwellian Scotland', in J. Dwyer, R. A. Mason and A. Murdoch, eds., *New Perspectives on the Politics and Culture of Early Modern Scotland* (Edinburgh, 1982), 116–32.

32. For admirable studies of the working of the kirk in its prime, see D.

Henderson, *The Scottish Ruling Elder* (London, 1935), esp. 100–45; W. R. Foster, *The Church before the Covenants 1596–1638* (Edinburgh, 1972), chaps. 4 and 5; W. H. Makey, *The Church and the Covenant, 1638–1651* (Edinburgh, 1978); and Graham, *The Uses of Reform*.

33. T. Burns, *Church Property: The Benefice Lectures* (Edinburgh, 1905), 1–65, and 193–268 (a list of church records then extant).

34. Calculated from Rayner, Lenman and Parker, *Handlist of Records for the Study of Crime*, 158–259. These totals include only volumes deposited in the Scottish Record Office or in Register House before 1980. It was then thought that about 130 more kirk-session records dating from before 1750 were extant in private hands. Most church records have since been moved from Edinburgh to regional archives, making it extremely difficult to update these figures.

35. David Hay Fleming's edition of the register omitted only some of the coarser exchanges between various sinners and the session. They were indicated by dots (. . .). Vol. I covers the years 1559–82 and vol. II covers 1582–1600. The original register for 1559–1600, filling some 300 folios, is still conserved at Holy Trinity Church in St Andrews. The session records for 1600–38 are incomplete, but five volumes cover the period 1638–1706 in some 1600 folios: HM Register House, Edinburgh, OPR 453/5–9. A parallel to Melville's diary also exists for part of the later period: see T. McCrie, ed., *The Life of Mr Robert Blair, Minister of St Andrews, containing his Autobiography* (Wodrow Society, XIII, Edinburgh, 1848).

36. Quotations from the excellent article of J. Dawson, ' "The face of ane perfyt reformed kyrk": St Andrews and the early Scottish Reformation', in J. Kirk, ed., *Humanism and Reform: The Church in Europe, England and Scotland, 1400–1640: Essays in Honour of James K. Cameron* (Studies in Church History, subsidia VIII, Oxford, 1991), 413–35, at 427; and *Register*, I, 198.

37. The events of 'Reformation Day' – quite a contrast to the Reformation process in other countries, which could take years – are discussed in Dawson, ' "Ane perfyt reformed kyrk" ', 415.

38. On the work of the superintendent's court in St Andrews see ibid., 431–3; Graham, *The Uses of Reform*, 81–92; and *Register*, I, xxvii–xxxv, for details. Superintendent Winram led an interesting life: a pillar of the Catholic church right up to 1558, when he witnessed the burning of Walter Milne for heresy, he switched sides fast enough to help draft the Scots Confession and the *Book of Discipline* in 1560, and took advantage of the new order to marry in 1562 at the age of 70. He died in 1582. On the work of the superintendents, see the definitive essay of J. Kirk, 'The superintendent: myth and reality', in idem, *Patterns of Reform*, 154–231 (on Winram's career see 176–9).

39. For details on the commissary courts before, during and after the Reformation, see G. Donaldson, 'The church courts', in *An Introduction to Scottish Legal History* (Stair Society, XX, Edinburgh, 1958), 363–73. On

p. 366 there is an interesting analysis of the business handled by the commissary courts of Scotland in the first half of the sixteenth century: appeals from lower courts made up around one-third and, of the rest, about one-third concerned wills, one-quarter broken contracts and one-fifth church property. The role of sex and slander cases, which became the staple of church courts after the Reformation, was negligible before 1560. In England, however, over 80 per cent of the cases heard by the London consistory court between 1470 and 1516 concerned either sex or slander: see R. Wunderli, *London Church Courts and Society on the Eve of the Reformation* (Cambridge, 1981), 81.

40. G. Donaldson, *The Scottish Reformation* (Cambridge, 1960), chap. 3. John Carswell, a local laird, was both superintendent of Argyll and apostolic bishop of the Isles: see Kirk, *Patterns of Reform*, chap. 7. For the hesitant installation of the Reformation in other towns of the kingdom, see I. B. Cowan, *The Scottish Reformation: Church and Society in Sixteenth-Century Scotland* (New York, 1982), chap. 8; M. Lynch, *Edinburgh and the Reformation* (Edinburgh, 1981); idem, 'From privy kirk to burgh church: an alternative view of the process of Protestantisation', in MacDougall, *Church, Politics and Society*, chap. 5; and A. White, 'The impact of the Reformation on a burgh community: the case of Aberdeen', in M. Lynch, ed., *The Early Modern Town in Scotland* (London, 1987), chap. 4.

41. Details from Dawson, 'Ane perfyt reformed kyrk', 427–30. The first cases in the register (both from 1559) concerned adultery; the first case of fornication was punished in May 1560.

42. *Register*, I, 294ff. (for sabbath breach); *Diary of James Melville*, 46 (on the witch) and 26 (on Knox's need to be virtually carried up into the pulpit, where he reached his full oratorical powers only after about half an hour).

43. See Donaldson, *Scottish Reformation*, 171, 176 and 183.

44. *Register*, I, 377–8. The fine was to be half the hiring fee agreed between master and servant; since servants made up the largest single category of sexual offenders, this measure was of considerable importance. The General Assembly of the church ordained in 1573 that no minister 'may dispence with the extremitie of sack-cloth prescryvit be the acts of the generall discipline, for any pecunnial sowme' (quoted in ibid., I, lii). See also p. 263 above.

45. *Register*, I, 373–4.

46. Calculated from ibid., I, 373–943. Annual totals are given in the appendix, pages 283–7 above. Although where possible information on punishments is given in the text, many entries in the register fail to state the penalty imposed so that quantification is impossible.

47. Quoted in Foster, *Church before the Covenants*, 72.

48. Based on the tables in Davies, 'Law and order in Stirlingshire', chap. 4. See also M. Black Verschuur, 'Enforcing the discipline of the kirk: Mr Patrick Galloway's early years as minister of Perth', in W. F. Graham, ed., *Later*

Calvinism: International Perspectives (Sixteenth Century Essays and Studies, XXII, Kirksville, 1994), 215–36. However, although sexual misconduct seemed as rife in sixteenth-century Perth as elsewhere, Dr Black omitted it totally, on the curious ground that it has received so much notoriety elsewhere (218)!

49. See Roodenburg, *Onder censuur*, 137 (although note that further minor infractions may have been dealt with by the elders locally and recorded in the – missing – *wijkboekjes*: 142–4); H. Schilling, 'Sündenzucht und frühneuzeit-liche Sozialdisziplinierung: Die Calvinistische Presbyteriale Kirchenzucht in Emden vom 16. bis 19. Jahrhundert', in G. Schmidt, ed., *Stände und Gesell-schaft im alten Reich* (Stuttgart, 1989), 265–302; and R. A. Mentzer, '*Disci-plina nervus ecclesiae*: the Calvinist reform of morals at Nîmes', *Sixteenth Century Journal* XVIII (1987), 89–115. There are further (somewhat frag-mentary) data on southern French, Rhineland and Swiss Calvinist church courts in J. Estèbe and B. Vogler, 'La genèse d'une société protestante: Étude comparée de quelques registres consistoriaux languedociens et palatins vers 1600', *Annales: Économies, sociétés, civilisations*, XXXI (1976), 362–88; and J. R. Watt, 'The reception of the Reformation at Valangin, Switzerland, 1547–1588', *Sixteenth Century Journal*, XX (1989), 89–104. Publication of the records of the Geneva consistory has begun, in both French and English, under the general editorship of Robert M. Kingdon. See *Registers of the Consistory of Geneva in the Time of Calvin. I. 1542–4* (Grand Rapids, 2000). This will eventually allow a comprehensive analysis of disciplinary activity. In the meantime, see the 'guesstimate' of Monter, 'The consistory of Geneva', 484; and the general remarks of H. Höpfl, *The Christian Polity of John Calvin* (Cambridge, 1982), 90–6, 115–21 and 188–206.

50. *Register*, I, 392–4. John Chaeplan *contra* Jonet Lawsoun, 19 May and 9 June 1584.

51. Generalization based on the survey conducted by Rayner, Lenman and Parker for the *Handlist* (see n. 2 above), but see Graham, *The Uses of Reform*, 220, 286 and 346.

52. It might be supposed that the presence of numerous university students in the town would have affected the picture; but this does not appear to have been the case, for all university members were subject to the discipline of their own officers and their own parish of St Leonards. Students therefore figured rarely among those tried by the kirk-session of St Andrews.

53. *Register*, I, 449.

54. Quoted by S. J. Davies, 'The courts and the Scottish legal system, 1600–1747: the case of Stirlingshire', in Gatrell, Lenman and Parker, *Crime and the Law*, 120–54, at 125. In the 1951 fornication cases recorded in various parishes of Stirlingshire between 1637 and 1747 only 26 women were not pregnant: see Davies, 'Law and order in Stirlingshire', 83.

55. The text of the oath was standard: see an example in Davies, 'The courts', 124 n. 13. In a survey of Scotish kirk-session records from the 1760s, 72 per cent of the men named as father by pregnant women owned up within a month: see Mitchison and Leneman, *Sexuality and Social Control*, 75.

56. *Register*, II, 656.

57. See, for an example, *Register*, II, 523: the case of Christene Mwir, 18 March 1584, 'quha grantis that sche, the xvij day of Marche instant [i.e., the night before!], in the nicht, past out with the South Gait Port of this citee, and thair committit the filthy crime of adultrie with James Neilsoun'. The record notes a previous adultery with Andrew, earl of Rothes, which produced a bastard child. The case was therefore referred to the presbytery. For numerous similar examples, see Mitchison and Leneman, *Sexuality and Social Control*, chap. 6; and G. R. Quaife, *Wanton Wenches and Wayward Wives: Peasants and Illicit Sex in Early Seventeenth-century England* (London, 1979), 48-56.

58. Sir W. Brereton, *Travels in Holland, the United Provinces, England, Scotland and Ireland* (Chetham Society, I, London, 1844), 107; A. I. Ritchie, *Churches of St Baldred: Auldhame, Whitekirk, Tyninghame, Prestonkirk* (Edinburgh, 1880), 86. Ritchie, ibid., indicates that the Aberdeen 'stool' was certainly capable of seating seven at a time – women and men at different times, of course. The St Andrews stool, still kept in the town church, was somewhat more modest.

59. *Register*, II, 850 and 766. 'Jokin' seems to have been a penalty found especially suitable for women. At Tyninghame, a second set of jougs was erected by the magistrates at the church door, on the special request of the minister, because 'there war sae many railers in the toun, especiallie women, and that they troublit the session sae aft'. See Ritchie, *Churches of St Baldred*, 88.

60. *Register*, II, 793, and similar cases in Mar. 1595 (794) and Aug. 1596 (819). On fines, see also Graham, *The Uses of Reform*, 212.

61. It was the same elsewhere: see (for England) J. A. Sharpe, *Defamation and Sexual Slander in Early Modern England: The Church Courts at York* (Borthwick Papers, LVIII, York, 1980); (for France) Mentzer, '*Disciplina nervus ecclesiae*'; and (for the Netherlands) Roodenburg, *Onder censuur*, 321-82.

62. See, for example, the detailed examination of Agnes Meluill (daughter of an elder and reader of the kirk in Anstruther) in July 1588: *Register*, II, 620-3. She was convicted (ibid., 799-800). For a successful defence against a charge of witchcraft in 1587, see Kirk, *Stirling Presbytery Records*, 247 and 249. On church and state sharing the cost of 'justice', see Ritchie, *Churches of St Baldred*, 105: the bill for burning two witches on the sands at Kirkcaldy in 1633 was shared between the town (which paid £17 for ten loads of coal,

some tar and tows, and the executioner) and the kirk-session (which paid £17 for the other expenses).

63. *Register*, I, 441: case of 24 Sept. 1579; and II, 785-6: case of 17 Apr. 1594.

64. Cameron, 'Godly nurture', 274-5, and L. Leneman, 'Prophaning the Lord's Day: sabbath breach in early modern Scotland', *History*, LXXIV (1998), 217-31, give a fine selection of offences. Some sabbath-breakers earned severe punishment, however: at least 51 St Andrews offenders were condemned to the stool of repentance and 6 were also imprisoned, while 7 were delivered for punishment to the magistrates.

65. The same preponderance of male offenders in this category has been found in other records, suggesting that, in this respect, perhaps women were more disposed to respect the church's commands and to fulfil its requirements than men. This phenomenon has been observed in other societies: see S. H. Brandes, *Migration, Kinship and Community: Tradition and Transition in a Spanish Village* (New York, 1975), chap. 8; and K. V. Thomas, 'Women and the civil war sects', in T. S. Aston, ed., *Crisis in Europe 1560-1660* (London, 1965), chap. 13 – but not, so far as I am aware, for Scotland.

66. Stuart, *Selections from the Records of the Kirk-Session*, 62-3 (1608) and 116 (1651) about covered faces; *Register*, II, 806 (1595: 'na persoun sall cum to the stuill of repentance armit with sowrd nor gun' – nor indeed to the session). See also K. M. Brown, *Bloodfeud in Scotland, 1573-1625: Violence, Justice and Politics in an Early Modern Society* (Edinburgh, 1986), 185f.

67. *Register*, II, 556-7 (James Lermonth, heir to the barony of Balcomie, alleged that he did not live in the parish of St Andrews in April 1585; it was one of his many appearances for various forms of sexual misconduct: see also p. 277 above) and ibid., II, 547-9 (Jhone Cambell's 'dispytful and opprobrius wordis' to the session in Dec. 1584). Note also the similar tensions and abuse in Auchtermuchty, somewhat later, recorded by di Folco, 'Discipline and welfare', 176-7.

68. Two for contempt and one each for homicide, adultery and sabbath breach. It is true that 28 more offenders were threatened with the ban but (in its own inimitable words) the session was 'nocht willing to be suddane to fulminat excommunication aganis ony person, if thai culd be brocht utherwyis to repentance and humiliatioun' (*Register*, II, 671: May 1590). It thus stood in stark contrast to the 300 excommunications and more issued annually by the consistory of Geneva in the 1560s (Monter, 'The consistory', 484).

69. See Gatrell, Lenman and Parker, *Crime and the Law*, 4, 49-75 and 190-237, on the methodological problems posed by 'labelling' and by 'panic prosecutions' in the historical study of crime. David Underdown has located a similar phenomenon at Dorchester in the early seventeenth century: following a great natural catastrophe – a devastating fire in 1613 – some of the same laymen who had previously resisted the work of their Puritan minister

suddenly became pliant and pious. See D. Underdown, *Fire from Heaven: Life in an English Town in the Seventeenth Century* (New Haven, 1992).

70. *Diary of James Melvill*, 89–90, and Graham, *The Uses of Reform*, 190–6 and 205–10. Calvin had also faced a determined group of opponents among the magistrates of Geneva in 1552–3, but they were vanquished: see E. W. Monter, *Calvin's Geneva* (New York, 1967), 82–8.

71. *Diary of James Melvill*, 90; *Register*, II, 559 n. 4 and 576.

72. Details from Graham, *The Uses of Reform*, 192–3 and 207–10.

73. *Register*, II, 760–3 and 904.

74. Graham, *The Uses of Reform*, 190–201, based on M. Smith, 'The presbytery of St Andrews, 1586–1605: a study and annotated edition of the register of the minutes of the presbytery of St Andrews' (St Andrews University Ph.D. thesis, 1986).

75. R. G. Cant, *The University of St Andrews: A Short History* (2nd edn., Edinburgh, 1970), 52; *Register*, II, 694–5, 760–1, 788–92 and 801–4. Two of these Melvillian sessions continued in office for two years apiece.

76. Ibid., II, 821; see also 929, 942 and 943. And see Graham, *The Uses of Reform*, 213–19.

77. *Register*, II, 767.

78. Similar considerations clearly operated in eighteenth-century England with regard to the game laws, after poaching became a capital offence: see D. Hay et al., *Albion's Fatal Tree: Crime and Society in Eighteenth-Century England* (London, 1975), and E. P. Thompson, *Whigs and Hunters: The Origin of the Black Act* (London, 1975).

79. The register records five persons fined £2 and two persons sent to the stool of repentance for concealing sins committed by others. (The punishment accorded to seven others is unknown.)

80. See some English examples of 'girls in trouble' unsuccessfully trying to flee from the hostile parish in which they lived in K. E. Wrightson, 'The nadir of English illegitimacy in the seventeenth century', in P. Laslett, K. Oosterveen and R. M. Smith, eds., *Bastardy and its Comparative History* (Cambridge, 1980), 176–91. There was at least one good reason for firmness: unless the father of a bastard could be found, the parish might become responsible for its upkeep.

81. *Diary of James Melvill*, 206.

82. Remarkably, bastardy seems to have reached a peak in other countries of Western Europe at precisely this time: D. Levine and K. E. Wrightson, 'The social context of illegitimacy in early modern England', in Laslett et al., *Bastardy and Its Comparative History*, 158–175 (for England), and M. del C. González Muñoz, *La población de Talavera, siglos XVI–XX* (Toledo, 1974), 109 (for Spain) both found an 'explosion of illegitimacy' in the 1590s. It is difficult to be absolutely sure what happened in St Andrews at this time because there is no usable register of births.

83. *Register*, II, 925–6. See also Leneman, 'Prophaning the Lord's Day'. There is some debate about the likelihood of short-run 'reformations of manners' in early modern times, however. Contrast D. Levine and K. E. Wrightson, *Poverty and Piety in an English Village: Terling 1525–1700* (New York, 1979), who clearly found something of the sort in the Essex parish that they studied (as did David Underdown at Dorchester: n. 69 above), with M. J. Ingram, 'Religion, communities and moral discipline in sixteenth- and seventeenth-century England: case studies', in von Greyerz, *Religion and Society*, 177–93, who looked carefully for parallels in other parishes but failed to locate any.

84. See *Diary of James Melvill*, 231, and Donaldson, *Scottish Reformation*, 222.

85. See the pertinent remarks of Mitchison and Leneman, *Sexuality and Social Control*, chap. 2, on the decline in 'discipline' in the mid-eighteenth century, balancing extrinsic changes in the economy and the intellectual environment against a softening in the attitudes of church leaders towards the necessity for discipline. Some 'softening' certainly seems to have happened in the Calvinist city of Emden at the same time: see the tantalizing remarks of H. Schilling, ' "History of crime" or "history of sin"? Some reflections on the social history of early modern church discipline', in E. Kouri and T. Scott, eds., *Politics and Society in Reformation Europe* (New York, 1987), 289–310, at 299.

86. For Sweden, see J. Sundin, 'Control, punishment and reconciliation: a case study of parish justice in Sweden before 1850', in A. Brändström and J. Sundin, eds., *Tradition and Transition: Studies in Microdemography and Social Change* (Umeå, 1981), 9–65; for Denmark, see T. Dahlerup, 'Sin, crime, punishment and absolution: the disciplinary system of the Danish church in the Reformation century', in Grane and Horby, *Die dänische Reformation*, 277–88; for Germany, see W. J. Wright, *Capitalism, the State and the Lutheran Reformation in Sixteenth-century Hesse* (Athens, Ohio, 1988), chap. 6; L. J. Abray, *The People's Reformation: Magistrates, Clergy and Commons in Strasbourg, 1500–1598* (Ithaca, 1985), chap. 8; Schilling, 'Reformierte Kirchenzucht'; and L. Roper, *The Holy Household: Women and Morals in Reformation Augsburg* (2nd edn., Oxford, 1991).

87. For Amsterdam, see Roodenburg, *Onder censuur*, 72 and 137. For the Inquisition, see sources cited in G. Henningsen, J. Tedeschi and C. Amiel, eds., *The Inquisition in Early Modern Europe: Studies on Sources and Methods* (De Kalb, Ill., 1986), 121f.; and G. Parker, 'Some recent work on the Inquisition in Spain and Italy', *Journal of Modern History*, LIV (1982), 519–32. The increased attention paid by the Spanish Inquisition to fornication (which made up 33 per cent of the business handled by the Toledo Tribunal in the later sixteenth century) is noted and explained by J. P. Dedieu, 'L'hérésie salvatrice: La pédagogie inquisitoriale en Nouvelle Castille au 16e siècle', in R. Sauzet,

ed., *Les frontières religieuses en Europe du 15e au 17e siècle* (Paris, 1992), 79–87.

88. The crucial importance of 'fundamental discipline', involving both secular and ecclesiastical institutions, in preparing Europe for rapid social and economic change was first highlighted by Gerhard Oestreich. See his studies, posthumously published in *Strukturprobleme der Neuzeit* (Berlin, 1980) and *Neostoicism and the Early Modern State* (Cambridge, 1982). See also the interesting remarks of Schilling, ' "History of crime" ', 293ff., and of V. A. C. Gatrell in Gatrell, Lenman and Parker, *Crime and the Law*, 300.

Text acknowledgements

The chapters of this book are based on the following earlier publications.

1. R. L. Kagan and G. Parker, ed., *Spain, Europe and the Atlantic. Essays in Honour of John H. Elliott* (Cambridge, 1995), 245–66

2. Co-authored with Jonathan Israel: J. I. Israel, ed., *The Anglo-Dutch Moment. Essays on the Glorious Revolution and Its World Impact* (Cambridge, 1991), 335–63

3. Co-authored with Mitchell Leimon: *English Historical Review*, CXI (1996), 1134–58

4. Based on an article in D. Buisseret, ed., *Monarchs, Ministers and Maps. The Emergence of Cartography as a Tool of Government in Early Modern Europe* (Chicago, 1992), 124–52

5. English version of 'Le traité de Lyon et le "chemin des espagnols"', *Cahiers d'histoire*, XLVI (2001), 287–305.

6. M. Howard, G. Andreopoulos and M. Shulman, eds., *The Laws of War. Constraints on Warfare in the Western World* (New Haven and London, 1994), 40–58 and 233–40

7. Co-authored with Rolf Loeber: J. H. Ohlmeyer, ed., *Ireland from Independence to Occupation, 1641–1660* (Cambridge, 1995), 66–88

8. J. D. Tracy, ed., *City Walls. The Urban Enceinte in Global Perspective* (Cambridge, 2000), 386–416

9. *Past and Present*, CXXXVI (1992), 43–82

10. Leah Leneman, ed., *Perspectives in Scottish Social History. Essays in Honour of Rosalind Mitchison* (Aberdeen, 1988), 1–32; revised version published in R. A. Mentzer, ed., *Sin and the Calvinists* (Kirksville, Mo.: Sixteenth Century Essays and Studies, XXXII, 1994), 158–97

Index

Page references for illustrations and tables are in italics

Acheh 28, 213
Adams, Simon 94, 311
Aden 201
adultery 269, 271–2, 273–4, 279,
    283, 283–4
Africa 19, 200, 2001, 254
Aguila, Don Juan del 176
Alba, duke of
    Dutch Revolt 156–7, 159–60,
        164
    maps 113–17, 115, 116, 118
    Spanish Road 129–30
Albuquerque, Afonso de 194, 202,
    203
Aldana, Francisco de 24
Allen, Cardinal William 55
Alvares Seco, Pedro, 106, 324n
ambassadors 72–3, 76
Americas
    artillery fortresses 205–9, 358
    colonial wars 166
    maps 107–8
    trade 34–6
Amsterdam 268, 281
Andalusia 51, 53
Andrew, Christopher 67
Angier, John 242
Anjou, Francis Hercules, duke of 71,
    78, 82

Anna of Austria 18
Annesley, Sir Arthur 191
Antonio, Dom 37, 74, 85, 89
Antrim 182–3
Antwerp 143, 160, 201, 355
Aragon 120
Ardlonan 182
Armada see Dutch armada; Spanish
    Armada
armies 161–2, 192
artillery 6–7
    Ireland 174, 176, 178–81
artillery fortresses 4, 6–7, 125, 172,
    192–3, 195–6
    Aragon 120
    England 190
    and European mastery 216–18
    evolution 196–9, 197
    Ireland 172–4, 175, 182–4, 183,
        184
    Netherlands 116, 117, 119
    non-Europeans emulate 208–16
    outside Europe 199–208
Arundel, Charles 79, 81, 84, 85, 87,
    314
Arundel, Philip, earl of 80
assassination plots 89, 91, 145–6
Aston, Sir Arthur 158
Atlantic 35

atrocities *see* brutality
Auchtermuchty 260, 388
Aurangzeb 211–12
Ayala, Balthasar de 148, 149, 160, 337
Ayhtta, Viglius van 117
Azores 17, 19, 23–4, 27, 50, 149
Azuchi 214–15

Ballyally 188, 189
Ballyshannon 183, *184*
Bandon 173, 349–50
banking system 130
Barreto de Resende, Pedro 200–201
Barry, Garret 176, 179
Bascape, Carlo 246
Batory, Stefan, king of Pland 248
Baxter, Richard 233–4
Beard. Thomas 29
Behr, Johann 198
Belfast 183
Bentinck, Hans Willem 45, 49, 58
Berden, Nicholas 81–2
Berlaymont, Gilles de, lord of Hierges 117
Berlichingen, Götz von 147
Bernaldez, Andreas 196
Bernier, François 211
Berwick-upon-Tweed 192
Bibles 225, 231, 237
Birr 188
Black, David 278, 281
Black Legend 143
Blake, Admiral Robert 190
Bocarro, António 200–201
Books of Discikpline 259, 261, 263
Borromeo, Archbishop Carlo 225, 244
Borromeo, Archbishop Federigo 244
Bosnia 144
Bossu, Maximilen of Hennin count of 164

Bottigheimer, Karl 224
Boyle, Richard, earl of Cork 173, 174
Boyle, Roger, baron Broghill and eal of Orrery 176, 198, 346
Braudel, Fernand 14, 35
Brazil 200, 205
Brito Nicote, Felipe de 213
Brittany 33–4
Broun, Nicholl 271–2
Brown, Judith 1
Brûlart de Sillery, Nicholas 133
brutality in war 143, 150–59
    justifications 165–7
    rebellion 149–50
    restraint 159–65, 167–8
Burghley, William Cecil Lord 92
    Cadiz raid 87
    and earl of Leicester 81
    and Mary Stuart 79, 80, 93
    and Spain 21, 313
    and Stafford 71, 75, 76, 77, 78, 81, 82, 84, 85, 86, 90, 94–5
    and Walsingham 69, 72, 83
Burma 213
Burnet, Gilbert 57, 59
Buzenval, lord of 80–81, 95

Cadiz
    sacking 34, 54, 69, 87–8, 317–18
    Spanish Armada 54
Cairati, Giovanni Battista 201, 354
Calvin, John 258
Cambodia 33
Camden, W. 73
Canaries 107
cannon 195, 196
cannon-founding 174, 176, 179
Cardinal-Infante Fernando of Spain 140–41
Carew, Sir George 176
Carlini, Benedetta 1, 2

Carlos, II, king of Spain 18, 37
Carlos, Don 18
Castello, Castellino da 245
Castillo, Fray Hernando del 21
Castle Coote 187
Castle Forbes 187
castles 185–7, 189, 218
Castro, Joã de 217–18
catechisms 231, 237, 368, 379–80
Catholicism 7, 225, 243–7, 266
Cecil, Robert 72, 93
Cecil, William see Burghley, Lord
Chapeaurouge, Françoois de 132–3
Charles I, Kikng of England,
    Scotland and Ireland 148
Charles V, Holy Roman Emperor
    20, 22, 127–8
Chaunu, Pierre 221, 253
Chichester, Lord 183
China
    brutality 338
    fortifications 195–6, 212, 352,
        360, 361
    military technology 216, 362
    proposed invasion 20, 25, 27,
        33
church courts 253, 255, 260–61,
    263–4
    see also kirk-sessions; presbyteries
Churchill, Winston 2
Civil War, English, see England,
    Civil War
Clausewitz, Carl von 2
clergy 232–6, 371–2, 278–9
    in armadas 303–4
    Catholic 244–5
    preaching 236–8
    Protestantism 251, 367
    Sweden 247–8
Clichthove, Josse de 250
Clusius, Carolus 99
Cobham, Henry Lord 75, 81, 313

Cock, Enrique 100, 102, 322
Coignet, Michel 138, 139
Collinson, Patgrick 231, 239
colonies see empires
conformity 224
conversion 224
Córdoba, Don Diego de 19
Corunna 34
countermarch 178
crannogs 187
crime 253–6
Croatia 144
Croft, Sir James 81, 93
Cromwell, Oliver 171, 237
    artillery 181
    brutality 4, 143, 158, 169
    siege tactics 184–5
Cruise, Walter 182
Cruso, John 198

d'Albeville, marquis 60, 62–3
Dartmouth, Lord 47–8, 64
Davis, natalie Zemon 1
Davison, William 83, 94
de Brito Nicote, Felipe 213
deconfessionalization 162–3
Delbene, Abbot 80
Derrotero de las costas 111–13
Derry 173
Dick, Janet 261
discipline 258–9, 388, 397
    see also church courts
Dögen, Matthias 176, 197
Domínguez, Francisco 107, 108
Drake, Sir Francis 24, 26, 28, 205
    Cadiz 54, 87–8, 317–18
drama 239–41, 242–3, 376, 380
Drogheda 153–4, 158–9, 182, 185,
    186
Dublin 173–4, 182, 183
Duncannon fort 174, 182, 187–8,
    188

Dutch armada 39, 40–41, 42–6,
    307
    invasion force 302, 303, 308,
        309, 310
    providence 62–5
    sailing orders 49
    strategies and logistics 47–9,
        57–61
Dutch East India Company 36
Dutch Republic 34–5
    and England 41–66
    Americas 205–6, 207
    clergy 234, 235, 236–7, 371–2
    English intelligence 74
    India 203–4
    Makassar 214, 215
Dutch Revolt
    artillery fortresses 192, 198
    brutality 3–4, 155, 156–7,
        159–60, 164
    clergy 236
    flooding plans 152–3
Dutch West India Company 36

eclipse, observation of 19–20, 108,
    325
education 234, 245
    Sweden 248, 249
Edwards, Peter 170
El Escorial, monastery of
    St Lawrence at 31, 56, 100
Eldredge, Niles E. 6
Elizabeth I, Queen of England
    assassination plots 89, 91, 145–6
    Cadiz raid 87, 88, 89
    court politics 94
    and Portugal 85
    Spanish Armada 54, 67, 69
    and Stafford 78, 80, 82, 92, 316
    succession 93
Elliott, John 1, 16—17, 126, 293
Elton, Sir Geoffrey 68, 311

Emden 268
empires
    artillery fortresses 199–218
    conduct of war 165–7
    Spain 19–21, 33
    trade 34–6
England
    church courts 281
    Civil War 147–8, 151, 154, 155,
        162, 181, 190–91, 343
    clergy 235, 372
    intelligence system 72–6
    invasions 49, 50
    maps 109–10
    and the Netherlands 41–66
    and Portugal 24
    religion 8, 250, 251
    and Spain 21, 34, 41–66, 70–85
    trade 36
    visitation records 228
    see also Dutch armada; Spanish
        Armada
Erasmus 234
Erasso, Francisco de 97–8
Ercilla, Alonso de 24
Escalante, Bernardino 110, 112
Esdcorial Atlas 104, 105, 106–7,
    323, 324
Espinosa, Cardinal Diego de 21, 99
Esquivel, Pedro 103, 104, 106, 107,
    323
Estado da India see India
Estau, Aquileo 106
Evertsen, Cornelis 58, 60

Fagel;, Gaspar 58
Fairfax, Sir Thomas 146
Farnese, Alexander see Parma, duke
    of
Faunt, Nicholas 75, 84
Ferdinand of Aragon 29
Fernández Álvarez, Manuel 14

First World War 163, 164
Fitzgerald, Pierce 182
Fleury, Abbe1 Claude 246
flooding, in war 152–3, 338
fornication 253, 260, 269, 271, 281,
 283, 283–4
 penalties 256, 272–3, 279–80
fortifications *see* artillery fortresses
France
 artillery fortresses 206–7, 358
 crime 254
 documents 126–7
 English intelligence 74, 75
 hostility to England 89
 languages 236, 373
 religion 250
 Spanish Road 131–4, 136,
  138–9, 140, 141–2
 Stafford 70
 trade 35–6
Franche-Comté 128, 131
 maps 114, *115*
Freitag, Adam 176
Friedrichs, Christopher 223
Fróis, Luis 214
Fuentes, count of 134, 135–6
Fulk Nerra, count of the Angevins
 218

Gachard, Louis-Prosper 118
Galway 182, 349
Gascoigne, George 143
Geminus, Thomas 99
Geneva 132, 134, 137
 consistoire 258–9, 268, 281
 Gentili, Alberico 149, 159
 Georgio, Luis 106–7
 Gerhardt, Paul 163
 Germany, religion 250
 Gesio, Giovanni Battista 20, 21,
  109
 Gifford, Gilbert 91

Gilbert, Sir Humphrey 165
Ginés de Sepúlveda, Juan 20
Ginzburg, Carlo 1
Glamorgan, Lord 162
Glorious Revolution *see* Dutch
 armada
Goa 19, 23, 28, 34, 201, 211
Golconda 211–12
Goldman, Nicholas 176
Gould, Stephen J. 6
Graham, Michael 255–6
Gravelle, Cardinal Antoine
 Perrenot de 128–9, 130–31,
 330
Gray, William, Lord 72–3
Great Britain
 brutality 150
 see also England; Scotland
Grégoire, abbé Henri 236
Grésin 133, 134, 136
Grimstone, Edward 84
Grisons 136–7, 138, 139
Guide and Godlie Ballatis, The
 238–9
Guerre, Martin 1, 2
Guevara, Felipe de 103
Guicciardini, Francesco 6
Guise, duke of 81, 84
Gulf War 143, 145
Gustavus Adolphus 157
Gutiérrez de la Vega, Lope 176

Haeyan, Aelbert *111*
Hall, Joseph 228
Hamilton, Robert 276–7
Hammen, Lorenzo van der 14
Handel, Michael 67–8
Harborne, William 74
Harfleur 154–5
Havana 205
Hawkins, Sir John 42
Heighington, Robert 110

Henry III, king of France 312
Henry IV, king of France 21–2,
  131–2, 133–4, 136
Henry V, king of England 154–5
Henry V 154–5, 168
Herbert, Admiral 45, 59, 60, 65,
  305, 309
Herrera, Diego de 20
Herrera, Fernando de 24
Herrera, Juan de 22
Herrera y Tordesillas, Antonio de
  13–14
Hitler, Adolf, 1, 2, 165
Hobbes, Thomas 125
Holland
  clergy 234, 235, 236–7, 371–2
  war in 152–3
hostages 145, 165
Howard, Admiral 85, 87, 88, 90, 93
Howe, Richard and William 150
Hume, Martin 68, 69
Humfrey, Laurence 73–4
Hutchinson, Lucy 155

Idiáquez, Don Juan de 85–6, 89,
  319n
imperialism 19–21, 33
Incas 208
Index of Prohibited Books 7, 225
India
  Acheh attack 28
  artillery fortresses 200, 201, 202,
    203–4, 211–12
  Mughals 216
  trade 34, 35, 217–18
  see also Goa
Indonesia 210, 213–14
insults 274–5, 281, 285
intelligence
and maps 109
Spanish Armada 67–9, 93–4,
  318, 319

Walsingham 72–5, 313
  see also Stafford, Sir Edward
Ireland 169–71
  brutality 4, 165
  court of claims 160
  language 237
  Military Revolution 171–91
  Spanish Armada 50, 52, 53, 54
  Tyrone rebellion 34
  see also Drogheda
Ireton, Henry 185
Isabella of Castile 29
Iskandar Muda 193, 210–11
Israel, Jonathan 39
Israel, Yom Kippur War 67

James II, king of England, Scotland
    and Ireland 44, 46, 47, 48,
    304
Japan 214–16
Jesuits 243, 244, 245
John III, king of Portugal 210
Johnson, Lyndon B. 153
Jonas, Justus 234
Jones, Michael 181
Juan, Jaume 108
jus ad bellum 144–5, 157–50
jus in bello 145, 150–68
just war 147

Kagan, Richard 16
Keingzo, James 273–4
Kenya 166–7
Kinsale 174, 185
kirk-sessions 255, 281–2
  St Andrews 255–6, 264–9, 270,
    271–5, 278–81, 279, 283,
    283–7
Kittelson, James 228, 229–30
Knox, John 259, 267
Kumamoto 215
Kyoto 214

La Boullaye–Le-Gouz, sieur de 184
La Noue, Francöis de 153
La Salle, Chevalier de 206–7
language 236–7, 373, 374
Laud, Archbishop William 1, 2, 228
Lavanha, João Baptista de 104, *105*, 107, 120
le Brumen, Geoffroy 74
Legazpi, Miguel López de 20, 97, 320
Leicester, earl of 81, 90, 92
    and Burghley 81
    death 92
    and Mary Stuart 79, 93
    and Stafford 84, 86, 94
    and Walsingham 73, 82
Leinster 182
Lenman, Bruce 253, 254
Leocadia St 31–2
Lepanto, battle of 21, 43, 216–17
Lermonth, James 277
Leycester's Commonwealth 79
Lichefild, Nicholas 176
Lilly, William 79, 84, 314
Limerick 174, *175*, 184, 185, 187, 188
Lisbon 51, 52, 54, 110
literacy 232, 382–3
Locke, John 163
Loeber, Rolf 169–70
logistics 128
Londoño, Don Sancho de 114
longitude, attempts to calculate 19–20, 108, 325
López de Velasco, Juan 104, *105*, 106, 107–8
Lorraine 140
Lotz-Heumann, Ute 224
Louis XIV, king of France 37, 43, 64, 213

Low Countries *see* Netherlands
Loyola, Ignatius 227
Luis de Granada 225
Luther, Martin 7–8, 226, 231–2, 239
Lynn, John 144, 192
Lyon, league of 138
Lyon, treaty of 127, 132–4, 142

Macao 201
McCue, R. J. 68, 311n
MacDonnell, Randal, marquis of Antrim 189
Machiavelli, Niccolo 196–7
Mackay, Major-General Hugh 60
McMahon, Jeff 144
Magdeburg, sack of (1631) 4, 153, 157
Makassar 213–14, 215
Malacca 19, 193, 201, 202–3, 355
Mallet, Alain Manesson 209–10
Mallow 188
Malta 50
Manila 204
Manucci, Jacomo 74
Manucci, Niccolo 211
Manuel, Nicholas 239–40
maps 96–9, 120–21
    English invasions 109–13, *111*, *112*
    Netherlands 113–17, *115*, *116*, *118*, *119*, *119*, 120
    Spain and possessions 99–109, 120, 322, 323, 324
    Spanish Road 134, *135*, 138, *139*
Marchaumont, lord of 78, 82
Mariner's Mirror *111*, 113
Mary, queen of Scots (Mary Stuart) 79–80, 82, 89, 93, 306, 315
Mary Tudor 18
Mather, Increase 208
Maynooth 173

Mechelen 156–7
Medina Celi, Juan de la Cerda duke
of 117
Medina, Pedro de 101, 322
Medina Sidonia, Alonso Pérez de
Guzmán 7th duke of
maps 110–13, 327
Spanish Armada 28, 48, 48, 51,
52, 53, 56, 57, 61, 307
Meinertzhagen, Richard 166–7
Meldrum, James 271
Melville, Andrew 277, 278, 280,
281
Melville, James 257, 264, 267,
276–7, 281
Mendoze, Don Bernardino de
Cadiz warning 87
Spanish Armada 88, 90
and Stafford 68–9, 84–6, 88, 91,
92, 93, 94, 316–17
Mentzer, Raymond 255
Mercator, Gerard 100, 109, 321
Mercœur, duke of 33–4
messianic views 29–33, 148–9
Methwold, William 211
Mexico 108
Middleton, Lord 44, 62, 63
Mildmay, Sir Walter 81
military intelligence 67
Military Revolution
England 190–91
Ireland 171–90, 191
see also artillery fortresses
Mirandola, Andrés de la 20
missionaries 225, 243–4
Mitrchison, Rosalind 255
Moluccas 19
Molyneux, Samuel 176, 346
Montano, Benito Arias 100
Moody, Michael 79
Morales, Ambrosio de 100, 103
Morocco 200, 210

Morone, Cardinal 250
Mountjoy, Lord 177
mystery plays 240–4

Nanking 212
Napier, John 251
Naples 107
Narragansetts 208, 358
navies 172
Ireland 189–90
see also Royal Navy
Neale, Sir John 68, 70, 94
Netherlands
maps 98, 101–2, 114–17, 116,
118, 119, 119, 322
religion 247, 250
and Spanish Armada 51, 53, 55,
56
see also Dutch Republic, Dutch
Revolt; Spanish Road
Neumann, John von 2
New Amsterdam 205–6
Nimes 268
Nobunaga, Oda 214, 216

Ohlmeyer, Jane 170
Olivares, Enrique de Guzmán, count
of 109
Olikvares, Gaspar de Guzmán,
count-duke 1, 2, 138–9, 140,
141, 329
Onderiz, Pedro Ambrosiko de 107
O'Neill, Owen Roe 177, 180, 181,
189
O'Neill, Sir Phelim 182
Opium War 212
Ormond, Thomas Butler, marquis of
and later duke of 158–9, 176,
186
Ortelius, Abraham, 98, 99–100,
111, 114, 120
Osaka 215, 316

Ottoman Turks 209–11, 216–17
Ovando, Juan de 102, 107, 108

Pacheco Pereira, Duarte 200
Páez de Castro, Juan 102
Palatinate 235, 236, 372n
Palvacino, Sir Horatio 75, 81
Parma, duke of
    Bourbourg conference 86
    maps 110, 117, 119
    prisoners of war 160
    Spanish Armada 50, 51–2, 53,
        55, 56, 57, 306, 307
    Spanish Road 130
Parry, Dr William 80
Parsons, Robert 79, 109
Parsons, Sir William 191
Peace of God 146
Pearl Harbor 67
Peasants' War 8
Peking 212
Pemble, William 237–8, 241
Pereira, Jacob 58
Perret, J. 176
Petty, William 183
Phelippes, Thomas 91
Philip II, king of Spain
    artillery fortresses 205
    documents 13–15
    Dutch Revolt 153, 159–60
    empire 20, 33–4
    Lepanto 21
    maps 97–8, 99–100, 101–4, 105,
        106–7, 109–12, 120, 322n
    marriages 18
    messianic vision 29–33, 149
    Portugal 17–18, 19, 22–5, 26, 37
    Spanish Armada 5–6, 28–9, 40,
        41, 49, 50, 52, 53–6, 61,
        307
    Spanish Road 128–9, 330, 331
    and Stafford 85–6, 89, 93

supports assassination plots 89
    and Switzerland 131
Philip III, king of Spain
    India 203, 204, 356
    Spanish Road 132, 133
Philip IV, king of Spain 142, 334–5
Philippines 20, 25, 27, 97, 204
Piatti, Giovanni Battista 52, 54
Pius V 18
Plays 239–41, 242–3, 376, 380
plunder 145, 151
Poland 246–7
Pollard, A. F. 68, 70
Porreño, Balthasar 14
ports 174, 181–2
Portugal
    annexation by Spain 17–18, 19,
        21–5, 36–7
    artillery fortresses 199–204, 205
    and England 74, 85
    Makassar 214
    maps 106, 324n
    witchcraft 380n
    see also Azores; Goa; Malacca;
        Moluccas
Pourbus, Pieter 116
Powell, Enoch 2
preaching 236–8, 241
presbyteries 255, 260–61, 278
Preston, Thomas 169, 177, 182,
    187–8, 188
prisoners of war 160–61, 164
propaganda 165
protection money 161
Protestant wind 41, 64
Protestantism 7
    discipline 258–9
    impediments 230–43
    and Peasants' War 8
    success and failure 26–7, 250–52
    Sweden 247–8, 250
providentialism 28–33, 162

puertos secos 22
punctuated equilibrium 6–7

Quiroga, Gaspar de, Cardinal 31–2

Rada, Martin de 20
. Randolph, Thomas 72
Read, Conyers 68, 70, 94
rebellion 149–50
Recalde, Juan Martínez de 51
Reformation 7–8, 224–6
  success and failure 226–52
Reid, Anthony 195, 218
Relaciones topográficas 102–3
relics 31
religion
  and war 153–4, 162–3
  see also Catholicism;
    Protestantism
Requesens, Don Luis de 117, 292
Reyes Católicos 29
Rhine Palatinate 235, 236, 372
Ribadeneira, Pedro de 22, 37
Ricci, Matteo 25, 195–6, 212
Richardson, John 237
Riche, Barnaby 1777
Ridgeway, Sir Thomas 174
roads 353n
Roberts, Michael 291–2
Robles, Gaspar de 117, *119*
Rochestown 188
Rogers, Thomas *see* Berden,
  Nicholas
Rois Soares, Pero 24
Roman Catholicism 7, 225, 243–7,
  266
Romans 218
Royal Navy
  Civil War 191
  Dutch armada 41, 44, 47–8,
    59–60, 305
  Ireland 190

Spanish Armada 41, 47, 86
Rupert, Prince 190
Ruthven, Lord 162

Sabbath-breaking 275, 278, 281,
  285
St Andrews 4, 8, 228, 282
  church courts 255–6, 264–9, 270,
    271–6, 283, 283–7
  population 257–8, 264–9, 270,
    271–6, 283, 283–7
  population 257–8, 386–7
  siege 154
  university 234
St Gotthard pass 131, 134
St Ninians 268
Saluzzo 132
Sánchez, Alonso 27
Sánchez, Ciprián 113, 327
Sande, Don Francisco de 20
Santa Cruz, Alaro de Bazán marquis
  of
  Azores 27
  Spanish Armada 50–51, 54, 55,
    56, 61, 305
Santa Cruz, Alonso de 110, 321
São Jorge da Mina 199, 200
Savoy 132, 133, 134, 136, 137, 138
Saxony, clergy 232, 233, 235
Scot, John 274
Scotland
  blood feud 147
  clergy 233, 235, 372
  crime 253–6, 259–64, 281–2
  Dutch armada 59–60
  English intelligence 74
  language 237, 374
  religion 228, 250, 251
  see also St Andrews
Sebastian, king of Portugal 17, 21,
  210
Second World War 164, 167, 193

Selden, John 242
Sepúlveda, Juan Ginés de see Ginés de Sepúlveda, Juan
Sessa, duke of 37, 38
Seville 101
sexual offences 253, 256, 269, 271–5, 279, 386
    see also adultery; fornication
'Sgrooten, Christopher 117, *118*, 119
Shakespeare, William 154–5, 168, 243
Shaw, John 240–41
shipbuilding 47
Siam 212, 213
Sibbald, James 260–61
Siberia 204
sieges
    and brutality 150–51, 154–6, 159
    English Civil War 191
    Ireland 184–6, 187–9, *188*
Sigüenza, José de 14
Simier, Jean de 78, 82, 316
Singapore 193
slander 274–5, 278, *285*
Smith, Sir Thomas 83
Snellius 234
songs 238–9
Spaanse tiranie 143
Spain
    artillery fortresses 204, 205, 206
    Civil War 167
    colonial wars 166
    maps 97–104, *105*, 106–7, 120–21, 322, 323
    religion 245
    see also Dutch Revolt
Spanish Armada 3, 5–6, 41, 42, 307
    and imperial security 28–9
    intelligence 46, 67–9, 93–4, 318, 319

invasion force 43, 303–4, 307–8
    maps 109–13, *112*
    sailing orders *48*
    Stafford 88–9, 90
    strategies and logistics 47–8, 49–57
Spanish Netherlands see Netherlands
Spanish R oad 3, 96, 125, 126, 128–9, 130–32
    bullion 130
    decline 134–42
    documents 126–7
    maps 113–14, *115*, 134, *135*
    postal artery 129–30
    treaty of Lyon 132–4
Spanocchi, Tiburcio 107, 120
spies see intelligence
Spinola, Ambrogio 133
Sri Lanka 33, 201, 204
Stafford, Lady 70–71, 75
Stafford, Sir Edward
    and Burghley 80
    gambling 315
    political career 70–72
    spying for Spain 68–9, 84–95, 315
    and Wade 312
    and Walsingham 75–84

Stafford, William 91
Standen, Anthony 74
Stirling 260–61
Stockwood, John 240
Strafford, Thomas Wentworth earl of 173, 174, 176, 177
Strauss, Gerald 222, 224, 226, 227
Sturm, Jacob 74
Sully, Maximilien de Béthune duke of 96, 132–3, 134, 332
Susquehannocks 208–9

Sussex, Thomas Ratcliffe earl of
71
Sweden 247–8, 249, 250
Switzerland 130–31, 134–5,
136–7
Sydney, Sir Philip 70, 83

Taiwan 33
Talbot, Richard, earl of
Tyrconnel 2
Tallow 182
Teixeira, Luis 110, 327
Terzo, Filippo 22
Testi, Fulvio 125
theatre see plays
Theatrum Orbis Terrarum 98,
99–100, 111, 114, 120
Tilly, Count 4, 157
Tod, Janet 273
Totenfresser, Die 239–40
trade 34–6
Trent, council of 7, 244
Trevor-Roper, Hugh 1, 8, 39, 290
Trier 141
Truber, Primus 232
Truce of God 146
Tufat-al-Muijâhidîn 200
Turriano, Leonardo 107
Tyrone, earl of 34

United States
Civil War 167
Pearl Harbor 67
universities 234
Unton, Henry 77

Valdés, Francisco de 150, 152
Valtelline 136–7, 139–40, 331
van Creveld, Martin 144–5, 146,
168
van Deventer, Jacob 97, 101–2, 116
Vanderipen, Antonio 182

Vauban, Sébastien le Prestre de 199,
217
Vázquez, Mateo 14
Venice 136, 138
Vervins, peace of 132
Vienna 210
Vietnam 153, 212–13
Viglius see Aytta
Virginia 206, 207
visitation records 221, 222,
226–30, 244, 248, 365
Vitoria, Francisco de 155–6, 157,
159

Waghenaer, Lucas 111, 113
Wales 237
Wallace, Robert 278
Walsingham, Sir Francis
death 92
intelligence system 72–5, 313
and Leicester 82
and Mary Stuart 70–80, 82, 315
and Spain 82
and Stafford 69, 71–2, 75–9,
80–84, 86, 87, 88, 90–91, 94,
316
war 125
and clergy 235–6
conduct of 143–4, 145, 150–68
Laws of War 144–7
legitimacy 144–5, 147–50
Waterford 174
Wellington, Arthur Wellesley duke
of 155
Wexford 180, 182, 185, 190
Wild, Job de 58
Wilkie, Robert 278
William I, king of England 50, 200
William III, king of England,
Scotland and Ireland (William
of Orange)
assassination plots 89

William III – *cont.*
  Dutch armada 6, 39, 40–41,
    45–6, 49, 56, 57, 60, 64, 65,
    305
Williams, Walter 75
Wilson, James 260
Wilson, Sir Thomas 83
Winram, John 266, 267
witchcraft 274, 380
Woodhouse, Thomas 150
Wotton, Edward 82, 83

Wotton, Sir Henry 138, 250
Wyngaerde, Anton van den 102

Yom Kippur War 67
Youghal 182
Yugoslavia 143, 165

Zúñiga, Don Balthasar de 134, 137,
    138
Zúñiga, Don Juan de 52–3, 54, 292,
    306